THE ANTI-BLACK C

THE ANTI- BLACK CITY

Police Terror and Black Urban Life in Brazil

JAIME AMPARO ALVES

University of Minnesota Press | Minneapolis | London

Portions of chapter 3 were previously published as "On Mules and Bodies: Black Captivities in the Brazilian Racial Democracy," *Critical Sociology* 42, no. 2 (2014): 229–48; copyright 2014 SAGE Publications, Ltd.; reprinted by permission of SAGE Publications, Ltd. Portions of chapter 4 were previously published as "'Blood in Reasoning': State Violence, Contested Territories, and Black Criminal Agency in Urban Brazil," *Journal of Latin American Studies* 48, no. 1 (2016): 61–87; reprinted with permission of Cambridge University Press. Portions of chapter 5 were previously published as "Neither Humans nor Rights: Some Notes on the Double Negation of Black Life in Brazil," *Journal of Black Studies* 45, no. 2 (2014): 143–62; copyright 2014 SAGE Publications, Ltd.; reprinted by permission of SAGE Publications, Ltd.; and as "From Necropolis to Blackpolis: Necropolitical Governance and Black Spatial Praxis in São Paulo, Brazil," *Antipode* 46, no. 2 (2014): 323–39; copyright 2013 Antipode Foundation Ltd.; reprinted with permission of John Wiley and Sons.

Published by the University of Minnesota Press
111 Third Avenue South, Suite 290
Minneapolis, MN 55401-2520
http://www.upress.umn.edu

The University of Minnesota is an equal- opportunity educator and employer.

Library of Congress Cataloging-in-Publication Data
Names: Alves, Jaime Amparo, author.
Title: The anti-black city : police terror and black urban life in Brazil / Jaime Amparo Alves.
Description: Minneapolis : University of Minnesota Press, [2018] | Includes bibliographical references and index. |
Identifiers: LCCN 2017020146 (print) | ISBN 978-1-5179-0155-4 (hc) | ISBN 978-1-5179-0156-1 (pb)
Subjects: LCSH: Police misconduct—Brazil. | Urban blacks—Violence against—Brazil. | Urban blacks—Brazil—Social conditions. | Urban poor—Brazil—Social conditions. | Urban policy—Brazil. | Discrimination in criminal justice administration—Brazil. | Brazil—Race relations.
Classification: LCC HV8183 .A48 2018 (print) | DDC 363.2/308996081—dc23
LC record available at https://lccn.loc.gov/2017020146

To Dona Maria, Betinho,
and the mounting number of black lives
shortened by police terror

CONTENTS

INTRODUCTION
ON OUR OWN TERMS

This book tells stories of suffering, hopelessness, and political resistance among black individuals struggling to secure a place in an *anti-black* city. In the Fundão da Zona Sul, a conglomerate of predominantly black marginalized communities on the south edges of São Paulo, Dona Cecilia tries to come to terms with the disappearance and later discovery of the body of her child, stabbed and wrapped in newspapers in a clandestine cemetery. Meanwhile, Dona Maria is engaged in an arduous effort to gain custody of the body of Betinho, her twenty-two-year-old son who was killed by a police-linked death squad. On the other side of the city, Dona Cidinha is still mourning the killing of her twenty-eight-year-old son Alexandre, who was choked by four policemen in front of her house as he begged for his life and screamed for his release. In a housing project on the east side of the city, Luana struggles to get by after spending nine months in jail for allegedly helping her brother in the attempted robbery of a supermarket. Addicted to crack, she spends most of her days outside her public housing project, selling drugs to other youth in the neighborhood. Back in the Fundão da Zona Sul, Serginho, who has recently been released from prison, tries to support his two little girls through what he calls *correrias* (hustling), a slang word for criminal activities such as robberies and muggings. Since his release from prison, his main source of income has been to

1

rob expensive homes in the upper-class neighborhoods of Morumbi, Moema, and Itaim Bibi in the prime area of São Paulo's Zona Sul. In downtown São Paulo, often overlooked by those passing by, black activists openly denounce what they describe as the "genocide of black youth." Led by black mothers whose sons had been killed by the police, these activists occupy the Patriarch Square to grieve the dead from yesterday, today, and tomorrow.

All of these fragmented stories share an intimate history of economic marginalization, residential segregation, police terror, and other forms of anti-black racism directly produced or energized by the state. Full of human suffering, the periphery of São Paulo offers an opportunity to unveil how the state produces geographies of death and privilege while celebrating Brazil as the land of the "cordial man."[1] This book aims to contest this celebratory approach by unshielding the economy of anti-black violence in the making of urban Brazil: spatial segregation, mass incarceration, and killings by the police are all constitutive dimensions of the reproduction of the urban order. Social theorists usually look at schooling practices and the workforce to understand how social hierarchies are reproduced in capitalist societies. Pierre Bourdieu, for instance, argues that the lack of cultural capital plays an important role in defining one's position in societies structured around capitalist values. Within this framework, children of working-class parents will barely succeed because they are socialized around a habitus or cultural setting that makes them internalize and naturalize their parents' position in society.[2] Cindi Katz, likewise, refers to "the expanded role of the state and capital in securing social reproduction," through immigration labor policies, particularly in relation to poor women from the global south coming to the north to work as nannies. Within contemporary capitalism, Katz notes, practices of social/biological reproduction produce local political ecologies—such as the disarticulation and rescaling of childhood at the household level—deeply connected to global economic articulations. From yet another perspective, feminist scholar Melissa Wright highlights the work of gendered terror (feminicide) in the reproduction and accumulation of capital. At the U.S.–Mexican frontier, poor women of color become integrated in the world neoliberal economy as cheap labor for multinational *maquiladoras*. Their gendered precarity provides the underlying basis for the expansion of the male-dominated neoliberal order. Feminicide is integrated in the logic of production and disposability of necrocapitalism.[3]

Although these critiques inform most of my concerns regarding the political forces that prevent the reproduction of black urban life, I am more specifically interested in examining the role of anti-black violence in mediating social, political, and economic relations of production in São Paulo and in Brazilian society at large. I argue that police terror is a symptom of neither dysfunctional nor failed democracies; rather, anti-black policing creates conditions of possibility for the making of the "city of man" (the *koinonia* of *politai*), an anti-black social formation where whites exercise their civil rights. Although my reliance on the Aristotelian terminology may sound anachronistic, my intention here is to highlight the antithetical relation between black urbanity and the political community that conforms civil life *(koinonia).*[4] The antagonism between blackness and civil society implied here may raise objections. It can be argued that civil society itself is not a racially monolithic category in Latin America and in Brazil's multiracial society. While the final chapter of this book takes on the question of black participation/exclusion in the public sphere, suffice it to say that civil society is thought here as a political community that replicates the colonial structure of power even when including some black and indigenous bodies. Although not homogenously white, civil society is essentially anti-black. Its diffused anti-blackness particularly interests me because it appears even among the working-class/subaltern politics that comprise nonhegemonic civil society in most of Latin America. In that sense, the state/civil-society domain may include some black protest but would such inclusion change the structural place of Otherness? At any rate, very few would deny that the Greek city-state continues to be the ideal type of Western political life. If in modernity's urban utopia the polis is the place where the citizen-state contract is sealed and social life lived, the permanent urban warfare against black Brazilians—considered menaces to public life—exposes the *politeia*'s anti-black constituency. As Steve Martinot and Jared Sexton remind us, the polis is a racial project produced through a dialectic relation of "terror and civility" represented by the black threat and "endangered civil society." Therefore, the polis is the spatiality where white life is produced and white supremacy comes into full display "for the sake of the social paranoia, the ethic of impunity, and the violent spectacle of racialization that it calls the 'maintenance of order.'"[5]

To unveil this "making" of the city through the "spectacle of racialization," I ask the following key questions: What are the spatiosocial practices that enable the (re)production of the city's racial order? What kind of political action is required for turning the city of death into a *blackpolis,* a place for a radical repositioning of black life vis-à-vis violence and victimization? Ultimately, by discussing police terror as a constitutive/productive dimension of the city, this ethnography deals with a critical and timely issue still underexplored in the prolific field of urban studies: the gendered and racialized politics of security. Over the past few years, scholars have paid more attention to what they identify as a shift from tough to "soft" neoliberal urban-governance projects. While the police continue to be the main feature of the security state, under neoliberal urbanism their practices have been increasingly framed through cultural/human rights discourses and urban development.[6] Moreover, as the shifts in the global economy turned so-called Third World cities such as Cape Town, Guatemala City, and São Paulo into competitors for foreign investments, securing the city has become a matter of securing urban development. In his analysis of Cape Town, Tony Samara notes that under this neoliberal security governance regime, the black urban poor are seen as a threat of underdevelopment, therefore the police and the criminal justice system are deployed not only to contain "black crime" but also to enforce development. In postapartheid Cape Town, "neoliberal governance is the result of bundling these related security and development agendas into a coherent government ideology and related set of practices in which so-called free-markets provide guiding principles and reference points for ordering urban life."[7] In the case of Brazil, how is race mobilized in this new paradigm of fighting crime? What are its gendered outcomes? Has it changed anti-black urban security logics?

In this book, I explore these questions at length using São Paulo as a case study. Since the late 1990s, the city has undergone a set of transformations aimed at reducing the high rate of violent crimes that compromised the government's efforts to compete with Rio de Janeiro as the main destination for urban investors. To reduce crime, the state has targeted the periphery of São Paulo with a set of "progressive" strategies that includes human rights training for its police officers, encouraging residents' participation in neighborhood-based security councils, implementing community policing, and launching campaigns in public schools to keep local youth out of trouble. Close your eyes and imagine a weekend in one of São Paulo's favelas: children playing soccer with police officers on one of countless small improvised soccer fields surrounded by heaps of trash while another officer drinks coffee and jokes around with elderly residents at a local bakery. Or, imagine a walk in the neighborhood where you encounter flyers on light poles calling on youth to participate in an annual marathon organized by the local police station. Not unique to this city, these real examples underscore the "human face" of the neoliberal state, aimed at selling a soft governing strategy to enhance urban development and to control "troubled" areas that endanger the city and spoil its international image.

In this new human-security-based regime, Paul Amar argues we are witnessing the emergence of a new form of governance—what he calls "a parastate formation"—in which moral politics replace or supersede the traditional rhetoric of the military/repressive state. Today evangelical groups, NGOs, and the police converge in a humanitarian discourse of saving the souls of prostitutes, rescuing citizens from drug traffickers, and improving conditions for the poor.[8] While Rio de Janeiro's ongoing program of pacifying its favelas and São Paulo's community-based initiatives fall under this new cultural/human-sensitive approach, they also support Amar's argument in troubling ways. How do we account for this new human rights security regime in the face of astonishing levels of incarceration and killing that remain in place in São Paulo's favelas? If it were ultimately a question of strategies of rule and discipline, how do we account for a population whose racial marks render them as inherently ungovernable subjects, or subjects governable only through the spectacle of death?

Necropolitical Governance

The paradox of "soft" urban governance policies existing side by side with state necropractices becomes clear when we consider the macabre spatiality of São Paulo's periphery. It was a Thursday morning when I visited the Luizão—the São Luís Cemetery—in the region of Jardim

Angela, in the Fundão da Zona Sul. Dona Maria, the mother of Betin-ho, told me that if I wanted to know how violent the region was, I should visit the Luizão. That morning I decided to do just that. The Luizão (or "Big Luís") is known for its size and for the profiles of the dead it houses. By some accounts, 80 percent of the 150,000 individuals buried there are young and mostly black men killed by rival gangs or police-linked death-squad groups in the 1990s, when the region was considered by the United Nations as one of the most violent in the world.[9] The cemetery's aesthetic does justice to the area surrounding it. Located on the hillside from where one can see the sea of unfinished brick shacks on the other side of the creek, the Luizão is filled with simple graves, endless lines of crosses bearing the names and ages of the forgotten dead.[10] "Here the elderly bury the young ones," the gravedig-ger Aurelio told me. He reminded me that things were even worse in the past, especially on the weekends when open confrontations among gangs and police raids would result in many deaths. "There were some Mondays when we would bury around ten young people, all at once."

As we walked through the endless rows of crosses and graves, I noticed mounds of freshly piled earth indicating that some individuals had only recently been buried. Six other holes, one after the other, were open and waiting for new dead bodies. Now, Aurelio says, he buries an average of five people per day. "It has become a paradise compared to the old days," he said. I asked if even this amount was too much and he chuckled, reminding me of when he buried many more bodies daily in the 1990s. While at first glance it appears that the periphery has left the "old days" behind, the cemetery continues to receive victims of violent death by gangs, vigilante groups, and the police. The region in which the Luizão is located now houses the bulk of community policing, and its residents are invited to participate in civic campaigns by reporting crimes and cooperating with the police. At the same time, it has—along with the east side of the city—the highest rate of killings by the police.[11] The Luizão operates, then, as a spatial metaphor for understanding the coexistence of two strategies of state governance in the periphery of São Paulo: promoting civic life while producing black death.

If it is true that in the last two decades the state has invested in a rhetoric of engagement that emphasizes civic life and human rights, it is also true that during this period the police has filled cemeteries like the

São Luís Cemetery in São Paulo's Fundão da Zona Sul. In the background, un-
planned and self-built terracotta two-story houses. Photograph by the author.

Luizão. The most conservative statistics suggest that 10,152 people were killed by the Military Police in the state of São Paulo between 1999 and 2014, and that at least 50 percent of these deaths occurred in the metro-politan region of São Paulo.[12] During this period, the state of São Paulo became known as the "Brazilian Texas" for its astonishing rates of incar-cerations. In 1994, the state had a prison population of almost 65,000, or almost one-third of the 210,000 individuals currently behind bars.[13] In the chapters that follow, I elaborate on the racialized spatial logic for killing and incarceration within the context of multiple forms of domination in São Paulo. I privilege the familiar face of state power cor-porealized in the work of the police and in its attendant consequences. While it may be odd to refer to the state as a uniform category within the neoliberal context of intertwining governing projects in place in São Paulo's periphery, the pervasiveness of police terror as a project of state control renders the anthropological question of whether the state is an idea or an objective force not of primary relevance in this book.[14] First, we must consider some key questions: What is the reconfiguration of the racial state in terms of discourses and practices under neoliberalism, and what does it reveal about the state's strategies for securing white life and governing the racialized geographies of the city? What insights might the apparently counterintuitive soft-governance approach provide for us to understand the predicaments of black urban life in Brazil? And finally, what would resistance look like in political environments where resistance itself is embedded in the logic of anti-blackness?

By centering these three questions, *The Anti-Black City* advances two major arguments that resonate in other racialized contexts of the African Diaspora. First, it suggests that the muted violence embedded in human-security strategies such as community policing, human-rights training programs, and civil engagement all collapse in the face of the "unruly" black body. I argue that in the Brazilian racial order, the favela is produced as a Fanonian zone of nonbeing (here named as a necropolis), a place where the commonly evoked distinctions between criminal and good citizen, worker and vagabond are blurred by the generalized work of police terror.[15] In the racialized zone of nonbeing, the favelado is a killable (and unsacrificeable) object. As Denise Ferreira da Silva puts it, "raciality immediately justifies the state's decision to kill certain persons—mostly (but not only) young men and women of color—in the name of self-preservation. Such killings do not unleash an ethical crisis because these persons' bodies and the territories they inhabit always-already signify violence."[16] The racial alterity of the favelados not only disinvests them from any political status (what Silva names as "no-bodies") but it also renders them, in the gaze of the state, as ungovernable subjects and thus subjected to the decisive power of state terror. Second, racialized police terror not only produces black bodies and black geographies but is also a productive form of imagining and enacting the Brazilian state. If the commonly accepted definition of sovereignty, "he who decides in the state of exception,"[17] is correct, it is safe to say that in the Brazilian racialized regime of law, state sovereignty relies on the uncanny capacity of state agents to terrorize black communities and produce dead black bodies. What does it mean for the black subject to be the raw material for the Brazilian project of state making? Here, race works as a political resource that enables the production of black enemies, civil society, and state sovereignty.

My claim is part of a larger set of concerns many scholars have expressed in response to the Foucauldian–Agambean blindness to enduring forms of gendered anti-black state violence vis-à-vis the making of sovereign power. Foucault's approach to modern sovereignty has provided social scientists with new analytical tools for understanding modern forms of statecraft beyond traditional and centralized forms of political authority. In Foucault's analysis of power, the state is thought of as "a regime of multiple governmentalities" produced not only through sovereign violence but also through distinct regimes of knowledge and technologies of the self.[18] Foucault argues that although power in earlier regimes was exhibited through the sovereign's theatrical performance of punishment (the public spectacle of death), the eighteenth century witnessed the birth of a new biopolitical regime that produced docile bodies and governing subjectivities. Sovereignty, discipline, and government became simultaneously deployed, constituting "a triangle in the art of government," a system of government that took the population as its main target and security as its central mechanism of ruling.[19] The management of humans, not as individuals but as a human species, established the emergence of an economy of knowledge and discourses on the improvement, fostering, and "calculated management of life."[20] Within this new economy of power, Foucault argues, the techniques of domination and control operate with a completely different logic from old sovereign power: "Now it's over life, throughout its unfolding, that power establishes its dominance. [The modern power operates in] the gradual disqualification of death."[21] While Foucault highlights an epistemological shift from the sovereign's right to kill to "the calculated management of life," which he calls "biopower," Giorgio Agamben sustains that the modern regime of power is founded on the "zone of indistinction" between the sovereign and the biopolitical body. Sovereignty and life are dialectically produced through normalcy and exception, the rule of law and its suspension. "In Western politics," Agamben argues, "bare life has the peculiar privilege of being that whose exclusions found the city of men."[22] The state of exception is presented, then, as "the dominant paradigm of government in contemporary politics"[23] and the refugee as its paradigmatic subject. In Agamben's conceptualization of modern politics, the refugee camp has become the *nomos* and virtually everybody *homines sacri*.[24]

Critics of Foucault and his heirs remind us that the original violence of black slavery founded modern state sovereignty and that "slavery's afterlife" creates the conditions of possibility for its contemporary reproduction. These critics have also interrogated Foucault's claim of the disappearance of the spectacle in the exercise of modern sovereign power by highlighting the spectacular display of beaten and dismembered dead bodies, which continues to haunt black communities in the African Diaspora. What Foucault fails to consider, Joy James forcefully writes, is that "bodies matter differently in racialized systems."[25] These critiques hold true in the context of Brazilian favelas where, as described above, a multiplicity of disciplinary projects (community policing, NGOs' human-rights and drug-prevention workshops, and community security activism) goes hand in hand with the sovereign's decisive power of death. This book joins these critics in exposing the limits of the Foucauldian theorization of modern power vis-à-vis the black experience. It also recognizes and engages with Foucault's inquiries on the "problem of government," for it opens the possibility for an expanded analysis of sovereign power's mundane practices, especially in the intersections of gendered racial violence and discourses of security in ongoing state-promoted governing projects in urban Brazil.[26]

Foucault does recognize the coexistence of multiple strategies of power (discipline and government) along with the old sovereign's power of death *in modern regimes centered on biopower, of which racism is regarded as the ultimate expression.* Even when considering racism as "a precondition that allows someone to be killed,"[27] however, Foucault and his followers work under a Eurocentric race-thinking paradigm that denies the colonial history of race at the expense of erasing the specificity of anti-black racism.[28] In Brazil, as black feminist scholar Sueli Carneiro suggests, Foucault's biopower can only be understood in relation to an ontological violence that produces White Being and black nonbeing subjects. In that sense, segregation in the favelas, exploitation as servants in the houses of white elites, incarceration, and killing by the police all illustrate how raciality produces blackness as an index of death.[29] These racial conditions suggest that in the Brazilian polity not everybody becomes *homines sacri,* nor has police terror created a zone of indistinction in which any Brazilian can be potentially subjected to the power of death. There is a particular subject of death that is the raw material for the project of state domination in Brazil. In other words, although blacks have a place in the national imagination (*samba, capoeira,* and *futebol* are some of the "cultural resources" mobilized in the name of the Brazilian *imagined community*), anti-black racial terror attests and secures Brazil's enduring colonial order.

A strong point has been made that the postcolony is "the space of raw life."[30] It is a "formation of terror" in which "disciplinary, biopolitical, and necropolitical" power converge in creating "death-worlds" or creating possibilities of "new and unique forms of social existence in which vast populations are subjected to conditions of life conferring upon them the status of dead."[31] Such claims may not find receptive ears in the Brazilian mainstream academia, but these necropolitical practices are constitutive—and expose the central paradox—of Brazilian national identity. Though racial lines are blurred, according to the official myth of racial democracy, in practice the state and civil society are consistently able to identify black bodies and thereby establish racial boundaries through everyday violence, incarceration, and death. Within that context, as enforcers of the racialized regime of law, the police are key actors not only in the production of the state but also in the production of racial alterities. Within the supposedly racially ambiguous Brazilian society, police killings and their attendant technologies of social management make racial identities acquire consistency in and through death. In a nutshell, if we accept that policing does more than "merely" produce dead bodies, then black dead bodies can be read as political symbols of the making of the city and the Brazilian polity.

The *Mundo do Crime*

Death occupies such a presence in the narratives presented in this book that one could argue that there is no political agency in these anti-black geographies. It could be said that this study centers only on human tragedies, encounters with state terror, and the omnipresence of death. It could also be said that death occupies such a central role in this text that it occludes the strategies people develop to reinvent life even in hopeless places. Finally, others might view this study as so invested in denouncing death that it reproduces the pathological narratives that correlate blackness with poverty, violence, and crime. Elsewhere, Fred Moten cautions us not to fall into a conceptual trap that unintentionally equates

blackness with a permanent "death-driven nonbeing."[32] He also argues
that the equation of blackness with death cancels alternative forms of
black political subjectivity that emerge in response to (or despite) racial
terror. Moten theorizes black agency as the "fugue state" or the lived
"para-ontological disruption" of the racial script of slavery.[33] Moten's insights resonate with this book's political project to make ethnographically
visible the agency of the socially dead in places as saturated by racial terror as Brazilian favelas. His critique is directed toward the so-called Afro-
pessimist project of demystifying civil society as a place for black politics.

In the context of ever-present anti-black terror, an incisive body
of literature takes on the Fanonian tradition of forcefully suggesting
that there is an "irreconcilable structural antagonism" between blackness and civil society since what we call civil society is the political space
for the heteronormative white male subject of rights.[34] According to
this theoretical orientation, civil society is not only the racial formation that makes the afterlife of slavery possible, but it also enables the
reproduction of whiteness as an all-encompassing category of sociality
and life itself. Since civil society implies and/or requires a contractual
relationship between the state and its citizens, and since blacks are not-
quite-humans and not-quite-citizens, the relationship between blacks
and civil society is one of *ontological impossibilities*. Black are nonbeings
reduced to physicality, and their bodies pose a permanent threat to the
regime of rights that governs civil society. As Jared Sexton, a representative of this school of thought, remarks, in the afterlife of slavery "black
life is lived in death."[35]

Many of the subjects depicted in this ethnography would agree
with Fred Moten's emphatic warning. While there is no doubt that their
lives are constituted in or through encounters with death, it is also true
that they are actively engaged in challenging the state in ways that may
assert their agency. For example, one can imagine what the mothers
portrayed in this book would think about theoretical claims that would
label them as "already dead," and what it would mean to act politically
if they were to accept *death* as a defining existential condition of their
being. Although I am skeptical about accounts that see resistance ev-
erywhere, and share the Afro-pessimist incisiveness in denouncing the
centrality of death in defining black experience, I believe it is also imperative to make ethnographically visible that those who are socially

dead are also politically alive subjects. Are we willing to listen to them? If the assertion that black life is lived in death is correct, then Sharon Patricia Holland's call is timely: "perhaps the most revolutionary intervention into conversations at the margin of race, gender and sexuality is to let the dead . . . speak from the place that is familiar to them."[36]

Rather than refusing the Afro-pessimist thesis, this book engages with its critiques and recognizes the so-called difficulties, contradictions, and ambivalences of making legible the political life of the socially dead in the anti-black polity. I join their political and theoretical challenge of unmasking the field of racial annihilation we call civil society, even as I also join Moten in calling attention to the risk of endorsing a *sterile politics of hopelessness* that may involuntarily undermine black political agency. One way to avoid this is to consider the diffuse, (in)coherent, and intertwined forms of black agency that are quite often seen as unintelligible or contradictory even from the point of view of progressive black social movements. There is an ongoing underground form of resistance that does not operate under the premises of the state/civil-society contract at all. This is why, although it is important to critique civil society as an anti-black formation, it is also theoretically pertinent and politically imperative to make ethnographically visible the political praxis of a transgressive black subject that never bought into the promises of civil society or accepted its grammar of rights in the first place. In various parts of the African Diaspora, black urban life is invented on the margins through a variety of underground strategies such as the decision to steal electricity, occupy public land in "illegal" settlements, and engage in the practice of drug dealing, sticking up, and carrying out retaliatory violence against state terror.

In this sense, this book is an invitation to further research about what constitutes resistance in hopeless places of racial urban precarity. What does black youths' involvement in the *mundo do crime* (the English equivalent is "world of crime") and their refusal to participate in state-backed urban governance projects reveal about the limits of traditional black mobilization vis-à-vis civil society? What counternarratives of space and violence are generated by black women's overtly political actions (e.g., occupying squares to reclaim the dead) or by their participation in the underground crime economy? In the context of mass incarceration and police killing, what do controversial responses to state delinquency—attacking police stations, burning buses and state facilities, and organizing riots—reveal about the nature of domination and strategies of resistance in urban Brazil?

I suggest viewing such practices as generative of an explosive political identity that, while not confined to the world of death, uses the rage that emerges from encounters with death as a political resource to make black urban life possible, even if precarious and ephemeral. The disruptive moment of black rage may be one of these "fugue states" from which one can locate forms of life that refuse to be governed by the racial security state. The focus on outlawed practices in the next pages should not be seen as a claim that crime is *the* radical black politics par excellence, though. As I explain in chapter 5, there are multiple, contradictory, and vibrant ways black organizers attempt to bring black matters to the center of Brazil's political life. Black activists have indeed been relatively successful at securing some citizenship rights, the most visible ones being affirmative action policies and welfare policies that took millions of black families out of poverty during the Workers' Party's government between 2013 and 2016. Yet, how do we explain Brazil's social achievement in these matters and its genocidal proportions of violent black death during the same leftist administration? This apparent contradiction, which has been described elsewhere as "granting rights and denying life,"[37] reveals precisely the racial conundrum of a nation that does not know what to do with its undesired unruly black population. More important, it reveals the limited impact of the politics of rights in challenging the black structural condition in Brazilian society. This liminal space of precarity may be well articulated in the troubling position of hegemonic black politics that regard the state as genocidal and savior. If racial progress continues to be a mirage, what are other options available at the political horizon?

In the next pages, I attempt to locate alternative black politics by paying attention to black men's participation in the *mundo do crime*. The expression refers to the symbolic and spatial division between the worker and the bandit, the favela and the city; in the context used here, it also refers to a claim of belonging to criminal life made by my interlocutors themselves. Much has been written about the dichotomy between bandits and workers in Brazil.[38] Some scholars emphasize that in the restrictive regime of Brazilian citizenship, these categories help to situate those caught in the crossfire between "bandits" and the police in a symbolic universe that protects them against urban violence. The favelados evoke their belonging to the world of work as an attempt to distance themselves from the world of crime when the police invade the favela. Moreover, it gives the police a moral guide to their work. After all, if one is not a worker, one is a bandit and thus deserves to be mistreated and even killed. Finally, it also guides the "criminals" in situating themselves in relation to the police and the *ze povinho* (hardworking citizens). The real criminal is one who respects the rules of crime: he or she does not rob workers and only robs the playboys—those who have real money.[39]

Significantly, the division between worker/bandit is made irrelevant in the generalized criminalization of black life. Still, when looking at black men's claims of participating in the *mundo do crime*, I began to unpack a set of transgressive practices that while at first glance fall into the category of petty crime and self-serving acts of urban survival, nonetheless open up a different venue for understanding alternative governing projects, black ungovernability, and black criminal agency in relation to the city's anti-black racial order. Black men's participation in a self-titled criminal band named Primeiro Comando da Capital (hereafter PCC or Partido) underscores this point. Let me be clear: PCC is not a revolutionary organization aiming to overthrow the structure of racial oppression in Brazil. It controls the drug business in the periphery of the city, imposes a system of domination that regulates every aspect of the favelados' lives, and usually establishes ties with corrupt police officers. From this perspective, PCC is more like a state entity than a self-governing initiative led by favelados. Things get more complex, though, when we look at the participation of marginalized and predominantly black youth as rank-and-file foot soldiers in the Partido. As will become clear in chapter 4, I propose a reading of their participation in PCC as black insurgency. My claims will only be understood if the reader is willing to read PCC's practices from below and recognize that the relation of the city with black youth is one of enmity. Rather than mere *lawbreakers*, black individuals are regarded as *enemies*. Thus, black resistance must be understood from such a location.[40] Only then can we begin to see black criminality not as a pathological practice but as a challenge to the city's enduring colonial order. The insurgent is not asking for inclusion in the city's politics; rather, his/her practice violently disrupts the city's political life. Regardless of the insurgent's intentionality or political scope, his/her actions could well be placed within Fanon's understanding of decolonization as "a program of complete disorder."[41] Thus, while I am cautious about not regarding criminality as the only form of black politics, black men's participation in the PCC represents different terms of engagement with the state and a different way of understanding what political life should look like in the black necropolis. Thus, the *mundo do crime* is considered here as a political formation that encompasses both the criminalization of black life and the black self-embracing of deviancy as a legitimate, albeit controversial, form of political action.

Racial Anthropophagi

"All this maritime coast is inhabited by Indians who, without exception, eat human flesh. They feel so much pleasure and sweetness in doing so that they often run more than 300 miles when they go to war. And if they hold four or five enemies captive, they return with great noisiness, parties and tasteful wine manufactured with roots. And eat them in a way that they do not lose even the smallest nail."[42] This excerpt, from the 1554 diary of missionary José de Anchieta, is one of the several classic texts about the anthropophagic practices of some indigenous groups in Brazil. The story of the legendary Bispo Fernando Sardinha (the first bishop sent to the colony) being devoured by an indigenous group in the northeastern coast of the country is a fable that continues to dominate the popular imagination. Instead of invoking orientalist narratives of indigenous groups as barbaric cannibals, the term *anthropophagi* in the context of this book helps to set the tone for a much-needed debate on racial terror that comprises historic and contemporary modes of social subordination in Brazilian society. To my knowledge, Brazilian scholar Darcy Ribeiro was the first to articulate a critique of what he calls a "máquina de triturar gente" (literally, a "grinding machine of human flesh"), a deadly machine of colonialism in which black and indigenous bodies were devoured.[43] Similar to Ribeiro, I use *anthropophagi* in a quasiliteral way: black bodies are exploited in the job market, segregated in favelas, incarcerated, beaten, killed by the police in what amounts to an anthropophagic economy of the flesh. In this sense, if Oswald de Andrade's anthropophagic manifesto—"anthropophagy is what unites us socially, economically, [and] philosophically"[44]—is correct, the mundane devaluation of black lives signals the central place of racial anthropophagi in Brazilian nation making.

Indeed, it is racial anthropophagy. By international standards, Brazilian society is a violent one. Approximately forty thousand people are killed every year in Brazil and the country now occupies seventh position in the world homicide rank. Between 1980 and 2012 at least a million individuals were murdered in a country that sells itself as a pacifist society. These deaths are unevenly distributed along the lines of age, race, gender, and geographic location. Most murder victims in Brazil are young men between fifteen- and twenty-five years old and 75 percent of them are black.[45] As a whole, black victimization is much higher than that for whites in Brazil. In some states in the northeast of Brazil (Paraiba and Alagoas for example), the black victimization rate is 1000 percent higher than the rate for whites. Even more worrisome, there has been a steady increase in black homicides in the country throughout the last decade, while homicides among whites have decreased. The combination of racism, violence, and impunity has increased the already-high difference in victimization rates between blacks and whites from 72.5 percent in 2003 to 147 percent in 2012. In the years between 2000 and 2012, at least 272,422 black individuals were murdered in Brazil.[46]

Despite this overtly explicit racialized pattern of victimization, the Brazilian scholarship on urban violence has relatively neglected the deeply racialized context in which urban violence take place. Only recently have scholars begun to consider the racial logic of urban security and the unmistakable color of the dead. Broadly speaking, the literature on the subject makes substantial contributions in critiquing the state as an agent of violence, crediting what is referred to as a Brazilian "ethos of violence" to colonialism, and regarding violence as a *medium* of social relations. The contemporary scholarship is extensive but can be loosely synthesized into three major lines of inquiry that overlap and converge in many ways.[47] The first is a class-based model of analysis in which scholars' main concern is to understand crime and violence in relation to both the structure of antagonism in capitalism and the role of the state in sustaining social control of the poor through its penal institutions. These scholars view social inequality as a decisive factor in the production of vulnerabilities to violence and see favela residents' participation in criminal activities as a strategy of urban survival. Despite the unsolved debate of whether or not one can draw a correlation between poverty and criminality, the main contribution of this body of scholarship has been to situate urban violence as a product of the rigid social hierarchy of Brazilian society.[48] A second scholarly approach relates the problem of urban violence to a supposed dysfunctionality of the Brazilian social order, referred to as a "disjunctive democracy."[49] Democracy in Brazil, it is argued, is unfinished because the ideology of authoritarian regimes still permeates social relations. The military dictatorship corrupted Brazilian institutions and its legacy explains the exclusionary regime of citizenship, disregard of the rule of law, and "social authoritarianism" present in the collective belief in using violent means to solve social conflicts.[50] Based on Guillermo O'Donnell's chromatic scheme, in which Latin American societies could be divided into zones according to the efficacy of the rule of law—blue represents highly stable zones, green represents relatively stable areas, and brown represents dysfunctional zones—this body of literature provides a critique of state delinquency (mainly of police violence) and criminal bands as threats to democracy.[51] This normative understanding, as I elaborate later, takes the state and the *rule of law* as the paradigms of conceiving justice and social order while overlooking the productive relation between democracy and racial terror in constituting the Brazilian social order.[52] What remains unaddressed is who is the subject of rights in the racially restrictive regime of Brazilian citizenship.

Finally, a more recent body of literature, mainly dominated by urban ethnographers, has centered on the everyday forms of political order in Brazilian favelas. Some scholars in this line of research have highlighted the instrumental use of violence in producing spatial cohesion and alternative sovereignties. They argue that in the Brazilian outskirts, state sovereignty is performed through a "symbiotic" and clientelist relation between the police, criminal bands, and state authorities. Within this context, the sociological category of violence is analyzed not only as the act of physical aggression per se but also as a medium of social relations. Violence organizes and structures social relations in the city and its margins. Violence is also taken as a cognitive-rational discourse that helps ordinary citizens, "bandits," and the police to situate themselves (as workers versus bandits, for example) in everyday interactions.[53] A critique of this field of analysis—provided by Alba Zaluar, one of the most prolific scholars on the subject—is that scholars draw a dangerous association between the favela and a native or emic culture of violence. The favela seems to produce a particular type of sociability (the violent) permeated by a particular "warrior ethos" and an endogenous (criminal?) way of life.[54]

Overall, although scholars are finally considering the racial aspect of urban violence in the country, this field of inquiry is still informed by an underlying belief that violence in Brazil is a cultural or class-based phenomenon. Such perspectives neglect not only the deeply racialized urban settings in which violence takes place but also gloss over the productive logics of racialized violence in Brazilian democracy. One could hypothesize that scholars have been resistant to bring race into the debate to avoid the "trope of urban pathology"[55] that equates blackness with crime, poverty, and vice. Plausible. However, the silence around racial violence goes hand in hand with a solid white imagination in Brazilian urban studies that denies racism while locating blackness in cultural (folkloric?) practices such as carnivals, *capoeira*, samba, and *futebol*. The favela itself, the main locus of theorizing urban violence while denying race, is also the place of fieldwork for ethnographers studying blackness. How can we account for the denial of race as a category of analysis and for the culturalist narratives of blackness so prevalent in Brazilian urban anthropology? This ambivalence has not only theoretical implications but also serious political consequences. The silence around racial violence informs color-blind public policies with no impact whatsoever on addressing long-standing state-orchestrated anti-black violence, and leaves black Brazilians with the responsibility to account for their own victimization.

This book differs from mainstream literature on violence in Brazil by exploring the troubling relationship between blackness and criminality within the current context of security strategies aiming to "pacify" urban geographies. In doing so, it aims to reposition the debate about black urban life beyond the redemptive narratives of black progress and the denial of racism. While the former is the main focus of the book,

I respond to the denial of racism in a somewhat different way. Rather than engaging with white academia's terms of the debate, in which it establishes the political terrain from which racial meanings are given and erased, black activists have urged scholars to take race seriously by stating explicitly: "If you want to know who is black or white in Brazil, just ask the police." To them, it is fruitless to discuss whether race matters because the statistics on black premature death, the recurring racial lynchings and disappearances, and the astonishing level of mass incarceration, to name just a few, demystify color-blind narratives of violence.

While the myth of racial democracy continues to inform mainstream social-sciences scholarship, an incisive scholarly work has pointed out that the myth itself reveals the existence of—and hence the need to hide—racial antagonisms.[56] In the Brazilian mode of racial relations, silencing and denying racism are strategies to both cope with the brutal reality of race and depoliticize its meanings while perpetuating white supremacy. The stories Brazilians tell themselves about race relations, Brazilian anthropologist João Costa Vargas notes, in fact reveal a "hyper-consciousness of the existence of race in structuring social life." This awareness is made manifest, for instance, in the creative deployment of 134 racial categories Brazilians use to avoid the term *black*. Expressions such as *café-com-leite, moreno, cor-de-burro-quando-foge,* and so on all suggest that rather than engaging in false consciousness, dark-skinned Brazilians know the cost of being black and thus try desperately to detach themselves from it. Vargas explains it well when he notes that "the abundance of color denominations as well as the deafening silence about racial matters . . . can be understood as a manifestation of the centrality that race occupies in Brazilian social structure and common sense. This is to say, the hyperconsciousness and negation of race dialectic is the mode through which the social construction of race in Brazil is manifested."[57] From apparently innocent denials of racial belonging— "Come on, you are not black, you are *café-com-leite*"—to the violent racial interpellation in everyday interactions as domestic servants in the kitchens of elites or in encounters with the police in the streets, it is assumed and expected that everyone knows his/her position in the Brazilian social order.

Consider for instance the spatial disruption caused by black youth coming from the periphery to "take a little stroll" in the shopping malls of the wealthy, predominantly white areas of São Paulo in June 2013. Called *rolezinhos*, these gatherings of dark-skinned and working-class teenagers in white elite centers of consumption received violent responses from government officials and the shopping-mall owners. The state court released a judicial order allowing mall operators to prohibit the youth from entering the malls and conservative governor Geraldo Alckmin quickly released the Military Police "to guarantee public safety." The police and armed private security at the mall beat and arrested dozens of youth accused of "endangering public order" and damaging private property.[58] The fear of black and brown bodies invading white spaces was yet another moment when the myth of racial democracy came into question. The police's attack on black youth during *rolezinhos* enabled state and civil society to reestablish the city's racial order that the black youth attempted to subvert. As black activist Douglas Belchior points out, by occupying prohibited spaces, black youth revealed the "racist structure of the Brazilian criminal justice system and the telling contradiction of the Brazilian state selling the myth of an inclusive society where everyone can have access to consumption while banning black youth from the right to the city."[59]

Epistemic Blindness

In the process of my research, I came to realize that my social position as a black man limited my understanding of the gendered dynamics of police terror in Brazil. In my work as an activist, and later as an academic, I endorsed what Devon Carbado has referred to as a "gendered construction of black racial victimhood." Carbado argues that by treating the heterosexual black man as the archetypical victim of racism, scholars have "left unarticulated the complex ways in which race, sexual orientation, and gender function as compounding categories of subordination."[60] Although I was sensitive to questions of gendered racism and sided with black female activists in the struggle for gender equality, the watershed moment for this process of transformation, both on a personal and intellectual level, came when I started closely following protests led by black mothers whose children had been killed by the police. With them, I had a first-hand engagement and was confronted with the question of how to research black men's fates in the hands of the police without overlooking the place of black women in such an economy of violence. Posed in different instances in my activism and my professional training as an anthropologist, this question came into full display when Brazilian activist Vilma Reis described the painful journey of black mothers burying their sons who were killed by the police. Vilma Reis's poignant lecture and a graduate-course seminar on black gender with radical scholar Joy James, both in 2008 in Austin, Texas, represented a paradigm shift not only in terms of my understanding of racial violence but also of how to conceive black resistance beyond the macho-black-warrior ideal-type.[61]

Still, I caution the reader that this book does not do justice to the complex and interlocking manifestations of gendered racial violence in Brazil. Things get even more complicated when we consider that most direct victims of killings by the police are unmistakably young black men. How do we account for their encounters with police terror without falling into an ungendered critique of racial oppression? One would argue that black men have a gender identity, and thus any analysis of their condition would necessarily be a gendered analysis. A fine and satisfactory answer, if black women were also recognized as victims of the police and if their experiences were not framed as by-products of black men's fates. They are only rendered visible through the heteronormative identities of *mothers, sisters,* and *girlfriends* of black male victims. This is so prevalent that even when society reacts against violence against black women, it reinforces their supposedly exceptional victimization. The killing of Claudia da Silva Ferreira, shot and dragged throughout the streets of the shantytown where she lived by Rio de Janeiro's Military Police in March 2014, is one example. Claudia's death caused an outrage on social media and even made Brazilian president Dilma Rousseff publicly express solidarity with her family. President Rousseff released a statement saying, "The death of Claudia has shocked the nation. She had four children, was married and used to wake up in the early hours of the morning to go to work in a Rio hospital." Like in President Rousseff's statement, what prevailed in the public outcries was Claudia's status as a wife and mother. The motherless children and the wifeless husband left behind were the categories mobilized even when human rights activists and politically engaged news commentators denounced black women's vulnerability.[62]

A growing body of literature by black feminist scholars considers the physical/emotional/psychological outcomes the state produces in the lives of poor, marginalized, and predominantly black women in urban Brazil. Much of this work drives our attention to the specific set of structural vulnerabilities determined by black women's ontological and spatial locations as favelada, women, and black. For instance, the most recent works of Raquel Luciana de Souza, Keisha Khan-Perry, Luciane Rocha, and Sonia Beatriz dos Santos, among others, break this male-centric perspective by providing ethnographic accounts of poor favelada's and mostly black women's encounters with state violence.[63] Sociological research by black women has also provided an informed analysis of state violence in Brazil. Maria Ines Barbosa's and Jackeline Romio's studies on access to public health and homicidal violence respectively have shown that black women have their lives shortened by preventable diseases, and police and homicidal violence in higher rates than their white counterparts.[64] And even when the final result is not physical death, the cumulative experience of state violence has a profound gendered impact. How do we measure, for instance, rape, abject poverty, long-term trauma, emotional distress, strokes, cancer, and other countless conditions that blur the line between living and dying?

This book does not deny the statistical evidence that black men's bodies are the objects of a very specific form of state intervention. Instead, it contextualizes black men's victimization within the broader economy of gendered racial violence that produces multiple forms of vulnerability to violence and death. My hope is that, inspired by black feminist thought, this book not only contributes to the denouncement of the slow-moving, structural, and ongoing Brazilian anti-black genocide but also challenges an "epistemological blindness" that places heterosexual black men at the center of struggles for racial equality while denying black women agency.[65] Even if I had not attended to black feminists' forceful critiques of these gendered dynamics, it would require being utterly blinded by hypermasculine notions of black male agency to neglect the overwhelming evidence of black mothers' prominent role in the struggle against black genocide in São Paulo. Frustrated with civil society's blindness toward their pain, they embrace maternal grief as the moral ground from where they hope to decolonize the white public sphere. In this way, the bodies of their children and their wombs are converted into political symbols to denounce the terrocratic regime of rights that governs black lives in Brazil. Through their tactics, I hope to show not only the spatial agency of black women bringing their points home in the white, heteropatriarchal, and male public space but also the ways they unmask the anti-black nature of the Brazilian democracy. Their children, in the words of one of the mothers I interviewed, are "victims of democracy."

Lived Knowledge

This work is politically situated within personal and collective encounters with state violence as I came of age in a Brazilian shantytown. While this is not an ethnography of the favela where I used to live, the experiences of my youth deeply inform my political and theoretical choices. I will never forget, for instance, the day when the police came to the hillside and dismantled the newly built shacks in the shantytown where I lived with my family in Vila Baiana, a hillside favela in one of São Paulo's beach resorts. Not long before, we had joined with other Northeast families and occupied the hills one night. The next morning, the city authorities sent the Defesa Civil (civil defense force) and the Military Police to remove the shacks under the excuse that this was an environmentally protected area and any new shacks would be destroyed and the material confiscated. The only way to secure a place was to build the shack at night and occupy it right away so it would pass as an older occupation. It eventually worked out, but not before we lost everything to a police raid. This was my first explicit encounter with the armed branch of the state. As helicopters flew overhead, some local residents hid in the bushes, others tried to save their few items of furniture, while still others tried to resist eviction and were beaten by the police. For several months, we lived suspended in a constant state of anxiety and uncertainty as we insisted on going back to the hillside during the night to rebuild what was left. We managed to continue living in the *illegal* city, and the favela remained vulnerable because of the heavy rains that caused constant deaths by mudslides or by the police's frequent raids to crack down on drug dealings in our surroundings. It has been many years since I moved away from the favela. Many of the youth with whom I shared those difficult experiences have ended up in jail; some were killed while others have managed to get by. Like many black Brazilians, I discovered my own "blackness" in these personal encounters and humiliations living in the favela and working as a yardman in the house of an Italian family in one of São Paulo's beach resorts in Baixada Santista. As a newly arrived resident from Bahia, in the northeast of Brazil, I discovered my racial identity through these violent interpellations. Perhaps afraid of James Baldwin's prophetic assertion—"to be black and conscious is to be in a permanent state of rage"—I denied my blackness to not look the dragon in the eye. However, I did not have a choice in the matter as the city pushed me further and further into the black spaces of residential segregation, police violence, and precarious jobs. From serving the white elites at the beach resort to the hillside favela to the constant stops and searches by the police, I was viewed not only as a poor brown *nordestino* (northeasterner) running away from hunger, but fundamentally as a black *favelado*.

I have no ambition or interest whatsoever in claiming originality or ownership in this work. All insights come from the interactions with those generous enough to share their experiences and ideas in different spaces. My academic training as an anthropologist enables me to translate some of my street capacity into academic jargon, but rather than seeking an authoritative voice in academia, where others have a much better command of the political lexicon and theoretical sophistication, I hope that my lived experience validates my interpretation of the stories presented in this book. They primarily came to me not as objects of a research inquiry but rather as part of my background and my work with Educafro and with UNEafro-Brasil, two black social movements in São Paulo. In the favelas, these organizations mobilize black and working-class youth through popular education projects, aiming to prepare them for highly selective entrance exams to public universities and advocate the human rights of those brutalized by the police. Operating within a political context in which the denial of racism leaves little room for organizing around racial identity, Educafro predominantly mobilized youth through tangible goals such as obtaining fellowships to study at a private university or securing a job in the highly selective service economy. From 1995 to 2005, Educafro provided fellowships for more than ten thousand young people to study at public and private universities and managed to bring to the public debate the discussion of affirmative action policies in higher education.[66] What had at first glance seemed

like a color-blind social movement was in fact a strategic way to mobilize a racialized group highly skeptical of the black movement's discourse around racial discrimination. Once they were drawn to Educafro
with the tangible possibility of improving their material conditions, students were exposed to what we referred to as the "pedagogy of anger."
Our work as popular educators was to expose the invisible barriers that
prevent poor and predominantly black youth from accessing public
education and hopefully make them angry at the "system." Students
were then invited to participate in public protests and in weekly forums
where we discussed key issues such as police violence, affirmative action,
and residential segregation.

It was at Educafro's headquarters, and later at UNEafro's, that I
began the more structured research for this book. Many of the young
people in these organizations lived in the favelas and had had a relative
killed by the police, a friend or brother serving time in a prison, or
been victims of police abuse themselves. In this way, my research was
not a conventional ethnography in which the researcher, the "subjects,"
and the place of fieldwork are well defined. It is not an ethnography
of a particular location, but rather a politically situated and multisited
account of black encounters with the regime of terror that produces
the city as an anti-black spatiality. This is a challenge because, contrary
to other disciplines, the anthropological method privileges microanal-
yses that enable close observation and "thick descriptions" of people's
everyday lives. In that sense, this ethnography is to a certain extent
one of black placelessness as much as it is an account of black spatial
captivities. During my research, most of my time was spent organizing
demonstrations against police brutality and mass incarceration in São
Paulo or teaching writing classes in one of Educafro's dozen local offices
in the periphery to prepare black youth for the highly selective admission exam to public universities. At other times, I was traveling by bus
across the city, going to court with the parents of young black men who
had been murdered by the police, or visiting individuals in prison. The
grassroots, the public protest, the favela, the street corner, the prison,
and the city itself were all "sites" of fieldwork. These multiple locations
inhabit spatial displacement and spatial agency.

Anthropologist Arjun Appadurai challenges the traditional ethnographic imagination that confines the research subject to specific

places—what he calls a "metonymic prison for particular places."[67] Under the anthropological gaze, the "subject" is confined to a particular location with an endogenous culture and, often, a particular cultural logic. By choosing the place of their fieldwork, anthropologists are themselves producing places and subjects.[68] This is particularly true to an anthropological imagination that insists on producing black communities as places of poverty, violence, and crime. This book is not committed to discovering this "racial truth" (i.e., poverty, dysfunctional families, crime, and vice) in Brazilian favelas, although the danger of reproducing such pathological narratives certainly exists. Following Appadurai's warning, I did not confine myself to a particular place or delimit my intellectual inquiry. As I crossed paths with black individuals trying to live their lives, I was led into prisons, emergency rooms, favelas, police stations, and cemeteries. As I followed the mosaic of fragmented encounters with state violence, riding buses back and forth across the city, I was forced to consider the multiple sites and diffuse practices through which racial domination finds its inscription in the city's geography. My interlocutors taught me that these fragmented, murky, and multifaceted practices are what make the Brazilian racial order so efficient in its promotion of life and (social) death.

Outlaw/ed (Activist) Anthropology

For those of us coming from and doing research in communities terrorized by the police, what should our ethnographic accounts look like? Where is the place for field notes and casual exchanges, for example, when the ethnographer is also a member of the same racial group as his/her "informants"? Does the ethnographer "take a break" to write notes on the spot? How does one negotiate between the academic bureaucracy and the urgency of those whose lives are on the line? Although many ethnographers have dealt with this set of questions,[69] activist anthropology attempts to address some of them by inviting self-reflection on the political implications of academic research to the communities in which one works. This call has been accepted, and more and more anthropologists are aware of the imbalance of power and the contradictions that emerge from their research. According to anthropologist Charlie Hale, a strong advocate of this approach, there are various methodological and epistemological challenges in conducting activist anthropology. It requires a political sensibility to "listen," learn, and design the research according to the needs of the community; researchers have to renounce the authoritative discourse of academia and recognize their research subjects as co-producers of knowledge. The researcher also has to accommodate academic and social-movement temporalities in order to prioritize the everyday pressing problems people encounter as they live their lives. Politically situated research requires patience, humility, and fairness.[70] That is not an easy call for those of us embedded in institutional practices that quite often demand the opposite: publish or perish, establish authority, and control the process of knowledge production.

Activist scholarship poses challenges but it also provides certain unique insights that traditional researchers may not have. My engagement with the black movement, for instance, afforded me the opportunity to identify urgent matters that would not have been visible to me had I followed a "traditional" path. The kinds of questions with which this book engages would be different had I not considered my "situated" experience of being black and my political alignment with the organizations I have worked with in the struggle against racial injustice. Likewise, the most revealing interpretations and insights in the text that follows come from the collective political struggle in which I found myself. That means, as Hale forcefully points out, activist scholarship is "a privileged source of theoretical innovation." It provides "special insights, insider knowledge, and experience-based understanding" hard to find in traditional research settings.[71] A practical example here is the ways black activists understand their encounters with the police. In sociological records, police violence is a deviant practice that undermines the Brazilian regime of law. In the eyes of many black activists, police terror is in accordance with what democracy has always been in the post-slavery Brazilian society. Against mainstream interpretations, my interlocutors insisted that "for the black favelados dictatorship never ended." As I explore in the following chapters, such an assertion has implications for my research inquiry. Informed by the collective struggle against police brutality, my research asks: What kind of political actions are required so that black matters become matters of democracy?

While I endorse activist anthropology as a decolonizing strategy, I do wonder about the limits of a black activist anthropology in facing anti-black police terror. My argument is that despite its incisiveness, activist anthropology is still stuck in institutional practices that cannot go further than civil society's politics, which are quite often politics that cannot account for the state of emergency in which black men and women live their lives. I do not aim to disregard activist anthropology as "reformist" or suggest that all activist research follows the script of civil society politics.[72] There are different forms of activist research, and embracing the grammar of rights is an important one in contexts where anthropologists' skills may be placed under the service of urgent matters. In fact, activist anthropology enabled me to navigate some institutional channels in different ways. For example, it allowed me to work with human rights organizations to assist parents of black youth who had been kidnapped and killed by the police. Likewise, it made it possible for me to attend public hearings and join other activists in advocating for prisoners' rights. At other times, I joined the movement in more radical approaches such as disturbing the public order with sit-in protests in downtown São Paulo.

Still, at the same time that the resources of activist anthropology were available and enabled me to join the black movement and demand police accountability, I found it hard to put activist anthropology to work in my interactions with "deviant" individuals facing the state in the margins of the city. If I were to be coherent with my reading of their transgressive practices as insurgencies against the city's racial order, why then could I not join them? The obvious answer is that to embrace such "unlawful" practices beyond the object of scholarly inquiry would mean breaking my bounds with the institutional and civil-society-based politics that granted me some right to the city in the first place. Doing differently would require me to embrace what Cathy Cohen refers to as "a radical politics of deviance," one that vindicates *outlawness* as a legitimate space for political action.[73] How would activist anthropology, as a political endeavor committed to "putting scholarship to the service of [our] communities' empowerment,"[74] include these marginal politics as part of its praxis? If we are to take seriously the Afro-pessimist claim that black political life (in the polis) is a seemingly impossible project,[75] then how would activist anthropology engage with black political life in the margins? Would the black anthropologist join the riots, storm state facilities, set buses on fire, and stick up the wealthy homes, so that civil society will pay attention to black suffering? How do notions of law-abiding citizenry limit activist anthropology? Although these are questions any activist anthropologist would face, they are central questions for black scholars who also face violent interpellations for their racial identity daily and who advocate for their experience as a privileged place in the production of emancipatory knowledge.

I was forced to grapple with these questions many times and in different ways by my interlocutors, including Dona Maria, the mother of Betinho, a young black man disappeared by the police. Dona Maria angrily interrogated me, asking which side I was on, when I counseled her to be patient with state bureaucrats who promised to help her bring Betinho's remains to a proper burial. In another occasion, I was accused by black men in the world of crime of being a *cuzão* (asshole) for "being too afraid to die," and then there were moments when they assumed I "kept it real" for my being from the favela only to be disappointed by my "too-straight" politics. At times, the black movement itself embraced such limiting politics, and I was then swept to the other side of the activism-while-black equation.[76] For example, black organizers warned me to stay away from PCC, and I was sometimes criticized by interlocutors in the favela and prison for being too close to the state.

While I refrain from disclosing the behind-the-scenes struggle that led to a split in Educafro, one of the organizations I worked with, one significant divergence was the terms of engagement with the police when a range of organizations tried to build a strategic alliance to denounce police terror. At Educafro, some individuals believed that working with the police department would be the best approach for combating police brutality. The organization defended the need for negotiations with the police department while other black organizations demanded an immediate firing of the police chief and a federal investigation of the crimes committed by the Military Police. Furthermore, a third and marginal group of individuals advocated an even more radical approach, saying that we should talk with black youth engaged in the world of crime. These tensions worsened when the leaders of the church-based black organization began unilateral conversations with the police department, demanding diversity initiatives and asking for human rights training in the police force. Most radical sectors of the black movement refuted these two measures and instead denounced the genocide of black people and demanded the end of the Military Police. I was a member of the organization until my antagonism came into full display, and conciliation between my agenda and that of the organization's leaders became too challenging.

In defense of activist anthropology, it can be said that these tensions are precisely what make this approach a rigorous, innovative, and compelling form of knowledge production. After all, activist anthropology does recognize "conflict" as a constitutive aspect of knowledge.[77] While that holds true to my experience, these encounters—my unsatisfactory answers to interlocutors who did not participate in formal politics, my frustrations with the organization I worked with, and my empty-handedness in helping other victims of police terror deal with state bureaucracy—all illustrate the tension between *activism* and *insurgency* for those of us aiming to be more than activists and scholars. Joy James and Edmund Gordon highlight a similar antagonism, arguing that what distinguishes the "radical subject" from the "activist scholar" is that while the latter is a coherent academic-bound subject, the former is a "fractured self." Although the radical subject works in the academy, she has no loyalty and does not seek legitimacy from within but rather from/in the struggle for social justice. The only way the activist scholar can become truly radical is by departing from academia or accepting the "fractured self" as a place of agency. The fractured self is a mobile subject seeking to exit.[78]

Beyond the skepticism of the "radical subject" becoming insurgent or not, James and Gordon's critique brings to light the constraints that prevent those of us with a foot in both places (academy and the community) from engaging in truly transformative practices. While my interlocutors in the prison and in the favela "asked" me to be insurgent, the leaders of that particular organization endorsed the politics of rights that civil society was more willing to accept.[79] And still, the clash of perspectives revealed precisely the constrained political terrain for articulating black demands in the Brazilian public sphere. My arrogance blinded me to the consideration that despite my frustration, my interlocutors at Educafro embraced a politics of urgency that, while contradictory and limited, also revealed the desperate attempt to stop killings by the police. This does not solve the impasse for activist anthropology, however. I do not pretend to solve it here, and as the reader will notice, this book itself reflects my ambivalent position within this political and methodological dilemma. Still, while the politics of rights is a "safe ground" for doing activism while navigating between the academy and the streets, accepting to embrace black insurgency on the margins of the city may indeed require definitive departures from places of privilege and legality. For activist anthropology, it may mean an outlaw/ed anthropology: one that if not willing to pay the price—since it is not truly revolutionary—is at least willing to dislodge itself from white civil society's morality. The question becomes, how far can we (and are we willing to) go? If dissociated from radical praxis, an activist anthropology of the current "crisis" of police terror is nothing but an anthropology of sorrow, lamentation, and pity.

A Methodological Note

In this book, I combine journalistic and ethnographic methods to recreate meetings I attended during formal fieldwork in the peripheries of São Paulo from May 2009 to December 2010. Data also come from my long-term involvement with the black movement. At times, quotations may not be exactly as they appear. While I devoted a great amount of care to reproduce them as close to the dialogues as possible, they are filtered by my inability to take notes on the spot when the events took place. In some cases, I relied on my journalistic skills to recount painful moments later, such as when I attended public hearings, joined task forces to help black mothers file paperwork to reclaim the remains of their loved ones, hung out in the *biqueira* (dope spot), and attended monthly police–community meetings. While this is not a conventional ethnography, I did take notes and record formal interviews with many individuals that appear in the book. These complement the notes I wrote on a daily basis to capture my impressions after meetings. In stressful situations involving parents terrorized by the police, I often refrained from grabbing records and instead wrote down notes later on my way home. At times, some dialogues and events that present recurring similarities (e.g., the several public hearings I attended with Dona Maria, the mother of a youth killed by the police) are paired with others for the sake of organizing fragmented ethnographic moments around key themes. They are represented in this book thematically but not necessarily in a linear direction. While this writing strategy may have decontextualized some dialogues, it helped me to piece together recurring themes that emerged from countless meetings that my ethnographic notes were unable to cover. This strategy also speaks to the very conditions of doing activist research in precarious sites overwhelmed by human tragedies, such as São Paulo's favelas or institutional meetings in which the parents of the dead expressed deep frustrations with state bureaucrats and with me. Writing on "the politics of truth," anthropologists Antonius Robben and Carolyn Nordstrom argue that "one can count the dead and measure the destruction of property, but victims can never convey their pain and suffering to us, other than through the distortions of words, images and sound. Any rendition of the contradictory realities of violence imposes order and reason onto what had been experienced as chaotic."[80] I apologize for possibly misinterpreting and trivializing these fragmented narratives as I tried to "order" their stories into an academic text.

Finally, readers may find some divergences in names of places, institutional settings, and individuals as they appear in my previous publications. As time went by, I made a deliberate choice to disclose the real names of some interlocutors from the black movement and parents of victims of the police when such disclosures did not pose a threat to their security. I also took additional precautions not to further reveal sites or provide full descriptions of activities that would endanger interlocutors in the world of crime. At times, I use the words Fundão da Zona Sul to describe the sprawl of *favelas* in the south side of the city where I did most of my activism. At other times, I use the fictional name "Dreaming City" to describe particular sites within the Fundão that I wish not to disclose. Likewise, I refrain from describing the name of the male detention center where I did my activism with the Prisoners Advocacy Network (here loosely referred to a coalition led by the progressive wing of the Catholic Church).

Book Outline

Each chapter of this book revolves around the set of mundane and institutional practices that makes the city an anti-black spatiality. The favela, the prison, the public protests, and the pitfalls of the black movement are the routes through which I take the reader on this journey. The first chapter situates the text within the black necropolis. In this chapter, I focus on the work of death in the constitution of the black urban alterity in the city of São Paulo. I analyze the macabre practice of police-linked death squads as a dialectic that works to unmake bodies and make spaces. By destroying and disposing of black bodies throughout the territory, the police produce the geographies the state aims to control. Chapter 2 focuses on a new urban governance framework launched by the state to redress crime and violence in the city. It analyzes the penal rationality that makes São Paulo a case study of the neoliberal strategies of urban governance in Latin America's racially divided cities. I further illustrate how the state advances these governing practices through soft-power strategies, best showcased by the Polícia Comunitária, while police terror continues as an enduring practice. As the urban poor are pushed out of the neoliberal economy, the favela suddenly becomes a laboratory where individuals are compelled, in diverse ways, to respond to the challenges posed by the neoliberal global city. They are invited, for example, to participate in security councils, workshops on domestic violence, and neighborhood watch initiatives. Interviews with police officers, participation in community security council meetings, casual conversations with young black men, and interviews with elderly men and women all provide the content for understanding the troubling relationship between soft governance and state necropolitics in the city of São Paulo.

In the subsequent two chapters, I shift focus to the prison as a site for exploring the issues of city making. I illustrate how the city becomes a prison and the prison becomes a city through the mapping of discourses and practices of black individuals serving time in overcrowded prisons in the heart of the city. Chapter 3 outlines the contemporary Brazilian penal landscape. I discuss the favela–prison pipeline, or how black captivity in the city (through unemployment, residential segregation, and low-paid jobs) energizes the prison system and vice versa. Killings by the police in the favelas, incarcerations in São Paulo's overcrowded prisons, and the overexploitation of black men and black women in low-paid jobs are seen as parts of a process of black surplus and disposability—intensified by the neoliberal policies adopted by the state and federal governments during the 1990s. These two chapters are not, however, ethnographies of the prison. They are routes for reading the centrality of incarceration and death within the urban-security paradigm that is in place in Brazil.

Chapter 3 pays particular attention to black women's encounters with the carceral state. It illustrates how black women's increasing incarceration for drug offenses reflects their captivities in other prisons such as the favela and the kitchens of white elites. I examine the racialized and gendered relations that lure black women into the drug trafficking economy as "human mules." Chapter 4 examines the ways black men grapple with notions of criminality, how to handle the police, and how to situate their criminal practices within their communities. This chapter explores the political agency of black men who are *primos* and/or members of Primeiro Comando da Capital (PCC), a self-described criminal organization that controls São Paulo's favelas. The concept of tragic agency is employed to account for their investment in particular notions of patriarchy and its gendered consequences for favela residents. Chapter 5 broadens the question of what constitutes political action for the marginalized black urban poor. It draws on my activism in the black movement, the protests launched against police violence, the occupation of the governor's office, and the political strategies employed by black mothers to reclaim the bodies of their children left behind by the police. The chapter explores the meanings of public mourning and grief, and it highlights the strategies deployed by the black movement to turn black bodies into political symbols in response to a general disregard for black life in public discourse. The shortcomings of these strategies—exemplified by the lack of public responses to ongoing black suffering—illustrate the limited options available for redressing racial violence within the anti-black Brazilian polity.

1

MACABRE SPATIALITIES
NECROPOLIS

The map of Brazil drips blood. My flag is not green and yellow. My
flag does not have stars. My flag [is the symbol of] a fantastic factory
of dead bodies. And the stripe where one reads "order and progress,"
it does not exist for the mother.

—Debora Silva, *Mães de Maio*

On May 30, 2008, a body was found in the bushes alongside a remote road in the sprawling conglomerate of slums in São Paulo's south
side. The mutilated body was headless with burn scars and bullet holes.
Only later did we come to know that it was the body of a twenty-two-
year-old black man named Betinho. The last time Betinho's mother,
Dona Maria, had seen him, he was leaving their house to visit his pregnant girlfriend, Geilsa, after a long day working at a carwash. The day
after Betinho's death, Dona Maria looked for him at the hospital and at
the three police stations surrounding Dreaming City, her neighborhood
in the Fundão da Zona Sul (the vast impoverished area on the south
side of São Paulo). She mapped out all of the surrounding state facilities
where Betinho could have been taken. She even mobilized neighbors to
look for him wherever they thought he could be. It was all in vain. At
the local police station, they dismissed her—the officer at the counter
did not even bother to look at her. They did not treat her any better at
the neighboring police districts. Dona Maria remembers the first question the officer asked her: "Does he have a criminal record?" She yelled
back, "No, and what if he had?" The officer warned her to calm down
and refused to fill out a missing-person report because Betinho had not
yet been missing for twenty-four hours.

No clues about Betinho's fate turned up until a friend broke the silence, revealing details about a police patrol in the area around the time of Betinho's disappearance. Assuming that Betinho had been killed by the police, Dona Maria began a new battle to find his body, though there were still no records of him at hospitals or police stations. Two years later, Dona Maria was still consumed with the struggle to bring legal charges against the police-linked death squad that had been investigated for her son's killing. In order to push the case forward, she had to navigate a morass of paperwork and bureaucratic obstruction and make endless trips to the public notary, the Medical Forensic Institute, and the police department. All the while, Betinho's remains were kept in a plastic bag at a local cemetery, waiting for the state's official recognition of his death. Without his death certificate, Dona Maria could not provide her son with a proper burial.

Dona Maria and I made arrangements to meet at 10 a.m. at Dreaming City's residents' association one Tuesday morning. She arrived almost two hours late, having come from the public clinic where she was picking up a prescription for depression. We went to the kitchen, where Dalva, one of the local leaders, had just made some coffee. Maria had brought with her an old newspaper displaying the faces of the police officers said to be responsible for Betinho's death: "These are the monsters. They took my son from me. No, they stole him from me. Now *you* tell me how I am going to live." She stressed the pronoun "you" to emphasize her hopelessness about and skepticism of my interest in her painful circumstances. Her raw emotion was accentuated by her strong voice. With tears in her eyes, Dona Maria cursed the Military Police with all the names one could imagine. After a long pause, she recalled Betinho's dream, among others, to buy her a house, although his salary did not even make ends meet: "The day before his death he said, 'Mom, I know I'll get you a house. I have no money, but I will do that.' To a car washer to have a house was already a big dream."

It was indeed an ambitious dream. Working in a car wash, Betinho made roughly 300.00 USD per month. He was the one who had put food on the table, as Dona Maria suffers from severe back pain and bronchitis from the years she worked cleaning floors in a supermarket. After his death, her health deteriorated and she began taking antidepression medication. She opened her purse and showed me the bills she had to pay. "Beto used to pay my rent. Now I ask you, what is my life going to look like?" Dona Maria's experience was far from unique. The favelas of Zona Sul had been targeted for a long time by death squads and other forms of vigilantism. Back in the 1990s, the region was well known for the high rate of homicides carried out by local business owners and off-duty police officers. The "social cleansing policies" are still in place: some human rights organizations have documented a consistent "politics of extermination" of black young men carried out by on-duty and off-duty police officers in the periphery of the city.[1]

One week after Betinho's kidnapping, fifteen-year-old Lucas was last seen being thrown into a police car patrolling the favela. Lucas was found in a trash dump fifteen days after his disappearance. The body was wrapped in newspapers that covered a deep cut on his throat. There were cigarette burns and puncture wounds all over his body. Dona Cecilia, Lucas's mother, was at the hospital due to complications in her pregnancy when she received the call from her ex-husband, Jonas, who informed her that Lucas had been arrested by the police. At the time, neither Jonas nor Dona Cecilia had known about his death. Neighbors told her that Lucas and a friend had been taken away by the Slaughters, a police-linked death squad said to be responsible for dozens of deaths in the Fundão da Zona Sul. In the days following his disappearance, Dona Cecilia followed the same path as Dona Maria, looking for Lucas at the morgue, the hospital, the police stations, and any other place she could think of. Even without any concrete leads to go on, she was certain that Lucas was dead. Lucas had a criminal record, and the police had warned him multiple times not to be on the streets or they would kill him. At first, Dona Cecilia thought he had been arrested once again, but when a neighbor told her that Lucas had been kidnapped by the Slaughters, she lost all hope and admitted to herself that the police had killed him. After fifteen days of searching, a friend of Dona Cecilia overheard a conversation on the bus about the discovery of the mutilated body of a young man in the neighboring city of Itapererica da Serra. It was Lucas's body.

I met Dona Cecilia through Dona Maria. Because Betinho's and Lucas's murders took place under the same circumstances, and seemingly by the same police officers, they both had been receiving support from the local Catholic church and knew each other. Like Dona Maria, Dona Cecilia feared retaliation; she had changed her place of residence and hid herself. It was Dona Maria who put me in touch with her after several warnings that I would not place either of them in danger. I met her for the first time at Sunday mass at the church. She was scared to talk about her son's death and told me that she would call me when she felt it was a better time to do so. Therefore, I waited. Almost two months later, she called and we set up a meeting at the church again. She explained that she was too scared to meet elsewhere because the police have been surrounding her house ever since her ex-husband filed a lawsuit against the Military Police for her son's murder.

Like Dona Maria, Dona Cecilia was a single mom struggling to raise Lucas and his seven-year-old sister Tamires. At the age of twelve, he ended up in a juvenile detention center for stealing from a woman in the wealthy neighboring district of Moema, where Cecilia worked as a domestic servant. After his release, Lucas tried to study, but the school board expelled him for misbehaving in class. At the age of fifteen, he was working with his mother selling yogurt on the streets. The day the police kidnapped him, Dona Cecilia was in the hospital; he had taken the day off and went for a ride with a friend. As they passed through, the police asked them to stop. Without the proper documents in the car, and each with criminal records, Lucas and his friend escaped through the tiny streets of the favela but did not get very far. The fact that Lucas was involved in criminal behavior, Dona Cecilia admitted, made his death almost certain. "I was expecting the worst. I told him, Lucas, stay at home, avoid bad *companhias* [friendships] and do not get into trouble." In fact, on the morning of his death, Dona Cecilia had warned Lucas to stay at home and be careful because a police patrol had been searching the area for days looking for drug dealers in yet another break deal, in which dealers fail to pay police bribes and the police retaliate by killing or arresting residents. During our conversation, she blamed herself for not being a "good mother" and letting him stay by himself. Jonas, her ex-husband, has always been absent, appearing now and then with something for the two children. With her little girl in her arms (she was pregnant when Lucas was killed), she said, "I am the mother and the father. What can you do when you are raising a boy in the favela and you don't have anything to offer him? I have to choose to stay at home and take care of him or go out to sell these things to feed them [Lucas and his sister]." Dona Cecilia makes a living by reselling at a higher price, door-to-door, yogurts she purchases in advance.

Black in the City

The deaths of Betinho and Lucas were in some ways expected. Killings by the police are so prevalent in São Paulo's periphery that there is a macabre certainty that raising a little black boy is a fatal investment. While their killings are an enduring and banal practice in urban Brazil, their fate at the hands of the police speaks to a much broader racial and gendered regime of domination that I call the *black necropolis*. Michael McIntyre and Heidi Nast argue elsewhere that in contemporary neoliberal capitalism, the world of production is divided into the biopolis and necropolis, in which the necropolitans (inhabitants of the necropolis) "not only supply much of the world's industrial labor, but (through migration) they carry out reproductive and productive functions for the biopolis as well." In their view, this necro(bio)political regime of production constitutes a "spatial unity" where profit and surplus population, accumulation and dispossession, life and death are dialectically produced.[2]

Like the authors mentioned above, I regard neoliberal São Paulo as a zone of symbolic, physical, and social death indispensable to the reproduction of the biopolis, the zone of being. I further complicate their argument, however, by adding the qualifier *black* to account for the necropolis as a spatial unity in dialectical relation not only to the world of labor, but also to political and civil life itself. The Brazilian neoliberal city stands as a zone of economic exploitation and racial annihilation. It is a zone of physical and *social death*. I borrow the last concept from Orlando Patterson's work on dishonor and "the natal alienation" of the black enslaved. According to Patterson, the enslaved were "socially dead" because slavery stripped them of their right to personhood, permanently dishonored them, and prevented the intergenerational reproduction of their cultural practices.[3] My take on Patterson's concept aims to call attention to the black *Brazilian* paradigmatic position in relation to the world of citizenship (not only in terms of access to economic opportunities but also to the very right of personhood, a right that could entitle one to claim, for instance, habeas corpus against police raids or, more broadly, to have the right to the city).

The paradigmatic social location of black women like Dona Maria and Dona Cecilia in the city's spatial order (mostly as domestic servants and faveladas, residents of the favela) provides a glimpse into the functional relationship between the necropolis and the biopolis. They participate in the biopolis as expendable bodies exploited in the city's division of labor, and are placed in the center of the necropolis as the gendered and racial embodiment of insecurity and crime. Although Dona Maria's and Dona Cecilia's grief for their loved children attests to the "impossibility of black motherhood" imposed by the state's murderous practices, which I discuss in chapter 5, it also points to the multiple forms of violence (symbolic, physical, structural) they face as favelada, black, and women. That is to say, gendered anti-blackness is the basis for the seemingly impossible blackpolis. Scholars have highlighted the marginal conditions of black women in Brazilian society from the period of slavery to Brazil's "racial democracy." Domestic servants, street vendors, and faveladas are all positions "naturally" ascribed to black women in Brazilian society.[4] Such positions are naturalized in a racial common sense that equates the black gendered body to mythic physical attributes such as hypersexuality and strength, and in doing so consolidates blacks in an inferior position in the Brazilian social order. Sueli Carneiro's assertion that there is a continuum from the master's house to the kitchen of white elites—"yesterday we were in the service of frail mistresses and rapacious plantation owners and today we are domestic servants for 'liberated' women and housewives or *mulatas*-for-export"—finds reality in the fact that the main occupation for black women in Brazil is domestic service in the houses of white elites.[5] Their bodies continue to be at best a supply of cheap labor and at worst disposable.[6] A 2008 survey by the government-based agency Fundação Seade revealed that black women represented 52 percent of domestic workers in the metropolitan area of São Paulo; 85 percent of the women were 25–60 years old, and 60 percent did not have elementary education.[7] The exploitation of black women in the labor force is another side of the accumulation of capital and dispossession of black families in the biopolis, as it enables white women to work outside the home and prevents black women from participating equally in the city's economy. Although in the last decade the salary gap between women and men has been reduced to 70 percent, black women make an average of 40 percent of a white man's salary and are the largest group of unemployed individuals in the informal economy.[8]

Even though Dona Maria and Dona Cecilia rarely speak about their conditions as black women, their spatial identity as faveladas and their position in the gendered division of labor in the city are defined by race and gender. Before working as a street vendor, Dona Cecilia had been a maid in the house of a white family in the wealthy neighborhood of Moema in southeast São Paulo. Dona Cecilia decided to quit the job because the *patroa* complained when she tried to take Lucas to work with her when he was still a little boy. The *patroa* warned her that the little boy would break things and be an extra mouth to feed. Without anyone to watch Lucas while she worked, she first left him with the children of a neighbor who also worked as a domestic servant. Then, she became pregnant again and decided to quit the job to take care of Lucas and Tamires, her now-seven-year-old daughter. When Jonas, her former husband, left home and refused to provide any kind of support for the children, she began buying goods to resell door-to-door for a higher price.

The details of Dona Maria's trajectory are not different from those of Dona Cecilia's life. At the age of twenty, Dona Maria migrated to the city in the 1970s from the bordering state of Minas Gerais to work as a domestic servant in the house of a white family in the upper-class district of Pinheiros. On arrival, she lived in a small room in the backyard, but then she met her soon-to-be husband, Pedro, and relocated to an *invasão* (clandestine settlement) in the Fundão. Pedro was an abusive alcoholic who left home one day and never returned, leaving Dona Maria to raise her two sons, Betinho and Thiago, on her own. Maria says very little about Thiago, who has been in and out of prison for charges of robbery and drug trafficking. It is a public secret that he is a member of PCC. Dona Maria now lives in Dreaming City, one of the Fundão's favelas.

Working at Educafro, I met other black women whose lives differed from Dona Cecilia's and Dona Maria's life trajectories despite this oppressive structure. For instance, Railda is another black woman and favela resident whose son was serving time in a detention center. Railda actively participates in the city's politics, runs an association for parents of imprisoned children, and is about to become a lawyer—"to advocate for the victims of the state," as she says. There is also Debora, who despite the pain of having a son killed by the police organizes mothers in São Paulo and beyond to bring the killers to justice. As I discuss in chapter 5, Debora's and Railda's encounters with the state reinforce the argument of black women's liminal condition in the city, yet their trajectories caution us about "the danger of single stories" that tend to inform the imagination of urban ethnographers.[9] The same concern can be voiced about the "single story" of black women's victimization as mothers and wives, as my account of Dona Maria's and Dona Cecilia's encounters with the state may suggest. In the subsequent chapter, the reader will find that Nina, Luana, Duda, and Elisa also challenge such reductionist interpretations.

There can be little doubt that black urbanity is lived through diverse practices and that black urban life is more than tragedies and suffering. Still, I focus on Dona Maria's and Dona Cecilia's experiences here because they are very instructive of the multiplicity of forces that produce gendered racial precarity in the city of São Paulo. Consider, for instance, Dona Maria's condition. She fought to bring Betinho's remains home and to secure a place to live since she was about to be homeless. One morning, I received a desperate call from Dona Maria, who had received an eviction notice from the landlord and had to move out by the end of the week. Four months behind on her rental payments, she asked me to help her get some money, or she would soon be living on the streets. I asked about Thiago, her son who was by that time out of prison, but as always she refused to talk about him. That same evening, I headed to her place—a two-room unit in the basement of an unfinished two-story home—to give her some money and encourage her to apply for financial assistance from the municipal housing authority to cover her monthly rent. She qualified for the subsidy because she was unemployed and had no source of income since Betinho's death. The next day we traveled across the city to try to obtain help, but this only increased her frustration with the government. It also reinforced her skepticism about the kind of legal activism I was doing (first going after Betinho's paperwork and now after a housing subsidy) in my efforts to mediate her claims with the state.

At the housing authority, after a long wait in line, the staff person heard her story. She was unable to pay her rent because the police had killed the person whom she had relied on for financial support. The official expressed pity but told her that he could not provide assistance. He explained that like everyone else, Dona Maria needed to apply for the subsidy and wait for a social worker to assess her condition to determine if she were indeed eligible for aid. The process, he explained, would take at least six months. Dona Maria became frustrated and demanded that he bring someone else to assist her. "How am I supposed to live without a shelter until my case is revised?" she questioned. The official responded that he was "just following the rules." Since she refused to leave and was blocking the line, he called his superior, who insisted that Dona Maria provide paperwork to prove that she was unable to pay rent. We argued with the light-skinned man, explaining that Dona Maria was unemployed, had no means of support, and had no paperwork to prove her financial condition since Betinho had had an informal job as a car washer. In the end, the official scheduled an appointment for Dona Maria to return to the office two months later. Empty handed and frustrated, we returned to the favela fearing that soon she would be without shelter.

Traveling across the city that afternoon, I realized how alienated Dona Maria was from the polis built by black slaves. I also realized how the city reproduces the colonial order through mundane encounters like the one we had just had in the housing authority or through organized dispossession such as the racialization of the job market. One could mention, for instance, the years stolen from Dona Maria, working as a domestic servant in the kitchen of white elites for much of her life, or even the practice of black mothers babysitting white children while the police killed their sons. Such examples, among many others, provide us with a way to think about how gendered racial precarity creates the conditions of possibility for the reproduction of the anti-black city. In that sense, Dona Maria's urban experience challenges the appealing fantasy of São Paulo as a land of opportunity; one could say that it is her exclusion from the city (or her inclusion as overexploited body and then disposability as permanently jobless) that makes the "city of men" possible. The denial of her "right to the city"—at even the most basic level of having a shelter—and her overexploitation as domestic servant are quite illustrative of the functionality of racial gendered violence to the reproduction of São Paulo's urban order.

Highlighting the economic functionality of state violence does not mean that black women's relation to the city is "merely" an economic one of overexploitation in the gendered division of labor. There is also an ontological condition of *placelessness* that renders their bodies as special objects of racial violence. While several actors enact the patriarchal order of the city (at home, in the workplace, and in the very constitution of the city), perhaps the spectacular violence of police raids, as I demonstrated in the introduction of this book, has the "merit" needed to unify the diffused gendered economy of racial violence that paints São Paulo as a macabre hue. In the following section, the reader will find several examples of direct and indirect violence perpetrated or facilitated by the state. Black women's violent interpellation by state policies indicates that a critical intervention in the necropolis would consider not only the astonishing levels of police killings of black men but also the intertwining project of urban governance that comprises policing, unemployment, economic dispossession, residential segregation, psychological pain, and more. An ethnographic examination of police violence must take into consideration these gender-race spatial dynamics because they ultimately inform the political, economic, and social rationality of anti-black violence in general. Perhaps Dona Maria's search for Betinho's body and her struggles to secure a place to live are indicative of the *place* of blacks within Brazil's urban modernity. It also renders the overlapping of police terror and mundane, gendered racial disposability even more visible: without any help from the housing authority, she relied on her neighbors' solidarity to prevent her eviction.

The following month, she was once again struggling to pay the rent. This time she did not seek out government assistance. Instead, she moved in with her niece Sandrinha. The move did not require much work. Dona Maria's possessions were few: an old sofa, an uncovered mattress, an old-fashioned television, a rusty refrigerator, and a stove tied with wire. Sandrinha helped us move the furniture into another tiny room in the backyard of someone else's house, where she still lives waiting for financial compensation from the state for Betinho's death.

The Racial Production of São Paulo

São Paulo is the largest metropolitan area in Brazil. It became the economic and political power of the nation in the second half of the nineteenth century, when the price of coffee increased on the international
market and the volume of production in the state turned São Paulo
into the center of the coffee export market. These days, the city alone
contributes 10 percent of the Brazilian national gross domestic product
(GDP) and houses roughly twelve million people, or 6 percent of the
country's population. The consensus among Brazilian scholars is that
three state policies are at the core of São Paulo's urban transformation.
The first is the Land Law of 1850, which reclaimed state control of
"unoccupied lands," regulated land prices above market values, and prohibited buying land other than through cash purchase. In practice, the
1850 Law prohibited blacks and poor Brazilians from having access to
land and property while the state invested the money acquired through
the "unoccupied lands" and the profit from land transactions to support
the coffee boom.

The second state policy was a new immigration legislation that
emerged in 1887 as a result of the abolition of slavery and the raising
of the Republic, two major political and economic changes in Brazilian
society. While black and Asian immigrants were banned from entering
the Brazilian territory, the country supported European immigrants as a
workforce that would solve two problems: the loss of the enslaved labor
force and the racial anxiety over the dark-skinned population.[10] With
the arrival of European immigrants, freed blacks would find themselves
unemployed, landless, and occupying slum tenements in the city's
downtown. It is not hard to imagine the racial antagonisms that arose
from the proximity of the white elite—still resistant to the abolition of
slavery—to the black territories. The third anti-black state policy was
the industrialization of São Paulo. As the coffee *fazendas* (plantations)
became the primary destination for European immigration, the incipient industries made the city of São Paulo particularly attractive. George
Andrews argues that while blacks were prevented from participating
in the new economy on the basis of supposedly meritocratic choices,
immigrant families not only counted on state subsidies but were also
given preference in the job market regardless of their labor skills. Racial

discrimination in access to the labor market was fundamental to the economic mobility of poor white Europeans: it allowed them to accumulate economic resources that would later be critical to their social mobility and access to urban land.[11] Indeed, the denial of access to the job market and to land were the main blockages to black social mobility in the postabolitionist period. As a result of the overpriced land, as well as state ownership of large portions of it and state support for large landowners' acquisitions, São Paulo's land market became very restrictive to both poor immigrants and the black population. However, the former still counted on state incentives and racial preferences that enabled them to secure access to housing and to create the net worth that may explain the persistent economic gap between the two groups.[12]

As the government welcomed white immigrants, the new arrivals replaced blacks in the labor force and also appropriated the traditionally black territories in the city. The ideology of whitening was spatially expressed in the state's urban cleansing policies. If the young republic were to embrace civilized standards and attain the status of a developed nation—insofar as its population looked white—its cities needed to reflect such changes in their landscapes.[13] In this new imaginary of urban modernity, urbanist Raquel Rolnick argues, the *quituteiras* (black female street vendors) should leave because they "disrupt traffic," the markets should be transferred because they are "an affront to the culture and pollute the city," and "the *pai-de-santos* ('father of saint,' or *orixás*) can no longer work because they are liars who pretend to be inspired by some supernatural being."[14] In fact, in 1886, the São Paulo city government introduced an urban planning program that prohibited selling items in the streets, outlawed informal markets, and demolished the old downtown where blacks had traditionally lived in slum tenements called *cortiços*.[15] The city was divided into two parts: the elite's New City—including the current upper-class neighborhoods of Campos Eliseos, Boulevard Alto Caguacú, Jardim da Aclimação, and Higienópolis—and the proletarian city in the surrounding districts of what is now Bexiga, Brás, and Barra Funda, where European working-class immigrants had settled.[16]

This remodeling of the city "swept away" the traditionally black territories of downtown, thereby pushing this demographic to faraway areas in the margins of the city.[17] As São Paulo consolidated itself as

Brazil's industrial center during the first half of the twentieth century, it also started to receive a wave of migrants, predominantly poor black and brown northeastern Brazilians escaping from hunger and from the drought that still plagues that area of the country. That is when the process of residential segregation intensified. Urban renewal policies—including subsidized mortgages for middle-class families, the privatization of public housing projects, and the abandonment of migrants to self-constructed houses—created a pattern of spatial segregation in which blacks and northeastern immigrants were pushed into "illegal" settlements in the far periphery. Unable to cope with the high cost of housing and lacking "good" credit history, they inhabited areas lacking basic infrastructure such as water, sewage services, pavements, and garbage collection.[18]

In *City of Walls,* anthropologist Teresa Caldeira contends that São Paulo's pattern of residential occupation cannot be explained solely by the center–periphery model, in which the poor are pushed out and the wealthy residents control the city's prime areas. Instead, she sustains that São Paulo's urban occupation is the result of three distinct yet complementary dynamics: spatial heterogeneity, spatial homogeneity, and spatial heterogeneity again. There was relative heterogeneity in the city during the first few decades of the twentieth century, given the presence of the black population in hyperimpoverished enclaves surrounded by the white elite in the downtown area. Between the 1940s and the 1980s, however, this population was pushed to the expanded periphery of the city, mainly due to the high cost of rent and the rapid increase in valuation of real estate. Joining the wave of northeastern migrants pressuring the demand for housing, these residents built houses on high-risk hills or on environmentally protected water-supply areas that were lacking basic infrastructure such as public transportation, sanitation, and electricity. Then, in the 1980s and 1990s, new favelas sprung up around prime São Paulo neighborhoods; the poverty of the periphery was again on the doorsteps of the city's elites. According to Caldeira, this trend may be explained by the diminishing supply of vacant land for the expansion of the urban frontier, and also by the high cost of public transportation for the working class to reach their jobs as domestic workers in the elite neighborhoods. Previously expelled due to housing costs from the city center to distant areas on the outskirts, where their spatial mobility was restricted, the working class began an inverse movement from the periphery to impoverished areas around rich areas, where they could mitigate prices of transportation and be close to their places of employment. In the new pattern of segregation, "different social classes live closer to each other in some areas but are kept apart by physical barriers and systems of identification control."[19]

Although the lack of institutionalized discriminatory policies and the current spatial heterogeneity of São Paulo (and Brazilian cities in general) demonstrate differences from South Africa's apartheid or from the ghetto model of segregation in the United States, São Paulo is a de facto racial-apartheid city. This is an approach avoided by scholars of spatial segregation in Brazil, who think that the weight of race in the pattern of segregation should be relativized. São Paulo's historical process of spatial occupation is indeed different from that of these countries, and "the model of segregation in São Paulo does not correspond to the [American] ghetto." But, as showed by the same literature that relativizes the weight of race, economic forces alone do not explain the uneven geographies of the *city of walls*.[20] As in many other spheres of social life, São Paulo's spatial dynamics are deeply informed by its racial politics. That means that to read the city's race-based segregation, one first has to consider how ideologies of race and skin-color privilege produce (as much as they are products of) the urban space even in the absence of racial discourses.

A way to unveil this de facto apartheid is to look at moments of spatial disruption such as the city's response to marginalized black youth "taking a little stroll" (the so-called *rolezinhos*) in the mall of a wealthy neighborhood in 2013, as mentioned earlier. In that case, black marginalized youth "invaded" unspoken yet socially expected spaces of privilege reserved for the white middle class. The reaction of the white middle class cohered to the popular Brazilian saying, "cada macaco em seu lugar" (each monkey to his own branch). The discursive arrangement of racial difference finds then its economic materiality in public space. Even in the common context of racial proximity, there is still a spatial relation of domination. In an economic sense, this proximity is functional as the predominantly black territory provides cheap labor, or in any case, a surplus population that is devoured by the carceral state. In the racial imagination of *paulistanos,* when one says "favela" one implicitly manifests a spatially grounded *racial truth*. Yet, there seems to be more to the contemporary spatial arrangement of racial difference in the city than just racist attitudes toward blacks. Hegemonic ideas about blackness, violence, and crime converge in the production of economically disinvested, politically marginalized, and militarily brutalized topographies of race. Thus, "racial truth" finds its material base in areas of privilege and social suffering that make up the city. There may not be overtly discriminatory racial policies in contemporary São Paulo, but similar to the United States, the "Brazilian apartheid" is *the result of the state's policies aimed at maintaining white supremacy* through the cumulative process of denying land rights, job opportunities, and black Brazilians' right to the city since the postcolonial period.[21]

The "Brazilian apartheid" is expressed also in the chromatic privilege that informs racial relations in the city; thus one has to relativize the class-based argument of a racially diverse urban periphery. To be fair, like the spectrum of skin color that composes Brazilian society, the periphery of São Paulo is not racially homogenous. Still, it reflects the social geography of opportunity and poverty in which the darker the skin color, the higher the likelihood of occupying places of urban precarity. I regret that I have no data to back up this claim, but considering the myth of racial democracy, one could imagine two spatial referents for the distribution of the racially "ambiguous" population: the favela as an undoubtedly predominantly dark space and the *jardins* as a predominantly white area of privilege, with the in-between as predominantly brown. Researchers at Instituto Nexus created an index of dissimilarity—a methodology that measures the intensity of racial segregation in a given geographic area—that revealed that São Paulo is the third-most-segregated capital city in Brazil. In a scale from 0 to 100, in which 0 is the ideal racial integration, São Paulo has an index of 35.9.[22] Although this number is much smaller than that for cities like New York, for instance, in which the dissimilarity is 81.4, if we consider that the data are based on the Brazilian census (in which respondents generally do not self-identify as black) there is reason to believe that this figure is understated. The map below illustrates the spatial distribution of the black population in São Paulo's periphery.

The darker areas on the map are boroughs where the black and brown populations represent more than 50 percent of the local

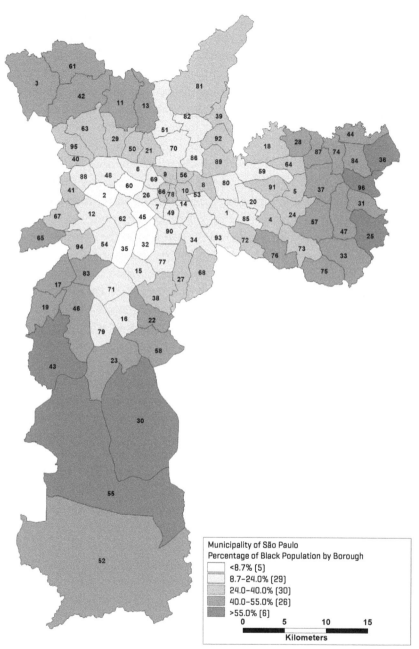

Municipality of São Paulo
Percentage of Black Population by Borough
- <8.7% [5]
- 8.7–24.0% [29]
- 24.0–40.0% [30]
- 40.0–55.0% [26]
- >55.0% [6]

0   5   10   15
Kilometers

Distribution of the black population in the city of São Paulo. Map by Fundação Seade, Census IBGE 2010.

population. In the intermediary/grey areas, the black population makes up an average of 30 percent, and in the lighter areas in the center of the map blacks account for less than 10 percent of the population. The reader should keep in mind that São Paulo's population is 60.6 percent white, 37 percent black, and 2.2 percent of Asian descent. Not surprisingly, the pattern of residential segregation produces uneven geographies of opportunity and exclusion. The lighter areas in the map, where whites present an average of 85 percent of the population, are also the areas with the highest levels of employment, income, and literacy, and the lowest levels of violent death. The income average in these areas is 2,500.00 USD, whereas in the predominantly black boroughs, the average income is only 800.00 USD. The difference in median household income between predominantly white and predominantly black boroughs can be as disparate as 5,400.00 USD (in the white district of Pinheiros) and 640.00 USD (in the predominantly black district of Parelheiros).[23] The black territories contain only 2 percent of the job opportunities, which means long public transportation commutes for those employed in the service economy (which represents the main occupation for blacks in the city). As for education, 23.6 percent of white youth have a college degree, while among the black population this number is as low as 6.4 percent. Even on the micro level, racial diversity among the poor does not authorize a reading of the periphery as a place for "racial democracy from below," because blacks are still the ones enduring the most state violence in these spaces. At least 65 percent of the violent deaths in the city are committed against black men between 15 and 39 years of age living at the edges of the city.[24] The phenomenon of whites living in high-poverty neighborhoods seems to be an accident, an accident that makes white bodies vulnerable to widespread policing practices against black and brown bodies in these territories. A question that begs further investigation, then, is what is at stake when a social group is victimized by its proximity to the black body?

Killing Bodies, Making Space

The remnants left by the Slaughters, a police-linked death squad terrorizing inhabitants of Zona Sul's favelas, are the dismembered bodies of their victims. After dismembering the bodies, the killers scatter them and hide them from sight. They are burned, buried in clandestine cemeteries, or disposed of in the garbage. During the course of my research, the dismembered bodies of Betinho, Lucas, nine other young men, and one woman were discovered on street corners and among bushes in slum settlements on the Fundão da Zona Sul, where the Slaughters operate. Far from being isolated events, targeted assassinations and disappearances have become mundane policing practices in São Paulo's favela. The Slaughters operate in an area also ominously referred to by residents as the "Bermuda Triangle" or "Triangle of Death," as it comprises the territorial jurisdiction of three police precincts that form a triangle. The "triangle" is located in a depressing area compounded by a sea of favelas that houses an average of 30 percent of those killed by the police in the city every year. A study by *Ponte Jornalismo* has shown that the police consistently kill in the same areas. The southside and eastside favelas accounted for 82 percent of all killings by the police in the city of São Paulo in 2014. The southwest of the city (where the white upperclass population is concentrated) registered 9 percent of killings by the police during the same period.[25]

The areas housing the most police terror are also the most stigmatized in the media. Consider, for instance, one of the Fundão's densely populated territories loosely referred to as Jardim Angela. Eight miles from downtown São Paulo, the region is integrated in the city's imaginary as a crime-prone territory where police violence is not only justified but also necessary for the preservation of the spatioracial boundaries of the "legal" city.[26] An analysis of news coverage in the late 1990s and early 2000s, for instance, reveals a criminalizing narrative of the region as "the most dangerous area of the city," "the champion of violence," and "a place scared by drug dealers." On May 7, 1997, the newspaper *Diário do Comércio* called attention to the "endemic" homicidal violence in the region with the headline "Jardim Angela bate Cali em homicídios" (Jardim Angela Beats Cali in Homicides). The news invests in the rhetoric of war, associating the neighborhood with the narco dispute that turned the Colombian city into the area with the highest homicide rates in the world during the 1990s. The race between the favela and the city of Cali also suggests that Jardim Angela is not a part of São Paulo, but a place out of control and under the domain of drug dealers. This is how Cali has been portrayed in the international media and in Hollywood—another instance in which some geographies are pathologized to protect white tourism.[27] A news report on August 29, 1997, in *Folha de S. Paulo* opened the front page of the section "Cotidiano" with the following headline: "PM is received under bullets at Jardim Angela." The text, based on the police report, presents a confrontation between drug dealers and the police to justify the use of force against local residents. The text reads, "The main goal, besides the verification of cars, motorcycles, buses, and pubs, was to try to apprehend clandestine guns." The journalist then presents an account of the military operation: 1,538 suspects were stopped, more than a hundred and fifty pubs were supervised, four guns were apprehended, and one alleged bandit was killed. The newspaper also quotes the commander in chief of the Military Police saying, "We are going to make *arrastões* (looting rampages) against criminality. Operations like this one will happen every weekend."[28] On March 4, 2004, *Diário de S. Paulo*'s news report, "Drugs Scare Jardim Angela," stressed the correlation between the high consumption of alcohol and homicidal violence among males, who, according to the journalist, spend many hours drinking. The news report ends by advocating strict alcohol regulations and an early-to-bed bar curfew to discipline local youth.

The city's concern over Jardim Angela has inspired journalists to live in the district in order to follow the infamous ROTA (the Rondas Ostensivas Tobias Aguiar, a special branch of the Military Police) at work in its harassment of Jardim Angela residents.[29] In "Night of Blitz in Jardim Angela," journalist Valdir Sanches narrates a "surprise attack" by the Military Police on the favela. Sanches, documenting the military occupation, writes the narrative from the perspective of the police. In the text, spectacular raids by the police seem to be the obvious approach to securing the endangered city against the favelados. Leaving no doubt about his agenda, Sanches ends his account with a melancholic note: "Individuals evade, running up the steep stairways . . . Soon the two officers who were in the vehicle receive a call on the radio. They run around the block at speed to the top of the stairways. But there is no time. The suspects escaped."[30] While homicide, violence, drug trafficking, and poverty are unmistakably part of the everyday lives of favela residents, what interests me here is the "collective authorship of space"[31] by the interrelated narratives of government reports, police raids, and the media. Collectively, the media and government produce the favelas of the Fundão da Zona Sul as an outlawed geography. Within this context, police killings are the materialization in bodies and spaces of discourses and anxieties around crime and violence in the city. In that sense, the black bodies killed, dismembered, and scattered by the Slaughters are polysemic signs in which one can "read" the collective authorship of black zones of nonbeing.[32]

Scholars have long considered the role of violence in producing spatialities. Anthropologist Allen Feldman argues that in Northern Ireland, the body, space, and violence were political commodities and "inscribed texts" that mediated both political domination and political agency. Space, he notes, is not a thing out there but rather "a power and an animated entity" or a "mnemonic artifact" that embodies the history of Belfast's religious-sectarian violence. Violence is the medium for ordering and colonizing imagined and disputed space: it allows political actors to perform their own narratives of spatial belonging.[33] Finally, the dead body is a spatial inscription that, in the face of territorial disputes, enables "unrealizable geographies" to come into being. As he notes, "the production of stiffs transfers territorial paradigms from topographic registers to the surface of human bodies."[34]

What is particularly useful in Feldman's work, as it relates to Brazil, is his framing of the body as an "instrumental staging" for political and territorial claims. In São Paulo, the disfigured bodies of Lucas and Betinho are instrumental in the production of São Paulo's black spatialities. The Slaughters seem to be very aware of this macabre sociospatial engineering. The strategy of dismembering and disposing of black bodies throughout the favelas has been effective for two reasons. First, and more obvious, without the evidence of a dead body police officers are rarely held accountable for the killings and can continue to terrorize the favelas with impunity. Second, and perhaps less explicit, by appropriating, destroying, and disposing of bodies, the police officers produce social life. Through killings, they demarcate the political terrain from which the dead emerge as a necropolitical spatiality, and, in doing so, produce the opposite biopolitical geography of privilege and sociality. As police terror strips the favelado of life, it also provides the political resources for imagining white and nonblack spatialities as the places where civil life is lived.[35] Finally, police terror is instrumental to the production of the *city-state* (here understood as the juridical-political *community* where contractual subjects/citizens exercise their legal rights). Thus, far from being a problem, policing is a solution. It produces racialized bodies and spaces as "instrumental staging" for *city-state* making. This can be seen in the embodied sovereignty of the Slaughters, and also in the increasing deployment of the Brazilian military's counterinsurgency strategies to "conquer" the urban territories under enemy control in most Brazilian metropolitan areas.

The question of mundane forms of state sovereignty has been at the center of current anthropological inquiries. Anthropologists have looked at everyday expressions of political authority in military checkpoints, airports, legal bureaucracies, or wherever some individuals hold decisive power over life and death.[36] While I discuss the political implications of such all-encompassing conceptualizations of the state in a later section of this book, I follow their path in thinking of the police as the embodiment of state sovereignty. In the peripheries of São Paulo, the state comes into being through a "bloody transaction"—to use Frederick Douglass's famous term—between the favelado as the enemy of public order and civil society as a threatened political community. In the absence of an external enemy, blacks embody the enmity that informs the boundaries of citizenship, the regime of law, and state sovereignty. And, because state sovereignty relies on a permanent anxiety about *aliens,* the production of the favela as a foreign and outlawed territory justifies decisive warfare, as seen in nationally televised and spectacular military raids organized to pacify Rio's favelas and in civil society's complicity (or tacit silence) about police killings in these foreign territories.[37] Police officers shooting at favela residents from helicopters, checkpoints preventing residents from getting in or out, and military raids without search warrants all illustrate the foreign land of the favela, where the law as protection never applies.

What is at stake here, therefore, is not so much the police embodiment of state sovereignty but also, and perhaps more pointedly, the racial *locus* in which the exercise of such embodied sovereignty takes place, that is, the black body. That is also to say, in this supposedly raceless city, that the police draw racial lines in bodies and in space through acts of killing. Police terror, then, becomes a tool for the spatial arrangement of racial difference. The uncanny capability of the police to produce racial alterities through death is something black activists have long presented in their critiques of the myth of racial democracy. They have insisted on examining the relation between the elite's kitchen and the master's house, the favela and the plantation, the police patrol and the slavery cargo.[38] These sites of racial violence, they argue, should be enough to disprove claims of São Paulo as a racially democratic city. More than a joke, the saying "If you want to know who is black and who is not, ask the police" expresses an awareness of the police's destructive creation of racialized bodies.

Legalized Killings

When I discussed the Slaughters with Francisco, a friend in Dreaming City, he warned me against treating the death squad as if they were an exception in policing practices. He was surprised that I was investigating the death squad, because killings by the police are common events in the Fundão da Zona Sul. When I suggested that the death squad comprises outlaw police officers who had been under investigation, Francisco became upset, insisting, "That is the problem, we continue to distinguish between legal and illegal police violence." "It does not matter if they were rogue police officers or not," Francisco added. He pointed out that the police have always acted this way in the favela: "You may not have the Slaughters, but you have the others [referring to the Police Special Unit famous for its lethal practices in Brazil]. At the end of the day, they are all the same."[39] Francisco had a point. The political lexicon that scholars use to describe killings by the police is part of the problem. We often rely on the legal grammar of the state, which turns police terror into police violence and targeted assassinations into legal interventions. In the same way, by focusing on particular stories, one may involuntarily regard police killings as isolated events rather than practices entrenched in the legal apparatus of the Brazilian state. Killings carried out by on-duty and police-linked death squads are so systemic that human rights organizations call the phenomenon a "policy of extermination," and the black movement has referred to it as "black genocide."[40] The intensity of these killings became even clearer to me in 2010, after I began to make regular visits to the Police Ombudsperson's Office (Ouvidoria de Policia) in São Paulo. I initially went to collect information on the death of Betinho, which I thought would be useful in Dona Maria's efforts to initiate a lawsuit against the state. I met Joaquim, the person in charge of the archives, in a room packed with countless boxes of complaints related to police killings. Joaquim welcomed me with a sense of humor: "Here, you pick the place. Just name the favela and we can give you something to have fun with.

Folders containing files on the victims of police killings were organized by year. It took me a while to find Betinho's file among others labeled "The Slaughters." I started collecting the material I felt would be helpful for Dona Maria's legal battle. I even tracked down some of the documents that the courthouse had refused to share with her: the police report, the autopsy report, the public attorney's filing, and the police inquiry. As I collected materials, I found myself surrounded by dozens of records on police killings and disappearances. The staff at the ombudsperson's headquarters kept receiving calls denouncing police abuse, thereby increasing the number of files. It was Joaquim who called to my attention what he describes as the "cinematic narrative" of police killing.[41] Pointing to a huge stack of papers on the table, Joaquim explained, "Here you will find all that trash with the same copy-and-paste text. All the same . . . The story is always the same. The police ask the guy to stop, he evades the checkpoint, the police go after him, he crashes into a wall, comes out of the car shooting at the police, and the police react by firing. He is taken to the hospital but doesn't make it." "It's like a Hollywood movie," he added.

Joaquim also kept an electronic file of autopsy reports with photographs of disfigured bodies: heads destroyed by bullets, backs riddled with gunshot wounds, legs and arms broken apart. When I asked him what he made of this evidence of targeted assassination, he responded, "This is going to be just another case number and then forgotten. This is included in the annual report as statistics, goes to the governor's desk, and then becomes trash." What most disturbed me about these pictures was the spectacular nature of police killings. The killings generally took place in public spaces such as squares and streets rather than in spaces hidden from sight, thus exposing a dimension not yet fully explored in the scholarship on police violence in Brazil. The police reports themselves reveal that the spectacle of death is a defining feature of state sovereignty in troubled urban areas of Brazil rather than a practice belonging to the past. If we were to universalize Foucault's claim that with the spectacular punishment of Damien for regicide we closed a historic period of torture as public spectacle and the body as "the major target of penal repression," then what are we to make of the public rituals of police terror in São Paulo's streets?[42] What Foucault failed to consider, Joy James points out, is that "some bodies cannot be normalized no matter how they are disciplined, unless the prevailing social and state structures that figuratively and literally rank bodies disintegrate."[43] In the Brazilian racial order, the disintegration of such "normalizing structures" remains to be seen, as black bodies are lynched in public spectacles. During the process of conducting research in the Ouvidoria de Policia, I collected dozens of descriptions of killings from the police reports that underscore such critiques:

> Arriving at the site, it was found to be a case of gang robbery. We started a police raid when we identified nine armed men. When we identified ourselves as police and ordered them to drop their weapons and surrender, they fired individual rounds toward the police, who retaliated against the unfair attack by firing their guns. Such individuals were shot and taken to the General Hospital of Taipas, where they did not survive the wounds. At the site, weapons were found, drugs and objects were seized and sent to technical expertise.

> The Military Police were patrolling the streets when they heard explosions and headed to the scene. In front of the bar, four people were injured. People reported to the PMs which direction the vehicle, a black Chevrolet Corsa, went on the run. Police pursuit began, at that time the driver lost control of the Corsa and hit the wall. The two defendants came out with guns drawn and shot the policemen. PMs retaliated with shots hitting them. The accused were taken to the Hospital but eventually died.

> The defendants, using . . . motorcycle, approached the victim and by using a firearm stole his phone. The victim called the police and immediately started pursuit. They were told they were under arrest, and they responded with gunfire toward the police, forcing the police to retaliate, injuring them. They were helped to the emergency room but did not survive the injuries and died.

The police were notified of a robbery at the shop. Undercover police were at the scene and went to catch the robbers, who escaped into the woods. The officers approached the robbers but they began to take shots at police. There was a counter-attack and a robber was shot, and immediately rescued to the Hospital. Didn't survive the injuries, he died.

The reach of these "cinematic narratives," as Joaquim calls them, goes beyond law enforcement practices. These narratives also permeate the medical sphere, where cases of wounded patients left to die for being "criminals" abound.[44] The multiple spaces in which deadly police practices take place—in the favela, on the streets, in the police car, or in the emergency room—creates a traceable network between the police raid, the rescue, and the refusal of medical attention in the emergency room. Joaquim refers to this as a "methodology of death." He explained to me, "The police kills; with luck, the victim makes it to the hospital; the doctor delays care, and the newspaper justifies the killing." The span between the street, the police car, and the hospital constitutes the scenario in which other state actors participate in this policing ritual of death. Although the state of São Paulo has passed a resolution prohibiting police from rescuing the wounded individuals—after Human Rights Watch pointed out that the removal of dead bodies on the way to the hospital is a way to clean up a crime scene and to cover up police killings—the connection between the police and medical interventions still begs attention from researchers on police violence.[45] In the Brazilian context of racialized access to health care, medical interventions reproduce patterns of racial discrimination ranging from lack of access to health care and refusal of care in the emergency room to medical errors and misconduct such as denying anesthesia to black mothers in childbirth.[46]

In the cases involving police killings, the scope of the officers' and/or doctors' complicity remains unknown, as both the police and the medical authorities have the last word on the so-called "death event." For instance, press accounts help to unveil the sinister power of the police to decide who is dead, who should be taken to the hospital, and who deserves to live. On August 24, 2011, the newspaper *Folha de S. Paulo* delivered a videotape featuring three police officers surrounding two handcuffed young men, shot and in agonizing pain on the streets of

São Paulo. The video shows an officer saying, "S.O.B, you have not died yet? Look at me! Damn you. Not dead yet?" Then another officer says, "Estrebucha! Filho da puta, estrebucha, vai! (rattle and throw to death son of a bitch). I hope you die on the way to the hospital. Are you not dying?"[47] Deliberately letting individuals die or denying them immediate access to the emergency room after having been shot is yet another face of the terrocratic nature of the Brazilian police force.

Black activists and the parents of the dead find it extraordinarily hard to challenge the legal narratives of police killings. After all, the police report, autopsy report, and even the prosecutor's documents do not deny the murders; in fact, they acknowledge them. Yet they do so in a manner that both criminalizes the victims in advance (the police appear as victims of those resisting arrest) and justifies killing as the "strict duty" of state agents. In the first excerpt above, for instance, the killing of nine individuals is justified as police retaliation against the criminals' "unfair aggression." Likewise, the police report states that the officers simply retaliated against "unlawful aggression," and that the deaths were incidental ("The individuals didn't survive the injuries and eventually died."). In the second report, I found important information buried in the file of the deceased at the Police Ombudsperson's Office: one of the two men who were killed by the police had used his cell phone to photograph himself in the back of the police car and had subsequently hidden the phone in his underwear. This photograph, when discovered by the victim's family, became evidence that he was alive in the police car rather than having been killed earlier in the crossfire, as described in the official police report.[48] Given that the police incident report is the primary document needed to open an investigation of possible wrongdoing, police officers place great emphasis on the culpability of the dead and the victimization of the officers when issuing the incident report at the police station. This blame-the-victim language places the responsibility to prove the police officers' misconduct on the families of the deceased.

Predictably, since the police essentially investigate other police, there is a systematic failure to prosecute officers.[49] At the Ombudsperson's Office, I identified a standard response to claims made by the family members of the deceased: "The shootings were motivated in response to the unjust aggression suffered by the police," or "There was no unlawful practice since the death was caused by the deceased themselves in using firearms against police officers."[50] To complicate matters even more, the Persecution Service (known as Ministério Público) that holds the power to oversee the police and to defend civilian constitutional guarantees under the 1988 Brazilian Constitution has a troubling record of closing cases involving police killings in the state of São Paulo. The cases that are investigated are quite often archived "pending further evidence" or deemed justified as the officer was "strictly performing his duties." As a report by Amnesty International in 2015 acknowledged, there is a shared belief among members of the judiciary that the police are just cleaning up criminals from the city. Thus, cases involving the police themselves are swept under the carpet.[51]

An incident from 2015 illustrates this culture of complicity and impunity. Stuck in a traffic jam due to a public demonstration against fare hikes for city buses in São Paulo, a public prosecutor responsible for overseeing criminal cases involving police officers posted the following message on his Facebook page from his car: "Someone tell the police that if they kill those motherfuckers I will close the police inquiry."[52] A similar view is publicly expressed by elected government officials in other parts of the country, who quite often respond to police killings of civilians as being justifiable because, after all, "one cannot make an omelet without breaking the eggs."[53] Even more troubling, São Paulo's police force holds strategic positions in political parties. Former officers have been elected to the city council and state and federal legislature by selling themselves as "killers of bandits"—they constitute the infamous "bullet caucus." In two emblematic cases, former Military Police commanders Coronel Telhada and Conte Lopes were reelected to the city council in 2016 and to the state legislature in 2014, respectively, advertising their sinister legacy: "Let's say, I killed forty," Conte Lopes admitted in a public interview. Telhada, who had admitted to killing thirty-one individuals, was nominated to the State Commission of Human Rights. He defended his nomination, saying that "police officers are the main human rights activists because they protect the lives of other humans."[54]

Some research on the sociology of policing argues that modern police have achieved such a high degree of bureaucratization and autonomy (in comparison to other state bureaucracies) that they can hardly be controlled. This theory suggests that the state's weakness or efficacy can be evaluated based on its police force's degree of autonomy. Mathieu Deflem observes that "the autonomy of state bureaucracies, ironically, creates the potential for bureaucratic activity to be planned and implemented without regard for considerations of legality, justice, and politics."[55] While no one could deny that the police maintain extraordinary autonomy and discretionary power in modern democracies such as Brazil, the police's "autonomy" in relation to that of other state bureaucracies should be viewed with caution. In Brazil, as shown above, the judiciary and other branches of the state are intimately connected to the legalization of police terror in the same way that police terror informs other government practices. Although the media portrays the police as an institution with a life of its own, and the state-elected government turns a blind eye to systemic police killings by individualizing police misconduct, police terror cannot be dissociated from other state practices—not even its less-repressive branches. In fact, policing is much more than the work of officers in the street. It is also a "program of government rationality."[56]

Police killings reflect and energize broader state ideologies. Even if one were to move away from the Marxist understanding of the state as an apparatus of the dominant class, or from the Weberian idea of state force, and instead agree with the poststructuralist approach of the state as "an abstraction," "a message of domination," or "an ideological artifact," the police would still stand as the organizing principle and paradigmatic materiality of the state idea, not as an independent force.[57] The problem of policing vis-à-vis state bureaucracy has been explored by the incipient scholarship on police subjectivity in Brazil. Who are the Brazilian police officers? Why do they kill? The police find moral and political justifications for their actions in the predictable legal-bureaucratic rationality of "just doing our job." Police who kill and torture have undergone violence training programs that have desensitized them to their victims' suffering and compelled them to "blindly obey" their superiors. These trainings "prepare police to become more effective at carrying out atrocities."[58] Another often overlooked aspect is that policing practices are socially situated within the larger political and ideological climate that establishes notions of crime, order, justice, and value judgment on who deserves to live. Police officers generally see their work as a civic duty to "clean up" the city. They usually work under the socially shared belief that so-called criminals should be killed because sending them to jail is a waste of taxpayers' money and perhaps a waste of their own time. Disturbing evidence from a 2015 national survey by the *Folha de S. Paulo* newspaper and the Brazilian Forum of Public Safety revealed that as many as 50 percent of Brazilians agree with the popular saying, "a good bandit is a dead bandit." Not new, this motto is found in strategies used by elected officials, the police, the conservative media, and a great part of civil society to justify extrajudicial executions, which are seen as a civic responsibility to do what the supposedly "failed" justice system cannot do.[59] Here, the police are given autonomy and are detached from the state in a convenient and fashioned way.

This ideology is so pervasive that officers who formerly were favela residents and potential victims of police abuse share the belief that killing "thugs" is a part of the police's duty. According to Roque, a young black man from Educafro who had been admitted into the Military Police, "one thing officers do not tolerate is to see a thug back and forth between the prison and the streets. It makes us feel like we are wasting our time. . . . It is frustrating [when] we arrest them and the justice [system] frees them."[60] The social profile of police officers like Roque may challenge some assumptions of the Brazilian police as a homogeneously white institution against the black population. While high-ranking positions in the rigid military hierarchy are predominantly white, the Brazilian police force is racially diverse.[61] In the face of such a reality, we must ask: What are police officers telling themselves when they kill individuals who quite often are from their own social group? The subject position of police officers in Brazilian society (mostly as poor black and brown men with few options other than joining the police) speaks volumes about the need to interrogate how race is lived and avoided by black Brazilians.

I was relieved when Roque, the young man from Educafro, told me in our last interaction that although he had been admitted into the São Paulo Military Police, he was now thinking of quitting the job. Roque had migrated to the city from a rural community three hundred miles away from São Paulo, hoping to study at a public university. He did not pass the highly selective entry exam but was fortunate to get a fellowship to study at a private university. Unemployed and sharing an apartment with five other unemployed students from the same rural community, he decided to apply to the Military Police. The salary was attractive (roughly 700.00 USD) and the exam required him to have only a high school degree. Roque was thinking of quitting, but he was also hesitant about losing a stable job in the public sector. When I asked him if he did not fear being killed, his answer was predictable: "Kill or been killed, I would be taking a risk either way, Jaime."

Indeed, as victims and victimizers, black and poor marginalized individuals are killed on both sides of law enforcement practices. Although at a much lower rate than civilian deaths, the mortality rate among the Brazilian police is much higher compared to other parts of the world. In the United States, for example, the annual civilian/police killing ratio is twelve civilian deaths for every police officer killed. In Brazil, this figure is much higher at a ratio of 21:1.[62] That said, to read the blurred racial lines between victims and victimizers in Brazilian urban policing as black-on-black violence—and thus as a matter of individual accountability rather than structural racism—is to overlook the normative framework in which police violence becomes accepted and even expected. Police practices in Brazil should be located within the "historic-racial and bodily schema" that structures urban imaginaries of crime, order, and fear.[63] In this sense, it is irrelevant that the police force in Brazil has become more racially diverse, because at the end of the day the bodies to be protected and the sources of threat are clearly defined.

Killing the Dead

What is it about the black body that makes it the target of multiple forms of killing? What else are the police killing when, besides shooting, they decide to dismember, burn, and hide the destroyed body from sight? Although set in a completely different context, anthropologist María Victoria Uribe's analysis of the period of political terror in Colombia called "La Violencia" provides some insights into the bodily economy of police terror in Brazil. In Colombia, the massacres followed a ritual that transformed the dead into a "macabre allegory." Bodies were turned inside-out as if in reverse of the world's order—for example, victims' intestines were inserted into their mouths; their throats were cut deeply and tongues brought out of the hole in an act called the "necktie." In this way, the process of killing was also a process of unmaking and creating a symbolic order that would distinguish humans (the killers) from *inhumans* (the annihilated victims were referred to as animals). Uribe argues that this process was threefold: to kill (biological death), counter-kill (beheading and reversing of anatomic order), and rekill (scattering of the body).[64] Unlike in Colombia's "La Violencia," where peasants were assassinated for their (supposed) political membership, and unlike in the political violence of the Brazilian dictatorship regime, in which leftist activists were tortured and assassinated, blacks in the Brazilian racialized regime of terror are killed for being blacks. Like in Colombia, the Slaughters' macabre ritual of repeated degradation (killing, rekill-ing, and counterkilling) seeks to destroy more than the biological life of its black victims. The dead need to be killed.

"The police kill the dead." That was how Joaquim, the public ser-vant responsible for the archives at the Police Ombudsperson's Office, explained the ruthless wrath of the death squads. Besides killing and destroying bodies, the police also invest a significant amount of energy in destroying the deceased's public image. In this context, death is just the beginning of a long punitive process that comprises the destruction and symbolic annihilation of the dead body. Dona Maria's and Dona Cecilia's struggle to defend the reputations of their loved ones exem-plifies how the state extends punishment beyond the mutilated bodies of its victims. More than once, Dona Maria showed me Betinho's em-ployment records to counter the accusation made by the police that he was a criminal. "My son was a *hard worker*. He worked all day long, from Monday to Saturday, in this car wash. He was not a criminal; he was a worker, he had a family, he had a girlfriend," she lamented. Dona Maria also complained that information about Betinho's employment status was missing from the paperwork related to his death, which pre-vented her from being able to prove his status as a breadwinner and therefore from receiving social security payments. Although the status of "hard worker" is a clear example of a restrictive conception of citi-zenship (i.e., only hard workers and good citizens deserve to live), for Dona Maria it was the only strategy to try to prevent her son's second death.[65] Black men growing up in a favela, including myself, quickly learn from their parents to never go outside without their identification cards, to memorize the telephone number of a relative, and to never leave their work papers behind. However, the rampant police violence is an obvious indicator that the status of "worker" fails to prevent one from being killed—one may be a "worker," but skin color overshadows occupational status. And yet, favela residents' investment in the worker-versus-bandit dichotomy is ambiguous and goes against their own interests. How can the very victims of the police invest in the rhetoric that justifies their killings?

Although I agree with scholars who locate such compliance within the diffuse authoritarianism that permeates Brazilian social relations, Dona Maria's and Dona Cecilia's claiming of the "worker" category seems like a conscious survival strategy rather than compliance with the restrictive notion of citizenship for which Brazil is known.[66] Joy James argues that the apparently nonradical forms of resistance that black mothers sometimes embrace reflect civil society's "biopolar stereotypes" of what constitutes a "good mother" and a "bad mother". As she contends, "most mothers, rather than school their children in radical resistance to dominance, teach them to get along in order to survive, with coping strategies that create new forms of covert resistance to subjugation."[67] In order to distance themselves and their sons from the discourses and practices that criminalized their lives, Dona Maria and Dona Cecilia embrace "working" and "good mother" as protective categories that they hope would give them and their loved ones some recognition from civil society and the police. Oddly enough, while society sends the message that those who work deserve to live, the job market is inaccessible to youth like Betinho and Lucas. Betinho began working at age thirteen to help his mother and sister survive. He followed the script society expects from "good" black men: he went to school, was a provider, worked stocking supermarket shelves and then at the carwash where he made a minimum-wage salary. Lucas, on the other hand, did not have a formal job. He helped Dona Cecilia sell yogurt on the streets, but always found a way to skip going and join his friends in smoking marijuana. Eventually, he started mugging pedestrians in the wealthy neighborhood of Moema in the *Jardins,* the same area where his mother had previously worked as a domestic servant. While Dona Cecilia links Lucas's death to what he has done "wrong" and to his friendships with other "criminals," she also complained that growing up in the favela made him particularly vulnerable to police violence. "When they come to the Fundão, be prepared because they do not go away empty handed. They don't look at who you are, if you are a hard worker or a mugger. They just come and shoot," she says.

Death haunts the black subject regardless of one's status as worker, churchgoer, or thug. Black mothers try to prevent their children
from dying once again, but the police often succeed in imposing an
official narrative that dishonors the dead. From the all-too-common
question relatives have to answer in police stations—"Does s/he have
a criminal record?"—to the struggle to claim the status of the dead as
"human being[s] that deserved a decent burial," as Dona Cecilia told
me, these experiences indicate that some deaths do not count as death
because "some subjects never achieve, in the eyes of others, the status
of living."[68] How does one navigate a social world in which life is lived
through a cumulative process of dying (day-to-day humiliation, depri-
vation, criminalization, and finally physical death), to the point that
bullets hitting black bodies are just yet another process of killing?

The phrase "killing the dead" is not rhetorical in this context. It
points to the postmortem violence the dead and their relatives have
to endure as the state holds their bodies and further deteriorates their
biographies.[69] Dona Maria explained, "They killed me twice, the day
that they captured Betinho and the day I discovered that his body was
totally spoiled. . . . Then they killed me again when the police said he
was a thug." The notion of killing someone more than once may sound
odd, but from the police's point of view it is an efficient strategy for
maintaining order by imposing a timeless death. This leaves the families
of the dead with an extra task to accomplish. Besides having to go over
all the bureaucratic battles to reclaim dead bodies, they have to fight
against the discursive dehumanization of their dead loved ones. I closely
followed Dona Maria's impossible battle to prove Betinho's innocence.
The police report on Betinho's disappearance highlighted that he "was
from a well-known favela where residents receive help from drug dealers." Dona Maria constantly complained to me that she had to remind
even social activists that Betinho was not a criminal, as they kept inter-
rogating her about her income and asking about how she could have
relied on the minimum wage of her car-washer son. "My son was not
a bandit, he was a worker," she kept insisting during our interactions.

Dona Cecilia did not have the energy to fight against the excuse
that Lucas was killed because he was a "criminal." She was aware that
Lucas's previous criminal record would make this fight even more depressing and frustrating. She just wanted "to bury him and let him

rest in peace," she said to me. Even in the hopeless fight against the criminalization of Lucas, she was conscious of what was at stake in his death. "Lucas was *presa fácil* (easy prey). I don't know if it was because he was black. . . . Now, think, two black boys in a car. I think they went to their [criminal] record. And to complicate matters, his friend has lots of tattoos . . . two black boys with criminal records. Too much violence they suffered." Jonas, her ex-husband, sued the state but also became discouraged by the fact that the police had threatened him; to complicate things even more, he also had a criminal record of his own. With no "proper credentials" to fight back, Jonas expressed his frustration to me with anger and tears in his eyes. "They may be protected by the law, but I will avenge my son, I will."

How does one recover the dead's biographies in the face of a regime of legality in which blackness is seen through the lens of criminality? Dealing with a similar set of concerns, Luciane Oliveira Rocha makes ethnographically visible some strategies black mothers embrace to recover the spoiled identity of their loved ones. If in the framework I presented above police killings are rituals of reiterating death again and again (killing, rekilling, and counterkilling), the parents of victims of police terror *dekill* the dead by stressing their positive qualities as "our children," "workers," "good citizens," and so on. Within that context, Rocha observes, black mothering appears as a political assertion of black biological and social life. In her words, "black maternity is the re-creation of black sociability in face of destruction."[70] While Rocha's intriguing notion of *dekilling* holds true to the mothers-led movement I have been working with in São Paulo—a topic I explore at length in chapter 5—I want to call attention here to the efficiency and success of the criminalizing narratives in killing the dead despite the painful and tireless efforts of the ones left behind. Commenting on the killing of five young black men by Rio de Janeiro's police on November 28, 2015, journalist Fernanda Escóssia called attention to the burden placed on the dead's families to prove their innocence. The young black men had rented a car to celebrate a friend's first paycheck as a stocker at a supermarket in Rio de Janeiro's periphery. While passing through a police checkpoint, they were shot one hundred and eleven times. The police reasoned that they had a criminal record and had attempted to shoot at the officers, who simply reacted to the aggression. They used the same "copy-and-paste" blame-the-dead narrative that Joaquim identified in São Paulo. Escóssia asks, "Why do the families [of the victims] have to explain? . . . We can hear the voices of mothers, fathers, brothers, and friends many times: he was innocent; he is studying English; he was taking a technical course; he was a good kid. I heard and still hear justifications and claims in defense of the honor of the dead children. . . . We are used to a twisted argument according to which families devastated by the tragedy of the death of their children are the ones who have to give explanations."[71] The constant need to reclaim the dead's dignity through discourses of respectability that go against their own community ("worker," "citizen," "good son," and so on) is in fact an indication that within the domain of the law, proving black innocence seems impossible. At least until now, Dona Maria's and Dona Cecilia's attempts to improve the dead's public image by appealing to their status as "workers" and "humans" have failed. The police have succeeded in destroying biographies and producing dead bodies, as the astonishing levels of killings under the label "resisting arrest" indicate, and as civil society's support of the "good thug is a dead thug" adage confirms.

Police terror is a main strategy of securing white life in São Paulo, but it is far from the only one. In the periphery of the city, there is also a set of everyday and apparently benign strategies of spatial governmentality. Aside from death squads, this "new" paradigm of policing has compelled favela residents to participate in their own policing by reporting neighbors, denouncing crime, and participating in community-based security forums. What if "community" itself were defined as an anti-black construct? What are the sets of practices put in place to govern the "unruly," predominantly black geography of São Paulo's periphery? I explore these key questions in the next chapter.

2

"POLICE, GET OFF MY BACK!"

And on the eighth day Devil created the Police.

—Popular saying, São Paulo

It then becomes necessary to consider the ways discipline itself bears the traces of what Foucault would describe as premodern forms of power but which perhaps are more aptly described as discipline with its clothes off.

—Saidiya Hartman, *Scenes of Subjection*

I arrived at the police headquarters early in the morning. After several unsuccessful attempts to interview the high commander of the Military Police at its central headquarters in downtown São Paulo, I was directed to the commander responsible for the Zona Sul area. In my e-mail request I emphasized that I was a researcher from a university in the United States. I was surprised by the cordial tone of the e-mails once I disclosed this information. The pleasant treatment ended, however, when I reached the checkpoint at the military building. When I tried to enter through the "civilian gateway," an angry police officer shouted, "Hey, what do you think you are doing? Step back, step back! You cannot enter here." I handed him the printed e-mail from the commander and he quickly apologized. He sent me to the main building, where I showed my identification and explained the reason for my visit to a police officer. She took me to a room where I waited for my interviewee, Commander Pontarelli.

On a wall in the Commander's office was a picture of a white man in his early fifties wearing a decorated uniform denoting his high position in the military hierarchy. It was Mr. Pontarelli. Written on the wall above his photograph was the Military Police motto: "We, the Military Police, are committed to the defense of life, physical integrity, and human dignity." The national, state, and military flags in the corner of the room added more formality to the environment. I was distracted by my survey of the decor when Commander Pontarelli arrived, accompanied by four other officials. I quickly stood up and extended my hand to greet him. We shook hands, but he could not hide his disappointment with my presence. I explained that I was a Brazilian researcher trained at a U.S.-based university. His disappointment was quickly matched by his curiosity about how I managed to study in the United States. He directed me to one of the two couches next to his desk and asked me to take a seat alongside his four male assistants. He did not join us. Instead, he went behind his desk to his computer and interjected corrections, clarifications, and other bits of information in between phone conversations. Based on his inattention, it was obvious that I was not the researcher he had expected to meet.

The Police Headquarters

As I sat down on the sofa, one policeman handed me an institutional bulletin highlighting an award the Military Police had just received in Japan for its innovative community-policing program. I expressed my interest in knowing more about the program and its impact on the reduction of homicides in the Fundão da Zona Sul. Naïvely, I forgot a basic journalism rule of thumb I had learned in my professional training—leave the more difficult issues for the end of the interview— and told them I was also interested in discussing the police-linked death squads operating in the Fundão. As soon as I mentioned the death squads, Commander Pontarelli turned toward me and protested, "Stop! Stop! Where did you hear that? From the media?" He stood up angrily and joined us on the couch. I had suspected this kind of reaction to questions about the Slaughters, even though the link between the police and the death squads had been widely publicized by the media and human rights organizations. Bringing up the issue at the very beginning of our conversation turned out not to be too terrible after all. My inter-locutors tacitly recognized that my position as researcher could be used to promote the "new" police and its commitment to the philosophy of human rights. At stake was a political strategy to promote a positive image of an institution associated with rampant acts of brutality and terror in one of the most violent areas of the city. One of the assistants emphatically questioned the media's descriptions of the death squad as the "Slaughters," arguing that it was just a word used in order "to sell newspapers." He cautioned me not to reproduce the nomenclature in my research. Commander Pontarelli chimed in: "You cannot say that they [the Slaughters] were Military Police. When they did that crap, they were not wearing military uniforms and they were not on the clock." I showed them a newspaper article with a photograph of twelve police officers suspected of murdering thirteen individuals, including Betinho and Lucas. An awkward silence descended on the room. One assistant took the newspaper and examined it closely. The commander resumed: "Some cases may be true. I am not going to tell you that it is impossible that we have police officers involved. But let's be clear, the Military Police has nothing to do with this. This is not a deliberate and intentional mission to go out there and kill these guys. You have to understand that."

Mr. Pontarelli and his assistants assured me they did not endorse the actions of the death squad and they energetically condemned these practices, which, according to them, threatened to damage the Military Police's public image. As one would expect, they expressed a strong af-fective identification with the institutional community to which they belonged and tried to distance themselves from the death squads by promoting the "polícia cidadã" (citizen police). It was clear that they wanted to avoid the gray area between legalized and unlawful assas-sinations by framing the widespread institutional practices of killing "suspects" as wrongdoings by individual officers. As Mr. Pontarelli high-lighted, "some bad apples should not be used to judge more than one hundred thousand men committed to promoting order."[1]

Commander Pontarelli acknowledged the existence of police-linked death squads but highlighted the *farda* (uniform) as a distinction between officers representing the institution and individuals supposedly engaged in extrajudicial executions. Based on the Commander's logic, if the police officers were not wearing their military uniforms when they committed the killings, their actions should not be connected with the institution. Although many killings by the police are committed by off-duty officers participating in undercover criminal bands, Commander Pontarelli and his men failed to consider that police officers feel entitled to kill because of the institutional protection they enjoy. Likewise, when an officer is killed on or off duty, the police force as a community responds to the death with indiscriminate revenge slayings. The disturbingly frequent, organized killings by police officers avenging the death of their colleagues indicate an expansive corporatist and punitive community that calls into question narrow and individualized considerations of police officer autonomy, misconduct, and brutality.

For the victims of police terror, it is irrelevant if the killers are on- or off-duty officers. Many of the victims of police assassinations, like Lucas and Betinho, are arrested by on-duty police officers, supposedly for a background check at a nearby police station. Yet they never make it to the station or make it alive to the hospital. I pressed the matter with Commander Pontarelli, reminding him specifically of Lucas's and Betinho's cases, where there was plenty of evidence that the victims had been kidnapped and killed by his men. An eyewitness last saw Lucas being thrown into the police patrol car. Betinho, neighbors told his mother, was stopped, beaten, and taken away by officers in uniform. Despite the abundant evidence that the Slaughters were Military Police officers, Commander Pontarelli and his assistants insisted on seeing their atrocities as instances of individual acts of misconduct. They also downplayed the fact that the officers accused of murder usually received protection from the institution by claiming that their actions were carried out in "strict execution of their legal duty." Finally, the Commander's explanation did not take into consideration the structural, rather than contingent, dimensions of racialized policing practices in Brazil.[2] In other words, while not every police officer is implicated in extrajudicial executions, the police officers who are involved are also part of the institution, and it is their loyalty to it that enables them to do what they do. Because the police force represents a legalized/organized form of state violence and a diffused rationality of government, individualized notions of accountability obscure the ways state practices and civil society's expectations are represented by those carrying out (il)legal killings.

I carefully asked Commander Pontarelli and his associates if officers involved in wrongdoings did not feel entitled to do so because of their position as state agents. I also questioned the implications of his narrow view of police misconduct as a matter of uniformed officers *versus* officers acting off the clock.

I reminded him that at the end of the day, what counted was the bodies left behind, showing once again the pictures in the newspaper. Fed up with my insistence, the Commander abruptly interrupted me, saying, "I cannot say anything else about this!" Addressing his assistants, he asked, "Do any of you have anything else to tell him about that? I do not!" Commander Pontarelli went back to his desk and after a disconcerting silence, one of his subordinates stood up and presented some maps of hot spots for crime on the periphery of São Paulo. Then, he began to share a carefully constructed presentation on the methodology of community policing. The assistants showed me photographs of the Military Police with Japanese police officers during a 2009 visit to a local police station in Jardim Angela, a neighborhood well known for its high homicide rates in the 1990s. They also showed me pictures of a conference where they were awarded a prize by Scotland Yard for their accomplishments in "reducing crime while promoting human rights." An officer complained about the treatment of the police by the media and human rights activists, who did not acknowledge their efforts to "bring the community to our side." Instead of focusing on the wrongdoings of a few police officers, Commander Pontarelli angrily explained from his desk, individuals like me needed to focus on the fact that police officers work as friends, not enemies, of the community. "They know the residents by their names, visit them, go to their schools, and talk with the teachers and the children."

The new approach that Mr. Pontarelli and his assistants were advertising can be better understood through what some scholars working in the global south have, following Foucault, termed "spatial governmentality," a paradigm of governing that seemingly supplants its old-fashioned necropolitical order by replacing it with a discipline-oriented and spatially based regime of subject formation.[3] A key shift here is how the state responds to urban challenges. In Brazil, for instance, the state deploys new forms of spatially organized techniques of governance such as enhancing community activism in security matters, founding

NGOs and Christian missions against drugs and domestic violence, and promoting *friendly* police occupation of favelas to rescue populations under the control of urban criminals.[4] Here, the (human) state is not invested in producing dead bodies—at least rhetorically—but is instead invested in fostering neoliberal subjects who engage in their own discipline, comply with the police, and participate in moral crusades against a mythic enemy cast as apolitical, uncivic, unruly, and quite often nonwhite.

This new urban-governance strategy is also a market-oriented response to the urban sprawl problems (that, in São Paulo, includes structural unemployment in the shifting industry-based economy, growing social inequality, residential segregation and thus occupation of mudslide-prone areas, chaotic public transportation, and street crime) precipitated by the neoliberal state itself. Although neoliberal urban governance is marked by necropolitics, scholars have argued that one of its main features is to promote life. As the enforcer of the neoliberal order, the racial state launches racialized forms of control that perpetuate structural inequalities while discursively (and selectively) promoting multicultural citizenship and social rights.[5] In fact, an important dimension of the neoliberal state is to recognize, at least formally, a right to cultural difference. It also grants popular participation in decision-making processes even in security matters.[6] Perhaps ironically, participation in security concerns has been one of the most granted rights by the neoliberal government of the right-wing Social Democracy Party (PSDB) in São Paulo. While the urban periphery is disenfranchised from basic services such as public transportation, sanitation, and health clinics, residents are invited to participate in the local security councils every month to express their concerns and "help the police do their job." In power since 1994, PSDB has advanced a multipronged approach to fighting crime, comprising the neighborhood security councils, community police stations, domestic violence prevention workshops, police visits to public schools to keep troubled youth away from drugs, and its support of NGOs working with "dysfunctional" families. At first glance, the core of this intertwining strategy for ordering urban space is "governing through community," or, in Mr. Pontarelli's words, "to bring the community to our side." The question that arises out of the humanly sensitive neoliberal urban-security regime is how to govern populations that have been historically seen as unfit to the very idea of urban life? What are we to make of the interconnected configurations of promoting human rights, inviting popular participation, and enduring police terror?

In the next few pages, I take a closer look at the state's attempt to mobilize civic crusades against crime in the periphery of the city of São Paulo. In the police's crime-fighting strategies, local black youth appear as the quintessential enemies of public order. This may explain why "soft" interventions such as security councils, community police, and workshops on human rights coexist alongside a brutal police force that caused the United Nations Security Council to recommend its abolishment.[7] While this study offers a local analysis of this "new" approach in urban policing, state-level dynamics of carcerality and death unveils its larger outcomes: as the state of São Paulo led the implementation of community policing in the country over the last twenty years (from 1995 to 2014), its prison population has grown steadily and its Military Police has killed as many as 10,379 individuals.[8]

Polícia Amiga

When I made my first visit to the local community police station (Base Comunitária de Segurança), I was welcomed with great enthusiasm by the sergeant in charge of the unit. Mr. Pereira served me a cup of coffee and started explaining the achievements that the community police had made in Jardim Angela, in the center of the Fundão, known in the past as one of the most violent areas in Brazil:

> Today the police are seen as a *polícia amiga* [friendly police], a *companheira* [a buddy], and ready to help in any situation. Here, the community comes to us not only to solve problems of security, but also problems like water supplies, electricity poles, and helping pregnant women give birth. They know that even if it is not our duty, we will help. Because, you know, if a person is well received here, he will spread the word talking to a relative, a friend . . . This *boca-a-boca* [word-of-mouth] strategy made our military base approachable. And there is no secret to our success.

Most of the accomplishments of the community police were credited to the relationship between the police and the schools. Teachers now work more closely with the police to prevent drug dealers from selling drugs at the school gates. Mr. Pereira gives regular lectures in the public schools on drug prevention and involves teachers and students in the surveillance strategy. "We ask teachers to be aware of any changing behavior in the students. And we ask students to tell us if they see anything wrong at home or in the neighborhood," he told me. Involving the community, the family, and the school in the soft-policing strategy has paid off, according to Sergeant Pereira. Now students, parents, and teachers know the police by their names, and the police officers also know everyone. "We participate in school-board meetings, go to visit people at their houses, drink coffee with them, and find a way to get integrated into the community." This strategy particularly targeted young children because most of the teenagers have already been "lost to criminals," he complained.

The Base Comunitária houses a small library and a computer lab where children come to do their homework or surf the Internet. Since Internet access is an expensive service in Brazil, and schools and libraries usually do not provide it for free, the police station is particularly attractive to young people. In my visit, I saw young children playing around the police station while others waited in the tiny room for their turn to use the computers in the station. Flyers on the wall reminded children about soccer games, marathons, and cultural activities promoted by the police. The setting was in sharp contrast to the ugly image of brutal police force exhibited by the Slaughters. Mr. Pereira was proud of this change: "Years ago, when a child used to pass by the station, her mother would say, 'Behave or otherwise I will take you to the police.' So, the child would grow up with the image of us as bad guys. Today you will not see scenes like that." The corrupt and violent police, Mr. Pereira told me, "became a distant memory."

Although the "new" police have been able to draw children and some residents to their side, the main challenge continues to be the lack of trust many residents, especially local youth, have in the "old police." He complained that many residents refuse to collaborate by handing over criminals to the police, which poses an extra challenge to his work. The strategy to get churches involved, launch cultural activities, and distribute rewards has not been as successful as he had wished. "Unfortunately, many people don't feel responsible for helping to protect the community," he lamented. Ironically, he added, the children are the ones collaborating with the police nowadays. "Now we have a little child herself giving us information. This is beautiful and shows that they are doing what the adults are still afraid to do." I asked Mr. Pereira if this mistrust was not because of the rampant police violence that continues to plague the region. How is it possible, I asked, that the community police and the police-linked death squad operate in the same area? Uncomfortable with my question, Mr. Pereira argued that some abuses occur because some police officers have not been trained under the human rights approach. A passionate advocate of this approach, Mr. Pereira was a fellow in an exchange program between Brazil and Japan to train the Brazilian police, organized by the World Bank in 2004. Now, his community police station is a showpiece for the success of this approach and he himself trains new officers. Before I left, Mr. Pereira handed me a police newspaper that featured a *cidadão do mês* (citizen of the month) in the center with several police officers. The monthly tribute is given to one member of the community in recognition of their effort to keep the community safer. "Now imagine who in the past would have wanted to take a picture with the police," he reasoned.

The community police were part of a comprehensive strategy that included undercover police officers, rotating military checkpoints, and monthly meetings between the police and the community. In addition, police officers and community activists ran drug reduction programs in public schools and introduced new legislation that mandated the closing of bars at 10:00 p.m. The initiative was created in 1999 as a statewide plan to reduce homicide rates and as a city ambition to clean up São Paulo's infamous image as a violent metropolis. As the city, like any global city, struggled to become an attractive center for international business and tourism, fighting crime became not only a matter of urban security but also a matter of urban development.[9] São Paulo's neoliberal state responded to the economic crisis provoked by its liberalizing and deregulating policies by framing insecurity as a collective problem. Now the urban poor were invited to voice their opinions on matters of security while the state turned a deaf ear to their protests against the violence of neoliberal structural reforms. They were welcome in the security councils and repressed while protesting in the streets. Likewise, at the same time that government and think-tank discourses sold the city as a security project that required the active participation of its citizens, shoot-to-kill policies and the incarceration of the predominantly black (surplus) population intensified. As many scholars of neoliberal urbanism have noted, there are no contradictions between enhancing individual civic participation and investing in a hyperpunitive criminal justice system. What makes the neoliberal program of government compelling is that "it must conform to some degree with social constructions of legality, ethics, and justice to maintain legitimacy, notwithstanding efforts to redefine social justice along neoliberal lines."[10]

Drawing from Canadian and Japanese policing models, while also adapting the U.S. Zero Tolerance program, the "new" police in Brazil set out to promote human rights and bring ordinary citizens into the crime-fighting crusades launched by the state. In 2010, São Paulo's community-based police were selected as one of the top five most innovative policing programs in the world by the UK's National Policing Improvement Agency. Since then, it has provided training to other Brazilian states and other police forces throughout Latin America. São Paulo's Military Police has trained police forces in Costa Rica, Nicaragua, Guatemala, Honduras, and El Salvador. It has also been widely promoted by both the media and mainstream human rights organizations as a successful crime-fighting intervention.[11] The seeds of this community policing initiative were planted in the wake of the dictatorship regime, when André Franco Montoro, the first democratically elected São Paulo governor, introduced a set of policies to reform the Military Police. Nonetheless, scholars on police violence in Brazil identify a landmark event that led to the adoption of the community-based police project: the 1997 Favela Naval scandal, in which the Military Police were videotaped torturing residents in a favela in the satellite city of Diadema.[12] The event raised public awareness of the torture, misconduct, and killings carried out by the Military Police. At a moment when state legitimacy was called into question by national and transnational human rights organizations, the state decided to respond by promoting an image of a police force that respects the democratic state of rights. Indeed, the new community policing approach was meant to clean up the police's public image, to share the responsibility for policing poor communities with schools, churches, and human rights NGOs, and to control impoverished urban areas under drug traffickers' control.

Although internal events certainly played an important role in shaping state security strategies, this new security paradigm needs to be understood within a neoliberal global context in which the so-called international community pushed forward neoliberal urban policies aimed at stabilizing crime-prone areas and "promoting democracy" in "underdeveloped countries." Policing technologies developed in the United States, Canada, England, and Japan were "sold" to the global south as police "reform" became the magic word for redressing "failed" state efforts to administer justice, bring down crime, and improve the economy. In the late 1990s, the World Bank and the United Nations began calling for police reform in nations such as South Africa, Uganda, East Timor, Kenya, Haiti, and Brazil as part of their human-security strategies, to promote "development" through the promotion of "human rights."[13] Under this new rationale, in the 2000s the United Nations Development Programme (UNDP) pushed forward what came to be known as a "citizen security" agenda for Latin America. More recently, the UNDP suggested ten recommendations to strengthen citizen security in the region, such as the promotion of active local "community" participation in security matters, youth opportunity, and international cooperation. This approach identifies insecurity as a decisive factor in preventing human development because it causes ruptures in community bonds and drains state efforts to fight poverty. An obvious question it does not ask is: who are the subjects of protection within Latin America's racialized regime of citizenship?[14]

As an important dimension of the citizen-security paradigm, community policing has been broadly defined as a new philosophy created to solve minor problems and to enhance the "quality of life" of members of the community.[15] Its immediate project is to mobilize the "community" to fight crime; more broadly, it aims to conduct social life toward self- and collective-policed neoliberal subjectivities. The state, in turn, promises to enhance and control the police by deploying "force" in a legal, strategic, and calculated fashion. Some scholars describe this form of governance as a neoliberal strategy to rule not by force but through *community*, or through a set of moral discourses that produce spatially contained and economically viable subjects.[16] Some suggest that in this new "ethicopolitics," the state, the market, and the citizens function as equal partners. The notion of partnership is very important here because in the case of the community-policing initiative, the state mobilizes citizens and NGOs as active agents in security matters. That such mobilization is based on collective vengeance against historically defined criminals indicates that the "new police" is an all-too-familiar technology of racial domination.

Indeed, assumptions about who belongs to the community should be interrogated here. As the *koinonia* of *politai*, the community is a restrictive, racialized, and gendered one. In his analysis of community policing in South Los Angeles by the Los Angeles Police Department (LAPD), Aaron Roussell remarks that "community is composed in opposition to an 'anticommunity' animated by racial preference and labor utility." In the neoliberal context of job shortage and spatial poverty, the "anticommunity" works as a political device to regulate the distribution of punishment and access to the job market for the Latino and black population.[17] As in Los Angeles, race and gender work as ideological devices to regulate surplus population, establish civic entitlements, and control the city's black geographies in São Paulo's neoliberal order. The favela may well be targeted by soft-governance projects, but these projects are aimed at protecting white and other nonblack bodies endangered by their proximity to predominantly black spaces. As the city's hyperperiphery is pushed farther to its edges, and as neoliberalism deepens urban poverty across racial lines, poor whites reaffirm their ontological condition as members of the polis by reaffirming their anti-blackness against the black neighbor next door.

At the same time, the state's attempts to *govern through community* may suggest a crossracial invitation to participate in this political project. Scholars enthusiastic about the "democratization" of security concerns in the racially diverse periphery—through community policing, security councils, and so on—may even be tempted to deny the weight of race in these dynamics. After all, anybody can potentially participate in this initiative. They failed to consider, however, that the body politic we call "community" mostly consists of nonblack individuals even if they live on the edge of the city (and increasingly share the predominantly black space of the favela). What are we to make of the fact that—even when occupying the same geography—the community and favela are situated on opposite sides of sociality? Community is conceived as the place for the assertion of "good civic life," while the marginal space of the favela is the place for the negation of not only civic but also biological life itself.[18] This is particularly true in the favelas of Zona Sul, where São Paulo's human-rights-sensitive new police approach goes hand in hand with its historical pattern of brutality and terror. In the Fundão, the making of community comprises apparently disparate strategies such as human-rights-trained police stations, community-based security councils, mobile checkpoints, helicopter raids, prisons, and killings. At the end of the day, it seems that in São Paulo's favelas, state governmentality takes the form of "discipline with its clothes off."[19] In the next section, I examine how gender, space, and racism conflate in the production of citizens and criminals, civic community, and disorderly spaces.

Homens de bem

In the poor and predominantly black Fundão da Zona Sul, the state divides the population between good and bad, *homens de bem* (good men or men of good will), and criminals. Although some black individuals invest in the politics of respectability and gain relative access to the body politic called the *homens de bem,* impoverished white and light-skinned men are the paradigmatic figures of the local civic community constituted around security concerns. They are the main collaborators with the local police and the main attendees at the local community-council meetings. At the police headquarters, Mr. Pontarelli first called my attention to the *homens de bem.* He praised them for being the only ones to stand by the police when the latter were "attacked" by human rights organizations and the media. He pointed out that "the population that really needs the police, the *homens de bem,* doesn't buy into these critiques. The *homens de bem* don't agree with these stigmas."[20] When I asked him to explain who the *homens de bem* are, Mr. Pontarelli told me: "They are the people who make the difference. You know, you always have the pig spirit [or the mean-spirited ones] that messes things up. They are there only to destroy the community. But thank God we also have the *homens de bem—pessoas trabalhadoras* [hard working people], the leaders from the community, [and] the church members who organize, participate, and help the police to do their job."

Only after participating in the Community Security Council's monthly meetings was I able to place a face to this racial and gendered figure often evoked by the police and conservative media. The *homens de bem* is a morally defined category of people, mainly comprising local businessmen, the staff of NGOs, individuals working for politicians, and churchgoers. Although they also live in precarious urban spaces, what defines them most is their access to politicians in the state apparatus and to the police in their role as informants or simply supporters of policing practices. *Homens de bem* is defined in opposition to the supposedly uneducated, poor, politically illiterate individuals usually associated with the underground drug economy, who live in illegal settlements on the edge of the city. They barely participate in local politics and refuse to collaborate with the police.

The Community Security Council (Conseg) meeting takes place in a different location each month. "The idea is to bring the police to the community, so instead of having people go to the Conseg, the Conseg comes to the people," explained Vicente, a light-skinned northeastern migrant in his early sixties from Ceará, who serves as president of the council and minister at a local protestant church. The first time I met Vicente was at a council meeting that took place in a high-school classroom in Dreaming City. As usual, he introduced the authorities and asked them to take a seat at the table. The Military Police captain, the Civil Police delegate, the president of the business association, the school principal, and a representative of the municipal government took turns introducing themselves and inviting the individuals present to share their concerns. There were approximately twenty mostly light-skinned people along with some racially mixed northeasterners and dark-skinned individuals.[21] I sat in the audience attentively listening to the authorities present. The president of the business association, also a northeastern man in his sixties, complained that he had called "190" (the phone number to reach the police) and had not been promptly assisted. "We pay our taxes and when we need the police it takes you forever to come. It is not fair. We want more police," he asked. The captain defended the police by saying that they are in high demand and underfunded, and are thus unable to attend to all requests. He also complained that in many instances the police had to attend calls that had nothing to do with their work, such as taking an elderly person to the hospital or even attending to a pregnant woman giving birth.

A representative of a local NGO supported by politicians got up and complained that when the police arrive, they do not protect the identities of those who have called them, thus leaving those people in danger. The man, whose last name is Silva, highlighted an incident in which a police officer arrived in his neighborhood yelling, "Who is Silva? Who is Silva?" after he had called. He said that if the police wanted their help they would have to be more careful not to expose informants, who would otherwise be in trouble with local criminals. A member of the residents' association said that the police should work more in the neighborhood, do more patrolling, and be more efficient in attending to residents' requests. He complained that "the guys" [drug dealers] party all night during the weekend, and that even during the week they keep loudspeakers on the streets until late at night. He requested that the police close the bars and confiscate the speakers because the bars are places for drug sales. "These are not *pessoas de bem* [good people]," he explained. "A good citizen doesn't stay out late partying during the week. For God's sake, remove this bar from there to show who has the power over this area because the dealer keeps saying that he is the boss, that no one will mess up his business," he shouted angrily.

The attentive captain took note of the complaints and urged the participants to continue collaborating with the police. According to him, the police depend on everyone's commitment to make the community safer, and if they fail to provide protection to the community, it is because council members did not take a more proactive role in denouncing crime and testifying against criminals. "You are here today complaining against the police. Fine. If you tell me that there is an individual committing a crime, we need to know more. You have to report who that person is, his color, his clothes, what time he approaches the area. Please make a report, don't be afraid. We are here for you." He ended his remarks with a warning: "That teenager that you hide today will be a drug dealer tomorrow." Someone interjected that although the police were asking for more cooperation, the majority of the attendees were already doing their work. A member of the residents' association, who was waiting for the police to close the bar in which drugs were sold, showed the captain a report that he had already filed. The president of the Conseg told him to stop by the community police station and "have a cup of coffee with the captain" so he could disclose information about drug dealers without placing himself at risk of being seen as a "snitch," which could cost him his life.

A common concern among the participants in the security council was that the police were unable to tame the favelas surrounding the "legal" and urbanized areas where most of the *homens de bem* live. In the words of the participants in Conseg, the police's mission should be to transform the favela into a *community*. The council is organized around a racialized regime of morality that aggregates the "good citizens" in a war against those associated with deviancy. One example of this regime of morality is how members of the council legitimize police violence against the "troublemakers," a relationship with the police quite different from Dona Maria's and Dona Cecilia's, for instance. In Dona Maria's words, "you don't need to think too much to know that the police are the problem. I can't trust the ones who wear the uniform in order to terrorize the Fundão." Yet residents like Dona Maria were the source of anxiety for the *homens de bem*, who felt threatened by the disorderly spaces of the favelas "infested" with criminals. To the *homens de bem*, police violence was framed not as a human rights issue but rather as a legitimate way to take back the territory under drug dealers' control. During the period when I attended the council meetings, I never heard the members voice any concern about rampant police brutality in the Fundão. On the contrary, it was common for members to demand tougher actions to protect their "endangered" community. In one instance, a local resident voiced his concern that the police had been too soft on a teenager who had allegedly shot at the police. He complained that instead of shooting back, the officers told his mother they would retaliate the next time but then never followed through. The teenager continues selling drugs and threatening people on the streets. "Were the police afraid of him? If this street had been cleaned up, we would not have this big problem now," he concluded, referring to the alleged increase in drug dealing in the area. Another individual agreed with him and blamed the municipality for not supporting the police. He complained that the geography of the favela prevents the police from being more effective in their incursions and, consequently, that city hall should give this issue more attention: "If the streets had been opened over there, instead of this tiny alley, they would already have been arrested. It would be difficult for them to escape from the police. But how can the police take them in if the patrol car cannot get there easily?"

Vicente, the president of the council, summed up all the requests by asking the captain to bring more police officers to the Fundão. He argued that the police leave too much room for the "artists" to take control of the favelas, and that unless the state takes a heavy-handed approach, they will have more control than the *homens de bem*. The state, he complained, has the obligation to protect the *homens de bem* because they are the ones who stand by the police when the media criticizes their work. Animated by applause from the audience, Vicente concluded with the conciliatory rhetoric expected from the president of the council: "We need more state, more police. Where is the cancer? Everyone knows where it is. We need to take out the cancer from the community because this cancer is like ants. If we don't extract it, it will eat the whole body." The evoked image of a cancer growing in the favela and threatening the body of the "community" is a metaphor that speaks volumes to the ways racism is articulated without race being evoked in these settings. In the Fundão da Zona Sul, the *homens de bem* establish a symbolic and physical sanitary boundary that divides the periphery of the city into good and evil people, and make claims for state intervention based on the discourses of territorial prophylaxis. In the virtual absence of race, and in the presence of some black attend-ees, the alternative vocabulary (the cancer, the bad/good citizen, the *homens de bem*) is a subtext that names a (social) geography produced at the intersections of spatial segregation, criminalization, and racial-ized police violence. Seeking full participation in the white biopolis, the law-abiding citizens that dominate the council distinguish themselves from the "people of the Fundão" not through racial identification but rather by expressing their loyalty to the state (the police) and by engag-ing with civil society's politics of morality that conflates race, crime, and space.

The Conseg was an anti-black but far from racially homogenous space. Impoverished Brazilians of various racial backgrounds whose experiences mirror those of the black male and female victims of po-lice abuse described in this book also attended the meeting. It was a model space for racial democracy and, as such, was informed by an-ti-blackness even with the presence of some black individuals who also participated in the stigmatizing narratives. Its racial dynamics were not different from other forms of political associativism in the city in which black presence becomes both an inconvenience to the assertion of racial democracy and a political resource to depoliticize race as a category of struggle. In the Conseg, crime and security were synonyms for anti-black racism, while the few black participants like myself were proof of the periphery's multiracial politics. It also cohered with the skin-color chromatic privilege that informs racial hierarchies in Brazilian society at large. With more access to formal education and better conditions for securing a job in liberal white NGOs, white-middle-class and light-skinned individuals not only controlled most of the agenda but were also the gatekeepers between the state and the local black population. As expected for a society organized around anti-blackness, other nonwhite individuals participated in anti-black politics. Some of them could unambiguously fall into the "negro" category of the complex schema of racial classification in Brazil, but would deny their blackness. For instance, the northeasterner *(nordestino)* president, who used the most persuasive moral rhetoric against the "cancer" that was "eating" the community, belongs to a social group (of undesired immigrants) that is racialized in popular discourse as a scapegoat for São Paulo's high rates of crime and unemployment, his light-skinned appearance notwithstanding. As Teresa Caldeira shows, in the *paulista* imagination, an individual from northeast Brazil is generally considered to be illiterate, backward, and uncivilized; at times these stereotypes are a "euphemism to black people."[22] The president's racial rhetoric suggests that anti-black racism is a political currency that at times grants other racialized and marginalized social groups in Brazil access to power. By actively participating in and expressing loyalty to the state, other people of color try to distance themselves from anything that resembles blackness in the racist imagination of the council members. The few black attendees were usually not as vocal, but they often clapped at the aggressive rhetoric of the Conseg's president. Rather than undermining the critique presented here, however, their presence further complicates how with such anti-black formations, the black subject position is, like any subject position, contradictory, nonlinear, and not necessarily progressive. Regardless of the skin color of its participants, the council is a racial formation in which the negation of race and the assertion of anti-blackness are articulated through the language of citizenship and law abidingness.[23]

The anti-black rhetoric of the council was articulated in multiple ways—the criminalization of black youth behavior was a prevailing one. In one of the monthly meetings, a member of the residents' association complained that the public school was hosting *baile funks* (funk dance parties) on the weekends. He complained that it was inappropriate for a place that was supposed "to teach our children how to become *homens decentes* (decent men) to instead be hosting parties with delinquents." He complained that the police should shut down the *baile funk* because it had become an event where people from the favela were getting together to sell drugs, plan crimes, and have sex. Other participants reinforced his complaints, saying that many people were hanging out around the corner the whole night drinking while playing loud music from their cars and smoking marijuana.

The link between *baile funk*, hypersexuality, and crime echoes a recurring theme in the Brazilian political landscape. The *baile* has been associated with moral decay and depicted as the setting in which black youth engage in violence, pornography, and crime.[24] As in American gangsta rap, the cultural practices of black youth are stigmatized as a security problem. Within these racist discourses, culture—as opposed to race—becomes the code language to condemn behaviors framed as urban pathologies. Any gathering with music, or even a simple get together, is a potential threat to the social order and thus justifies the intervention of the Military Police. Take for instance a set of legislation approved by the City Council of São Paulo in 2013 and in the state legislature in 2015. The law tries to control *baile funks* on the grounds that they were the loci of drugs and violence. It curbed the *baile funks* by requesting previous authorization and the presence of the police at the events.[25] According to the chief commander of the Military Police in São Paulo, Reinaldo Zychan, "We receive a very large demand of calls from people complaining of the noise and in many situations, when the police attend these calls, there are crashes. It is not uncommon that the police are met with shots, potions, and stones. Too often we find people selling drugs, armed, and stealing vehicles."[26] The council members endorsed these stereotypes and asked for harsh measures to protect local families menaced by urban black culture. The peculiar concern that the *baile funks* endanger "our children" and "our families" echoes the state's urban-governance policies aimed at building civic community around a racialized moral panic. Living near a drug-selling hot spot, listening to loud music on weekdays, or partying "too much" on the streets disqualifies black residents from the realm of respectability and citizenship. It is not by chance that the good citizens identified schools as the main area of concern for the council and the police. Strategic intervention in the schools sought to "save" the children from the unredeemed youth and to help the dysfunctional families that are unable to educate them at home. As Mr. Pereira, the police officer in charge of the local community policing station, told me, "Our focus is on the children because they are the men of tomorrow. It is through the kids that we break the ice and get into the family, the school, the community."

Indeed, the male-dominated council took as its mission to educate the children to become *homens de bem*. This apparent willingness to "protect" the children while criminalizing their parents and leaving them childless at some point is evidence of how black sexual and reproductive life was the main target of the security council's racial anxieties. Of special concern was black women's sexual behavior. Vicente, the evangelical minister and president of the council, insisted that "teenage girls are going to *baile funk* and getting pregnant by criminals." According to him and the other members, the police should already have closed the *bailes* because they were the source from which the "cancer" disseminated into the community. When we take into consideration black feminist scholars' concerns with the historical place occupied by the black female body in urban mythologies of criminality, it becomes clear why the council's concerns center around black children and black parenthood.[27] The "myth of a lascivious black woman," legal scholar Dorothy Roberts argues, provides political justification for the criminalization of black urban life. Within such a racial imaginary, black children are seen as potential criminals, black women's sexual behaviors are seen as practices that endanger civil society's morality, and the black community is seen as a threat to urban values and thus in need of disciplining and policing. Associated with prostitution, vice, and crime, black women's bodies became the site from which the economically and morally threatened (white) patriarchal civil society criminalized black urban life.[28]

This racial anxiety is so prevalent in discourses of security in Brazil that in 2007 Rio de Janeiro's governor, Sergio Cabral, made the following comment on the relationship between black women, reproductive rights, and violence in Rio's favelas: "[Abortion] has everything to do with urban violence. I am in favor of women interrupting an undesired pregnancy. You look at the number of children born at Lagoa Tijuca, Méier and in Copacabana [Rio's prime areas]. Now, you look at Rocinha, Vidigal, Alemao [favelas]. Zambia, Gabon standards. That is a factory of criminal[s]."[29] Cabral's rationality provoked heated debate on his eugenic politics, but these statements are part of an African-diasporic racial-security knowledge that associates blackness with crime. In the governor's mind and in the heteropatriarchal imagination of the *homens de bem*, black women were blamed for not taking good care of their children, while the killing of their children by the police was justified as a prophylaxis against crime in the periphery. The battle over criminality was a battle over (black) families unable to raise their children in a proper way. That was why, according to the president of the security council, it was important to hold council meetings in schools, churches, and local organizations "to bring these children to our side." No problem that the patriarchal rhetoric of rescuing "trouble children" stands in clear contradiction to the symbolic violence black kids and their families face in the Conseg and the physical violence they endure at the hands of the police.

Perhaps the most revealing aspect of the anti-black security formations in the periphery of São Paulo is indeed the obsession with black women's sexual behavior. In the heteropatriarchal discourse of protecting "the city of men," black women are seen as endangering figures to urban security, as voiced by the *homens de bem* in relation to the *baile funk* and in broader ideological discourses about their wombs as "factories of criminals." While helping Dona Maria move out of her place after her eviction, I met her niece, Sandrinha. Without my knowledge, Dona Maria had told her I would help her find a job since I was involved with organizations she referred to as "o povo dos direitos humanos" (those human rights folk). Filled with expectations, Sandrinha told me she was trying to find a job in order to get her three children out of the state orphanage. She complained that her children had been taken from her because people from the community security council reported her to the government, claiming that she did not take care of her children properly and, even worse, was dealing in one of PCC's *biqueiras* in Dreaming City. She was running out of time to find a job as a precondition for getting her children back, as she had been warned about by the social worker who visited her. I started to bring the Sunday newspaper to Sandrinha in order to look for jobs in the classified advertisements. However, she did not fit into the highly competitive job market. She was a twenty-eight-year-old single mother who had dropped out of school and had no professional qualifications. The only job listed on her resume was a "domestic worker" position. She refused, however, to go back to that kind of work not only because she found it humiliating but also because the image of her sick mother working as a domestic servant was too recent to forget. Sandrinha was still mourning her mother's premature death due to chronic bronchitis made worse by the long early-dawn commutes she had taken for almost a decade to and from Vila Madalena, another prime area of the city.

Ironically, as Sandrinha tried harder and harder to find work, the same forces that required her to have a formal income in order to get her children back kept pushing her out of the job market. Sandrinha tried to participate in a state program for unemployed individuals—one that offered training for menial jobs such as making cakes, cleaning shoes, and working at call centers—but she did not secure a slot and had to wait for the next turn. To complicate things even more, she did not have a formal address, which made it difficult to convince an employer to give her a job. Sandrinha lived with Dona Maria and moved from place to place unable to secure a place of her own. Finally, with three kids, she did not have time to complete the last year of high school, which would have increased her job options. A neighbor told her about the call center at Santo Amaro (the shopping hub closer to the Fundão), but they rejected her application for her lack of a high-school diploma. The state itself produced most of the conditions for Sandrinha's social vulnerability, then suspended her parental rights when she was unable to overcome the structural barriers that had been placed in her way. Sandrinha was held responsible for "her" failure to become integrated into the city's neoliberal economy and thus penalized for not being able to "properly" raise her children. Options were so limited that having the children in the orphanage "was not that bad," Dona Maria reasoned. When Sandrinha complained of missing them, Dona Maria harshly responded that she should give thanks to God, because nobody would feed them, "unless you sell your body to bring food home." In one of our conversations, Sandrinha told me that she would not visit her kids until she got a job because her anxiety grew each time she visited them and they asked her if she had found work. After a while, it seemed that Sandrinha had accepted the hardship and length of time it would take her to get her children back. She finally secured a slot in the training program for unemployed workers. She participated in workshops on hair styling, cooking, and baking. She was afraid the children would be placed on the adoption list if she did not show proof of professional progress.

In my last visit, however, Sandrinha was still looking for a secure job that would allow her to reclaim custody of her children. The social worker was not convinced she would able to afford the costs of raising three kids with the twice-a-week job as housekeeper. She continues to share a tiny room with Dona Maria, and both women remain dependent on Dona Maria's older son, who appears every now and then with some money to cover basic necessities. Sandrinha's experience is instructive of the ways in which black sexual politics (and black motherhood) become inscribed in the security strategies of the Brazilian state. The Conseg demanded the police prevent girls from attending *baile funks* so that they would not get pregnant. In Dona Maria's and Dona Cecilia's cases, it was reasoned, the police were responsible for their sons' deaths. As for Sandrinha, her children are held captive in a state orphanage. All these instances are examples of the racial gendered project of policing black bodies, regulating sexuality, and preventing the reproduction of black urban life.

Color-Blind Community Activism

The neoliberal state's attempt to govern through community places human rights activists within the anti-black structure of urban security in São Paulo's Zona Sul. Black favelados are invisible at best and are viewed as victims of black-on-black violence at worst. Besides the Conseg, neighborhood activism in the Fundão comprises several church-based NGOs, left-wing social movements, and public universities' research-based projects. With a strong tradition of leftist politics, the region also houses several forums that bring together demands as diverse as public transportation, housing, environmental protection, and security. The central political hub of the Fundão is Jardim Angela, the once-infamous neighborhood considered the most violent in the city back in the 1990s. "At that time, we had at least ten deaths every weekend. On Mondays you would see ten, twelve coffins passing to the cemetery," Sr. João, a local shopkeeper, told me. According to him, most of the deaths were caused by rival gangs and by death squads formed by the police. It was the time of *limpeza social* (social cleansing), in which the *homens de bem* would take charge of security in a very peculiar form of vigilantism still in practice in Brazil. But then the neighborhood grew; most of its areas are now urbanized and it is the center for an exciting political life. "Now Jardim Angela is a pacified community," Sr. João added.

With the expansion of the city's frontiers, Jardim Angela became a center of commerce and the place where nonprofit grassroots organizations hold most of their meetings and events under the umbrella called "Forum in Defense of Life." Led mostly by white or light-skinned middle-class NGO professionals, the Forum, formed in 1996 when Irish priest Jaime Crowe began gathering local residents to organize against violence, has taken a prominent leadership role as a civic crusade against violence and poverty in Jardim Angela. Besides providing several free services to the community, including education and health care, the Forum is said to be one of the main forces behind the reduction of violence in the region. Lurdes, one of the Forum's organizers, defined it as a political space for everyone who wants to struggle for better living conditions: "Everyone that feels part of the community is invited to participate, regardless of your race, class, or place of residence." Like Sr. João, Lurdes celebrates the fact that homicide rates have consistently declined since the community began organizing in the late 1990s. She celebrates the fact that Jardim Angela has left behind its reputation as one of the most violent places in the city.

Since its creation, the Forum has been active in urban politics and closely works with the leftist municipality on several state-funded projects in areas such as education, drug prevention, and health care. These projects directly benefit the black favelados—especially black kids and women—around Jardim Angela's hub. The Forum is an instance of civil society mediating the favelados' claims for basic rights and the government agencies' calculated distribution of services and aid. They also provide workshops to help develop the skills of impoverished residents so that they can participate in debates and demand a fair participation of the Fundão in the city's budget sharing. The Forum is a space where NGO staff members, university-based activists, and local politicians train impoverished local residents to access their citizenship rights in the neoliberal city. State authorities come, as invited, to public hearings organized by the Forum: they generally provide information, take notes on local demands, and leave. The Forum plays the role of mediating residents' concerns as an interlocutor recognized by the state. Its participants have creative and effective ways of bringing to the forefront concerns that would otherwise remain invisible in the city's political discourse. Although the district continues to be plagued with poverty and violence, the Forum has been relatively successful in convincing state institutions to bring public funding to secure the community. Like the Conseg, the Forum mobilizes the language of rights and citizenship to bring the state in. Yet, contrary to the Conseg's monolithic view of the state as a military force, there were also apparently contradictory moments in which Forum participants demanded more police and more social welfare. According to Lurdes, it was not contradictory because "public safety is not just to have the police around the corner." Other members would always reiterate the need for more police, health clinics, and job opportunities for local youth. One could say the Forum was one of those instances in which the state appears through a multiplicity of discourses, aspirations, and governmental practices.

One of their effective strategies has been the partnership between the progressive wing of the Catholic Church, public universities, and the Workers' Party (PT). During PT's decentralized government in the earlier 2000s, the Forum received great attention and was recognized as an important political actor mediating local concerns with the city government. Given the Forum's commitment to organizing the poor in a civic community to make claims for citizenship rights, what makes it blind to black politics? To be sure, this is not an argument against the agency and good will of community organizers in the constrained political terrain of São Paulo's periphery. It would be wrong to deny that the Forum is one of the most important political actors in the periphery of Zona Sul. Rather, I want to direct attention to this question, for it

is precisely within this community-based activism that we can ethnographically make visible the conflictual relationship between class-based
politics of rights and racial justice.

This question becomes more complex when we consider the Forum's role in reducing homicide rates in Jardim Angela. Even though its
members recognize that there are multiple explanations for the downfall in violent deaths in the region, among them the emergence of a
criminal band (PCC) as the de facto authority with decisive power over
life-and-death matters, they celebrate the creation of the community
police stations as a watershed in the region's reputation as the most violent part of the city. Now that Jardim Angela is "pacified," the Forum's
ambition is to expand its successful experience to other parts of the
Fundão. Although blacks continue to bear the brunt of police violence,
the Forum's "culture of peace" (as the members advertise it) was able to
mobilize the state and the community in defense of life. Its focus was
primarily on intracommunity violence. Again, closing bars, campaigns
against youth pregnancy, public lighting of dark areas, and the police–
school initiative to keep children out of drugs all amount to strategies
supported (and sometimes led) by neighborhood-oriented activism.
Perhaps the most expressive example of its capillarity in the periphery is
the annual Caminhada da Paz (Walk for Peace). On this day, residents
of the borough, from all class and racial backgrounds, walk together to
São Luis Cemetary (the Luizão) to remember the old violent days of the
1990s, when homicides were rampant.

At the same time that such events enable racial and class solidarity
and provide a means for members of the community to unify around
the common vulnerability to violence—"all of us are victims"—they
also overlook rampant racialized police violence in the region. This is
particularly true because of the Forum's endorsement of civil society's
color-blind politics of rights and for its racialized moral politics. The
Forum uses mostly pedagogical practices that aim to transform the favelados into "good" and efficient citizens. It has mobilized a conception
of "community" and "civic engagement" that unintentionally excludes
individuals like Dona Maria, Dona Cecilia, and most of the local black
youth. If in the progressive Forum, the right-wing *homens de bem* (of
the Consegs) were replaced by a leftist subject that participates in electoral politics, obeys the police, and protests under the banner of hu-

Annual "Walk for Peace" parade organized by the Forum in Defense of Life. Photograph by the author.

man rights politics, individuals like Dona Maria, on the other hand, see the Forum politics as distant from (and at times against) their needs as black favelados. As I show in the next pages, black young men criticized the celebration of the community policing initiative, arguing that it covered up the brutality of the militarized branch that continues to terrorize them.

While the Forum has been successful in organizing local residents around the broad concept of citizenship, it has been less successful in bringing specifically *black* matters to its agenda. In its defense, one can argue that in Brazil, *class* is a stand-in term for *race* and that the experience of local residents is clearly structured by a complex entanglement of racial and class-based oppression. Fair enough. Still, even the most celebrated achievements of the Forum (such as the decline in homicides) invite a careful consideration of the limits of community organizing with little consideration for the specific vulnerabilities faced by blacks, particularly in a district with a long-lasting history of racial violence.

The fact that homicides in Jardim Angela have dropped consistently in the last decade (the 2000s) while killings of black youth by the police in the region have continued to skyrocket underscores the disturbing and perhaps mutually constitutive relationship between pacified community and anti-black terror. Although the police–community relationship was credited for curbing homicidal violence among the favelados, Jardim Angela and its surroundings never stopped producing dead black bodies as police-linked groups like the Slaughters never stopped acting in the region.[30]

I participated in monthly meetings of the Forum and, although members from different racial backgrounds voiced concerns against police violence, the Forum nevertheless maintained its ties to the Military Police. In one of the meetings, the priest in charge of the Forum articulated the need for more community police stations in the region. There should be stations in strategic areas of the district, he argued, so as not to lose the battle against violence once again. He stated that police stations should be as prevalent as health clinics, and that the Forum's political goal should be to have a community policing station at every corner. "Here in the region we have thirty-five daycare health clinics. We should have thirty-five police bases as well." The priest invited the Military Police commander general to attend the meeting and discuss how to expand police stations to all areas of Jardim Angela. I sat in the back of a crowded room next to Silvia, a hip-hop organizer. We were curious to hear from the police chief. He introduced us to the new program the police were developing, called *Polícia Legal,* and explained that it had been created to attract children to the community police philosophy and to "instill notions of citizenship, environmental education, safe driving, and respect for the law." He gave a lengthy speech addressing the sociological origins of crime and argued that the problem of urban insecurity is the result of a lack of solidarity, the loss of family values, the chaos of the expansion of favelas, and the concentration of poverty. Silvia looked at me and shook her head, signaling her disapproval of his speech. While his explanations about crime and poverty did not appease Silvia, it was compelling to the individuals demanding more police in the favelas.

After defending the police as the "símbolo da ordem" (symbol of order), he invited us to celebrate the fact that the region had become the showpiece of a smart approach to crime fighting. He also fully endorsed the priest's request for more community police stations in the region. While his officers distributed the police newspaper, he went over the philosophy of community policing, showing pictures of officers in their daily practices. Silvia indicated with her eyes the six policemen at the back of the room: "I am uncomfortable with these guys standing here in military uniforms. Do you see anyone from the *quebrada* [the hood] here? Do you see who is here? I don't see anyone from the Fundão. The real people know who is who, and they don't buy this shit." As the colonel ended his speech, I raised my hand and asked him why there were so many critiques from the people from the Fundão against the police. He did not have a chance to address my question, as one of the organizers interrupted me, saying that the colonel had to leave. He left, and we were approached on our way out by two officers who wanted to follow up on our question.

Silvia reminded them about the ongoing complaints from black youth regarding the police. A common complaint was that the community-based police play the role of the good cops, but then they call special units to do the dirty work of cleaning up the area. These two special police units are responsible for most of the cases of "killing following resistance," in which the police employ lethal force, and they were the ones said to be involved with the deaths of Betinho and Lucas. Silvia told them, "the philosophy of the [community] police is good but in practice its role is to identify suspects and prepare the area for the others." The police officer responded to Silvia by arguing that the conflicts between police officers and black youth are due to the latter's lack of respect for authority. "This is a problem they themselves create when they challenge our authority. If they don't have respect for author-ity, what should we do?" he rhetorically asked, then responded to his own question: "Try to educate them. That is when the conflict arises." I pointed out that favela youth have a very negative image of the police, who to them are more of an occupying force than a "polícia amiga," as the colonel's presentation suggested. The officer ended the conversation by suggesting that those complaining are involved in criminal activities. "If they were *cidadãos de bem* [good citizens], they certainly would be here discussing, trying to help the community. Instead, they are in the *biqueira*." They were not there, and for Silvia and me, it would be un-thinkable to have them discussing "better" policing practices.

Contrary to the Conseg, the Forum members embraced a critical perspective of the state and of the city's economic powers that structured local conditions. They did not support police violence against local youth and did not invest in the explicit rhetoric of the good versus bad citizens. Their refusal to consider race as a category for social organizing, their embrace of a law-abiding religious leftist subject, and their silence over rampant anti-black police terror, however, underscored the roadblocks for black participation in the community unless they were to leave their blackness at the door entrance. Like in the security council, in the progressive Forum the problem of urban violence was crafted as a problem of poor state presence. The difference between the two political formations was that while the members of the Conseg saw brutal police patrolling as the most effective way to reclaim territorial control over the troubling areas, the Forum advocated bringing in the state through a combination of soft military presence and the state-funded pedagogical/disciplinary work of NGOs. The problem of violence in the Fundão was seen mainly as an ecological and public-health problem that could be solved by directing the conduct of the poor to become good citizens, subjects competent in the politics of rights.

Within such a paradigm of social organizing, there was no room for launching critiques against racialized police brutality because doing so would require the activist to disinvest themselves from their dependence on policing in the first place. If they were to consider policing as instrumental not only to state sovereignty but also to community making, they would have had to confront the disturbing question of how anti-blackness becomes an underlying or muted base for defining good civic life in the periphery of the city. To make its conflicting claims to the state, the Forum first had to express loyalty to state-led governing projects at the expense of those seen as enemies of the public order. The Fundão da Zona Sul is at once home to a vibrant NGO/community activism, the human-rights-oriented police force, and astonishing rates of police killings.

Strategic Compliance

While local businessmen, churchgoers, and representatives from local NGOs participated in the council on a regular basis, most of the black favelados showed up at events on rare occasions, generally to interrupt the official agenda with topics of their own. When this occurred, the president of the council would become very upset. Because the council's monthly meetings provide the only opportunity for poor residents to speak face-to-face with representatives of the government, this setting was seen as a strategic place to voice urgent concerns and make specific demands of the state. When they did show up, the favelados from the Fundão would unapologetically dismiss and disrupt the council's planned agenda.

In one of those meetings held in a public high school classroom, a group of shack residents from the hillside shantytown of Dreaming City attended in order to raise an urgent matter. They were demanding a plan to help residents threatened by an imminent disaster. It was the rainy season, and many people had died in mudslides in favelas throughout São Paulo; they were afraid they could be next.[31] The council, as always, began with the president presenting the agenda and asking the other participants to include their concerns. Calls for more police officers, complaints against the *baile funks*, and concerns about PCC's drug-selling points were all written on the blackboard as topics to be addressed in the two-hour meeting. Sitting in the back of the room, the individuals from Dreaming City refused to engage with any other topic. Alarmed by rumors that local authorities would be removing them from their houses without providing any shelter, they came to the meeting upset, demanding an immediate solution.

Adriana and her husband, Cesar, a dark-skinned couple in their early forties, voiced the favelados' concerns and threatened to file a lawsuit against Moises, the representative of the city government, if the worst happened. Cesar explained that when he called the Civil Defense Office, he was asked to provide more information, including the official addresses of the houses in danger. However, Cesar explained, "there is no such thing as numbers on shacks or street names in the favela." He demanded a response from the council: "So we have to cross our arms and wait for the shacks to crumble? And then call you to come to collect the bodies?" Moises told the group of favelados that all he could do was to listen to their complaints, take notes, and hand them over to the housing authority. Irritated, the group of local residents shouted at Moises, explaining that they did not attend the meeting just for people to listen to them. They wanted something to be done about their concerns. Adriana said, "I ask all of you, why is the mayor massacring us? Are we not living in a democracy? Why do we have to wait for another mudslide before you guys take action? The government is doing nothing for us." Moises dismissed them by saying he had not previously seen Adriana or the other members of her group participating in the Conseg. He went further to argue that if she had attended the Conseg's meetings consistently she would not be "telling lies about the mayor." The president agreed with Moises and expressed his frustration with the people that "only come when needing help but refuse to dedicate time to the common good."

Tensions escalated, with shouts in the back of the room. Moises had crossed the line. Cesar asked Moises to be humble and admit he did not know "shit" about the region. Visibly angry, Cesar demanded that Moises apologize and asked him to put himself in his place because "no one is a liar here." Afraid of the public's reaction, Moises conceded: "I didn't call you a liar. I just think this is an unfair accusation. We are listening to you. Look, I am right here, right now." Adriana interjected: "It is one thing to listen to us. It is another thing to respond to our demands, Moises. It is like a child crying and you give water instead of milk. We don't want to wake up in the middle of the night with a tragedy because you didn't prevent a mudslide from happening."

The Conseg president tried to delegitimize their demands, highlighting once again their lack of interest in participating in the monthly meetings. He also protested that the group did not come with proposals to address the problems they complained about. Attempting to squash growing tensions in the meeting and giving an indirect message to the favelados, the president thanked Moises and the other participants for attending the council every month, and then tried to move to the next item on the agenda, arguing that they were "wasting time with vague complaints." Before Moises could respond, Adriana eloquently interjected: "Wasting time? We are not asking for a job, a paycheck, or salary. Nothing. We just want you guys to do the job you were supposed to do. It is easy to talk about security, but the authorities need to know that security is not only the police patrolling the streets." She then turned to the people around her and told them that the government is insensitive to their problems and that officials would only act if they embarrass the authorities publicly. Moises interrupted her, saying "the government is doing a lot." "Even if they want to," he explained, "it is impossible to attend to so many demands in the rainy season." Adriana reminded him that it was not a matter of time but a lack of political will. To drive her point home, she gave Moises an example. "How about the bridge that we have been demanding for years? How many people have died there? Now you went there and put some wood out just to pretend you are fixing it. With all due respect, you are not serious."

Adriana's words made Moises step back. He promised the *subprefeito* (submayor) would provide *quatrocentros* (roughly 150.00 USD) in monthly stipends to help residents move out from risky areas and rent a house during the rainy season. Everybody, including myself, laughed at the offer. Under the barrage of shouts and name calling, someone shouted from the back of the crowded classroom, "We don't want this help, Moises." Another person added: "With such little money we can barely pay for renting a shack in another risky area." Ashamed, Moises scheduled a meeting with the residents for the upcoming week. In the back of the classroom, the new participants cheered. They had had a momentary victory.

The favelados' unpredictable participation in the council can be interpreted in several ways. One way to interpret their interactions with the *homens de bem* is through the framework that Partha Chatterjee describes as "the politics of the governed." According to Chatterjee, people do not refuse to participate in practices of governmentality but rather engage with governing programs on their own terms, using their own vocabulary, and with their own agendas. At strategic moments, they engage with the state, but they chose how and when to do so. When doing so, the urban poor expand politics far beyond what civil society regards as appropriate terms of engagement and instead open a disruptive popular domain for politics, what he calls *political society*. From this space, the poor demand, in disruptive ways, democracy from below. In the case presented here, I suspect Chatterjee would argue that the state and the favelados [population] maintain a pragmatic relationship in which "the demands of electoral mobilization, on the one hand, and the logic of welfare distribution, on the other, overlap. . . ."[32] That means that at times the favelados responded to government interventions by pragmatically mobilizing the political resources available to them, in this case their condition as potential victims of an imminent mudslide.

That was a way to be legible to the state.[33] Another strategy was threatening to not participate in elections "when the cara-de-pau [shameless] candidates come to ask for votes," a threat the city government could not afford to ignore despite Moises reprobation of the favelados' unruliness. The council was an open space for the favelados to participate insofar as they could speak in the institutional language and abide by the informal rules concerning their behavior in meetings. The homens de bem viewed the council as an official space where members of the community could make their claims to the state in what they deemed to be a civilized manner. The favelados clearly challenged these rules and when they decided to attend the meetings, they engaged with another kind of state—not the penal one pushed forward by the police and the homens de bem. Instead of buying into the state-centric rhetoric of crime and security, they strategically selected battles that spoke directly to their everyday experiences as favelados. In doing so, they challenged the civic community of homens de bem and, in Chatterjee's possible interpretation, made the state be in a "constantly shifting compromise between the normative values of modernity [civil society] and the moral assertions of popular demands."[34]

How does blackness, as a form of political organizing, fit into subaltern politics? Black favelados do participate in governmentality programs and embrace political society to make claims otherwise denied in civil-society politics. Their precarious position in such popular domains is rendered visible, however, in the fact that while favelados can at times be legible to the welfare state as population, they are also already and always legible as subjects of gratuitous violence fundamentally for being blacks. Perhaps that is why most of the black residents of Dreaming City cautiously focused on everyday demands, steering clear of matters of security. Pragmatically, they did engage with state and electoral politics by appealing to other governing categories such as "worker" and "voter," leaving race aside. In Adriana's words, "are we not in a democracy, Moises?" One could say that all these categories fit into the political society framework as the restrictive job market, lack of public transportation, the lack of housing projects, and overcrowded public hospitals were results of discriminatory policies that affect the poor population overall, not just black favelados. There is evidence to support this interpretation, and I do not wish to dismiss Chatterjee's optimist formulations on the potential for democracy from below. That is not an argument against poor people's politics, either. What I want to call attention to is the liminal place occupied by blacks in relation to the state, civil society, and even in relation to popular politics. To participate in subaltern politics, the favelado had to embrace, at least rhetorically, a *grammar of rights* that quite often collapsed in the face of their liminal condition as blacks. Although the favelados managed to have some "small victories," the council's identification of them as enemies of public order underscored a security-knowledge that produced them as nonbeing, to which neither civil society nor working class politics is able to fully accommodate. As a theoretical concept, while political society is conceived as the place in which the governed establish the terms of how to be governed, the racial alterity of the favelado places them in a condition of ungovernmentality, or governability only through terror despite the government's momentary recognition of their political claims—by offering them a subsidized rent for the rainy season, for example.[35]

While there were some strategic attendances, most of the favelados

A protest against police brutality by the Committee against Genocide in downtown São Paulo in May 2015. The banner says "Police get off the favelas and the hills." Photography by UNEafro-Brasil.

did not bother to attend Conseg's meetings even to disrupt them. Black young men were particularly explicit in their dismissal of anything that required contact with the state or community activism because they were seen as enemies in these spheres of politics. I read their critique of such channels of participation as a "radical refusal" to be governed.[36] If the traditional channels for making political claims are colonized domains that negate black life while opening some possibility to subaltern politics, then perhaps the refusal to participate in such channels of negotiation could be better crafted as black ungovernability or, in the words of H. L. T. Quan, "the *ungovernable* intent of impeding and negating 'governmentality' or [negating] the organized practices that render subjects governable."[37] While structural black expendability indicates that the state is less concerned with managing black life than with eviscerating it, the government's multifaceted techniques of control (biopower and necropower) in the urban periphery of São Paulo are indeed met with multiple forms of black ungovernability. An overtly explicit one is through the world of crime (analyzed in chapter 4), but there are also less visible and apparently contradictory politics of refusal, like dismissal and strategic compliance. Take Dona Maria's example: her son Thiago was a member of PCC. She, on the other hand, relied on the rhetoric of human rights to make claims against the state. At the same time, when I invited Dona Maria to the downtown protest against police brutality or to participate in the regular meetings in the Forum in Defense of Life, she told me, aware of her precarious position in such a political game, that she does not "give a damn about it." She also would often challenge my participation in the council, reminding me of her condition as a black mother favelada: "I wish that the people who participate in this shit were in my shoes to know what violence is about. They know nothing about what it is to have an innocent kid kidnapped and killed by the police." She had a point, because even though she had strategically endorsed the politics of rights and at times appealed to political society's strategic disruptiveness—so the state would recognize Betinho's death and provide her financial compensation—the state continued denying his death and her living. Dona Cecilia did not care to attend the council or engage in any form of formal politics. Besides being too busy struggling to raise her children, she kept herself apart from anything referring to human rights because it was "a waste of time." The tragic irony here is that "it was a waste of time" because in the eyes of civil society "human rights are for those deemed humans"; Lucas's wrongdoings disqualified his mother from embracing human rights to make political claims. And yet, if on the one hand the subject-positions of "black mother favelada" and "thug" complicate and limit political society in resounding ways (underscoring the Afro-pessimist critique), on the other hand they also unveil another form of political life of the socially dead.

Putting the Police in Their Place

The residents of the Fundão viewed the security council and the Forum in Defense of Life as *panelinhas* (cliques) and as spaces "where snitches get together," as they consistently told me during our interactions. When I asked questions such as, "What do you think about the Conseg? What are your thoughts about the community police?" and, "Why don't you participate in the Forum?" other Dreaming City residents also responded as if these inquiries were offensive. Usually they would immediately respond: "Are you a snitch?" The question, though asked in a joking manner, illustrates the general distrust between most of the favelados and those who regularly participated in the state-supported Conseg and their skepticism of the community-based activism of the Forum. They were skeptical about the Forum because, as nineteen-year-old Edu told me, "they don't know, or don't wanna know, the *other* face of the police."[38] Edu referred to those like me attending these meetings as *zé povinho*. The term *zé povinho* has two meanings within this ethnographic context. It is both a pejorative term the elite generally use to address the masses and a street slang term used by those in the world of crime to separate themselves from the people who "play the police's game," or who buy into the trope of respectability. The residents who attend the Forum and the security council are considered *zé povinho* because they are not from the world of crime; they are viewed as "too naïve, too straight, and too afraid to die," in the words of one of my interlocutors referring to my participation in these spaces. To put it bluntly, and in my interlocutors' own words, the *zé povinho* were viewed as *cuzão* (chicken shit).

To participate in the council is to be associated with the state, and even worse, with the police. Mistrust of the police seems to be the main dissonance between black young men hanging out with me on the curb and the *zé povinho* attending the state-backed spaces of political organizing. While these spaces asked for and celebrated the "new" community policing, in the eyes of individuals like Edu "there is nothing new about the police." According to him, the new logic behind policing Dreaming City was just a strategy to get more information about the *biqueiras* and harass black youth on the streets. "The community police play the 'good guys.' They come and drink coffee with you in the bakery. They invite you to soccer games. At the same time, they give your information to the *Special Unity*. So when they come they already know everything about you. And you better run away when you see the Special Unity because they will kill you," Edu warned me.

The Special Unity, said to be responsible for killing Betinho and Lucas, practices a more aggressive form of policing than the community police. However, in Edu's words, "the community police is a fraud." Activists in the community would disagree with Edu's statement and perhaps regard it as the black man's antagonism toward the police, but like many favela residents, he dismissed the "new police" because his day-to-day encounters with this branch of the state continues to be marked by surveillance, extortion, torture, and killings. That Edu celebrated the fact that he was alive speaks for itself: "The police shot at me two times. I was on the corner with some pot to deliver, and the cops came out of nowhere. Then I quickly threw it away. I ran and they fired two shots. I fell in the alley where they caught me . . . it was the Special Unity. . . . I was spitting blood. They didn't find the pot but fetched me. They thought I'd snitch on somebody but I'm not a snitch." Edu managed to deceive the police and avoid a criminal record. His decision to hide the drugs before being approached saved him from being arrested or killed.

The Special Unity was famous for its decisive use of force to maintain public order. It was deployed in moments of public disturbance in the legal parts of the city and in the hunting of "criminals" in the favelas. The considerable amount of time I spent hanging out with black young men on the curbs of Dreaming City gave me an overwhelming opportunity to listen to their day-to-day experiences with the Special Unity. In one of those moments, I was with three other men in their early twenties—Amaro, Fernando, and Júlio—during the break of a televised soccer match in a local bar that I am calling "O Ponto." As we sat in the chairs outside the bar, members of the Special Unity slowly passed by in front of the bar while displaying their guns and staring intently at us. O Ponto was located in front of the neighborhood association and since José (a white middle-aged individual who served as the president of the association) was a good friend of mine, we would always meet at the bar to catch up. That period of time was particularly tense because of a new wave of police-led massacres that resulted in the deaths of dozens of black men in several bars in Zona Sul.[39] The slaughters followed a persistent and "mysterious" pattern: the police patrol would pass by, and minutes later a car would pull up outside the bar and hooded men would shoot at the youth seated at the tables on the sidewalks. I was visibly nervous as the police car drove by that afternoon as I sat chatting with Amaro, Fernando, and Júlio. However, José waved at them and as they drove away, he told us they had been around earlier that day, looking for two individuals accused of robbing a store in Santo Amaro, the commercial hub in midtown. Since José was a local leader and they knew him well, I felt at ease, but the incident gave me the opportunity to speak with my associates about their encounters with the police.

With the exception of José, who at first avoided expressing his opinion and then left to attend a meeting in the neighborhood association, there was a unanimous understanding that the police were to be avoided at any cost, even when one is also a potential victim of intra-community violence. Fernando told us the story of a friend who had had an electronic guitar stolen and went to the police station to file a report, hoping to recover it. "Instead of helping the poor guy, the officer at the counter asked him so many questions that he got frustrated and left." He recounted that they asked if he had a job, where he lived, if he had a criminal record, and even where he bought the guitar. Without mincing words, Fernando asked me, "Who the fuck goes to the police? Do *you* go to the police when something happens to you?" "I don't go," he continued, "If you go to the police station as a victim, you will probably leave as a criminal." Fernando's statement is supported by the disturbingly common police practice of invading residences without a warrant to search for drugs and their usual practice of seizing cell phones or any electronics if the favelado is unable to show a receipt proving he or she paid for it. When I asked them who they turned to for help, Fernando explained: "Now it is the PCC who calls the shots. If something happens to you here you don't look for the police, fool. You go to the 'brothers.'" And then he started elaborating on how the PCC handles wrongdoings in the favela and why the favelados seek it out to solve everyday problems. His was an accurate assessment. Although neither the Conseg nor the Forum avoided talking about the criminal organization, it is a public secret that the PCC retains de facto authority in most of São Paulo's periphery. The Partido has replaced the state in regulating social life in a very complex and controversial system of justice. While I discuss the Partido's participation in São Paulo's regime of urban governance in a later chapter, I want to highlight the black young men's refusal to comply with the police and their participation in the criminal organization instead. The Partido is far from a political response to their everyday problems, but, as Fernando told me during another conversation, "[with PCC's justice] you can disentangle things. It is not as if the PCC goes crazy and kills a person just for the sake of killing. No! You have the opportunity to talk and defend yourself. Now you tell me if one can do that with the police." Perhaps his statements reveal why many black favelados refuse to engage with the security state even when it tries to approach them through human rights discourses and cultural activities.

The police had created a stage near to the police station where they promoted marathons, hip-hop music, street dances, and musical competitions under their watch. Ironically, at the time of our meeting, Amaro was under probation (he had to appear in court once a month and was completing community service as an assistant in the resident association's library) for playing loud music on the streets with other black youth and for breaking curfew legislation. His black funk style and loud music had crossed the border of what the police allowed as culture. Amaro was not swayed by these new efforts to bridge the gap between the police and black youth: "When I see an officer from the community police station and he comes to me with bullshit I just put him in his place. 'Good morning,' 'Good evening Sr.,' and that is all. I don't shake hands or talk with the police. I don't like them. I know what they want."

Amaro's avoidance was not just a lack of trust in the police, as law-enforcement policy makers and security think tanks may want us to believe. "Mistrust" suggests a mere state of mind or (mis)interpretation of

Stage for cultural activities in the main square of Jardim Angela in São Paulo's Fundão da Zona Sul. The community police station is located in the back. Photograph by the author.

someone's (good) intentions. Black youth's "reading" of the police was based on the lived experience of racial surveillance that turns their bodies and cultural practices into threats to the civic community. Júlio's story gives us a way to think about the collapse of "soft" law-enforcement policies in the face of black threat. One night when he was coming home from work, a group of police officers in a car suddenly appeared around the corner and began pointing flashlights into his face. Júlio froze and the officers shouted, "Vagabond, freeze and put your hands on the wall!" Júlio described what happened next: "So I went straight to the gate [of a nearby house] and put my hands on the wall, under the doorbell. They came to me with this stick and I was basically pissing myself. Then they started searching me, and I was pressing the doorbell. Each time they poked my body, I pushed the doorbell for someone who was inside the house to know that I was being beaten." Meanwhile, two police officers poked him with the stick while the others asked him questions and checked his identification. Assuring them he was coming from work and that he had no criminal record, Júlio was released. "I was feeling like trash." Júlio considered asking for apologies but he was smart enough to let it go. "There is nothing you can do in the middle of the night, four guys with a gun in your face." Júlio's life was spared that night, and he did not consider looking for help at the local human rights organization or the security council as even a remote possibility. He did not consider these spaces because he was very aware of the place he occupies in local activism and in the city's security politics.

This afternoon at the bar, my interlocutors gave face to the racialized regime of security in place in São Paulo's periphery. The police's treatment of the playboys in the Jardins, the wealthy neighborhoods of the city, is very different from how officers treat black youth in the Fundão, they said. "*Da ponte pra cá* things are very different," Fernando explained. *Da ponte pra cá* can be translated as "on this side of the tracks." Literally, the bridge above the Pinheiros River that separates the geographies of opportunity and exclusion of the predominantly white wealthy and the poverty-stricken, predominantly black Fundão da Zona Sul also informs different entitlements and policing strategies. "In the Jardins, if you walk around the block twice you are stopped. You take two laps and the bastard doorman calls the police," says Júlio. Fernando also elaborated on the differential treatment that the police give to youth from different parts of the city: "In Moema they say, 'Please, sir, hands on your head.' Here, [the police say], 'Hands on your head, *ladrão* [thief], or I'll bust you!'"

This bodily spatial consciousness suggests that the police are also enforcers of economic and social boundaries. Black youth attempting to subvert spatial frontiers by taking a little stroll in the well-off neighborhoods are met with harsher policing. The belief that they do not belong to the city is widely shared, as seen in the 2013 *rolezinhos* crisis, in which the police were called to protect mall clients against black and working-class teenagers from the favelas. It is also a belief shared by guards and officers that may well be from the same racial and territorial backgrounds as their victims. Black men constantly complained about black officers. "They are the worst. They beat you really good and call you a 'monkey,'" Fernando complained. He added that he knew a black officer who says "I prefer working in Fundão. You can beat up the *neguinhos.*" Trained under the same racial ideology that informs larger society, black officers protect the white elite *against* black men like Fernando and Júlio. Their brutality is usually seen as an indication that racism does not play an important role in informing policing practices in the periphery of the city. After all, some believe, the victims and victimizers are from the same racial group. That my interlocutors are aware of the "racial epidermal schema" involved in the exchange with the black officers, aware of their skin color and aware of the racially coded insults they are subjected to, complicates such simplistic explanations.[40] Why do black officers incorporate naming black youth as "monkeys" into their policing practice? Answering this question may further illuminate, rather than undermine, how policing is energized and how it reflects the much larger ideological domain of anti-black racism that structures Brazilian society. Race was so evident in my interlocutors' experiences that neither they nor I bothered to discuss the matter or prove its existence. We took it for granted. In the same way that race was never explicitly evoked in the Forum and the security council—it was enacted through coded words such as *cancer* and *criminals*—these issues emerged on a day-to-day basis, often through the territory-based language of being favelados and being from "other side of the track." The racial underpinnings of these dynamics are taken for granted because it was mundane, lived experience from my informants' perspective, not because they lacked racial consciousness. Crafted as "the problem" of insecurity, black young men live their policed lives suspended in a predictable chain of criminalization that makes questions about racism redundant.

This chapter shed light on the gendered and racialized structure of urban governance in São Paulo's periphery. I have also discussed the ways black favelados respond to the governmentality projects that target the Fundão. Although local NGOs and the city government have spent a lot of time and money trying to sell fantasies of a police force committed to the democratic state of rights, to the favelado nothing has changed under this new system of policing. Moreover, by contrasting the favelados' experiences of racism and community-based activism, I demonstrate how black young men and black women are positioned within security-state projects and how their social location informs how they respond to community activism. Whether through killings by the police, the "soft knife of routine processes of ordinary oppression," or through community making, state-led strategies of urban security exposes the conundrum of how to govern bodies and territories rendered unruly for their racial marks.[41] In the next chapter, I explore another particular technology of domination that has remained consistent in Brazilian history since colonialism: the penal system. In order to understand racial violence in this country, one cannot overlook how the prison system structures black urban life in Brazilian society at large and how neoliberal policies fueled the expansion of the prison system in São Paulo. What narratives come to the surface when we view the prison as a favela and the favela as a prison?

3

THE FAVELA-PRISON PIPELINE

Now, the slave quarter is the favela, the slave catcher is the police,
and the whip are the bullets that kill our people.

—Douglas Belchior, UNEafro

Prison is not that much different from the street . . . cells are not
that different from the tenement and the welfare hotels they live in
on the street. . . . The police are the same. The poverty is the same.
The alienation is the same. The racism is the same. The sexism is the
same. The drugs are the same and the system is the same.

—Assata Shakur, Women in Prison

On Friday nights women form a long line along the fence at the Centro de Detenção Provisória (Pre-Detention Center, hereafter CDP), a
men's prison in the heart of the city of São Paulo. Coming from all
over the city, they tell jokes, laugh, smoke cigarettes, and feed their
babies while waiting to visit their loved ones. Some take the opportunity to ask for a fee for watching belongings or renting out pants
and sandals to visitors unaware of the prison's strict dress codes and
rules regarding what visitors can and cannot take with them into the
detention center. The misfortune of some becomes an opportunity for
others to make money for the bus tickets back home. Getting ready
for the humiliation that generally comes at checkpoints, these women
prepare to meet the center's overbearing regulations. On the sidewalks,
they take out the food they bring to their relatives, cut cakes into small
pieces, unpack cigarettes and candies, and take soda out of its original

packaging. Everything must be transferred into transparent plastic bags. It does not matter what kind of food the women bring or how it looks in these plastic bags: these are the rules, and those who do not follow them are prevented from entering the prison. While waiting, there is no shelter and the only available bathroom is kept in unsanitary condition. With no other choice, women are forced to share the sidewalk with dirty water leaking from the broken bathroom while stray dogs sleep nearby.

I began visiting prisoners in the CDP in 2010 when I joined the Prisoners Advocacy Network for prisoners' rights.[1] As a member of the Network, a Catholic-based activist group, my duties included facilitating communication between prisoners and their relatives and guiding them through the process of calling on the public defender to take up their cases. On this day, I came to the prison in response to a special request from Gustavo, a young black man serving time for drug trafficking. He urged me to come on the family visitation day so I could meet his mother at the prison gates, as she was concerned about his judicial case. I met his mother, Dona Dina, a black woman in her early sixties, standing in the long line with Gustavo's five-year-old son, Raul. Dona Dina received me with excitement and was surprised that I was interested in her son's fate. Perhaps my affiliation to the prison advocacy group made our meeting cordial and very accessible. As I greeted her and Raul, the child asked me, "Is your father also here?" I replied, "Nope, but I visit some friends in here." "I am going to see my father," he replied. Dona Dina and Raul come from one of the favelas of Zona Leste, where they live with Dina's four daughters. She says she only visits Gustavo once a month because the atmosphere is too depressing and she feels sick after leaving.

Gustavo had been convicted of drug trafficking, sentenced to five and a half years in detention, and was waiting to be transferred to the penitentiary. The family did not have a lawyer to take his case and relied on a public attorney whom they had only seen once before the hearing. I gave Dona Dina the paperwork with information about Gustavo's sentence and the phone number of the Advocacy Network. She complained that Gustavo had been trying to do the "right things" but had been harassed by the police for his criminal record. "He even got a job at the supermarket, but the police were on his case and warned that they would make him go back to prison," she explained. Another woman in the line joined the conversation, nodding in agreement with Dona Dina's comment about the police harassing her son as well. Assuming I was a journalist, she began complaining that the prison guards treated the women in line "like criminals." Dona Dina told her it was better not to complain because if a prisoner's relative makes disturbances, the prisoner would receive a *gancho,* a term in the carceral universe's vocabulary that means the prisoner won't be allowed to receive visitors for two to four weeks. The woman agreed: "It is like *puxar a pena junto* [doing time together]."

Dona Dina remembered that a particularly harsh prison guard, whom the women referred to as *cabeça de porco* (pig head), would be working that day. The humiliation that began on the streets with the long lines would continue with the discretionary power of the prison guards over the prisoners' families. The women standing in line provided dozens of examples of how the visitors had been humiliated and terrorized by prison guards. The most common complaint was about the aggressive body searches they endured as they were viewed as potential *mulas* (mules) bringing cell phones and drugs to inmates. They protested that their complaints were routinely ignored since they were seen as *mãe ou mulher de bandido* (a thug's mother or wife). Afraid of retaliation, Dona Dina kept reminding us about the *gancho.* If prison guards believed the visitors were disturbing the prison order, they could suspend the latter's visitation rights for fifteen to thirty days at their discretion. As the guard opened the gate and the line started moving, I let Dona Dina and Raul walk into the monster's belly and took the bus home myself. This chapter asks, what work does the prison do to the social and political reproduction of the Brazilian racial order? How did prisons become central to the spatial arrangement of racial difference in São Paulo? And finally, what is the place occupied by impoverished black women within such an economy of urban security?

Carceral Violence

Brazil's prison population is the fourth largest in the world following the United States, China, and Russia. The country has one and a half million people under the supervision of the criminal justice system, half a million of whom are confined behind bars. According to the Brazilian Ministry of Justice, the prison population increased 410 percent—

jumping from 148,000 to almost 607,000—between 1995 and 2015. As for its racial profile, 53 percent of Brazil's imprisoned population is black, 46 percent is white, and 1 percent is classified as "other." Although men make up the majority of the prison population, the female population is quickly growing. In the last fifteen years, from 2000 to 2015, the female population grew 567 percent while the general prison population grew 119 percent. Black women make up 68 percent of the female prison population, white women account for 31 percent, and "others" comprise the remaining 1 percent."[2] Crimes against property (20 percent) and drug offenses (59 percent) account for the majority of arrests of women. According to a report from the Pastoral Carcerária, 38 percent of women arrested for drug offenses spend more than four years in prison, while the comparable rate for men is 22 percent. The report concludes that "the incarcerated woman in Brazil is generally young, a single mother, black, and in the majority of cases, they are arrested for drug-related crimes."[3]

Although the extraordinary growth in Brazil's inmate population and expanded prison system corresponds temporally and spatially to the country's adoption of neoliberal economic policies in the 1990s, the current Brazilian carceral state is historically and ideologically linked to the "peculiar institution" of slavery. Like in the United States, where prisons became the new plantations, prisons have always been central to the control of the black population in Brazil.[4] Scholars have long documented the set of legislation (the Criminal Code of 1830 and its updated version in 1890) that integrates the black population into the penal system. Curfew legislation and the prohibition of *capoeira* and bearing arms were among the laws established during the 1830s to control the circulation of blacks in the cities. The penal code also established the death penalty for slaves participating in revolts or threatening the physical integrity of their masters.[5] Slavery was abolished in 1888 and a few years later, the Brazilian congress passed a new penal code that, among other things, further criminalized black spiritual and cultural practices (e.g., *candomblé,* samba, and *capoeira*) and the "unproductive" and "vagrant" free black population. The new legal provisions targeted the "repression of crimes that threaten the social order due to, most of the time, the relaxation or depravation of morals, generally having its cause in idleness." Anyone found engaged in "idleness" was arrested and released upon signing a form that promised they would find a job within fifteen days. Residents were punished with three years in a penal colony.[6] The code also set the basis for the current prison system by structuring rural correctional facilities to house the undesirable population. The penal code had an economic rationality. As the formerly enslaved population migrated to urban centers like Rio de Janeiro and São Paulo, a major problem haunted the white elite: what to do with a growing black urban population made superfluous by the abolition of slavery and the European migration? The state was able to regulate the surplus population (keeping them as a reserve of cheap labor ready to be exploited) by threatening freed blacks with incarceration. Denied land rights and withheld access to the labor market now open to the European immigrant, the former slaves became feared urban criminals to be tamed by the "new" penal legislation. The formal change in the political–economic order of slavery society turned the black person from "good slave to bad citizen."[7]

While this brief description does not do justice to the complex historical process of the criminalization of black urban life, my intention here is to call attention to the ideological basis of what became the main technology of racial domination in contemporary Brazil. Following the lead of Joy James, I refer to the Brazilian society's current prison–police regime as a "penal democracy."[8] Like police terror, the ongoing domestic dynamic of black carcerality calls into question the class-based, prison-reform arguments so prevalent among mainstream human rights groups and Brazilian prison studies scholars. Penal (racial) democracy seems to be an accurate portrayal of a country obsessed with the surveillance of black bodies while celebrating blackness. In that regard, although the argument posed by radical black scholars that prisons are modern-day plantations sounds like an overstatement to a tradition of prison studies in Brazil that privileges the lens of class, the "criminalizing program" of black life in Brazil and the United States' Black Codes have stark similarities.[9] U.S. scholars often cite the Fifth Amendment, which outlawed slavery except in cases of punishment, as the underlying logic of mass incarceration in the "land of the free and the home of the brave." They highlight that the criminal justice system fulfills its historical role as part of an enduring racial project that sustains "Amerika." Postabolition Amerika, in turn, was never meant to be "the land of the freed" black and brown population, a population whose political status poses a challenge to liberal democracy. And still, black captivity and democracy are not in opposition to each other because in postslavery societies, the nonlegal or infrahuman black subject continues to be the negative reference that defines the white subject of rights.[10] Rather than comparing both racial trajectories (in the United States and in Brazil), putting them into perspective helps to situate the current stage of the Brazilian carceral state, seen by black activists as a sign that the "abolition of slavery is unconcluded."

Although Brazil's history is one of racial captivities, the current dynamics of mass incarceration correspond temporally and causally with the adoption of neoliberal economic policies at the federal and state levels. Beginning with the unstable government of President Fernando Collor de Mello (1990–92) and his resignation two years later, the Brazilian state promoted major reforms aimed to turn the country into a more competitive economy in the international market throughout the 1990s. Collor described his government as a "pacific revolution" that would clean up Brazil's "culture of corruption" and bring the country to the world stage as a modern nation. His short-term government was replaced by that of Vice President Itamar Franco (1992–94), who pushed forward the neoliberal agenda by promising to bring down the astonishing inflation rates of the previous decade. He attempted to make Brazil more attractive to foreign investment and sought to modernize the country's half-century-old labor legislation.

Although Fernando Collor de Mello and Itamar Franco initiated the process of neoliberalization, it was during Fernando Henrique Cardoso's two terms (1995–2002) that the country instituted drastic structural changes in line with the Washington Consensus: the opening of the economy to the global market, inflation control, modernization of the state, privatization, limiting of public spending, and increased investment in defense and police technologies. By the time Cardoso left the presidency in 2002, the federal government had privatized more than one hundred national companies.[11] Cardoso also forced the neoliberal agenda on state governments by passing a fiscal law (*Lei de Responsabilidade Fiscal*) that imposed drastic federal control of already tight state and municipality budgets and made federal funds conditional on structural adjustments at the state level. Unprotected by trade liberalization policies and unable to compete with imported goods, local industrial activity slowed and left millions unemployed. Seven million jobs were lost during Cardoso's administration, passing from 4.5 million unemployed in 1994 to 11.5 million unemployed in 2002.[12] While Cardoso's government was relatively successful in controlling inflation (keeping it at a two-digit figure throughout his term), he left his successor a scrambled economy with an interest rate of 25 percent, a poverty rate of 38 percent, a foreign debt of 230 billion USD, and a national public debt of 700 billion BRL in 2002 (it was 59.4 billion BRL in 1994).[13]

The rise to power of the Social Democracy Party (PSDB) was marked by a progressive shift toward developing an incipient welfare program. Cardoso also officially recognized the existence of racism in Brazilian society during the Durban Conference against Racism in 2001.[14] At the same time, the bitter side of his neoliberalizing agenda was felt most acutely by the black urban poor, as unemployment and cuts in social expenditure programs had a disproportionate impact on this already vulnerable population. As poor Brazilians unsuccessfully struggled to find jobs, Cardoso's administration was highly successful in pushing forward conservative penal policies that would have drastic impacts on the country's criminal justice system. Inaugurating a trend that would be followed by left-wing president Lula da Silva, the Brazilian government (federal and state levels combined) spent an average of R$24 billion each year (from 1995 to 2005) on law-enforcement policies. By 2009, security spending had grown to R$47 billion. Spending on the expansion and maintenance of the prison system alone increased 63.3 percent, from R$1.7 billion to R$2.8 billion, between 1995 and 2005.[15]

The periodization of Cardoso's government in matters of security is illustrative. Cardoso's national public-security strategy came into full display following several nationally televised events: the slaughter of nineteen landless workers in the state of Pará, and the killing of residents of a favela by the police in São Paulo and Cidade de Deus in Rio de Janeiro. Caught on camera, these incidents revealed to the international media an ugly side of the young Brazilian democracy, embarrassing Cardoso's internationally sold image of a government committed to the democratic state of rights and himself as a sociologist identified with progressive politics.[16] After the incident, the government created the National Secretary of Public Safety and gave the Brazilian army unprecedented power over public security matters. It was the first time since the dictatorship regime that the army would be deployed to "police" the urban crisis, and what was supposed to have been an exception has since then increasingly become a rule. The strategic alliance between the national defense forces and state-level secretaries conveyed a political move toward the increased militarization of public safety in a country that had just emerged from a bloody twenty-five-year military dictatorship. The army supported state governments in dealing with "crisis situations" at a moment when activists occupied the streets to end Cardoso's disastrous privatization program.[17] With leftist-communist insurgents no longer a threat, the "internal enemies" were recast, in Cardoso's words, as "neobobos" (neosilly activists) against his neoliberal agenda.

At the state level, São Paulo replicated Cardoso's neoliberal policies by cutting social programs and privatizing state-owned electricity, water, and telephone companies. At the same time, the state of São Paulo sold its public assets under the justification of meeting its financial obligations: the public debt of the state that was 3.4 billion BRL in 1992 skyrocketed to 50 billion BRL in 1997 and to 192 billion BRL in 2013.[18] Corresponding to these reforms, the state of São Paulo experienced consistent double-digit unemployment over that decade (15.1 percent in 1996, 19.3 percent in 1999, and 18.7 percent in 2004).[19] Simultaneously, the municipality of São Paulo passed through major transformations in its labor market, turning from an industrial base into a service economy. Brazilian economists Lucia Garcia, Mário Rodarte, and Thaiz Braga note that it was precisely Brazil's most industrialized area (the São Paulo metropolitan region) that suffered the most with the trade liberalization policies of the 1990s. According to them, the region's industry contracted 4.2 percent yearly. By 1999, the service-based economy represented 74 percent of the metropolitan area's job market while industrial activity accounted for only 19.9 percent. Years earlier, in 1988, the industry sector had represented 32 percent of the workforce.[20] This shift had a profound impact on the urban poor struggling to enter the new specialized economy, particularly the black population. According to *Map of the Black Population in the Job Market* by Fundação Dieese, unemployment among blacks in the metropolitan region in 1998 was 41 percent higher than among whites. Among the employed, black workers' incomes were half of the salaries that whites earned. Black women had an unemployment rate of 25 percent, the highest of any social group, and their earnings were 67 percent lower than white men's earnings.[21]

Neoliberal Carcerality

As the Brazilian economy shrank, the prison system grew steadily during the 1990s. Incarcerating the disenfranchised urban poor became a political response to social and economic insecurities generated by the neoliberal restructuring program imposed by Washington. As structural unemployment deepened urban poverty and spatial segregation, disseminating fear and fighting crime became the state's governing strategy as it withdrew from providing its already precarious network of social protections. Here, there may be a distinction from the aggressive neoliberal policies of the United States. While the U.S. neoliberal state dismantled public services and criminalized poverty through what Loïc Wacquant calls a "double punishment" of welfare turned into "restrictive workfare and expansive *prisonfare*," there was no welfare state to be dismantled in Brazil. We jumped one step as the timid social state that emerged from the 1988 constitution was put at risk by the violence of prisonfare.[22] The state responded to social suffering with more prisons and more police. São Paulo's neoliberal urbanism was particularly revealing in this regard. The country's leading economic power was the center of neoliberal economic and penal policies (with the PSDB controlling both the federal and state government). Simultaneously, the state privatized state-owned companies, "modernized" itself, and launched a multifaceted law-enforcement program based on mass incarceration, police brutality, and . . . community police.

The seemingly counterintuitive neoliberal approach to crime—mobilizing the language of citizenship and enforcing hyperpunitive and necropolitical state practices—has been the object of vigorous intellectual debate. Scholars have particularly analyzed the connections between violence, gendered racism, and the reproduction of capitalism under the neoliberal order. They usually agree that neoliberalism is not just *an economic project to restructure the power of global elite—it* is also a gender- and race-based system of governance.[23] At the same time that neoliberalism seeks legitimacy through the universal discourse of rights (to personhood, cultural difference, citizenship, and so on), its violent articulation of race and gender subordination enables the production of a surplus population increasingly stripped of any utility within the world of production, and thus expendable and devoured by the carceral state.[24] Neoliberalism's subject formation is based on the strategic recognition of minority rights even as it renders these very subjects unproductive and thus unworthy of living. It goes without saying that the rhetoric of "rights," "justice," and "community" all amount to discursive formations that aim to "secure white life" by eviscerating black bodies.[25] Dylan Rodríguez puts it this way: "the social formation of the current epoch is aggressively normatively white, to the extent that [neoliberal] multiculturalism is based on an empirical production of 'diversity' fostered and sustained by a white-supremacist organizing logic, and, as evidenced in the formation of the prison regime, premised on an astronomically scaled institutionalization of black and indigenous civil and social death."[26]

In São Paulo, the neoliberal "astronomical scale of social death" is nowhere more pronounced than in the state's heavy investment in the expansion of the criminal justice system.[27] The neoliberal government of Fernando Henrique Cardoso provided the state of São Paulo with a steady stream of funds to expand its prisons and restructure its police force. Between 1995 and 2003, the state grew its police force from 73,000 officers to 124,000, making it the largest police force in the country. The state also invested R$435 million in new equipment and another R$110 million in building twenty-one new prison facilities in the countryside.[28] The prison expansion continued over the next decade, and the state had doubled the number of correctional facilities (from 88 to 164 penal institutions plus 19 under construction under the "Plan of Expansion of the Prison System") by 2014, although it would need another 105 prisons to meet the incarceration boom.[29] In ten years (1995–2005), the state of São Paulo's security budget doubled from R$4.3 billion to R$8.9 billion, and it achieved the impressive mark of R$10.3 billion in 2014.[30] Although under opposite parties, federal investments in São Paulo's security system continued under the presidency of Lula da Silva (from 2003 to 2010). Under Lula's National

Public Safety Plan, São Paulo received R$230 million from the federal government between 2003 and 2009 to expand its police force and prison system.[31] In 2009, São Paulo's conservative governor, José Serra, announced a R$1.5 billion plan to build forty-nine new prison facilities in the countryside, designed to hold forty thousand new prisoners. In 2012, Governor Geraldo Alckmin announced a new plan to open thirty-nine thousand slots in prison facilities throughout the state.[32]

The expansion of the penal system has a geographic, economic, and political rationality. In *Golden Gulag*, political geographer Ruth Gilmore argues that California's prison boom in the last three decades was a sociopolitical and "geographical solution to political economic crisis, organized by the state, which is itself in crisis."[33] According to Gilmore, California's "prison fix" attended to a problem of surplus land, labor, and state technology created by the steady public investment in high-tech military industry and tax incentives in the marginal hinterland of the country. This "military Keynesianism" boosted the economy and helped to establish a welfare system that would crumble in the early 1970s with the global capitalist crisis. Astonishing prison growth since then, Gilmore forcefully argues, had much more to do with the necessity of putting capital and land to work than with the dominant explanations for prison growth, such as the rise in crime, drug epidemics, and urban poverty.

Despite the differences in scope and temporality in the role of the Brazilian state in promoting economic growth though military spending, the state of São Paulo's unprecedented expansion of the prison system is clearly also a "geographical solution" for creating a new job markets in economically depressed small cities forgotten in São Paulo's uneven development. The state has prioritized the construction of new facilities in agricultural regions particularly vulnerable to international fluctuations of crop prices (mainly coffee and sugarcane) and low economic performance. The expansion of prisons in the countryside increases public spending on security, roads, and public infrastructure, thus making the region particularly attractive to other economic activities. A few mayors have resisted the idea of opening prisons in their towns, but now small cities with poorly developed infrastructure fight among themselves to host these new facilities in their efforts to attract private and public investment. To break the resistance of some cities to housing new prisons, the state government has granted fiscal benefits under the "friendly municipalities" incentive program.[34] In February 2013, during the inauguration of a new prison in Cerqueira César—a small city of nineteen thousand people five hundred kilometers from the city of São Paulo—Governor Geraldo Alckmin revealed that "now there is a line of mayors wanting to bring prisons to their municipalities" because they know that "in a small city it means five hundred jobs with initial salary of R$2,700." Alckmin's speech also revealed how abandoned cities find in prisons a way to revitalize infrastructure that otherwise would be neglected by the state:

> The roads from Cerqueira César to highway Castelo Branco [one of the main highways crossing the state] are 18 km, and it is 6 km asphalted. So we'll authorize [asphalting] 6 km more and the next year we will asphalt the other 6 km. And then conclude the 18 km of new asphalt to Castelo Branco. The municipality has already signed the childcare school, has it not? Already signed. And you need a basic or primary school? We're going to write down the name of the neighborhood just to provide the school. And we will strengthen health care. We had a lack of doctors, but we made a new career plan with physicians, and this applies to all doctors, hospitals, clinics, police, forensics, prisons.[35]

Another example is Alta Paulista, a region in central São Paulo where ten prisons have been built in the last decade (2000–2010). The region has been suggestively referred to as the "Brazilian Texas," an allusion to the state infamous for one of the largest prison systems in the United States.[36] Passing through an agricultural crisis due to the fluctuation of coffee commodity prices in the international market, the poor region found an opportunity to boost its economic growth in the fiscal incentives granted by the state for hosting the prisons (in addition to the carceral tourism it generates with inmate families travelling eight to ten hours on weekends to visit their relatives). The federal government plays an important role in this Brazilian "carceral Keynesianism" by offering low-rate loans through the National Bank for Economic and Social Development (BNDES) to state governments and private corporations interested in administrating prisons in economically depressed regions. It is expected that with federal fiscal incentives in the present decade, São Paulo will not only be able to address the urgent need to create new slots in its overcrowded prison system but also decentralize job opportunities to the countryside. The so-called private–public partnership—in which the government lends money to private companies to build and in some cases to manage the prisons—is already in practice in the states of Minas Gerais, Pernambuco, and Bahia. The government of Minas Gerais has offered R$78 million to a company to administrate its prison system. In Bahia, the private company Yumatá profits R$2 million each year managing four prison facilities in the state. Left-wing Bahia governor Jacques Wagner justified transferring taxpayers' money to Yumatá, saying that the company has created seven hundred job slots in five years. The fact that seven hundred jobs within a five-year period represents absolutely nothing in one of Brazil's leading states in unemployment rates went unmentioned.[37] The figure below shows São Paulo's prison expansion plan. While the state is famous for its "uneven development" (with its concentration of industry in the metropolitan area), prisons have been distributed throughout its territory in the last twenty years and more are planned to be built, especially in central São Paulo, an area marked by poor economic performance.

Although Brazil itself is experiencing an expansion of its prison system, the state of São Paulo is particularly "addicted to incarceration." Between 1995 and 2010, the adult prison population jumped from 65,000 to nearly 180,000. This pace is accelerating even more, as the average daily rate of incarceration increased from around twenty-six to more than eighty individuals between 2011 and 2012.[38] As a result, São Paulo now has the fastest growing prison system in the country. There was nothing exceptional about São Paulo during the last two decades that could account for the high rate of incarceration, aside from the multifaceted "govern through crime" strategy that I addressed in chapters 1 and 2.[39] The state's "new" approach relied on human rights rhetoric to enhance community-based security activism while also investing its police apparatus against a well-defined urban threat crafted as drug dealers and street criminals who did not deserve to live. São Paulo's endogenous version of New York City mayor Rudolph Giuliani's zero-tolerance programs comprised increased police presence in the streets "to increase the sensation of safety," public accountability meetings where the police present their achievements to "civil society," closer ties to the community, and public relations strategies that covered the brutal face of the

The state of São Paulo's prison expansion program, which aims to create new prison facilities to accommodate its fast-growing prison population. Map by Secretaria da Administração Penitenciária.

"old" police. Like Giuliani's model, which selectively targeted black and Latino youth as the main sources of insecurity, São Paulo's government centered its efforts on cracking down on small misdemeanors and drug-related crimes in the periphery of the city, reinforcing hostilities against already-marginalized black youth.[40] As far as the state was concerned, the program was a success. In a public statement, the state secretariat of public safety celebrated the program, arguing that its performance beat its New York counterpart: "São Paulo's effort to reduce homicides is evident when comparing the results of the city with the ones obtained by the known New York 'zero tolerance' program. The fall in the percentage of homicides in the third trimester of the last seven years (1999 to 2006) was 64.14 percent, overcoming the percentage achieved by New York during Rudolph W. Giuliani's term (1993 to 2000)."[41]

The state's account does not reveal the real causes of the reduction in homicides and the hidden social costs of mass incarceration in São Paulo. While crime reduction and prison expansion may be appealing explanations, their relationship merits further examination. First, crit-

The Growth of Incarceration in the State of São Paulo, 1995-2015

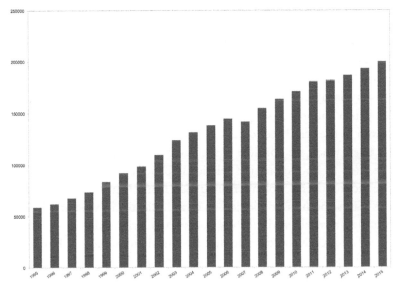

Dynamics of mass incarceration in the state of São Paulo during the neoliberal turn between 1995 and 2015. Data from InfoCrim-National Penitentiary Department; cross tabulation by the author.

ical criminologists have long argued that "crime" is an elastic category that acquires meaning in specific social and political contexts. Take, for example, the government of São Paulo's attempt to outlaw *baile funks*, as described in chapter 2. The genre, influenced by the U.S. funk, jazz, and soul movements from the 1960s, became part of the cultural repertoire and political struggle of marginalized Afro-Brazilians. Through *baile funk*, black youth denounced police violence and their day-to-day racial discrimination on the job market. As *baile funks* became popular and more black youth participated in the collective gatherings in the city's periphery, the government and the media began to depict the gatherings as places for sex, drugs, and violence. Journalist Jessica Diaz-Hurtado writes that "the criminalization of *baile funk* is a pattern the Brazilian government has repeated against other Afro-Brazilian forms of art, such as samba and *capoeira*. With the police shutting down shows and the government passing laws banning the music and parties in the early 2000s, criminalization transformed from social to legal rejection."[42] While samba, *capoeira*, and *baile funk* continue to be "legal" on paper, the state's attempt to crack down on these gatherings and the frequent police invasions and arrests point to the ways some behaviors and practices are criminalized and punished under the far-reaching category we call "crime." Crime against public order, narrowly defined as any antisocial behavior, has become a device for regulating the presence of black youth not only in shopping malls, as the *rolezinho* crisis illustrates, but even in the very inner cities to which they are confined.

Even when we consider a specific and indisputable category of crime such as homicides, the relationship between incarceration and the reduction of this violent crime in São Paulo is not self-explanatory. There was a boom in homicides—a clear indicator of violent crimes— in Brazil as a whole in the 1990s, and particularly in the state and city of São Paulo. One could argue that the drastic reduction in homicides during the following decade (the 2000s) would be the result of astonishing levels of incarceration in the previous decade, but scholars have consistently shown that São Paulo's reduction in homicides (particularly in the metropolitan region) was the result of several factors. One such is the phenomenon that Graham Denyer Willis calls "the killing consensus," in which the police and criminal organizations have a mutual agreement not to kill. Another explanation is what sociologist Jacob Waiselfisz calls "the interiorization of violence," a trend first noticed in 1996 when all Brazilian metropolitan regions reported small yet steady reductions in violent crimes while small- and medium-sized cities had an inverse trend.[43] Even more troublesome, São Paulo's celebration of its extraordinary reduction in violent crimes (homicides in this case), would have to account for the fact that most victims of violent crimes in the 1990s were young black men—the main targets of the state's zero-tolerance approach and its mass incarceration.[44] To accept the argument that *the state was incarcerating black men to protect black men against black men* would mean endorsing the racist imagination that black men were the main actors committing crime at that time. Following the national trend of the 1990s, São Paulo's juvenile homicide rates increased 57 percent over the course of the decade only to begin to fall in the next decade, although the rate of victimization for black youth continues to be more than 100 percent higher than for whites of the same age.[45]

Therefore, the ones portrayed as agents of violence were also the main victims of homicide and mass incarceration.

Finally, if mass incarceration were a response to the violent deaths, the decline in homicide rates reported during the 2000s—from 42 percent in 2000 to 13.9 percent in 2010—should at least lead to a downward trend in incarceration rather than the opposite (as can be seen in the graph on page 131, incarceration grew 184 percent in the same time period).[46] It was the moral panic around a black urban criminal, generally viewed as a drug dealer, that fueled the dramatic escalation of incarceration in São Paulo during the same period in which there had been a decline in violent crimes. Even as violent crimes decreased, arrests for drugs and robberies increased under the zero-tolerance regime, which had a profound impact on incarceration rates. In response to the urban mythologies of violence amplified by the "populism of fear" of conservative politicians and the media, the national legislation instituted harsher sentences for drug-related crimes and denied convicts benefits such as alternative sentencing and early parole.[47]

Although the punitive trend in drug-related crimes had begun much earlier in the 1960s and 1970s, it was in the 1990s that drugs passed from a public health problem to a security problem. A series of laws modernized the previous drug statute, decriminalizing the use of drugs while introducing a new set of concerns into the public safety agenda. Federal laws and decrees controlled the trade of toxic substances that could become raw materials for cocaine, provided a legal definition and penalties for "organized crime," and established international agreements to combat international drug trafficking.[48] A law in 2006 further depenalized drug consumption and established alternative punishments for first-time and repeat drug offenders. Those whom the state determined to be drug *users* were sent to rehabilitation programs, rather than to prison. As in the previous legislation, the 2006 drug legislation sought to "protect" users by heavily punishing drug traffickers. It established a sentence of five to fifteen years for those convicted of transporting, selling, or trafficking drugs, and penalized those vaguely defined as "associated with traffickers" with three to ten years in prison. To determine which category a person fits into, the judge considers the individual's criminal history and the quantity of drugs in their possession. Given that police reports are the primary documents that judges consider, the police hold an impressive amount of power in defining who deserves to be sent to prison and who receives clinical treatment. Similarly, the catchphrase "association with drug traffickers" was used to include relatives and friends in communities where the police had arrested a "drug trafficker." Legal scholar Luciana Boiteux writes that "the selectivity of operation in Brazil's penal system is clearly notable. While there are various degrees of importance in the drug trafficking hierarchy, the actions of authorities seem to be directed at the least fortunate levels of society, which are overrepresented in Brazilian prisons."[49] In the overwhelmingly white Brazilian law-enforcement system, officers, persecutors, and judges are guided by social vengeance rather than principles of justice.

This is particularly true when one takes into consideration the population most affected by drug legislation. Like that of the United States, the Brazilian war on drugs turned into warfare/prisonfare waged against impoverished and predominantly black urban communities. The war on drugs was a political program designed to control territories and populations by further criminalizing specific behaviors (such as attending *baile funks* or hanging out on street corners) and specific social groups (black youth). Following the inverse trend in the reduction of violent crime, São Paulo's Military Police have steadily increased arrests for drug-related crimes. In 2014, homicides represented 3 percent of incarcerations while drug-related crimes accounted for 25 percent of those serving time in São Paulo's prisons. Crimes against property (burglaries, robberies, and car thefts) account for the majority of arrests, with drug trafficking being the fastest growing cause of arrest and sentencing in the state. Between 2005 and 2010, there was a 195 percent increase in incarceration for drug-related crimes in the state. This is also the primary reason for female incarceration, which has increased 225 percent during the same period. Almost half of the current female population of São Paulo's prison system has been convicted of either drug-related crimes or burglary/robbery.[50]

The correlation between social exclusion and incarceration is perhaps revealed in statistics regarding the educational achievements of prisoners. According to the Brazilian Ministry of Justice, in 2011, 75 percent of the São Paulo prison population did not have a high school

degree (57.9 percent did not have primary education) and only 2 percent had college degrees; 75 percent of prisoners were between the ages
of eighteen and thirty-four.[51] A 2006 census of the infamous Febem
juvenile detention center (now Fundação Casa) revealed that 43 percent
of youth inmates had another family member in prison, 29 percent had
experienced someone killed in their family, and 75 percent had previously been convicted for nonviolent crimes (such as robbery, burglary,
or drug use). Prior to being arrested, 46 percent had been working low-
paying jobs (making no more than R$361.00 per month) and 54 per-
cent had been unemployed.[52] As far as race is concerned, while whites
also fall into the hands of the penal state, São Paulo's prisons are predominantly black spaces. Among the juvenile inmates at Febem, 67 percent were black, 31 percent white, 1 percent indigenous, and 2 percent
classified as "other." Among the adult population, blacks comprise 53.4
percent of inmates but only 31 percent of the state of São Paulo's population. Whites make up 46.34 percent of prisoners and 67.9 percent
of the general population. Young black men remain the largest inmate
population, making up 50.86 percent of the whole prison population.
Although women only make up 4.77 percent of São Paulo's inmates,
black women comprise 53.17 percent of the female prison population.[53]

Researchers have identified a disproportionate element in the
punishment of black women for property crimes. An analysis of arrests and prosecutions for robbery in São Paulo between 1991 and
1998 by the Brazilian Institute of Criminal Science (IBCCrim) showed
that 60.47 percent of white women were absolved during the judicial
process, while among black women this rate was only 38.21 percent.
Although there is no consistent difference in the number of robberies
perpetrated by white and black women, the latter are convicted of such
crimes twice as often as the former. During each stage of the criminal
justice system (police investigation, arrest, prosecution, and sentencing), the proportion of black women increases while that of white wom-
en diminishes. Blacks are more frequently arrested than whites are, their
judicial processes are more frequently expedited, and they are convicted
and sentenced far more often.[54] São Paulo's obsession with incarcerating
black women made the state rank number one in Brazil's female incarceration rates.

Luana and Nina

Placed in the lowest position of São Paulo's gendered division of labor, many poor black and brown women are pushed into the world of crime. As far as PCC's high-profit drug business is concerned, these women occupy mostly low-ranking positions as dealers and mules who smuggle drugs across the city and into the prisons. When the women are caught, the Partido replaces them with other impoverished women desperate to make ends meet. Desperate. That is how I found Luana and Nina, a young black lesbian couple living under the shadow of the police in a public housing project in Cidade Tiradentes on the east side of the city. Luana and Nina share a tiny apartment in an ugly housing project with Luana's father, Mr. Raimundo, a sixty-two-year-old man lost in his addiction to alcohol. Luana spends her time between the *biqueira* and the scrapyard where she and Nina work sorting recyclable materials. The first time I met Luana, she was selling cocaine in a PCC-controlled *biqueira* at the gate of the public housing building. Luana is a high-school dropout, and Nina began college with a fellowship from Educafro but gave up because she could not afford the 50 percent tuition rate. Nina worked in a call center for a while and Luana worked as a babysitter, but they soon decided to work on their own as recycling collectors. "More freedom and less humiliation," Luana reasoned.

In *Colored Amazon,* historian Kali Gross observes that most of the literature on black female criminality overlooks their criminal agency. In nineteenth-century Philadelphia, black women were victimized by white society but they also responded by developing strategies of resistance beyond the realm of respectability and citizenship. Such strategies included prostitution, vice, robbery, and even the assassination of their oppressors. Gross invites scholars to see their practices as "texts possessing palpable voice, one that effectively speaks of values, ambitions, and frustrations and also one that contains rare clues about black women's past experience of trauma."[55] I concur with Gross and see Luana's engagement with such crime as a strategy for coping with the everyday gendered racial discrimination that denies her the right to the city. Within that context, highlighting her "criminal" status also accounts for her resistance to the city's sociospatial order. As a structurally superfluous group in the labor market having their strategies for survival—as street vendors and recyclers, for example—criminalized, black favelada women like Luana and Nina find in criminal activity a way to *insurge* against the forces that drive the city.

As these forces keep trying to bring Luna and Nina to their knees, they punch back by embracing transgressive behaviors that give them some control over their lives. They refuse to work as maids and continue to work as recyclers during the day and drug dealers during the night. The "control" over her life that Luana emphasized compensates for the risk of being caught by the police. As a reference to her refusal to play the roles expected from her in Brazilian society, Nina insisted several times that she did not want to end up like her mother, "who is today sick, old, and unemployed" after spending most of her life as a maid. Despite their political agency, Nina and Luna's urban experience is structured by the city's punitive urban order. As they attempt to open a tiny space for (economic) autonomy, their lives are policed and circumscribed by state carcerality.

The intersection of their race, sex, class, and gender identities as black lesbian working-class women makes them particularly vulnerable to the penal state. Luana was nineteen years old when she spent nine months in the women's penitentiary after being convicted of participating in a robbery with her brother and another friend. She was caught in possession of a gun. The Military Police shot her brother and his friend in the back. Luana was forced to sign a confession under torture because both black young men were minors. One police officer threatened her, asking, "Have you ever been raped?" Luana defended herself: "I said, 'No sir, I have never hung out with scumbags. I was hanging out with decent men.'" The officer slapped her across the face and threw her into the patrol car. Before going to the police station, the officers took her for a tour, "threatening to rape and kill" her. Then they went to her home to search for drugs. Her mother, who still lived with her at that time, was at the gate of the housing project. Luana did not say anything to her but raised her tied arms to let her mother see that she was under arrest. The police officers told her mother, "You have to take care of this one because the other (referring to her brother) has been sent up already." Her mother began crying while the officers invaded the home, searching for drugs. Later, Luana discovered that her brother was alive. He had to have his kidney removed because of the injuries he sustained when the police shot him and then beat him with a baton.

Luana went to trial and was found guilty of illegal gun possession, gang participation, and armed robbery. She did not argue against her arrest or complain about the arbitrary conditions under which she signed her confession. "It would not make any difference to say that I was tortured. It was my voice against the paper that I signed." The "paper" she referred to was the official accusation presented in court by the prosecutor in charge of her case. Since she had no prior criminal record, the judge decided to release her on parole months later under the condition that she report to the parole office every month, abide by a 10 p.m. curfew, obtain a job, and stay out of trouble. If she violated any of these conditions she would be locked up again. Luana recalls the time she spent in prison as a learning experience: "To a certain extent it was good because I used to be a shoplifter. You know how teens are, you want something, your mom doesn't have it, and your father is drunk all the time. You will get it. And I did. In prison I learned a lot 'cause there you don't have nobody to help you. It is you and yourself." While Luana refers to shoplifting as "teenage behavior," she is engaged in other illegal activity as an adult. Unemployed and with a criminal record, Luana deals cocaine as her main source of income; it is also the main source of income for Nina, Mr. Raimundo, and Michael, Luana's fourteen-year-old son.

Luana's and Nina's lives were also policed by neighbors in the housing project who associated their nonheteronormative behavior with promiscuity, drugs, and crime. During a long conversation about the discrimination they faced as lesbians, both women spoke about their encounters with churchgoers and neighbors who condemned their sexual behavior. Luana explained: "They think that just because I don't go with men I am sick or a bad person. But nobody comes to my house and pays my bills. Nobody knows what I have passed through and they judge me based on what? My pants?" Nina, whose dress is non–gender conforming, faced police violence when residents of a well-off neighborhood on the Eastside "assumed" she was about to rob an ATM. Nina had naïvely decided to "take a little stroll" in the neighborhood. When she stopped at an ATM to get some money, the police patrol arrived and armed officers commanded her to stand against the wall:

> I was in front of [the bank] *Itaú* trying to get in the bank. The door was blocked and I was insisting on entering because I wanted to make a deposit. So then the police officer came saying "Put your hands on your head! Hands on your head, thug! Spread your legs, spread your legs!" I quickly told him, "Is this for my boyish appearance? I'm not a man, OK?" I kept saying, "I'm not a man" to discourage them from searching me. They are not allowed to do that. So one of them said, "We know you're not a man." And they started asking a lot of questions, What did you come here to do? So they started saying a lot of things about the way I am and I started crying. Everybody in the street was thinking that I was about to rob a bank. The other one told me, "You are going down! *Quantas passagens você tem* [How many criminal records do you have]?" I told him, "No, I never went to prison." He said, "You know what happens with people like you in the prison, right?" I told him, "No, I never was arrested, how would I know?" And he replied, "Well, then I will throw you in there and you will see how it works."

Nina and Luana's encounters with the police were yet another manifestation of the ways policing informs and entrenches everyday violence against black women in the periphery of São Paulo. The police–prison regime articulates a multiplicity of violence, of which threats of rape, incarceration, domestic abuse, and further stigmatization are just a few examples. Even when the police are not directly implicated in such practices, police ideology fuels larger systems of domination that in São Paulo's periphery are based on the intertwining racial, sexual, and gendered constructions of deviant bodies. These multiple locations of criminalization indicate that for black women like Luana and Nina there was no safe space, as they deal with violence in the job market, on the streets, in the police patrol, in the housing projects, and at home. That the expanse between society, home, and prison is barely recognized, Angela Davis argues, reveals the normalization of domestic spaces as spaces of punishment as much as the prison is normalized as a space that both "reflects and further entrenches the gendered structure of the larger society."[56] Indeed, one of the most painful aspects of Luana and Nina's experience is that despite their efforts to rewrite their histories, they saw their lives crisscrossed by the same pattern of violence their mothers suffered a generation before. Nina was five years old when her mother was killed by her husband, who justified the murder as an "honor killing." At this time she lived in the northeastern state of Bahia, coincidentally, in the same region that I migrated from in the 1990s. She had been sent to live with her aunt in São Paulo until she turned seventeen, when she left home to live with a friend. She had just came out as lesbian and started dating Luana when her friend kicked her out of their home. Luana's mother had suffered years of domestic abuse from her alcoholic father until one day she left home to live with a relative nearby. This backdrop is important not only for contextualizing their experiences within the larger context of patriarchy but also for underscoring scholarly claims that domestic violence is a driving force that pushes women into crime and prison.[57] Policing and domestic violence fuel each other and produce the same gendered (state) effects: if women were terrorized by officers in the streets, they were also brutalized by abusive fathers and male partners at home. In both places, the state comes into being through the intimate violence produced by the patriarchal performance of power that the police and the father represent.

In one of our meetings, we were interrupted by someone violently banging on the door. It was Luana's father, Mr. Raimundo, drunk on the doorstep. He entered, yelling at Luana and Nina. They told him to shut up because there was a guest in the house. Turning to me, he asked, "Did they tell you which one is the man and which is the woman?" Nina asked me to ignore him because he was drunk. Luana seemed not to bother anymore. "When is he not drunk?" she asked. Later, a neighbor whispered into my ear that Mr. Raimundo used to beat Luana and her mom. Luana herself told me that when she was "coming out" Mr. Raimundo had been particularly violent. He had once expelled her and her battered mother from their home. Later, when Luana started dating Nina, she had to move out because her father had threatened them both with death if they did not "become women again." Now elderly and unemployed, Mr. Raimundo depends on their income to survive, just as they depend on him for a place to live. One could be tempted to say that Mr. Raimundo finds in his violence against them a way to assert his patriarchal role, undermined by his "inability" to participate in the city's economy and thus be the "provider" for the home. It would infer, however, that only poor and marginalized men commit violence. Like him, Brazilian men socialized around patriarchy from all social class and racial belongings do the same.

Nowadays, Luana and Nina continue to share a room in Mr. Raimundo's apartment in a predominantly black neighborhood stigmatized as a crime-prone zone; it is hyperpoliced and consequently economically disempowered. Entangled in a corrosive cycle of social marginalization and criminalization, they find their attempts to be incorporated in the city's economy much like trying to drain the sea. As they struggle to secure a place in the city, the horizon of death and incarceration continues to haunt them. Luana, her brother, and her ex-husband have all been to prison, and she fears that her fourteen-year-old son, Michael, could be next. The tiny apartment, their place in the city's division of labor, the abusive father, and the constant police harassment all push them further into marginalization, leaving little room for living other than participating in the world of crime as dealers and shoplifters. The world of crime, however, is not just another place of gendered vulnerability. It is also one of the "fugue spaces" where black women reinvent urban life by subverting the racial gendered criminalization of their reproductive and social labor.[58] In the case of Luana, even though the world of crime enabled her to raise Michael, she teaches him not to follow in her steps because she does not want him to live the same "bad life" she lives. In our conversations, she paused several times to warn Michael about staying away from the *biqueira* and "não ficar dando bobeira" with the police. Teaching the child how to navigate the hostile city was another arena for making black life possible. While society stigmatized her as a "bad daughter" and "bad mother," Luana told me she has only Michael to make her life meaningful. For him, she would "kill or die."

While I return to the question of black criminal agency later in the remainder of this chapter, I take on an incisive scholarly critique of prison as a *political regime* rather than a physical space to argue that in Brazil prisons provide the material and ideological means to reinforce spatioracial domination. Like police terror, the prison's overreaching arms inform social life, connect dispersed geographies, and sustain a regime of domination that takes the form of a black necropolis in São

Paulo. As a result, incarceration and killings by the police all amount to the state's double strategy: to "govern through crime" and through death.

The Favela as Prison

One way São Paulo's sprawling favelas are connected is through the confinement of individuals from different marginalized communities in the same prison. Detention centers are geographic matrixes where dispersed territories of exclusion are put together by caging bodies from such localities. The inverse is also true. The favela entails a racialized geography of confinement. Black mother activists refer to this carceral unity this way: "Our *senzala* is the favela, the slave-catcher is the police, and the whip are the bullets that kill our son . . . slavery hasn't ended." As I will show later in this book, this is a fair picture of Brazilian cities where favelas, like prisons, are at the center of neoliberal urbanism as they house and make invisible the surplus black population suffering the consequences of neoliberal policies. Demystifying the separateness of both geographies is important because, in Assata Shakur's words, for the urban black subject "prison is not that much different from the street . . . cells are not that different from the tenement and the welfare hotels they live in on the street. . . . The police are the same. The poverty is the same. The alienation is the same. The racism is the same. The sexism is the same. The drugs are the same and the system is the same."[59]

The continuum between the prison and the favela is made manifest in the punitive rationality that transforms both spaces into geographies of symbolic, physical, and social death. As in the United States, in the Brazilian social order the favela feeds the jail and the jail feeds the favela through the punitive rationality—"the prison regime"—that dialectically produces both spaces as black territories.[60] My focus on the synchronicity of prison and urban peripheries is hardly new. I join other scholars whose work on the *school-to-prison pipeline* demonstrates how neoliberalism has turned racialized communities into spaces of hyperpunitiveness and prisons into political devices that enforce neoliberal urbanism. In Brazil, I name the cognitive and material making of such punitive geographies the "favela–prison pipeline."[61] In the Fundão da Zona Sul, these spatial dialectics are produced through a race- and gender-based spatial violence. Most of its residents are alienated from their rights to spatial mobility due to high bus fares, a poorly designed public transportation system, and the lack of infrastructure (neighborhoods located far away from the city's universities, public health care, and job opportunities). Adding to that, constant police raids result in killings, disappearances, and arrests that further disempower black communities. The police are enforcers of a bodily and geographic condition that renders the favelado as a nonbeing subject defined by its punishable/disposable status. One way to see how the prison feeds the favela is to consider the obvious ways it prevents the caged bodies from any possibility of participating in the city's formal economy. The high recidivism of black youth for drug offenses speaks volumes about imprisonment as a self-perpetuating condition for reproducing race-spatial conditions of oppression. Pushed out of the city by the very "prison regime" that placed them in an ontological condition of outlawness, black youth come into contact with the prison system through their experiences as favelados and then become permanently tied to the criminal justice system by their stigma as former prisoners. Their criminal records not only prevent them from securing a job but also give the police the socially sanctioned license to kill them. Once in the system, they are forever condemned to the popular Brazilian adage, "a good thug is a dead thug."

Another way to see how favelas are turned into prisons is to look at the process of outlawing all favelados regardless of their "criminal" status, as seen in Dona Maria's and Dona Cecilia's fruitless battles to prove their sons' status as workers as opposed to "thugs." The "collective search warrants" increasingly issued against favelas throughout Brazil allow the police to conduct searches in entire communities based on assumptions that residents are associated with drug trafficking and other illegal activities. Despite complaints from human rights organizations about the flagrant violations of the Fifth Amendment in the Brazilian Constitution, which expressly prohibits the search of one's home without consent, judges issue collective warrants to search homes in favelas based on the loose justification of "maintaining public order."[62] Take, for instance, the example of *Paraisópolis*, a community far away from Dreaming City but also in the Zona Sul of São Paulo. In February 2009, I visited the favela as part of Tribunal Popular, a human rights work group organized to document police abuses against favela residents. After a meeting with local residents in a public school, I joined Marisa, a human rights activist, in a meeting with some residents about their experiences living in a community where the police were carrying out a major military operation called Operação Saturação (Operation Saturation). The favela had been invaded just days before our visit by five hundred police officers who occupied the streets and entered houses searching for "criminals" from PCC, whom they thought were being protected by local residents. The police carried out collective search warrants, blocked the main entrances of the favela where residents coming in and out would have to hand over their ID cards, and established curfews for local businesses. The day after the invasion, the secretary of public safety visited the favela and defended the military operation, stating that it was a "civilizing mission to protect the good citizens." He also indicated that the police would stay "until the favela was safer and the bandits were surrounded and arrested."[63]

Along with Marisa, I went to see a young black man named Josias who had been threatened with death by the Military Police. He publicly complained about the police invasion and denounced the illegality of the search warrants carried out without a judiciary order. While we talked to Josias on the sidewalks of the tiny favela streets, police officers on horses stopped on the other side of the sidewalk. When the police headed away from us and turned the corner, Josias exploded. "Damn, man! They will pass by here again and again to intimidate us. Yesterday, they went to my house. They came to wreak havoc. I can't live like this." Josias told us that the police went to his house because they were looking for drug dealers. After being tortured, a drug-addicted teenager with a criminal record had told the police that Josias was a dealer.

Josias explained, "They took the *noia* [short for *paranoia,* a common nickname for drug users] and scared him, saying 'Either you give us a name or we will pull the trigger.' The kid didn't think twice and took the maggots to my home." The three police officers invaded Josias' shack and searched for drugs all over the place. They destroyed everything and didn't find any drugs. They insisted Josias was a drug dealer, although he insisted he was clean. They said, "*Perdeu neguinho, entrega a fita!* [You lost little black, give it up!]." Josias told them to search for the drugs if they were certain he had them in his possession. All the while, they continued mocking him. Fearing that the officers would plant evidence, Josias's wife started screaming aloud so the neighbors could hear and come to rescue them. Everybody walked out of their shacks and the officer walked out of Josias's shack threatening him with death. Marisa offered to help Josias bring his case to the media and the police ombudsperson. However, he was afraid that doing so would bring more police attention to him and instead decided to look for help from members of PCC, the criminal organization that controlled drug trafficking in most of the favelas in the region.

While I expand on the favelados' reliance on PCC in the following chapter, suffice it to say that Josias's status as a favelado placed him and the whole community into a carceral space ironically called "Paraisópolis," or "heavenly city." By the time Operação Saturação ended, the police had apprehended thirty-one guns, seized ten kilograms of cocaine, and arrested ninety-three people, while also searching approximately 90 percent of the favela's nearly 60,000 residents.[64] Just as Paraisópolis residents were about to celebrate their "freedom," the state announced a permanent occupying force to "pacify" the community. In 2012, the right-wing governor Geraldo Alckmin toured the slum community alongside the deployment of five hundred police personnel and announced investments in schools, housing, and public transportation.[65] The governor's "new" operation was launched after the eruption of violent protests against the killing of a teenager by the Military Police. With helicopters flying overhead, frequent checkpoints, collective search warrants, detentions, and killings, the entire favela had been transformed into a prison. As black bodies were spatially confined in the favela and pipelined to detention centers, the division between the two geographic references became blurred.

The Prison as Favela

It was 1:30 p.m. when I arrived at the front gate of the male detention center for my weekly visit. Along with Sister Maggie and three other friends from the Catholic-based Prisoners Advocacy Network, I displayed my ID card to the guard and crossed through the heavy prison gate toward the checkpoint, where we were subjected to an x-ray before entering the main building. The guard took our IDs, looked at us, wrote down each one of our serial numbers from the documents, and directed us to the corner where we would wait for him to give us authorization to enter. On this day, a guard with a reputation for being aggressive with prisoners and harsh with visitors was in charge of the gate. It was 2:30 p.m. when he finally inspected our papers and allowed us to pass through the electronic door. This was just the first checkpoint. We were led through another door, where another guard would finally give us permission to get into the prison yards where inmates were located. Some of the prison guards maintained animosity toward the Advocacy Network because they viewed our advocacy for prisoners' rights as "supporting bandits." We were, as one guard told me, "the people from human rights who want to make our work difficult." More than once, prison guards deployed harsh treatment, abusive language, and even arbitrary denial of access to the prison with the excuse that there had been an escape attempt and that the prison was under heightened security. Some days, the two-hour visiting window would almost run out while we were still waiting to receive permission to enter.

On that day, after our group had passed through the first two checkpoints and split up to visit prisoners in the courtyards, I was surprised by a guard who came up to me to complain about a news report in which a quote from the Advocacy Network denounced the arbitrary treatment and torture of prisoners in São Paulo's prisons. Angry, he asked me if we were not ashamed to defend bandits. He said that "instead of giving leeway to thugs," we would do better helping "the victims of those angels," sarcastically referring to the inmates. I responded by telling him that the denunciations were not new as prison advocacy groups received dozens of complaints from prisoners every week. Relentless, he insisted that we were defending bandits. It was pointless to argue with him because he did not see inmates as humans who deserved any amount of respect. Prison agents did not see prisoners as subjects of rights and saw their work as a waste of time due to the constant in-and-out flow of inmates. During my interactions with other prison agents, I came to understand that their attitudes were consistent with the socially shared logic of vengeance expressed in the maxim, "a good thug is a dead thug." The logic was: If the "hardworking" citizens were having a hard time, why should we make prisoners' lives easier? Under this logic, wrongdoers should be eliminated by the police or, if they survived, be subjected to extreme suffering in prison. Within that context, we were seen as those who defended the "rights of bandits" who should be left "to learn the lesson."

Even in the Brazilian judiciary system these violations are rarely questioned, as judges usually work under the overarching premise of vengeance rather than on the strict application of the law. The prison's inhumane conditions were seen as a natural part of the inmates' sentences not a violation of their rights. This shared belief was particularly true with sick inmates who were denied habeas corpus or who were dying while waiting for their case to be analyzed. The prison did not have any infrastructure for dealing with the several sick individuals lying in unbearable, overcrowded, dark cells waiting for doctors that never arrived. There were also several cases of injured inmates who had survived "resisting arrest" and were sent to the detention center after the hospital. The prison had one doctor visiting inmates on a weekly basis. However, that had not been a regular occurrence. Nurses often functioned as doctors, distributing medicine and taking care of minor sicknesses. When the doctor did arrive, he generally stayed for only a few hours, letting the long waiting list of inmates with complicated health problems—such as tuberculosis, HIV, depression, skin wounds, and infected colostomy bags—go unaddressed. For the Advocacy Network, it was very hard to arrange for an inmate to be sent to the hospital because it involved several bureaucratic steps, from requesting police escorts to special arrangements in the hospital. It is not hard to imagine how such demands could get lost in the precarious public health system—even more so when the patient is an inmate.

After visiting the detention center for several weeks, I knew by heart the names of those inmates in the *raio* (courtyard) I used to visit who were still in need of medical treatment. Instead of seeing a doctor, they generally received pain medication and in some cases psychotropic drugs. With Sister Maggie, I closely followed the case of an inmate who had an external colostomy bag and who also suffered from depression. After dozens of requests for him to be relocated to a hospital, the only treatment he was given was a daily tablet of Diazepam to help him cope with anxiety. Our requests to the prison authority resulted only in moral judgments: "We placed him on the waiting list. He has to have patience. When it was about committing wrongdoings he didn't think about that." Other times, they responded with long explanations of the bureaucratic procedures that would be required to move someone to the hospital. Often, officials blamed an invisible "system" for delaying the request for a hospital transfer or the slow processing of parole paperwork that many prisoners were legally entitled to. "There is nothing that we can do. We release one and tomorrow we receive ten." That is how Doutora Fabiana, the white lawyer and public servant responsible for overseeing the judicial cases of the inmates, would respond when my colleagues and I complained about the slow bureaucratic procedures that guaranteed inmates basic access to information about their legal condition.[66] She blamed the "system" for the precarious situation in the prison and seemed hopeless with so many court cases lying on her desk. In this web of blame, neglect, and dismissal, it was not enough to arrest and place individuals in jail. The prisoners were also subjected to the humiliation of having to beg for help from state employees who performed the duties of the state when they made decisions regarding food, visits, and access to medical help and legal aid.

Because poor inmates heavily depended on the state's legal aid to make their claims, the likelihood of their requests being met favorably was very small. They knew that as well as I did. Still, our arrival every Wednesday afternoon was received with hope as the prisoners believed we could beat the system and move their cases to the top of the judge's or the prison administration's list of priorities. We could not. Each visit was a source of frustration: we would stand at the gate to the *raio* (the courtyard) and someone would start crying out "Network, Network!" The prison guard would open the gate, and a group would form around us in the hope that we had some good news regarding their legal paperwork. We would split the advocacy group; I would go to the corner of the *raio* and spend the next half hour providing information about cases, documenting complaints about abuses or health conditions, and sharing disappointing news with those who had waited to hear from the public attorney appointed to follow their case (in Brazil the entity responsible for legal aid is called Defensoria Pública). Trying to fulfill a role that should have been carried out by state officials, my colleagues and I were always exhausted and frustrated with both the inmates' expectations and the empty answers we provided in response to their demands for a revision of their cases. Many did not qualify for parole or a reduction in their sentences under the new drug legislation, but they kept asking us to calculate their remaining time, hoping that the judge would give them an earlier release. The injustice of the system was as overreaching as it was insidious. Cases abounded of inmates who had been caught in a dope spot and sentenced to long prison terms for drug trafficking and gang membership even though they were first-time offenders: small-scale dealers rather than members of PCC. Others were drug users accused of being drug traffickers by the police only after they had refused to hand over someone the police were looking for. Many of those "lucky" enough to have had their judicial hearing were already serving most of their sentence in the detention center while waiting to be sent to a penitentiary, while others were still waiting for their futures to be decided. The pretrial detention center was in fact a permanent (detention) camp.

When I first visited the detention center, it was home to nearly two thousand inmates even though its intended capacity was around eight hundred persons. The inmates were housed in small cells called *barracos* (shacks), with as many as forty individuals packed into a concrete room designed for six. The reference to the prison cell as a "shack" is not coincidental. The cell resembled the favela shack in its abject misery, human tragedy, and confinement. Visitors never go to the cells to see inmates unless authorized to do so, but given the Advocacy Network's free pass to inspect their conditions I was able to visit some of them very easily. Although the high turnover of prisoners transferred from detention centers to prisons made it hard to keep up regular and sustainable conversations, I was able to maintain weekly contact with some of them. I asked Sister Maggie not to rotate me from *raio* to *raio* too much, and to instead allow me to conduct my repeat weekly visitations in the same courtyard when possible. In the "shack" where Gustavo, Eliseu, and Cleyton were placed, the walls were covered in pictures of naked women, Bible verses, and lyrics from the hip-hop group Racionais MC's. A small curtain made up of old clothes covered what was supposed to be a bathroom: just a hole in the wall through which a trickle of cold water ran constantly, with a dirty broken toilet bowl and a small water tap. The temperature in the cell was around forty degrees Celsius and there was an unbearably strong, nauseating smell in the air. Above our heads, ropes made with old clothes and plastic bags created a hammock in which some of the prisoners slept; others slept on the floor.

Eliseu offered me some orange juice in a very dirty white mug. As much as I wanted to refuse it, I could not decline his kind gesture without offending the prisoners' rules.

Eliseu is serving a twenty-three-year sentence for murdering another black man in the favela where he lived in the Fundão da Zona Sul. He had already been tried and had served part of his sentence in the detention center while waiting for his transfer to the penitentiary, where he will serve the remainder of his sentence. Depressed, Eliseu spends most of his time reading or distracting himself by giving haircuts to other inmates. One of eight children of a domestic worker and a mason, Eliseu wanted to become an engineer but he "was not good at school"; he quite wanted to try to become a soccer player, something he had never seriously done, although friends pushed him to consider applying to professional teams. When he was fourteen he began leaving the favela to take little strolls with other teenagers to the upscale areas of Santo Amaro, in Zona Sul. That was when he discovered he was not welcome to the "legal" city as security guards harassed him in the malls. When Eliseu was eighteen, he was caught stealing from a supermarket. The private security guards took him to the back of the store where they beat him and called the police. He was sent to prison and spent six months inside. After leaving, he tried to live what he calls a "decent life," but that did not work. Unemployed and soon with a pregnant girlfriend, he went to work in a *biqueira*. However, when he became addicted to drugs, the *patrão* (drug boss) gave him an ultimatum. He was beaten and told he had to leave the favela or be killed. Eliseu moved to a public housing project in the east side where he started a new life with his wife Lia and their little boy. The family was doing well and Eliseu had been making plans to move out of the project. While watching a soccer match one Sunday afternoon, Eliseu got involved in a fight and ended up killing another black man whom he refers to as a friend. Drunk and upset that his preferred soccer team had lost the game, Eliseu's friend slapped him across the face. Eliseu responded in anger, shooting him twice in the chest.

The life trajectories of Cleyton and Gustavo did not differ much from Eliseu's experience. Cleyton showed me the bullet scars on his body as the proud marks of his undeniable street cred and his tough masculinity. His first conviction was for drug offenses, and he served two other terms for robbery and attempted murder. He served three and a half years of his eight-year sentence for drug trafficking before receiving parole. After the temporary release, Cleyton worked as a street vendor, a car washer, and then as a cleaner in a bakery before being arrested again for beating his girlfriend while under influence of drugs. His parole was revoked and he began another sentence for attempted murder. Cleyton's father was killed when he was thirteen years old, and his mother died just after he had turned seventeen. After his mother's death, Cleyton moved from northeastern Brazil to São Paulo to start a new life. Like many young migrants, he became another favelado in the hypersegregated and violent periphery. Gustavo's way into the prison system started with a cell phone he had stolen from a woman in downtown São Paulo. His mother is Dona Dina, the woman I met standing in line in front of the prison. Although she is still angry over Gustavo's "first mistake" that led him into prison, she thinks "he has already paid his debt to society." She struggled to raise him and his three siblings in a favela on the north side of the city, relying on her monthly income as a maid. She now struggles to raise Gustavo's five-year-old son, Raul. A tattoo on Gustavo's right arm spells his son's name. Relying on state legal aid, Gustavo was hoping to get an earlier release to see Raul grow up. I had to once again remind him that under the new drug legislation he did not qualify for parole since he was a repeat drug offender. He had given up on trying to prove his claim that the police officers had framed him by placing drugs in his pocket. He did not want to antagonize the police because he feared for his family. He tried to bargain for his freedom or ask for a lesser charge but did not have enough money to pay a bribe to the officers. When he gets out, Gustavo told me, he will devote more time to Raul, try to get a job, and seek reconciliation with his ex-wife, who left home when he was arrested.

These three life stories may reinforce the stigmatization of black men as natural-born-criminals, predatory males, and absent fathers, as if there were no black men who decide to live alternative scripts of their gender identities. To challenge these too-common racist imaginations, one may simply ask: What forces are black men responding to when engaging in deviant behavior and what, if anything, is exceptional about these individuals' trajectories? By bringing their stories to the forefront, I want to present black men as neither simply victims nor agents of violence but rather as individuals whose gender identity becomes a *strategic field of intervention*—to use Foucault's expression—for urban security policies. Thus, refusing to engage in a moral judgment (on whether their criminal records are important) allows their life trajectories to help us understand the entangled context of structural violence, policing, and self-destructive behavior in which black men live their gender identity.[67] One important role prisons play in relation to black masculinity is that they translate society's racial phobia with the black male body into a *spatial truth*. The ideological construction of the favela as a dangerous place controlled by criminals is only one manifestation of a gendered spatial politics of carcerality. The "pathological script" of black masculinity finds its spatial inscription through policing and mass incarceration. In the face of undeniably astonishing proportions of incarceration, the predictable result is that by locking up black men, the carceral state is disempowering black communities, deepening poverty, unbalancing the gender ratio, and creating a socially dead category of individuals.[68] This gendered spatial politics of carcerality also produces *the city of men* (the biopolis) as a white heteropatriarchal community and the favela as a genderless black necropolis. While the urban threat of black masculinity is a political resource mobilized for the production of the polis as the object of white patriarchal protection, the black necropolis is a space where the gendered differences between black men and black women are erased through the generalized criminalization of black gender. Black women's and black men's incarceration reaffirms the black feminist critique of how racial violence makes and unmakes gender.[69] Race enables some gendered bodies to be protected and causes some ungendered bodies to be locked up.

The prison regime "secures" the white male city and provides a tragic "spatial fix" to individuals like Cleyton, Eliseu, and Gustavo, whose relations to the city are ones of criminalization and social displacement. Black incarcerated men make sense of their displacement through spatial references such as the *quebrada* (hood), the *biqueira* (dope spot), and the favela. A common question inmates asked during my weekly visits was revealing of their "spatial consciousness": "From which *quebrada* are you?"[70] This was not just out of curiosity. Rather, the territorial identity within the prison provided protection and a sense of community to prisoners from the same geographical areas. At the same time, being from *any quebrada* was a sign of a marginal urban identity marked by the shared experience of being policed. As I spoke to inmates and their relatives, I could map the carceral landscape of the city: Eliseu was from the *Fundão*; Cleyton lived in a housing project in the east side of Zona Leste; Gustavo belonged to a favela in Brazilândia, the north side. To me it was clear that the hood was (in) the prison.

This space-based oppression and consciousness also informed the internal dynamics of the prison. Even as prisoners used the words *favela* and *quebrada* as signifiers of police violence, they also expressed pride for their territorial belonging. *Quebrada* was also a synonym for the world of crime, street cred, and skills of urban survival. When inmates considered me someone from the *quebrada*, I felt invited, at least momentarily, into their community. I was much more welcome when they realized I was not "just" an activist from "human rights" but also someone who lived in the favela. Internally, the prison guards' practices were also informed by the broad and bodily spatial awareness that regards the *quebrada* as a crime-prone zone. They refer to prisoners as *ladrãos* (thugs). The *quebrada* is, for the prison guards, an evil geography from which the *ladrão* emerges. This automatic association is, of course, informed also by the racial script of whose bodies fit into the *ladrão* category. While the guards refer to inmates as *ladrão* as a strategy of dehumanization and to highlight their legal status and territorial origins, prisoners have to call the guards by the title of "mister."

The prison's spatial design itself produces subjection and a hyperspatial consciousness. When inmates walk from one side of the prison to the other (for instance, when going to the nursery or to see a lawyer), they have to stand with hands behind their backs, looking down, behind a yellow line on the floor that demarcates where they are allowed to walk. I sometimes pretended not to know the norm and defied this spatial order by interchangeably walking between the yellow lines reserved for inmates and the other area reserved for visitors on my way out. Prison agents never asked me to stop doing this, but I could see their discomfort as I challenged the spatial hierarchy. It was a privilege I exercised as a small protest. While walking on the yellow line did not disturb the guards, they always gave me a hard time when leaving. My white activist friends and I were subjected to the same harsh inspections when entering the prison. However, when we attempted to leave I always felt subjected to additional inspections of my ID, perhaps because my physical appearance, haircut, and body resembled that of most of the inmates.[71] Inmates often brought up my resemblance to them. In one case, a prisoner was sure I was also "from the *correria*" (also meaning from the world of crime). Another prisoner insisted that he and I greatly resembled each other and begged me to exchange clothes and trade places with him. He insisted that since I was "from the *direitos humanos*" (human rights people) I should help him to go visit his family, and he pledged to come back the following Wednesday. His offer was clearly not intended to be taken seriously, but it gives us a way to think about how some bodies are read within the carceral economy due to territorial belonging and racial marks. Despite my privileges, being a black working-class male from a favela raised suspicion from the prison agents and created empathy with other black young men with similar backgrounds. For the latter, our common identity seemed to provide both of us a momentary, and admittedly unequal, *black sense of place*.[72] These instances not only revealed the emotional bonds prisoners retain with each other but, more important, underscore a territorially based identity constituted by the racial conditions of bondage in the city.

Serving Time Together

The women's penitentiary houses a small childcare unit where incarcerated mothers spend time with their newborns while state authorities decide where to send the little ones. One day, Sister Maggie and I came to visit a young Angolan woman who was about to lose her baby because her time with her little girl had expired. Sister Maggie was working with the Brazilian and Angolan embassies to contact the woman's family in Angola, trying to at least send her back to her home country with the baby. Because she had been charged for international drug trafficking as she tried to leave the country with drugs inside her body, the deportation would be a long process under Brazilian law. I did not speak with her. In panic, locked in her cell, the woman would only accept Sister Maggie's visits. Sister Maggie's intervention with the authorities and long talks with her family would result in her departure weeks later. Like the nameless Angolan mother, there were several women from different nationalities and from different racial backgrounds serving time with their newborns. Because the prison's rules allow for babies to stay with their mothers only until they are weaned, the babies are sent to a state orphanage or put in line for adoption. Although the women's penitentiary has women from all colors caught carrying drugs, black and brown women are subjected to special surveillance in Brazilian immigration policies. The Brazilian policies on drugs target some individuals from countries such as Nigeria, Haiti, Angola, Colombia, Bolivia, and Paraguay—said to be transit routes of international drug trafficking destined for distribution in Europe and the United States—and specific bodies (black and brown tourist women) as bearers of criminality.[73] Disadvantaged in the global economy, they participate in international drug trafficking as "mules." The gendered dynamics of global poverty can be seen, then, in the social locations black women and black children occupy in the neoliberal racial penology, of which "black caged bodies" are the main symbol.[74] Domestically, the Brazilian patriarchal state's control of black newborns reveals something else here: an intergenerational captivity and a deadly circle of racial injustice that prevents the reproduction of black (social) life. It is this aspect that I focus my attention on in this section.

Dona Gloria, another Network volunteer, and I attended to a request from Val, an inmate who was recovering from her delivery. We went to Val's cell, where she sat crafting some handmade souvenirs with old newspapers. She came outside with vases and started displaying them in front of her cell in the corridor. There are a lot of visitations on Saturdays in prison and, with luck, some visitors might buy one or more. The nice vases indicated careful and patient work. She offered us one and we declined. We could not enter the prison with cigarettes (the prison's currency) or money. The police arrested Val in the hospital bed as she delivered her little boy. Four years before, she and her husband were wanted by the police for drug trafficking. They had started serving their prison sentence but did not return to the prison after their first temporary release on Mother's Day and became wanted by the state. Val planned to have her baby at home in the tiny apartment they rented from a friend in the housing project in Cidade Tirandentes, the same neighborhood that Nina and Luana live in, located in the outskirts of the east side of São Paulo. Afraid of getting caught at the hospital, she asked her husband to help her deliver the baby at home. "I did not want to go to the hospital but he was afraid because I started having contractions and too much pain. The sac started leaking and he took me to the hospital. I knew that something would go wrong," she said. She recalls that in the emergency room they asked for her documents and she told them she had lost them. Used to similar situations, the hospital staff became aware that she was wanted. Her husband was afraid to stay with her and get caught, so she told him to go. "If I were to be arrested, at least he would stay with the child later." The hospital staff finally got tired of demanding her ID and took her to the delivery room. While she was giving birth to a little boy, her husband was arrested in front of the hospital. She was kept under supervision, and twenty-four hours later she and her baby were put in a police patrol car and sent to the police station where the police reopened her file. In the hospital, Val had been harassed by a hospital volunteer who asked for the baby: "They were already with the eyes on my son." When the police gave her a chance to make a call for someone to take the child, she had no family to leave him with. The hospital volunteer was the only solution.

The other "option" was to bring the baby with her. Val did not know that she had this "right" and the police did not tell her of it. We reminded her that the law would give her the right to stay with the child for one hundred and twenty days in an appropriate space, and that our group would file a formal request if she allowed us to do so. Val was ambivalent about leaving her son with an unknown person whom she thought might steal him, and she was fearful of bringing him into the hostile space of the prison that she knew very well. Her prison mate, who had been quiet until then, told her it was her "right" to stay with her son in order to feed him. The prison mate warned that Val had not slept all these days and that she was depressed. Then, Val reasoned: "It will be worse if I stay with the baby and have deep feelings for him. And when they take him away, what I will do? So, I am thinking, why prolong the anguish?" Val refused to bring her baby into the prison walls. Her refusal of our "help" showed the limited scope of our advocacy work. What kind of activism were we doing trying to bring her baby into the prison instead of taking her out? It also shed light on our understanding of what "choice" really means in the context of state confinement. In such a context, the suspension of her parental prerogative meant the persistence of perpetual black captivity. It was not only her body that belonged to the state but also her family's bodies, her child, her future.

The termination of parental rights has been regarded as an extension of a prisoner's punishment onto their children. In *Invisible Punishment,* legal scholar Jeremy Travis calls attention to the "collateral consequences" of punishment to families and communities from where prisoners are taken. Some of the consequences that Travis outlines are poverty deepened by caging economically active members of the community, social exclusion by denying ex-felons access to welfare benefits such as food stamps and housing projects, and the political disempowerment of communities whose members are prevented from voting due to their criminal records. Children are especially targeted by an invisible chain of injustice from the denial of their parental rights to the dismantling of the social and psychological safety that family represents.[75] Scholars have also noticed that children whose parents are sent to prison are most likely to live in poverty, drop out from school, and be in the criminal justice system at some point in their lives. Given the fact that women are the main caretakers of children, the termination of women's parental rights is the extension of their punishment to their family members, who usually have to take care of the children despite lacking the economic capacity to do so. In many cases, economic hardship plays an important role in placing the kids of incarcerated parents in foster care for an extended period.[76] The increasingly common imprisonment of newborns and the expanding teenage prison system in Brazil, however, indicate that beyond the collateral consequences of adult arrests, children are also subjected to the same penal rationality that targets their parents. If children are seen as the most vulnerable people and entitled to protection by the state apparatus in humanist discourse, black children carry a mark of "danger" that prevents them from being entitled to state protection.[77] In fact, their captivity, whether in orphanages or in prison-like facilities for teenagers, illustrates the programmatic cycle of punishment, social exclusion, and vulnerability to premature death that marks black urban life in Brazil. Thus, one (in)visible outcome of prisons is that they deny black children innocence through the hypersurveillance of black bodies, no matter how young.

Children are indeed part of the *captive community.* I met children sharing prison cells with their mothers or in the wombs of pregnant inmates, and heard of a mother and daughter simultaneously serving time in different prisons. I followed Sandrinha's despair at having her three children sent to the state orphanage. I met children waiting in line at the prison facility to visit their fathers, and I met them waiting for parents who would never come back. Among them was five-year-old Henrique, whose father, Mateus, died in prison. Dona Maria, Betinho's mother, invited me to visit Liz, her sister and Henrique's grandmother. It was Henrique's fifth birthday and Liz had invited us to have a special pasta dish. Mateus, Liz's only child, was found dead in prison months earlier, one and a half years after the police had killed Betinho, his cousin. Liz had very little information about what had happened to Mateus since she never received an official explanation or any documentation from the prison administration. We barely talked about him because Liz hid from Henrique the cause of his father's death. She thought it would be important to keep him away from this painful conversation. "When he asks me, I say, 'Your dad became a star, look in the sky,'" she whispered to me while Henrique watched television. Liz was preparing herself to go through the legal battle to hold the state accountable for Mateus's death and demand a monthly stipend to care for Henrique. When we met, she was consumed with raising her grandchild and getting a divorce from her now-ex-husband, whom she blamed for doing nothing to prevent Mateus's fate. Liz had suffered a lot with Mateus's involvement with drug trafficking and was left to endure it alone. Now, like Dona Maria, she was taking psychotropic medication. "I am caged like Mateus was," she said, referring to her dependency on drugs to keep living. Liz and little Henrique were "serving time outside" in the favela.

Liz was dealing not "merely" with grief but also with anger, isolation, and frustration. Donald Braman argues that incarceration destroys social bonds that are vital to the reproduction of social life in the context of urban poverty. "While families in poor neighborhoods have traditionally been able to employ extended networks of kin and friendship to weather hard times, incarceration constrains these sustaining relationships, diminishing people's ability to survive material and emotional difficulties," he writes.[78] His remarks resonate with Liz's condition. She was facing hard times when I visited her and her grandson. After Mateus's arrest, Liz moved out of the favela where she lived and left the evangelical church where she had worshipped. According to

Dona Maria, Liz had felt judged and could not cope with the shame of having her son in prison. Now Liz occupies her time trying to provide for her grandchild and herself as a domestic servant in the Santo Amaro neighborhood. Before his arrest, Mateus had helped the family with income earned from his work as a small-time dealer for PCC. Dona Liz tried to get him out of the world of crime, but he got more and more involved until the police invaded the *biqueira* (dope spot) and arrested him. His imprisonment broke the family apart and deepened her already precarious economic condition. Eventually, she secured a spot for Henrique in the public day-care center, which allows her to take new shifts between her two jobs as a domestic worker.

Like Raul, the five-year-old boy I met at the prison gate on his way to visit Gustavo, his father, Henrique has had a boyhood deeply affected by racialized policing. Black boys know from an early age that they are part of the captive community. As the state incarcerates and kills black men, the experience of children like Henrique and Raul reveals how racist stereotypes about black absentee fathers come true through the work of the very forces that place the blame on their parental labor. The state produces mythologies that produce truths that produce death. As the favela is turned into a place for doing time outside, imprisonment and policing blur the lines between boyhood and manhood.

Pornotropes

At Eliseu's request, I had brought flyers about prisoners' rights and a timetable to help them calculate how much time they needed to serve before requesting parole or early release. I was quite conscious of the limited scope of the support that I could offer, but my colleagues at the Advocacy Network kept convincing me that in the context of desperation and the total suspension of legal rights, these small gestures have enormous significance. Eliseu took the flyer from me and asked the *faxina,* a gang member in charge of discipline in the prison courtyard, for permission to hang it on the wall. I also talked with the *faxina* about some prisoners' requests to make a collective petition to the public defender office asking for revision for their court cases. The idea was to group cases of inmates with overdue decisions, inmates who had already been sentenced but were serving their time in the pre-detention center, and those who had been denied parole and other benefits for no apparent reason. I gave him a template for writing a petition and promised that I would return the following week to retrieve them and hand them to the Advocacy lawyer. Then someone asked me to visit the cell of William, a new prisoner who had just arrived from the hospital and who complained about his severe pain. After asking permission from the *faxina*, I entered the *barraco* and took a seat in the corner of his cell. William had a colostomy bag in his stomach and a cast on his arm. "Another case of resisting arrest," I thought. And I was right. The police had been conducting a raid in his favela when he and his friend ran from them. The police pursued them, firing at them and hitting William in the back. Luckily, the bullet only punctured his intestine. The arm, he said, was broken during the torture session in the police car on the way to the hospital. To complicate his situation even further, William had a criminal record. According to him, the police checked his status and then showed him a handful of cocaine cubes. "We are going to charge you just because you are a *folgado* [slacker] and you ran away," William recounts. As I listened to William that afternoon, I took notes on his case, jotting down his family's phone number, and promised to talk with the nurse about his heath situation.

Like William, most of the men in prison carry bullet scars on their bodies, the result of "confrontations" with the police in the favelas. Just as the police produce racialized spaces and state sovereignty by scattering and dismembering bodies in the periphery, the bullet marks in the bodies of prisoners are bodily practices through which the state comes to life. The body is placed as the *interstice* of the favela–prison pipeline as such racialized spatial unities are mediated through the racialized violence of raids, bullets, scars, colostomy bags, and the dispositions of the bodies in the cells that prisoners call "shacks." Within prisons, the prisoners' bodies carry histories of spatial violence, criminalization, and state claims.

Thus, a common denominator between the bodies of those serving time in prison and those serving time outside is that they are the locus of state making through carcerality and evisceration. Many inmates' relatives live in dying conditions not only due to the psychological pain of waiting for the return of those held captive in state facilities but also through the bodily disintegration caused by the cumulative and eviscer-

ating everyday practices of state violence. Like the bodies of those killed
by the Slaughters and the wounded bodies of prisoners, I read the injured bodies of those serving time outside through what black feminist
scholar Hortense Spillers identifies as *pornotroping*. The pornotropic is
the body-to-flesh transition produced by "the calculated work of iron,
whips, chains, knives, the canine patrol, the bullet."[79] Running the risk
of oversimplifying Spillers's highly influential work, I contend that the
captive bodies marked by police bullets, segregated in the favelas, or
dying in bed due to state-produced slow deaths are "hieroglyphics of the
flesh." They are, in Spillers's conceptualization, surfaces on which one
can locate the afterlife of the original violence of slavery and the modern
exercise of state sovereignty. If then black woman was the "quintessential slave" occupying the double position of an ungendered object (slavery blurred the gender line) and the main target of repeated violation
(sexual-gendered-racial terror), now the current punitive turn reasserts
her liminal position. The expanse of state carcerality in São Paulo relies
on its uncanny capacity to make and unmake gender through a generalized and gender-specific regime of terror.

The reader should recall instances in which these dynamics come
into play in this book. Think, for instance, how the state granted Dona
Maria a *tragic* gendered identity through the racial mythology of the
term "mother of criminal," or how Nina's and Luana's bodies were ungendered in their encounters with the police. In those cases, they were
seen as "black lesbian criminals" not conforming to gender expectations,
thus unable to claim belonging to "womanhood" even as the threat
of rape ("to make you women again") brought female-gendered vulnerability back into the equation. The pornotrope is the "zero degree"
in which the captive community becomes a community of genderless
(neo)slaves. In Spillers's terms, "this body, whose flesh carries the female
and the male to the frontiers of survival, bears in person the marks of a
cultural text whose inside has been turned outside."[80] If in the juridical
order of liberal democracy the right of personhood is defined by the
capacity to claim one's right over one's own body as an inviolable home,
what are we to make of those whose bodies are "suspended" in a permanent zone of violability and expendability by the technologies of state
carcerality? Once again, the pornotrope gives us a way to locate those
instances that "escape conceptualization" within the legal grammar of

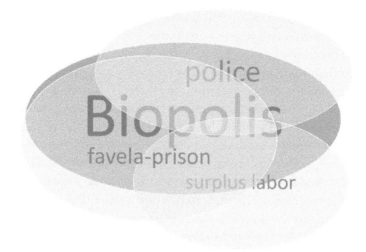

Necropolitical governance and the making of the anti-black city.

rights and personhood. Moreover, when situated within the larger political economy of urban governance, the pornotropic unmaking of black bodies through police terror, incarceration, labor precarity, and spatial segregation has a well-defined political purpose. Thus, as surfaces of power and domination, gendered racialized bodies and spaces are articulated in the name of the biopolis.

The experience of Dona Júlia, a seventy-four-year-old black woman dying while waiting for her son Jairo to come home from prison, is instructive of my take on Spillers's concept of the pornotrope to understand the intersection of race and gender subjugation in the making of the biopolis. Following Jairo's recommendation, I arrived in front of Dona Júlia's house around 10 a.m. one Sunday. It was supposed to be the day his brother would be at home. It took me a while to find the *barraco* (shack) in a narrow alley in the favela in Brasilândia, a poor community in the north side of the city. I asked a little girl on the street about Dona Júlia and she pointed me to another alley in the back of a half-built little house. I knocked on the door and a light-skinned woman in her early forties partially opened it. She asked me what I wanted with an angry tone. I identified myself as a member of the Prisoners

Advocacy Network and told her that I had come to talk with her about Jairo. She did not open the door. Standing between children playing loudly, she told me her husband was out working and that she could not talk about Jairo. I opened my backpack and gave her a letter from him. She opened it and started reading. Just as I was preparing to leave, she apologized for her harshness and invited me into her home.

Her name was Patricia and she was the wife of Jairo's brother. Their home was a tiny space with a torn sofa, an old television, a shelf with some souvenirs, and a Bible that lay open. A flag representing the Santos Soccer Club and an old picture of a little black boy in a school uniform marching in an Independence Day parade hung on the wall. It was a picture of Jairo. Patricia's three children were playing on the floor. She invited me to sit down and we started talking. I told her that Jairo was depressed and in need of some clothing. She expressed her concern about him in a way I had not expected. "Look, I feel bad to say that we hope that he stays there for a while. The reason he is not dead yet is because he is in jail." Then Patricia recounted a story about the local dealers who tried to kill Jairo for having debts for his drug addiction. Jairo was a drug user sent to prison instead of to a rehabilitation center. His brother tried to find a clinic for him but there were no free drug-rehabilitation clinics in the periphery of São Paulo, and his brother did not have enough money to cover the expenses. At twenty-five years of age, Jairo was in the prison system for the third time and had no hope of being released. Jairo's mother spent all her savings trying, in vain, to get him out of prison. Nonetheless, the last time Jairo was out, he started smoking crack and became even more aggressive. He sold everything he found at home and placed the whole family in danger because the police constantly harassed them while searching for him. Now that he was back behind bars his main complaint was that neither his mother nor his brother came to visit him anymore.

Patricia took me to a dark room in the back of the house where Jairo's mother lay in bed. Her arms and legs had atrophied and her mouth hung open because of the stroke she suffered a few months after Jairo was last arrested. Dona Júlia looked at me as her daughter-in-law introduced me, saying that I brought news from Jairo. She also advised me that Dona Júlia could no longer talk since the disease had severely hit her nervous system. Jairo did not prepare me to find his mother dying in a bed in the backyard of a shack. Seeing this elderly black woman's body deteriorating gave me another way to think about the invisible place of black women within São Paulo's carceral regime. The heartbreaking image of Dona Júlia dying in bed while waiting for her prisoner son to come home captures in some ways Spillers's critique of "female flesh" as the *interstice*—the bodily political territory—that symbolizes the intersection between life and death, humanity and its Others. Spillers writes that black women's bodies became "the principal point of passage between the human and the nonhuman world. Her issue became the focus of a cunning difference—visually, psychologically, ontologically—as the route by which the dominant male decided the distinction between humanity and other."[81]

The theoretical and political implications of Spillers's ideas have not been fully appreciated yet, particularly regarding contemporary forms of racial violence in urban black communities of the African Diaspora. Living in societies born from slavery, black people continue to struggle to have ownership over their *bodies* and to have a *place* in what we call the "human" community. Humanity is a relational terrain that places the white male property owner and black dispossessed "no-bodies" in opposition.[82] Within the context of the Brazilian prison regime, Spillers's idea provides a theoretical tool to account for both the black ontological condition and for the centrality of "female flesh" in urban security and carceral practices. Any conversation about racialized punishment must consider "the zero degree" of black women's bodies as the total expression of otherness. I situate experiences like Dona Júlia's within this security politics that places black women in the center— as a "primary narrative"—of security concerns whether manifested in the anxieties about black motherhood raised in the community security council, in the killings of Dona Maria's and Dona Cecilia's children by the death squad, or through Dona Júlia's bondage in a deathbed. This is not to reify claims that black women experience violence through their "gender" roles but rather to call attention to the making and unmaking of black gender in the making of the secure polis. Before Jairo, there was Dona Júlia.

Patricia wished that Jairo would remain in prison because he would likely be killed outside it. Perhaps she also wished that Dona Júlia would stop waiting for Jairo to return home. "She is only hanging on to life waiting for him to come to visit her," Patricia told me. Before leaving the home, I told Dona Júlia that Jairo missed her and sent his regards. She averted her eyes and eventually returned to staring at the ceiling. After some silence, Patricia walked me to the front door, where I gave her my cell-phone number and she promised me that Jairo's brother would contact me the following week to discuss his brother's situation. I was already outside when she called me back to ask for a favor. She told me once again that if I really wanted to help Jairo, the best solution would be to keep him in jail. Otherwise, the guys in the favela would kill him. The family had been through too much trouble because of him and his arrest was a kind of release. She showed me a bag full of medication that her husband had to buy out of his own pocket for Dona Júlia, who has very little left to support the children with. There was very little they could do for Jairo, she explained.

In this chapter, I have mapped out how spatiocarceral practices form the core of São Paulo's socioeconomic order. Through the lives of inmates and their relatives, I unpacked the racialized and gendered logic of domination that extends punishment far beyond the prison's walls. Through interviews with mothers of black inmates, interactions with children of the incarcerated, and accounts of black women's struggles to stay out of the shadow of the penal state, I have also tried to deconstruct male-dominated accounts of mass incarceration that often overlook the experiences of black women within and outside the prison walls. The overrepresentation of black men in prison statistics notwithstanding, gendered outcomes can be located not only in the "invisible (secondary) punishment" of those whose sons, brothers, and partners are affected by the penal state but also in their own (primary) criminalization and punishment as black women. Still, as another strategic "field of state intervention," black masculinity and its relation to narratives of criminality and practices of policing deserve special attention as matters of theoretical and political inquiry. In the next chapter, I draw on my weekly visits to the men's detention center to analyze the set of discourses that produces black men as a "social problem," black men's criminal agency, and their own investment in predatory masculinity as they try to fend off the state.

4

STICKING UP!

Decolonization, which sets out to change the order of the world, is, obviously, a program of complete disorder.

—Frantz Fanon, *The Wretched of the Earth*

To be black and conscious . . . is to be in a constant state of rage.

—James Baldwin, *The Fire Next Time*

Between May 12 and 15, 2006, the city of São Paulo was under attack. What began as a prison rebellion quickly spread throughout the city. Buses were burned, police stations were destroyed, and police officers were killed during this period. The city went into chaos as commuters tried to get home and metro stations shut down. In the periphery of the city store owners were ordered to shut down their businesses, shots were fired at community police stations, and police officers were gunned down. The government declared a state of emergency and deployed the full police force to control the urban riot that would become known as the "Crimes of May." The criminal organization Primeiro Comando da Capital claimed responsibility for the attacks, saying they were in retaliation for the inhumane treatment of detainees in the state prisons and for the "cowardice of the police officers" who had kidnapped and killed relatives of PCC members in an attempt to dismantle the organization. Within a week, 505 civilians and fifty-nine police officers were killed in a series of confrontations.[1]

In the aftermath of the killings, the right-wing state governor Claudio Lembo surprised everyone in the city by saying that the attacks were caused by the white elites' refusal to share their wealth. More explicitly, he asserted, "We have a very bad bourgeoisie, a very perverse white minority . . . It is a country that, when the slaves were freed, the masters received compensation, rather than the freed slaves. National cynicism kills Brazil. . . . The purse of the bourgeoisie will have to be opened in order to eliminate the Brazilian social misery."[2] Despite Lembo's critical remarks, he did nothing to end the slaughter of mostly young black men by on-duty police officers and police-linked death squads. As human rights organizations denounced the kidnapping and killing of black youth, black bodies filled the city's morgues and the favelas became an open cemetery, with the bodies of alleged PCC members on the streets.[3]

While favela youth hid from the police and families of the dead looked for their bodies around the city, journalists called for a swift, forceful response to the "terrorist acts" of the Partido. The right-wing parties and think tanks accused the Partido of using minors to carry out its "atrocities" and called for changing the penal code so that minors could be held accountable for their crimes. Media analysts accused the state of being "weak" and not responding to PCC with the strength necessary to put an end to the organization and to free the periphery from their dominion.[4] What was missing from the debate, however, was a consideration of what the shooting at police patrols, storming of state facilities, and bombing of buses meant not for "threatened" civil society but for the marginalized youth who carried out such acts. What are the racialized and gendered conditions that make the PCC so appealing in São Paulo's impoverished outskirts? How does racial terror enacted by the police inform the outlawed practices of poor and black youth under the PCC's domain? Why did PCC's antipolice rhetoric resonate with them? What does retaliatory violence against police mean in a society addicted to and supportive of police delinquency? And, just as important, how can we ethically respond to both police terror and outlawed responses to it?

In this chapter, I examine the criminal agency of young black men participating in PCC's criminal activities. Despite the chapter's primary focus on PCC's male members, it is important to note that while women were not directly involved in the organization's confrontations with the police during the attacks, they played a considerable—and dangerous—role in exchanging information and hiding the ones hunted by the police. While there are individuals from all racial and class backgrounds in PCC, black men and black women occupy rank-and-file positions in the drug-trafficking economy dominated by the Partido. I relate their participation in PCC to both their attempts to build economic autonomy in relation to their precarious positions in the job market and to their refusal to comply with the anti-black governing strategies that are embedded in the city's security logics. Methodologically, I center the discussion on the male branch of PCC because of my access to them during my work as a human rights advocate in a male detention center. Although access to PCC members was never easy and conversations about the Partido were always precarious (the latter often came to me as elusive secondary narratives), even these were impossible to achieve during my brief exchanges with female inmates in the women's penitentiary. If nothing else, my focus aims to respond to a gap in studies of masculinity and urban violence in Brazil that recognize the victimization of black men yet refuse to acknowledge their place in black urban politics of resistance.[5] Their experiences may illuminate a form of black protest that, while not the only one, points to the irreconcilable relationship between blackness and the regime of law, and thus to different terms of engagement with the state and civil society's norms of morality.

Within the current political climate, in which the urgent struggle for "black life" is received with the cynical response that "blue life matters," it is important to clearly state here that I am not advocating for violence against police officers. Neither do I romanticize PCC's violence or overlook its controversial and cruel politics. My intention here is to make visible some undertheorized attempts to challenge a raciospatial order that denies black urban life. If the political forces that make up the city mark black lives as expendable, black criminal activities seem to be a "fatal way of being alive."[6] In opposition to a mainstream debate that often regards black men as victimizers, or at best as passive victims of violence, the invitation here is for a consideration of how *some* young black men (who participate in PCC or otherwise) respond to their systematic criminalization. Referring to them as black insurgents not only accounts for their political agency but also calls attention to the principle of *enmity* that informs civil society's and the state's relation to them.

Considering this racial enmity is central to this chapter as it allows us to make a critical distinction between "lawbreakers" and "enemies." Building on Carl Schmitt's definition, Paul Kahan has made this distinction clear, arguing that while the criminal belongs to the domain of law (he or she can be punished by legal violence and claim protection from state abuse), the "enemy" is avenged with death and subjected to the decisive power of the sovereign.[7] In urban Brazil, rampant killings by the police through counterinsurgency and warlike tactics may well affirm the status of black "criminals" not just as lawbreakers but also as foreign enemies of the state.[8] As the weeklong police slaughter of alleged "criminals" in the streets of São Paulo in May 2006 demonstrates, the state responds with terror rather than violence when confronted with the black body.[9] Even when the state responds with incarceration, black prisoners do not stop being enemies of the state as they are not just mere menaces to public safety but also permanent threats to the core values of Brazilian society. That is why the black movement has been vocal in denouncing killings by the police as "targeted assassinations" and mass incarcerations as "political arrests" to highlight the ideological underpinnings of policing practices in Brazil. Within the Brazilian racialized regime of law, the black enemy is subjected to the state's decisive power through police terror or permanent confinement in zones of nonbeing.

Still, the zone of nonbeing is more than "an extraordinarily sterile and arid region" produced by the colonizer. It is also a liminal space of resistance "where an authentic upheaval can be born."[10] Like the favelas, São Paulo's racialized prison system is also one of those zones of violent interpellation where upheavals are born. It is mainly in the prisons where the Partido recruits its members and organizes urban riots that try to fend off the state. To be clear, PCC is not a revolutionary "party": not all its members are black and its leaders do not frame their rhetoric around race.[11] To regard the organization as a form of black protest and its members as racial warriors is to miss both its multiracial composition and its overarching ambition to establish territorial control over the periphery and to expand its profitable drug business. What makes PCC a politically and theoretically important subject in the current context of racial violence is its power to mobilize black and poor youth terrorized by the police and marginalized in the city's political life. The Partido operates in a social setting that is fundamentally structured by racial injustices, its raceless rhetoric notwithstanding. That is why, contrary to other scholars who place much emphasis on the bureaucratic, state-linked, and hierarchical structure of the PCC, I concur with Karina Biondi's perspective that the PCC should be understood within its social setting, its capillarity, and its resounding impact on restructuring social life in the outlawed periphery.[12] In the next section, I focus on the everyday practices of the marginalized and predominantly black urban youth sympathizers of PCC or serving as its rank-and-file members, known as the "brothers." What are the implications of this particular form of agency for understanding black politics within the context of Brazil's racialized regime of law? Before addressing this question, I shall first provide the context of PCC's emergence.

When a Brazilian congressperson asked him to explain how the Partido emerged, Marcola, said to be one of the leaders of the PCC, replied that "it was an awakening . . . the prisoners woke up [and] became aware their rights would never be granted." Marcola also elaborated on the members' discipline and willingness to carry out military operations against the state. He insisted that it was their structural condition and intimate experience with violence that made them unafraid of dying. "We are all sons of poverty, we all are descendants of violence . . . We are forced to live in misery, violence. So, in any favela you will see bodies every day," he replied.[13] Although Marcola portrayed the organization as an army of disenfranchised youth, the very emergence of PCC long before the 2006 riots allows us to think about the racial animus informing its practices. There are conflicting accounts of PCC's origins but according to the most widely accepted version, PCC was born as a response to the 1992 massacre, in which 111 prisoners were killed in the Carandiru Penitentiary, by then the largest prison in Latin America.

On October 2, 1992, São Paulo's then governor, former public prosecutor Luiz Antonio Fleury Filho, ordered the police to invade the Carandiru Penitentiary to put an end to a prisoners' riot the day before the national and state elections. Fearing the riots would cause his party (the Brazilian Democratic Movement Party) to lose the elections, Fleury Filho refused to negotiate with the inmates and instead ordered the Military Police to use lethal force to end the conflict, which resulted in 111 inmates killed by gunshots fired by police.[14] The massacre became a watershed moment for the prison system as images of piles of predominantly black and brown dead bodies exposed the ugly Brazilian prison system to the world. Many of the current PCC members were survivors of the Carandiru Massacre who began organizing themselves against the constant threat of police invasions. Another version, sustained by writer Josmar Josino, suggests that the organization was born after a 1993 soccer game between rival groups of prisoners at another prison, the Taubate Custody House. A fight between the teams resulted in a rebellion and in the aftermath, PCC emerged as a self-styled criminal organization to advocate for prisoners' rights and promote "paz entre os ladões" (peace among the thugs) in São Paulo's highly violent prison system.[15]

The versions are not mutually exclusive. Scholars agree that as the state of São Paulo rushed to incarcerate the (black) urban poor in the name of its "war on drugs," PCC found in victims of mass incarceration the means to establish itself as an army against the violent and corrupt São Paulo prison system. Whether rhetorical or not, the Partido's message was well received by a population historically subjected to the brutality of the "system." As the state continued to prove itself unable to control its police force and as the courts turned a blind eye to extrajudicial killings by the police, PCC appeared as a real possibility for counteracting widespread state delinquency.[16] These findings are important because mass incarceration has been justified by the state as a response to PCC's control of urban peripheries, when the PCC emergency was in fact a "collateral effect" of the state's political choice to "govern through crime," as discussed in previous chapters.[17] To restate: mass incarceration was not a response to PCC; rather, PCC's emergence was a response to state carcerality. The temporal coincidence is revealing: in the period between 1994 and 2012, during which the prison population skyrocketed, the Partido expanded its presence in most of the prison system, the periphery of São Paulo, and beyond.[18] Increasing incarceration, along with astonishing levels of police violence against disenfranchised youth, provided the political opening for the Partido's control of prisons and favelas to the point that the organization has nearly ten thousand members and 90 percent of the state's prisons in its domain today.[19] PCC's appeal is powerful. The Partido provides protection to prisoners by imposing a moral code that combats the scourges of rape, torture, and murder within the prisons. This was a huge achievement in a prison system notorious worldwide for its record of human rights violations. Deco, a thirty-four-year-old black former prisoner explained that loyalty to the Partido is a response to the PCC's work to "humanize the prison." According to Deco, before the PCC there had been "a lot of cowardice," with prisoners tortured and poisoned by prison guards. The Partido also established strict rules to protect inmates' relatives against prison guards and other inmates during visits and helped sick inmates purchase medicine. "The system treats us like animals and PCC advocates for us and for our families," Deco explained. Outside the prisons, the Partido provides protection to urban communities subjected to constant police raids and offers economic opportunity in its highly profitable underground drug economy to poor individuals like Nina and Deco, whose criminal records place them outside the city's labor market. It also helps the relatives of prisoners visit their loved ones serving time in correctional facilities far away from home through financial support for public transportation.

I did not anticipate having PCC as part of my research interest. Inmates at the detention center were very reserved in talking about the Partido, and I was even more careful not to raise questions that would compromise them under the watchful eyes of the *faxinas,* the PCC members in charge of the prison courtyard. Still, the PCC was a public secret. The Partido's control of the prison and advocacy for prisoners' rights were quite visible during my work with the Advocacy Network. Although the prison authorities would never admit it, it was an unspoken rule that if we wanted to distribute flyers or talk with inmates on the other side of the gate, we would have to ask the permission of the *faxina.* Because we were seen as "the people from human rights," PCC let us in and generally sought our collaboration in helping prisoners in need of legal or medical assistance. Some individuals would first deny their membership (members are called "brothers"), and others would refer to themselves as *primos* (cousins, those loyal to the Partido but not members of it). I managed to establish consistent interactions with one *faxina,* some "brothers," and several *primos,* who were in the PCC's controlled detention center awaiting their trial. I heard their personal stories from before they got into the world of crime, their motivations for participating in it, and PCC's rationale for governing the prison and the periphery of the city.

For inmates like Eliseu, Gustavo, and Cleyton, PCC represented much more than a criminal organization. It provided them protection against brutality within the system and helped their families cope with the economic insecurity their incarceration represented. In the prison, the Partido disciplined prisoners and protected their families against abuse by prison guards during visitation days. "The party is against oppression. Before PCC it was *malandro* [hustler] killing *malandro* during the night, prison guards abusing our families, treating us like animals. Now, from this gate onward they can't enter. Now is *paz, justiça, liberdade, e igualdade* [peace, justice, liberty, and equality]," said Eliseu, echoing the Partido's Manifesto. The manifesto establishes liberty, equality, justice, and peace as its moral principles. It also states that PCC's main goal is to "shake the system and make the authorities change the dehumanizing practices within it." Its most appealing principle is that all members should be treated equally, and that whoever causes division within the "brotherhood" will be excluded from the organization. The manifesto further mandates that all of PCC's "freed members must financially contribute to the organization by paying a monthly amount, and obey the Partido's orders to protect the community in which he lives."[20] That meant that members were bound to the Partido even if they wanted to be rid of the world of crime since they had a permanent debt to the criminal organization. Even prisoners who were not members of PCC recognized that the state could no longer afford to ignore the Partido because it "has changed the way the state treats us." PCC members selected the criminal justice system, personified in the "porcos" (pigs, meaning officers) and in the prison guards, as the enemy. Vander, the *faxina*, stressed that "PCC is a family against the oppressors," as I expressed curiosity in understanding the "political" scope of its practices.

The vague word "oppression" materialized in the riots of May 2006, which were seen as the turning point in PCC's history because, in Gustavo's words, it was a remarkable moment when "the Partido taught a lesson to those hiding under the uniform to kill." The killings, beatings, extortions, and kidnappings of drug dealers by the police were used by prisoners to justify the bombings and shootings at police stations during the May riot. These longstanding, corrupt police practices, they argued, left them with no other alternative than to rely on

PCC to protect them within and outside prison. The stories of individuals who were brutalized by the police for their territorial proximity to the *biqueira*—and of the police planting evidence and forging arrest warrants against youth—that I recounted in previous chapters relate to these terrocratic police practices that pushed Eliseu, Gustavo, and Cleyton into the PCC-dominated "world of crime." Prisoners expressed frustration and disapproval with the police's unpredictability regarding the "rules" of the game because, unlike themselves, they considered the police unable to follow a war protocol to protect the innocent. The police were considered "cowards" because "they hide behind the uniform" and do not discriminate between "thugs" and "workers" when invading the favela. The Partido, on the other hand, not only had a clear set of rules one could follow—and expect to be *cobrado* (held accountable) if not followed—but also organized a safety network to protect the community from constant abuse by the police. PCC's protection includes intelligence work to gather information on police operations, bribes for police officers to avoid military raids, and open military-style confrontations like the May riots.

Although it sold itself as a "crime union" that helped many prisoners and their families navigate the system, PCC also tried to manipulate or capitalize on the humanitarian work of organizations like the Prisoners Advocacy Network.[21] One day I went with two other prison activists to file a complaint with the director of the prison about glass in the inmates' food. Some inmates had just brought us the complaints, arguing that it was not the first time this had happened and asking us to intervene with the prison administration. The director was a black man in his late forties who kindly received us in his office on the second floor of the prison building. We had a conversation about the overcrowded conditions of the prison, and he told us about the governor's plan to build new units. He expressed his frustration with the fact that even new prisons would not solve the problem, since "when one prisoner is released, ten are arrested." Then, he admitted that the government had lost control of the prisons because there was no way to administer the system without negotiating with PCC. I asked the director about the prisoners' complaints about glass in their meals, and he changed his friendly face to a serious one. He resolutely refuted the accusations. He told us that there had been several recent escape attempts and argued

that PCC was using us to advance their case because the prison administration had adopted more severe rules to avoid rebellions and escapes.
Although most of the inmates' complaints were more than fair, this
particular one seemed to be an attempt to use us against the prison staff
as the guards had just prevented some escape attempts when food was
being delivered.

There were legitimate concerns we tried to address. One day,
Vander handed me a list with the names of prisoners who were seeking
information about their judicial condition, in need of legal assistance
with tasks such as filing paperwork for their parole requests, or seeking
a transfer to a prison closer to their families. I would bring their claims
to Dra Fernanda, the prison lawyer, or pass their names to the Advocacy
Network's lawyers. During other visits, Vander requested me to visit
sick inmates in the "shack" who needed medical care, as was the case
with William, the depressed young man with a colostomy tube. I was
conscious that Vander's mediation between me and other inmates was
"problematic" at times, as he "used" our work to establish more power
over the prison population, the fairness of his demands notwithstanding. Although I was aware of that and followed the Network's advice to
avoid his gatekeeping as much as possible, it would still have been impossible to overlook PCC's control of São Paulo's prisons. Regarding the
inmates as mere victims of PCC's dominance would be equally wrong.
In the next few pages, I focus on the complex and at times controversial
agency of black men living under the prison regime. I argue that PCC's
extraordinary growth in São Paulo's periphery is a political response to
the favela–prison pipeline as it represents the willingness of marginalized and predominantly black youth to set other terms of engagement
with the penal state.

Evading the State?

Is the Partido an autonomous form of authority or a caricature of the
Brazilian state? Does PCC colonize state practices or does it represent
an attempt to keep the state away from the favelas? Is it a symptom
of the crisis of the state or a sign of its symbiotic reproduction? Most
of the theoretical debates about the state and criminal bands in urban
Brazil revolve around the question of whether gangs are localized forms

of sovereignty (which, like the state, establish spatial order and coercive control over the local population) or antistate illegitimate delinquent enterprises. Some scholars tend to see gangs as parallel states that are the ultimate result of the state's failure to maintain social order. Under the implicit assumption of the state as the ideal type of order and political authority, other scholars argue that criminal bands' functional connections with the police, community leaders, and politicians could be better characterized as a "perverse symbiosis" constituting a necessary condition for the governance of the Brazilian peripheries.[22] Desmond Arias observes that the premise that violence is due to the state's failure overlooks the fact that the state itself is implicated in the production of criminal networks. The problem, Arias states, is not state failure but rather how the state comes into being through intimate connections between state actors and criminal bands.[23] More recent works take a more relativist approach, arguing that neither the police nor drug traffickers attain complete domination over the favelas, nor are they able to create an alternative mode of governance. Instead of providing stable order, criminal bands govern through a permanent state of *orderly disorder* that sometimes takes a performative form. In other words, rather than through stability, criminal bands rule through a *state of exception* in which the unpredictability of violence and spectacular displays of power become the norm and dictate social relations.[24]

Although these approaches represent important attempts to make sense of competing and/or overlapping forms of political authority that inhabit locations like the Brazilian favelas, I argue that they are severely limited by the "state-centric" assumptions of what constitutes social life, political order, and legitimacy.[25] The underlying logic is that there is no legitimate political life outside the state–civil-society construct and the state seems to be the final aspiration for anybody, anywhere. In the case of Brazil, such a theoretical perspective has serious implications for how urban ethnographers interpret the relation between populations historically deemed as "outlaw" and the state apparatus. What are we to make of the antistatist discourses of black radical groups throughout Brazilian history? For instance, is black criminality merely a self-serving act of resistance or can it be interpreted as a form of political refusal? H. L. T. Quan contends that the refusal to locate forms of politics outside the normative domain we call the "state" is the result of a scholarly "state addiction." She suggests that within such a state-centric paradigm, all forms of critique (even against the state) converge on a script that renders the state as the referent of justice and sociality with no consideration for "self-organized forms of life" that refuse to be controlled by the state.[26]

Things become more complicated, though, when we consider how the state is imagined and enacted in everyday life. At times the state is evoked in diffuse and contradictory ways, as seen in the community security council in the Fundão da Zona Sul. While the members of the council argued that they pay taxes and therefore need the state's force to be more present in protecting them, the favelados protested to demand their rescue from a mudslide and for housing policies from the social state. In all these instances, the state is thought of as a multifaceted entity embodied in the work of police officers, doctors, teachers, government bureaucrats, and so on. The theoretical debates on meanings of the "state" also reveal the difficulty of coming to terms with this historically situated political project. How to theorize the state when it appears in seemingly contradictory and overlapping practices of governance in the periphery of São Paulo, or in the pragmatic approach of the black movement denouncing state genocide and seeking state protection? How might we "break state addiction" without losing a grounded perspective on the sinister effects of this historically hegemonic power in the everyday lives of the black urban poor? How might we account for forms of political order that at first would fall into the "state-idea," yet represent a threat to the hegemonic Brazilian project of state domination?[27]

While these concerns remain ongoing, and I admittedly fall into a taken-for-granted idea of what the state should be and do throughout this book, my inquiry is informed by some interventions that have criticized certain scholarly blindnesses (or refusals to engage) with forms of social life that refuse to be governed by the hegemonic "thing" we call the state.[28] If we consider the structural antagonism between black life and the state-promoted white civil life highlighted by the so-called Afro-pessimist radical tradition, this critique becomes even more important, for blacks have always been ontologically displaced from the nation-state. In dealing with the question of black autonomy, Abdias do Nascimento recuperates the history of Palmares—Brazil's largest maroon community—to propose the concept of *quilombismo* as a utopic place for cultural and physical resistance against "the state of terror organized against black people." The quilombist liberation, Nascimento sustains, is founded in a black moral community seeking a "radical transformation" of Brazil into a national quilombist state. He visualizes an inclusive educational system, an economy based on the "African" principles of communitarianism, and the submission of the state apparatus to well-being across life's domains as among the principles of the "new" Afro-Brazilian praxis. In his vision, "The quilombist revolution is fundamentally antiracist, anticapitalist, anti-imperialist and antineocolonialist."[29] Whether through Nascimento's perspective of transforming the Brazilian state into a black state from within or through the radical refusal of state structures that James Scott locates in the stateless and self-governing people of Zomia, Palmares, and some Native Americans, the problem of black autonomy continues as a challenge for our political imagination: To what extent is it possible, and what does it entail, to live life outside the reach of the state?[30] What does it mean to seek state incorporation when one's relation to the state is a relation of enmity? Can (black) criminality be regarded as an attempt to create a space outside the political order funded by the state? While I focus on the black movement's apparently contradictory approach in the next chapter, here I want to understand the world of crime as an (extra)state space.

Again, PCC is not a revolutionary and state-escaping project. In fact, one is tempted to say that PCC is a *state effect* that in many cases mimics state power: its leaders hold privilege, it establishes pragmatic ties with corrupt police officers, and it controls drug trafficking and imposes a rigid model of discipline and surveillance in the city's periphery. Graham Denyer Willis has noted in his ethnography that there are some pragmatic relationships between PCC and state officials in the governance of the city's periphery. Most of the public-safety work in São Paulo is made possible because the police and PCC establish a mutually sanctioned system of urban governance that enables a certain stability that may be lacking in other Brazilian cities. What makes the periphery of São Paulo relatively peaceful is not so much the work of the police or of PCC but rather their capacity to be "morally and practically nested operating in mutually beneficial and symbiotic ways."[31] PCC also builds its legitimacy through politics with local grassroots and community organizers. Jose, the president of the local residents' association in Dreaming City, explained to me how this unfolds. He noted that there was no conflict between the association and the Partido because each part knew its place in local governance. "If there is something like a fight between two neighbors or someone complaining about the potheads, I let the Partido take care of it. I don't stick my nose in it. Now, if someone is requesting public lighting, someone is sick and needs an ambulance, or when we need help with our soccer school for the kids, I go to the *vereador* [councilman]." When asked about the place of the *vereador* in the PCC-dominated periphery, he responded that the *vereador* was elected with the help of PCC and the residents' association, and was obliged to attend to their requests. Jose was also a frequent attendee at the security council, but the *Partido* did not bother him because he assured them he was "just involved in politics" so he could legitimize his authority as a representative of the community when he needed to reach out to the city's government.

During my time in the association, I paid close attention to the interactions between Jose and Magno, who was known as the *piloto,* the primary PCC leader in the neighborhood. In one of these interactions, I went with Jose to attend a *capoeira* presentation in the yard of the local public school, and Magno was there with his assistant Tatú. José asked for some money for the Mother's Day event we were organizing. Magno promptly acquiesced and asked Jose to rent the Association Hall to host a *baile funk.* Jose said yes, but noted that he would have to look at the calendar to make sure there were no conflicts with the dates. Then Jose raised concerns about the youth who were storming the local school. The teachers had asked him to intervene, but the parents did not take care of it, and the problem continued to escalate such that the school principal asked him to talk to Magno. He carefully asked Magno to "just give a *reclamação verbal*" (verbal warning) to the youth.

Like the president of the residents' association, the favelados also established a pragmatic relationship with both PCC and the state authorities. Contrary to the hill people of "Zomia," total escape from the state was not an option (nor desired) for most of the people of the favela. They relied on the Partido to resolve conflicts and provide security against police abuse even as they called for state intervention in areas where they knew PCC could not help them. In this way, they identified two arenas of power through which they learned to navigate. While they recognized PCC's authority and refused to engage with the *homens de bem*'s security-centered discussions in the monthly meetings, the favelados also tried to be legible to the state by embracing a discourse of rights and citizenship (as illustrated in Cesar and Adriana's interventions in defense of the favelados threatened by mudslides, in chapter 2). Of course, the tiny space opened for the favelados within "political society," as shown so far, was closed by the negation of their fundamental right to life that the state consistently denied them through the work of rotten police officers and through structural violence.

This is precisely the dimension of PCC's politics that resists the state-centric approach. In matters of life and death, PCC enables a space of resistance, regardless of intent, against the state and civil society's anti-black regime of legality, however momentary. Locating these practices may shed light on another phenomenon: the terms of engagement with the state for black urban enemies to whom traditional spaces for claiming rights (such as political participation in community-based activism) are usually closed. When viewed from a top-down and normative perspective, PCC's rhetoric seems to be "nothing but a smokescreen" of a rogue state aiming to "terrorize society" and control the highly profitable drug trade in São Paulo's periphery.[32] A view from below, however, enables us to identify a point of fracture—"a zone of insubordination"—occupied by individuals historically seen as threats to urban order.[33]

Here is where I see the potential for transformative politics at the intersection of the Afro-pessimist critique of civil society as an anti-black zone of terror and the spatial agency of those whose criminal behaviors represents a "para-ontological disruption" of Brazil's structure of antagonism. If we consider the formulation that the black subject is defined through the double negation of being neither quite human nor quite citizen, what kind of political practice is necessary to bring black matters to the attention of civil society?[34] The answer is quite pessimistic. The term "resistance," the argument goes, implies the recognition of the human and civil status of those who are resisting; they must be seen as subjects acting as autonomous individuals in the struggle for (counter)hegemony. The political terrain (civil society) where the struggle for social emancipation takes place cannot incorporate the black agenda because, contrary to the working class or subaltern subject, blacks' relation to the political sphere is a "relation of terror as opposed to a relation of hegemony."[35] Some contend this paradigmatic position, in which the black nonbeing comes into life only to the extent of her/his "criminal liability," asks for a radical reframing of the ways we understand black agency in relation to law and to the politics of rights.[36] Would black criminality in São Paulo's periphery be one of those practices able to bring the socially dead black subject to life and thus make black suffering legible? Could black favelados' hesitation to participate in security-centered community activism be an *escape* from the program of government that regards them as *no-bodies*?

Not all black residents refuse to comply with the state, nor are all black youth engaged in criminal behavior. However, those in the world of crime and those criminalized by their proximity to the former found in PCC's shadow a way to protect themselves and their communities from the constant organized police terror that haunts the favelas. The most important aspect of PCC's governing practices is its predictability. Contrary to the arbitrary practices of the police, the favelados could guide themselves through the set of rules established by the Partido and be protected or charged through such codes. One of my interlocutors highlighted the difference between the police and the new rule of law by bringing to my attention the decrease in crime in the favelas after the PCC took control. According to state officials, the dramatic reduction in homicides in the city's periphery in the last decade is due to community policing, mass incarceration, and tough antidrug legislation. However, residents offer an alternative explanation, noting that PCC challenged the police's right to kill and claimed for themselves the responsibility of distributing punishment and justice. In Dreaming City, Fernando explained the PCC's approach to me: "The truth is that nobody can mess with the favela anymore. Do you remember when people used to kill each other all the time, all these deaths during the weekends? Now if you want someone's head, you need to get permission from the *piloto* [the PCC member responsible for maintaining discipline in the block]. Then, the *piloto* will call all the parties involved to have a fair judgment. You will have the right to defend yourself." Fernando's explanation made sense to me. The unpredictability of the police and the degree of its delinquency pushes the favelados toward PCC. For many black men, this may be the only way to escape from the hands of the police. Although the Partido also endangers black lives, one should not forget the astonishing rates at which black youth are hunted and killed by the Military Police. The police themselves constrain the further reduction of homicides in São Paulo, as the police commit a quarter of all homicides and 66 percent of these victims are young black men.[37] Here is the political puzzle that black activists find themselves in: disturbingly, it is not PCC but the police that poses the most prominent and lethal threat to black youth in the racialized periphery. It is never enough to highlight that while black men are the main victims, they are far from the only endangered social group. Throughout São Paulo, predominantly black communities are hunted by the terrocratic regime of policing. Take, for example, Paraisópolis, the community under military occupation that I visited in 2010. It had been one and a half years since the police launched the military "saturation operation" aiming to free the community from the Partido. Allegedly supported by PCC, local youth set buses on fire, ordered stores to close their doors, and blocked streets in protests following the killing of a youth by the police. The police operation was meant to free Paraisópolis from PCC, but residents complained about the terror the police brought to the neighborhood.

When I first visited the favela in 2009, I heard several stories of residents terrorized by the police and very few complaints against PCC. While not all residents openly supported the Partido, their anger toward the police, seen as an occupying force, was very clear. This was the case with Josias, the black man whom a colleague from Tribunal Popular and I tried to help. Days after the police invaded Josias's shack, police officers threatened to kill him if he did not leave the favela. When Marisa and I visited him, he had decided to look for protection from PCC. "I cannot leave my place, I have my family," he told us. Josias was not a member of PCC, but for him the *irmãos* (brothers) offered the only option to escape death. We offered to bring his case to the police ombudsperson or to the human rights organizations in the city, but Josias strongly refused, asking us a sound question: "Who is gonna protect me when you leave?"

"Meter o Louco" [Sticking Up]

The May 2006 riot was a hypervisible and organized attack against the state. It was also an expression of black rage. My interlocutors were evasive when I asked them if they had participated in the attack. Understandably, they recalled friends who participated and expressed sympathy for those brave enough to put their lives on the line to face the *"vermes,"* meaning "maggots" (another pejorative term for the police). The large majority of the young black men who were killed by the police in the aftermath of the attack were not members of PCC and did not participate in criminal activities.[38] Twenty-nine-year-old Serginho had participated in the attacks and was proud of it. Although he preferred to *correr por fora* (hustle outside PCC's circle) with his own *firma*, Serginho attended PCC's call to shoot at the police station in Zona Sul with a friend. He then joined another group and set a bus on fire at the bus terminal close to his favela. Contrary to other youth who were "dando mosca" (slow) in celebrating the attacks, Serginho was "esperto" (clever) and hid himself in his shack, spending time watching TV with his two little daughters. He recalls that the favela was "hot" with the police "pegando os pretinhos" (picking up the niggaz) in the street. The *pretinhos* even didn't know why they were being killed, but "who would explain to the police they were innocent?" he asks. Although the police killed hundreds of *pretinhos* in the aftermath of the attacks, he still celebrates because he sees the riots as a moment of rage in which youth from the favela took revenge against the "oppression" that they associated with the police and the criminal justice system.

Although Serginho was at first reluctant to talk about his personal experiences and always talked in the third person, our common friend Fabiano gave me further details about his work in the world of crime. Fabiano also helped to "break the ice," emphasizing the similarities in our backgrounds: "Jaime é da *quebrada* Sérginho, ele é firmeza, ele chega junto [Jaime is from the *hood*, he is for real, he keeps it real]." Only then did Serginho give me further details about his work, his sympathy for the Partido, and his fury toward what he called "the system." The first time I met Serginho was on a Saturday morning at a park near the favela where he lived. He had suggested meeting there because it would be a neutral place for both of us. Serginho arrived with his two little daughters, Mariana and Marcela. As they played with their bicycles, we sat under a tree and started our conversation. Serginho had been in prison three times; the last time, he had been sentenced to an eight-year prison term for aggravated robbery but managed to escape and change his identity. He was living clandestinely with a fake ID card. After escaping from prison with a criminal record and being wanted by the police, he had no choice but to continue participating in the world of crime by robbing supermarkets and houses in the elite neighborhoods of the Jardins. When I met Serginho, he was feeling particularly hesitant about his involvement in the *firmas* (as he calls criminal transactions) because of the constant raids the police were carrying out in the favela. Just a few minutes into our conversation, Serginho's telephone rang. He stepped away from me to take the call and spent almost half an hour on the phone in what seemed to be a *firma*. He seemed desperate, cursing at someone on the other side of the line. He came back to apologize that he had a *correria* (a hustle) to take care of. He took his two daughters and left. One month later, we met again. This time, he suggested meeting at his *barraco* (shack), a tiny one-room brick house among many in the narrow streets of the shantytown. Serginho's living situation gave no indication that he had made money from the *firmas*. The only things he possessed were a bed, a dirty old stove, a small bathroom, and a small refrigerator. Later, he explained to me that the *correrias* were risky and not profitable because even when they were successful in robbing a great amount of money, he had to share it with three others, leaving them with only enough to fulfill their obligations as fathers. He gave me a beer. I sat on the side of the bed and we spoke for almost two hours.

Hunted by the police and without a source of income, Serginho dedicated much of his time and energy to stealing from white elites' houses in the same neighborhoods he went to as a kid with his mother when she worked as a domestic servant. Like many other black men I interacted with, and contrary to a common assumption about their "lack of consciousness," Serginho was very aware of the city's inequalities and referred to himself and others like him as *pretinhos*; he referred to those living in the well-off districts as "playboys" (the white upper-class young men). Within the city's politics, these are coded racial and gendered categories that demarcate positions of entitlement to protection and vulnerability to death. Spatially, Serginho was caged in the favela as much as he was in the detention center where he had served time. Now "outside," he was very selective in his movements around the city, particularly after PCC's attack on the police. He spent most of his time in his *barraco,* had very few friends, and stopped going out at night. With a fake ID, he sometimes took the risk of taking a little stroll in the hood, but the police had recently created a checkpoint in the main access to the favela. When it was impossible to avoid the police, he focused on not showing signs of submissiveness and made sure he did not use prison jargon to hide the lingering marks of his time there. "If you want to avoid problem, when they stop you look at them in the eyes and don't say 'yes, sir' because they will ask right away, 'why did you fall [into the prison system]?' When you have a chance, look at their badge and call them by their name," he said. Serginho's strategic assertiveness of looking police officers straight in the eye and calling them by name was an attempt to prevent assumptions about his criminal background. He refused to refer to police officers as *senhor* (mister), because that could tip them off that he had spent time in prison.

I was very aware of these strategies. I have witnessed several moments in which the police stopped black youth during my work in the periphery of the city. The immediate reaction of bowing the head, putting the hands behind the back, and immediately assuming a submissive position while responding to the officer by repeating "yes, sir" is part of the survival kit. I myself have been stopped by the police several times and could see the police searching for clues of a criminal background in my speech patterns or for signs of tattoos on my body identifying me as belonging to the world of crime. Although the lack of criminal background does not protect one from being arrested or killed, language and bodily marks play a relevant role in these violent interactions in public spaces. Knowing that a criminal record could become a death sentence in moments like riots (when killings by the police were justified in the media as "cleaning the city"), Serginho carefully calculated each of his movements in the city. Even being in the favela's streets was extremely risky for someone like him. As he himself acknowledged, "we are living a life of Tom and Jerry. We are the little rats. They go, we come out. They come, we hide, and they take over."

For Serginho, the world of crime was much more than a transgression of law, for at least in the eyes of "endangered" civil society he was an outlawed subject. He made sense of his existence within this ontological enclosure: when I asked him about the future, he inadvertently invoked God to say that there was no other future ahead except in the world of crime "until God wills." Whether God's will was to keep him in the world of crime or not, ironically, it was through the church that Serginho began his street life. When he was fifteen, a member from the evangelical church congregation that he and his mother attended accused him of robbing the church's money. Serginho was furious; he cried and swore to God he did not steal from the church, but no one believed his innocence and he never went back. Later, he began to hustle by stealing from small stores, pedestrians in the rich areas of the city, and then the houses of the elite where his mother used to take him so she could keep an eye on him while she worked. Serginho has nothing but the little he has from his robbing. "I make my living from crime. That is my work. Everything that I have, everything that I give to my daughters I take from the *vida do crime* [criminal life]. That is my living."

Serginho tried to get a formal job after leaving prison for the first time. His mother got him a job delivering medicine, but he was fired as soon as the boss discovered his criminal record. Without an educational degree or job, he would most likely have to accept a low-paid job as a doorman, car washer, or supermarket worker. However, he refused these subordinate positions and preferred the world of crime because it gave him control over his time and his life. It was through his mother's work as a maid that he became aware of the privileges of the playboys. It was also through witnessing his mother's exploitation by the rich that Serginho saw the spatial injustices in the city. "I was a *pretinho,* favelado without a job . . . so *corri atrás do meu jeito* [I hustled my own way]," he says. The two geographies of opportunity and exclusion were tied through his mother's position as a black favelada, the playboy's maid, and the mother of a *pretinho.* His anger toward the rich playboys may offer important clues for understanding black youth's frustration with the structural barriers that prevent them from participating in consumer society. This, however, is just a partial explanation of the political subjectivity constituted in danger, frustration, and suffering. Hardly ever do we see youth participating in criminal activities appear as subjects capable of launching a racial gendered critique of their situation.

That is not to say their protests are not free from contradictions such as their investment in the patriarchal discourse of providing for the family. However, in the context of the structural devaluation of black lives (in low-paying jobs, the segregated favela, and police hunts), Serginho's critique goes beyond a demand for incorporation into the sphere of consumption. His refusal to take a low-paying job and to rob elites in the well-off district where his own mother works as a domestic servant instead may well be a political response to the forces that prevent the black right to the city. In everyday encounters with these forces the black body, expectedly docile, becomes an insurgent and ungovernable outlawed subject.

In her ethnography on a favela in Rio, Donna Goldstein explains, "in many cases, gang members' decisions to join a gang and their anger against the wealthy *bacanas* were based on a clearheaded analysis of the injustice of the system."[39] The *system*—this broad category that in the lexicon of marginalized urban youth includes the police, the economy, the political system, and the legal city—was precisely Serginho's target. In that sense, the playboy—again, a marker that, like the term *bacana,* denotes a racial and class division—personified the system for all it represented in terms of longstanding injustices in the city. Serginho suggested that the playboys feared him because they were conscious of their own responsibility in sustaining the city's inequality. Then, he speculated why the elite spends a lot of money on fences and security guards. "They are afraid because they know they have more than a lot of people, and the people perceive that." Urban fear, as some scholars have noticed, is a political resource mobilized by different actors to organize the social world into exclusive forms of sociability and community.[40] Still, at least for those seen as feared objects like Serginho and the other individuals in this book, fear must be severely qualified not only because distinct social and racial groups experience it differently in a qualitative way but also because fear is politicized as bodily agency.[41] From the perspective of the black urban enemy, fear is a political purchase that they embrace to drive their point home. The fear they originate in their "vulnerable" white "victims" brings about a political moment in which the dehumanized black criminal achieves the status of human being.

According to Serginho, the fear PCC produced in the city during the May 2006 attacks changed the ways society interacted with the periphery. Everybody knew about the "oppression of the system," but nobody paid attention to what was going on in the favelas until the Partido set the city on fire. "We were saying, we are here, if we want we stop everything," he says. Serginho told me it was not only the brothers that participated in the attacks, contrary to the media and the police's accounts. Residents also participated indirectly by giving them support and hiding them from sight when the police came. To him, PCC's attack was successful because they were able to speak directly to "the anger of the favelado suffering in the hands of the police." Although many young people just went with the flow of the riot, Serginho told me "everybody was fed up with the police coming to the favela, kicking the door, raping women . . ." While the legal city was caught off guard, the attack was not news for many in the periphery. "When it happened many folks already knew and even helped because they didn't agree with the oppression of the police in the favela," he says. Likewise, the PCC built on the carceral turnover to organize the attack in a synchronized way between prisons throughout the state and the peripheries. The order to "sentar o dedo" (to "slap the leather," giving permission to shoot someone) spread like fire throughout the periphery in ways that even the most sophisticated state-intelligence system could not intercept. The outcome of the riot was the bloody massacre by the police—"the rope always breaks on the weaker end," he reasoned—but it was still meaningful because PCC was the only force able to bring unity to the favela against the system.

Although Serginho knew black young men were in the expendable and volatile lower ranks of PCC's hierarchy, he defended the Partido because it alone was able to bring the "thugs" together. It also effectively organized dispersed criminal practices (like his) by making everybody comply with a set of rules that, in his words, "made the favela a better place to live" in. In fact, Serginho evoked one of PCC's moral codes, of not stealing in the favela and treating everybody equally, to defend his acts of sticking up in the other side of the city. Contrary to the hustler who makes a living stealing things in the streets, Serginho's actions were well planned. He and his peers strategically chose where to "meter o louco." In his language, *metendo o louco* was a phrase used to describe someone crazily sticking up (when someone decided to employ violent means to carry on the *firma*). While others occupied their time with dealing drugs or stealing from pedestrians, Serginho and his men were busy sticking up the playboys in the middle of the night in their homes. When I asked him how his apparently self-serving act of stealing from the rich helped to change his and his community's condition, Serginho once again brought his mother's domestic work and the police raids in the favela into the equation. As I pressed him further to try to find glimpses of what I judged to be a "political" discourse, he reminded me that my question did not make sense because I was judging his practices according to the *system*. He rationalized his "job" in the *mundo do crime* with a different logic. In this way, he asserted that contrary to the police, who are bound to the system through the law, he operated *outside* of it. Serginho's sense of justice is defined in opposition to a delinquent state that claims to be "fair" but humiliates, extorts, and does not provide economic opportunities. Under this reasoning, the *correrias* were legitimate since they never claimed to obey the law as the police did.

Serginho's qualification has important theoretical and political significance. His distinction between his and the police's places in relation to the law invites reflection on the positionality of the black subject vis-à-vis the law. Coherent to this ontological position, he positions himself not as a lawbreaker—after all he does not recognize or claim to obey the law—but as an out(of)law subject whose outlawness makes his existence possible.[42] Abolitionist Luiz Gama's remark that "a slave who kills his master does not commit a crime" is restated in Serginho's understanding that he commits no crime because he has no commitment to the law as the police do; because of his displacement in relation to the domain of law, the world of crime is a politicospatial reference that repositions himself in the anti-black world. In this line of reasoning, the "feared black man" represents an insurgent political actor, one who refuses to comply with the law not as a choice but rather as a way to refuse to live "blackness-as-victimization."[43]

What are we to make of someone whose outlawed body is the condition of possibility for the regime of law? What kind of blackness is generated in that context? Serginho's experience suggests that the black "criminal" that scares civil society is a subject who refuses to be "a good slave" in the (post)colony and instead embraces an explosive and deadly identity constituted in frustration, suffering, and rage.[44] The challenge here is not to fall into the attempt to judge Serginho's practice through what it should offer in terms of social change but rather through how the political–juridical order of the city informs the meaning, scope, and intensity of political action in the *arid zones of nonbeing.* It was his outlawed practices that enabled his momentary existence in the city other than in the traditional places of black subjection.

Serginho knew that life was an ephemeral project even in the tiny zone of insubordination opened by the world of crime. During our last meeting, he told me he considered himself a winner who was "profiting for being alive." "To be honest, I didn't think I would live to be twenty-nine years old," he said, showing me the bullet scars on his body. Serginho was conscious that death was always around the corner. Although he had already warned his family that they should not visit him if he were caught, he confessed to me that he would rather die in a confrontation with the police than go back to prison. His prediction turned out to be true. A few days later, our common friend Fabiano called to give me the news of Serginho's death. Serginho had been on his way to another stickup in a stolen car with two other black men when they came to a surprise police checkpoint in one of Zona Sul's main avenues. When the group tried to escape, the police shot and killed Serginho and one of his partners. I tried to contact his family after his death but they had moved from the favela to an unknown location. When Serginho's fate is considered in the context of the precarity of black urbanity, his death actually does not register as death at all. From the favela to the prison, and then to the cemetery, he had permanently occupied the ontological space of alienation from the world of living. The world of crime was a fragile space that he had managed to open within the black necropolis. I did not know what to make of them, but Fabiano's only words about his friend's death were that "he lived short and yet intensely."

The *Biqueira*

The urban riots organized by PCC were one manifestation of the struggle against the system, but there were also less-overt ways in which the Partido provided a means for black and other marginalized youth to assert themselves. Dealing was certainly one. As these youth become a surplus population to the service economy of São Paulo and are devoured by the state's penal system, PCC provides protection within the prison and economic security outside of it. Drug trafficking in the favelas has been regarded as a tragic way for poor urban youth to be integrated into the capitalist system. Like a firm, the *biqueira* employs people and generates profits. Its profits are high, its employees volatile, and its structure hierarchical. One can compellingly say that marginalized youth participating in such enterprises do so because they are harassed by drug traffickers, who find in them a marginal group craving participation in the capitalist economy. Drug trafficking offered a pass into the sphere of consumption—or a "perverse integration"—for youth tempted by the easy access to "guns and tobacco, money in the pocket, pretty clothes, and the willingness to kill."[45] Although true in many cases, this argument leaves no room for recognizing the political transactions that the *biqueira*—the dope spot or drug-selling point—represents as a place where vulnerability, spatial agency, and legitimate aspirations to have access to "goods" come together. What if, instead of looking at their practices as mere attempts at integration, we pay attention to the political spaces they open to transgress the city's racial order? Is not that the case that the *biqueira* enables, even if momentarily, some territorial and economic autonomy for a racialized surplus population not worthy of even exploitation in the neoliberal service economy of São Paulo? As I have shown, this resonates in the urban experiences of black individuals such as Serginho, Nina, and Luana, who made a living doing *correiras* and dealing in the housing projects. Racially ambiguous individuals like Fabio, a twenty-something-year-old migrant from Ceará in northeast Brazil, who works as a dealer at PCC's *biqueira*, also helped me understand the *biqueira* as a spatial metaphor for racially constituted disposability, economic autonomy, and territorial agency.

One afternoon, I was with Fabio in a bar on M'Boi Mirim, the main avenue bordering Dreaming City, where he works a twelve-hour shift trading cocaine. The *biqueira* is busy and Fabio does not take a break. The dealing was intense, with playboys and *patricinhas* (a common Brazilian term for upper- and middle-class white young men and women) stopping by to buy cubes of cocaine. Located on the other side of the drug-trade chain, the playboy "consumers" had the spatial mobility, economic capital, and personal security to cross the city to buy from small "dealers" like Fabio. While this circularity, in which whites exercise their privilege as consumers by default, is another frequently overlooked aspect of the "war-on-drugs," I call attention here to yet another way the *biqueira* is integrated into the racialized periphery's political and economic life. Fabio explained to me how PCC's underground drug economy works in the neighborhood: the Partido divides the territory into *biqueiras,* a term that sometimes refers to a street, an entire residential block, or a single corner. The *biqueiras* alternate between selling marijuana or cocaine. Most of the *biqueiras* are directly controlled by PCC, which controls the distribution of drugs to be commercialized on a small scale. PCC distributes the drugs through a franchise, in which the owner of the *biqueira* pays a monthly amount to the organization for the right to deal in the favela. He usually employs between ten and twelve people, who each work twelve-hour shifts for three days in a row. Those who work during the week cannot work on the weekends when the establishment is busier, and vice versa; Fabio explained that this is "to guarantee that other people also have the opportunity to work." As for the earnings, workers sell packets of cocaine containing thirty-five cubes and take five cubes from each packet as payment. When I spoke with Fabio, a cube was sold for R$10 (5.00 USD at this time). The average daily sale for one worker was three packets, or a hundred and five cubes—fifteen of which were for the worker's pay. This brought in a daily income of R$150, or a total of R$450 for the three-day work block. It made a monthly income of R$1800.00 (or 900.00 USD for twelve days of work in the month), a very attractive salary considering that the minimum wage was 300.00 USD at the time. Without a college education and with a little son, Fabio made a higher wage than his housekeeper mother or his doorman uncle. With irony, he asked me a rhetorical question: "The *ze povinho* [the hard worker] stays there in the sun, being exploited, gets slapped in the face by the police, and what does he earn?"

Even as the Partido provided job opportunities to youth like Fabio, its work placed them in the center of the PCC–police feud. When I talked to Fabio, he was anxious because he had received a death threat from police officers who came to extort from him, as he refused to pay the bribe. Under PCC's strict code, the dealer is responsible for the drug if he or she fell in the hands of the police, and a golden rule for staying alive is to "not mess with the boss's money." Being the weaker part of the extended drug-trafficking chain, individuals like Fabio (or Nina and Luana) are easily replaced when they are caught by the police so the drug business can continue running. Fabio's mother, Vilma, was particularly concerned with his position between the PCC and the police, and attempted to get him out of the world of crime. She also fought with the police multiple times and literally took Fabio out of their hands when they came to her house to take him because he refused to pay the weekly bribe. She denounced the police officers to human rights organizations, but that was a bad idea. They came back, took Fabio for a ride, and tortured him until he paid the bribe. Fearing his death, Vilma offered Fabio the possibility of sending him to the Ceará, where her mother lives, but Fabio decided: "I prefer to die than leave my *quebrada.*"

His experience reminds us that racially ambiguous individuals (e.g., a Northeastern immigrant) are also caught in the sinister economy of black disposability due to their proximity to black spaces and black bodies. It may also be the case that Fabio's encounters with policing and state violence in general are shaped by the dynamics of anti-blackness that inform life in the periphery. It also further helps us understand the transgressive practices of resistance inhabited by racialized youth living in liminal spaces of anti-blackness. I consider the practice of selling drugs on street corners of the favela a spatial praxis much like sticking up "playboys" in well-off areas of the city, for it reveals the active role of black(ed) youth in transgressing spaces that are not in their favor.[46] Despite its limited scope and precarious conditions, dealing is neither alienating nor merely instrumental. At the core of the favela–prison pipeline, the *biqueira* is the spatial form of state carcerality. It is also the concrete manifestation of a "transgressive politics of space" in clear opposition to the morally coded and space-based security strategies represented, for instance, by the security council, the community police, and civil society at large. While there is no doubt that dealing is a job occupation like any other, scholars should pay attention also to the alternative spatialities this deviant form of political and economic life enables. The outcomes of these practices can be as oppressive as those they challenge. Drug addiction, further policing, stigmatization, and intracommunity violence all carry intimate relations. However, I label them as alternative because in the context of urban siege, claiming the *biqueira* as a political entity opens up a world of possibilities to investigate what kind of spatial subjectivity emerges from the intertwining context of economic dispossession, racial violence, and deviant politics.

Katherine McKittrick's critique of traditional geographers' depiction of blackness as "despatialized" is important here. The black experience has been conceptualized as one of dispossession and displacement to the point that black people are imagined as a people without a "sense of place." Challenging this view, she writes: "[b]lack subjects are not indifferent to practices and landscapes; rather, they are connected to them due to crude racial–sexual hierarchies and due to their (often unacknowledged) status as geographic beings who have a stake in the production of space."[47] Like McKittrick, I contend that black agency in São Paulo's periphery is informed by a profound sense of place. This is not necessarily a fixed and stable (sense of) place but one that enables marginalized black youth to fight back against the forces that deny them urban life. I do not claim that dealing and engaging in criminal behavior is the only way black youth articulate a language of spatial agency, though. It would be a serious omission to overlook the broad political repertoire, ranging from graffiti and hip-hop to self-help initiatives in the educational programs offered by black organizations like UNEafro-Brasil and Educafro. Even though I encountered several individuals dealing and sticking up, there are several stories of black young men and women struggling to get a college degree, participating in formal political groups, and complying with the law. However, I privilege these marginal voices in the world of crime because their practices rarely achieve the status of political action, even to urban activists struggling under the banner of the "right to the city."

Black Rage

There is a common expression used by black youth in São Paulo's periphery that sets the tone of black political protest in the city. It is *sangue no raciocínio,* or "blood in reasoning." I heard the expression in demonstrations, in the *biqueiras,* and in the prison. In one of my visits to the detention center, I asked Eliseu what the expression conveys. His experience growing up in the favela under constant police raids, falling into prison, suffering the injustice of being fired for his criminal record, and observing his parents' daily struggle to make ends meet built up to a constant anger that exploded in his behavior of crazily sticking up. Eliseu's entrance into the world of crime began with stealing in Santo Amaro (the commercial hub separating the Fundão from Zona Sul's prime areas), mugging the playboys, and then dealing drugs in the *quebrada*. In fact, these transgressive practices provide a map of the spatial injustices that characterize most of the city's geographical landscape. Eliseu's only relation to the other side of the city was through his mother, who worked as a maid, and through his incursions into the commercial hub to rob stores and pedestrians. Eliseu's criminal acts were attempts to redraw the city's geography of exclusion. To him, pointing a gun to the head of a playboy meant more than just stealing something from him. This act, rather, is informed by an acute awareness of the city's dramatic racial, spatial, and class disparities. He referred to such hyper-consciousness of one's social condition as having *sangue no raciocínio*. Pretending to have a gun in his hands, Eliseu pointed to me and bluntly explained the rationale of his actions: "Shit, this is for me and for the bros in my *quebrada*. This is for *minha velha* [my old mother], changing the playboy's diapers, that son of a bitch." To Eliseu, having "blood in reasoning" is employing violent means to take revenge for the daily exploitation and humiliation that he and his mother faced.

Like Serginho, Eliseu robbed to serve his family's and his own everyday needs. In response to my attempt to understand "the political" in his actions, he made a key qualification. There was "the revolt of the belly," a phrase used to describe someone going out and hustling to meet his/her personal needs, as well as the cumulative rage against the *system,* here referring to urban poverty, police violence, and prisons. While the revolt of the belly and bloody consciousness are not the same, the former was an everyday manifestation of the latter and the latter was a cumulative expression of the former. In this reasoning, bloody consciousness came into full display during the May riots, when the rage of the system exploded into violence. The idea of "blood in reasoning" resonates with some studies on blackness, crime, and everyday resistance in the United States. These studies rely on James Scott's critique of normative accounts of resistance usually thought in terms of a leftist-oriented and radical subject protesting against oppression. Resistance, Scott notes, should be thought of as a "cumulative force" embodied in less overt practices such as sabotage, refusal to comply with authority, and even strategic negotiation with systems of power. Building on Scott, Robin D. G. Kelley proposed a reading of black urban resistance as "politics from below." Kelley did not deny the effectiveness of organized black protests but also asked for a scholarly consideration of ordinary strategies that the black urban poor embrace but that are disregarded as apolitical. According to Kelley, "Politics comprises the many everyday battles to roll back constraints and exercise some power over, or create some space within, the institutions and social relationships that dominate our lives."[48] Other scholars also build on this tradition to propose a reading of black "criminality" as a form of resistance. They argue that black youth's deviant behavior (of which the figure of the gangster has become an icon) should be understood not only as a counterhegemonic protest against racism and discrimination but also as a radical refusal to comply with white civil society.[49]

While I join these scholars in considering the "small and subversive acts" of everyday resistance (in opposition to the teleological constructs of resistance embraced by the Marxist tradition), my emphasis is not so much on the ordinary politics of the subaltern but on what Saidiya Hartman has identified as a "closure of politics" as far as black matters are concerned. I am not arguing that everyday practices of resistance are not acts of defiance against the system. Nor am I disregarding the role of "black cultural practices" in informing black resistance. All of these elements are certainly present in the periphery of São Paulo and manifest in actions such as stealing electricity, attending the security council meeting to shame the authorities, strategically complying with the community police, and producing cultural repertoires that challenge police authority through hip-hop and *baile funk*. However, black participation in PCC's politics suggests, in a non–mutually exclusive way, that to be legible in the context of racial terror black political life needs to take a *fatal* form. I read this strange form of politics as an insurgent one that aims to create life outside the anti-black regime of law.

Tragic Agency

Reading black criminality as black agency is an insufficient analytical approach if we fail to consider the ways black men engage in social relations that facilitate violence against those already vulnerable in the favelas. How do we account for black men's agency in the face of their investment in patriarchy, for instance? How do we deal with contradictions that arise from internal power dynamics among the oppressed without reproducing narratives that further criminalize them? Social anthropologist ethnographers Philippe Bourgeois and Donna Goldstein confronted this issue in Rio's favela and New York City's East Harlem, respectively, when their informants expressed no regrets and even laughed about the rape of girls in their territories. As both scholars show, the misogynistic practices of marginalized urban youth may empower them in relation to other marginalized groups, but it also further marginalizes their community. While both ethnographers do not downplay the political agency of black and Latino youth engaged in gangs and drug trafficking, they invite researchers to not only deconstruct pathological narratives of subaltern masculinities but also unveil how the symbolic purchase of masculinity comes into play even in these contexts. Similarly, I faced this challenge when reflecting on ethnographic moments that highlighted what I refer to as *tragic agency.* I should warn the reader that by adding the term "tragic," I bring an involuntary judgment on "agency." Against this misstep, scholars have contended that political agency is not necessarily progressive and without contradictions. Because "agency" is usually equated to resistance against structures of domination, there is a tendency to avoid the contradictions that arise when the oppressed participate in their own oppression. Therefore, subordinate practices that do not lead to social transformations are rendered as false consciousness rather than resistance. Black men's criminal agency is full of contradictions that point to the limits of conventional scripts of resistance rather than indicate "false consciousness."[50] I consciously employ this term to account for the political subjectivity produced by the everyday interpellation of black men as enemies of public order, and to explain these men's defiance of the state and their investment in reproducing domination along gender lines.

During one of my visits to the prison, I spent some extra time joking around with Eliseu, Gustavo, and Cleyton while another college activist attended some inmates in the other corner of the prison yard. My usual interlocutors were discussing the case of Bruno Fernandes de Souza, a nationally known goalkeeper from Flamengo Soccer Club who had been accused of murdering his ex-girlfriend Eliza Samudio. Cleyton asked me if I had been following the news about the case and wanted to know my opinion: "Was she innocent? Tell me, if your wife was cheating on you, would you not do the same?" Before I could respond, he justified the murder, arguing that after the Lei Maria da Penha, Brazilian women had become "too audacious" and no longer respected men. The Maria da Penha Law was enacted in 2006 by President Lula da Silva and was designed to reduce the domestic violence and *feminicide* so prevalent in Brazilian society. I contemplated arguing with Cleyton, but then decided to let Eliseu or Gustavo intervene before I did. However, they did not, and Cleyton kept going.

He told us how he was very jealous of his ex-girlfriend. She had once proposed to him that they have an open relationship. He said, "I grabbed her neck . . . and told her, 'If I suspect that you are cheating on me, I will break your ribs and twist your neck.'" In a flashback, he then realized that she had been crying. "Now that I think about it, this bitch was cheating on me and that's why she was afraid. When I get out of here I will kill her, Jaime. I'll do it." Eliseu started laughing about how Cleyton's girlfriend had cheated on him, bringing the hypermasculine mythic figure of the *Ricardão* into the conversation: "The *Ricardão* is fucking your woman and you are here, fool." After joking and challenging Cleyton's masculinity, Eliseu agreed that the new law was "giving too much freedom to women." Cleyton added that because of this sense of empowerment, his girlfriend went to the police and filed a case against him. Eliseu laughed, "If they arrest every guy who beats his woman, there will be no space in jail." Looking for my brotherly solidarity, he turned to me and asked if I had ever beaten my girlfriend. I shook my head no, showing disapproval, and before I could answer, he added, "At least some slaps are good. . . . If you are too nice, at the first opportunity she will put a guy in your bed." Gustavo was also thoughtful; he saw that we both did not like the conversation and asked them to "shut up," adding that they had no regard for their "girls" coming every weekend to visit them. He explained that some women were "folgadas" (slackers) but to defend killing them was crossing the line. "You two are psychopathic. . . . Bruno is a monster." Cleyton did not like being called a psychopath and harassed Gustavo for not displaying tough masculinity. Gustavo's "soft talking," Eliseu said, was proof that he was a "bicha enrrustida" (closeted faggot). Noticing my clear disapproval, Cleyton apologized and asked me not to "get hung up on this" because he was "just kidding."

Eliseu held his ground, insisting that anyone would kill a person in a moment of fury and thought it was too naïve to "think that a man would respond with flowers when his woman was cheating on him," a statement that was followed by laughter from other inmates who had overheard the conversation. He went back to the story of the goalkeeper who had assassinated his girlfriend. I grew upset with Eliseu and told him that Gustavo was right, men should have no right over women's lives. There would be no justification for Bruno killing his girlfriend, I explained. I also let them know that they were very clever in criticizing the "oppression of the system" but held misogynistic views about women in the favela. Eliseu and Cleyton continued laughing. "Man what the hell are you laughing about? You are all the time repeating the same story about police violence in the *quebrada* and now . . . what is the difference?" I boosted. Gustavo supported me, saying that his mother suffered at the hands of his abusive father and that he never "raised the hand against a woman." Eliseu quickly responded that he did not trust his "wife" because "your woman is not your mom." As the conversation got heated, I excused myself by saying that I had to go to the other prison yard.

In my interlocutors' narratives on violence and crime, masculinity was defined by toughness and women's bodies were portrayed as weak and liable to be abused. Even as he refuted Cleyton and Eliseu's argument, Gustavo had in mind an ideal woman exemplified by his own mother, who is raising his son and who is coming to visit him every weekend. The women nurturing, taking care of the home, and diligently visiting them in the prison were those who should not be subjected to violence; they were "good women." Black men's embracing the rhetoric of violence against women was a means of showing off their masculinity in the highly contentious space of the prison. Broadly, it was also a fair picture of black men participating in a brotherhood or patriarchal community imagined in and through the devaluation of women's bodies.[51]

Some scholars have argued that black men's investment in patriarchy is a way for them to affirm themselves in a white-supremacist world.[52] If this explanation is correct, such a search for affirmation not only has drastic consequences for black women, who are subjected to multiple layers of vulnerability, but also complicates the ways black men relate to each other. In the prison, masculinity was defined by the capacity to inflict pain and to withstand pain, and those individuals who failed to do so were seen as feminine. Under this framework, a real man should be able to "segurar o bagulho" (hold his own) and "segurar a cana" (withstand the time in prison). Naldo was a prisoner who was known as a "mariquinha" (little sissy) and considered weak for failing to meet the prison's stereotypes of tough maleness. During one of my visits, Eliseu pushed me to the corner and whispered in my ear, "Do you see that guy over there? *Se a prisão virar* [If there were a prison riot], he will die." According to Eliseu, this individual was living on a "fio da navalha" (knife's edge) because he had given the names of friends who had acted with him in a robbery when he was arrested. The brothers did not forgive him, which meant that he was by himself. What was surprising to me was the rationale that Eliseu used to explain the imminence of his friend's death. "This is the law of the criminal world, Jaime. Imagine if tomorrow someone else decides to do the same. In crime you have to be trustworthy. Jail is a place for machos." Naldo's fellow prisoners evoked gendered stereotypes assigned to women to describe him, mocking him for being "too emotional," "fearful," and "weak" to withstand pain under torture.

Violence against other men is rationalized by feminizing them, and by feminizing them, victimizers normalize gendered violence as a natural feature of punishment. Those who are committed to punishment are also committed to marking bodies with gendered inscriptions. This rationale, Angela Davis argues, is why "sexual abuse—which, like domestic violence, is yet another dimension of the privatized punishment of women—has become an institutionalized component of punishment behind prison walls."[53] The prisoners are gendered as female by prison guards in the daily humiliation to which they are subjected, and also by other prisoners like Eliseu and Cleyton to whom the inability to endure pain was a "woman's thing." These gendered dynamics were clear in the prison when the prison guards punished the prisoners by sexually assaulting "their women" with strip searches as the prisoners themselves complained. In fact, one of PCC's main complaints against the system was that "the prison guards make the wives pay for the prisoners' wrongdoings." In the same vein, in their attempts to fend off the state, the brothers also invested in a set of practices that particularly affected black favelada women. This holds particularly true for black women relying on PCC's underground drug business.

Nina and Luana's stories illustrate that as black women are particularly affected by the city's service economy that further constrains their insertion into the job market, the *biqueira* appears as an opportunity to make ends meet. It is also the most vulnerable place for sexual violence, extortions, and arrests by the police. This vulnerability is further intensified by PCC members, who rely on women to transport drugs and cell phones inside their bodies to prisons. To clarify, I do not intend to undermine the role of women who participate in PCC as mere victims. Nonetheless, their position as mules, for instance, should be understood within the constrained context in which brutal domination dictates the scope and intensity of political agency. The symbol of the mule, the animal used to carry heavy loads, is itself very revealing of their expendable position. Whether they became mules for a small amount of money that would complement their family income or because they were forced to do so to pay their husbands' debts to other prisoners, black women's bodies have become a currency within the sinister racialized prison economy.

In my visits to the women's prison, I met several women who *caiu* (fell into prison) while trying to enter the prison with drugs. Elisa was one of these women. My meetings at the women's prison were facilitated by my position as a member of the Prisoners Advocacy group. My male identity severely limited my access to these women but in my visits, I managed to maintain contact with Elisa every other weekend. Elisa was arrested while attempting to bring cocaine to her husband, Mario, in the male prison in Sorocaba in the São Paulo countryside. She had traveled hundreds of miles with small portions of cocaine wrapped in condoms and placed into her vagina. This was the first time Elisa had done this, as she struggled to resist Mario and the local dealer's harassment to bring cell phones and drugs into prison. Mario finally convinced her by saying that she would make some money and the dealer in the *biqueira* would look after her and the children. Although terrified, Elisa went through the violent bodily process and took the long bus ride to visit Mario. She had had second thoughts while still in line to enter the prison, listening to stories of women caught with drugs. But it was too late to back out.[54] In my dispersed notes after our meeting, I wrote down Elisa's fragmented narrative from when we sat at the curb in the prison patio where inmates sat in the sun during visiting hours. Duda, her cellmate, followed us and made fun of the situation. Here is my attempt to recuperate their narrative:

ELISA: The agent asks you to open your mouth, then shake your head. Then he sends you to the next room where this woman just points for you to take your clothes off, and then she wants you to open your legs because she wants to see inside.

DUDA: *Peladinha* [completely naked], squatting three times, front and back. Open your vagina with your hands. They see into your womb. *Mulher de cadeia sabe de cor e salteado* [Jailed women know by heart]. Now *zé povinho* trying to play hustler will certainly be fucked [Duda gestures and makes fun of the situation].

ELISA: And you have to blow air into a bottle, so if you have something they are gonna see it right away. If they find something, you are slapped across the face just to start with. You are gonna be beaten until you take it out by yourself or they threaten you with a piece of iron.

DUDA: Do you want me to take it out with that, *vagabunda* [tramp]? You choose. Without crying [Duda mimics a prison guard with a piece of iron].

ELISA: And you end up in the men's jail until they transfer you to a police station, and then to here [the female prison]. So here I am. You go to visit someone in prison and end up there also. Now, imagine the fear if there is a rebellion and these men [the male inmates] come to your cell.

Elisa wanted to know if she qualified for parole since she was a first-time inmate, but she was not eligible. She was convicted for association with drug trafficking—under Article 33 of the new Brazilian drug statute (Law 111.343/2006), she had to complete at least two-fifths of a sentence lasting five years and eight months before applying for any benefits, depending on her behavior. Frustrated with my papers, Elisa kept saying how she regrets the moment she accepted the "offer" to smuggle and angrily recalled the judge, a *playboizinho* (a young playboy), who had lectured her. Duda expressed solidarity by evoking a common saying among the prisoners: "The law is for the three p's: *preto, pobre e prostituta.*" These words rhyme in Brazilian Portuguese, producing a reiterated "p" sound for black *(preto)*, poor, and prostitute.

It is clear that Elisa's incarceration is intimately connected to the larger political economy of punishment in which structural violence, racism, and misogyny throw black women into crime. The opportunity to make ends meet in the world of crime reflects what Julia Sudbury calls "the feminization of poverty and punishment." Within the structural changes in the global economy, black women like Elisa and Duda are pushed into poverty and crime, have their lives policed, and then become the "raw material" for prison expansion as the case of São Paulo illustrates.[55] Their condition is also related to the investment of black men in practices that place black women's lives in positions of further vulnerability. The message I got from my meeting with Elisa and Duda was that scholars and social activists must denounce state violence yet address the explosive combination of anti-blackness and gender domination that undermines efforts to redress black suffering. Recognizing these shortcomings is not to deny "black women criminality" as an insurgent practice but rather to make visible the troubling relation between racism and gendered violence energized by but not unique to the penal state. While black men's political status as *enemies* of public order makes them live in the shadow of death, and while we should be cautious not to infer that all men participate equally in the structure of gender domination, reducing their experience to that of victims and insurgents against racial violence ignores another aspect of their agency— one that reinforces the gendered system of domination that degrades the lives of black women like Elisa and Duda. An important question for a black radical agenda against anti-black urban-security regimes, then, would be the following: If violence is a condition of possibility for the reinvention of black urban life, where is the place for gendered racial justice within *radical* politics of inclusion?

This question is also relevant for analyzing the alternative system of urban governance in the racialized peripheries of Brazilian cities, for which PCC is well known. As some scholars have shown, PCC regulates life and death in the city's periphery in controversial ways. Although there are multiple explanations for the sharp fall in homicide rates in the city, PCC has imposed a harsh control of punishment in prisons and in the favelas. This control includes everyday matters from street crimes, domestic conflicts, and disputes among neighbors to serious offenses like child abuse and domestic violence. In each case, the Partido holds a trial (called a debate) in which offenders, witnesses, and victims are heard.[56] Fernando told me, "to kill someone one has to ask permission from the Partido," and that is the reason why the homicide rate fell in the periphery. This was old news to me and to most of the residents in the periphery of the city, although government officials credited the reduction in homicides to its community-policing and mass-incarceration approach.[57] In a city with high levels of homicides throughout the 1990s and early 2000s, PCC's regulation of violence had positive outcomes particularly for blacks, given its domain over the predominantly black periphery. Favelados do not kill each other and, insofar as PCC is concerned, death is not a banal punishment but rather one regulated and deployed in the extreme cases. "Now we are a family. All for all," the *faxina* at the detention center told me.

Perhaps ironically, while mainstream civil society turns a blind eye to one of the most lethal police forces in the country, the right to live— the main priority for black activists—has been guaranteed by PCC.[58] Whether through a "killing consensus" between the Partido and the police or through PCC's real investment in creating a zone free from the state, the Partido's emergence has made the periphery safer for victims of state delinquency.[59] Neither the police nor the PCC holds absolute support from the favelados, but the widespread association of the police with a delinquent entity that terrorizes black favelados makes the latter consider PCC the kind of organization that is "illegal but not illegitimate."[60] PCC's legitimacy is built on its capacity to mobilize a language of justice and fairness that speaks to the favelados' frustration with the historical denial of state protection. To them, the promised democratic state of rights is delivered as a terrocratic state of policing.

Still, one cannot overlook the troubling ways in which PCC's attempt to mobilize poor and black young men through the antistate discourse of shared vulnerability ends up falling into the punitive logic of the penal state. Let me invoke once again my encounter with Josias, the resident of Paraisópolis, to shed light on this complexity. After being threatened to death by the police and refusing our help to take his case to the Police Ombudsperson's Office, Josias went to the Partido to ask for protection from the police officers and asked them to go after the drug-addicted teenager who had handed him over to the police. I asked Josias what happened to the teen. "*Crocodilagem* [snitching] in the favela means death," he said straightforwardly. Josias took the case to the PCC's debate. "He put my family on fire. Now he has to pay for that." I contended that the teen was just a tortured child with no choice but to snitch on him. Bringing him to the debate would mean a harsh punishment—maybe even death, my friend Marisa added. Josias responded that the teen knew well what he was doing and that he was not a little kid. "He is a snitch, a slacker who deserves to die."

Josias went to the PCC and spoke to the brothers, asking permission to "bump him off." At the debate, a brother assigned to defend the teen tried to soften the deal, saying he was "high" and had no notion of what he was doing. He asked Josias to forgive him. The PCC brothers wanted to beat up the teen, but Josias had already done this when he discovered who handed him over to the police. The brother who acted as the teen's lawyer used this fact against Josias. He argued that Josias had stepped out of line: he should have sought permission from PCC to punish the teen instead and that, he, Josias, should also be punished for "doing justice with his hands." Josias had violated the rules of the Partido. Josias reacted: "What is that about, brother? Is that right? If the Partido preaches fairness, don't I have the right to send up someone who wronged me? You must set the record straight. That is not right. I will not be protecting a tramp." The teen's father sent a message to Josias, asking him to forgive his son. Josias had been acquainted with the family for a long time and this request softened his heart. In addition, he later admitted that the teen's cries at the debate "stirred the feelings of the *irmãos.*" Since the teenager had already been severely injured by Josias, Josias agreed to forgive him and the PCC gave him an ultimatum: get out of the favela or Josias would have the right to "send him up." He disappeared from the favela, leaving his family behind. There, we had a case of two black individuals trapped in the PCC–police contest.

I listened to stories of individuals killed by PCC in the debates and of others made to commit suicide in prison through the sinister technique called the "Gatorade," in which the prisoner is forced to drink a lethal mixture of Viagra, cocaine, and Gatorade. Since the very nature of the Partido makes it difficult to provide an account of those moments without relying on secondary narratives, the debates have yet to be analyzed in depth by scholars of urban violence in Brazil. What these ethnographic moments reveal, however, is that while black men participating in PCC are clearly engaging in transgressive behavior that challenges the racial logics of urban security designed by the state to govern the favelas, PCC's necropractices call into question any naïve interpretation of the Partido as a revolutionary entity. It is not! Even when looking at PCC from below, as I propose, a question remains: What are we to make of its rank-and-file black soldiers who, despite posing a challenge to the city's racial order, also participate in dynamics of violence that target their own community? My interlocutors' disturbing justifications for violence against women, for instance, may be derivative of a political context produced by state terror, but their actions cannot be explained solely in those terms (as though black men merely reproduce white patriarchy).[61] Equally important is the need to acknowledge their *tragic agency* in building endogenous relations of domination that undermine efforts to build autonomous spaces for black life outside the structure of violence they actively resist.

This chapter began by analyzing an urban riot organized by PCC, a male-dominated organization that controls most of São Paulo's prisons, and sought to understand the underlying logic behind PCC's attacks. It argued that the seeds of the urban riot that unfolded on May 12, 2006, may be situated within black men's cumulative frustration with a regime of rights in which they are seen as enemies of the state and civil society. Their participation in the *mundo do crime* is an attempt to build autonomy in relation to their criminalization and disposability embedded in the city's security logics. Within that context, crime appears as a possibility of redrawing the city's geography of exclusion and reasserting their political agency. Crime, however, is only one response to racial oppression in urban Brazil. In the next chapter, I explore another form of black politics by analyzing the black movement's attempt to bring black matters to the (white) public sphere. Whether their voices can be heard through traditional and formal politics is the question I take up in the final chapter.

5

BRINGING BACK THE DEAD

> To find the flesh, the author and the critic must acknowledge no
> borders, must walk the space of death unafraid and uninhibited by
> a language that says such an outing is both a physical and imagina-
> tive impossibility.
>
> —Sharon Patricia Holland, *Raising the Dead*

After several attempts, I finally managed to set up a meeting with
Dona Maria, a group of human rights activists, and state authorities to
discuss the death of her son Betinho. With the help of a lawyer from
the black movement, we created a task force to assist individuals like
Dona Maria with bringing their cases to the judiciary and claiming a
monthly stipend for their families. The day before the meeting, Dona
Maria called to inform me that she was unsure about attending the
meeting. She mentioned a conversation she had recently had with PCC
members in the Fundão da Zona Sul, in which they had advised her
to be cautious since Betinho's case involved several police officers and
they could not guarantee her security in the downtown area where the
meeting would be held. If she decided to attend, they told her, I would
be held responsible if something went wrong. She was not exaggerating.
The relatives of other victims of the Slaughters had faced threats to their
lives and had to leave the favela when they publicly denounced the
death-squad group.

Only after her niece Sandrinha's insistence and my explanation
that the meeting would take place behind closed doors—without police
authorities and the media—did Dona Maria decide to attend, but not
before making two straightforward demands of me. First, she wanted to
get possession of her son's remains so that she could give him a proper

funeral. Second, she and her family needed financial support from the state because of their loss of Betinho's income. With anger and frustration, she warned me that she would not respond to endless inquiries about Betinho's death because "these people from human rights talk a bunch of hot air" and "at the end of the day they will not bring my son back." Bringing Dona Maria to the meeting was a victory from my side. Until then, she had been very reluctant to attend the public hearings organized by human rights organizations to discuss strategies against police violence. The last time she did attend a meeting in the Council of Human Rights, I had hoped she would take the opportunity to speak out, but she remained silent or cursed quietly at the human rights activists in the podium. When the presenter invited the parents of the victims to take turns on the microphone, she refused to talk and instead pulled me aside to say: "And this one with a horse face, what? I just want to know if he is going to bring my son back alive." With me it was no different. Sometimes she would ask why I was doing this research if I were not bringing Betinho to life. With my predictable answer, she would say, "So." And that would be the end of that conversation. Other times she would practically blame me for Betinho's death, using the pronoun "you all" to refer to his assassins, human rights activists, and individuals like myself. It was not easy to get along with Dona Maria.

And yet, she hoped that I would find paperwork that would prove Betinho had been working at the time of his death so that she could get her financial compensation from the state. With an old folder containing some news reports and Betinho's photograph, Dona Maria continued asking me to go after his file in the courtroom to find out where it stopped. On other occasions, she would call in the middle of the night with panics of anxiety to ask me to come to her in the morning and to go into a cybercafe with her to see if there had been any update on the trial's schedule. Any news on TV about a police trial, and Dona Maria would call me asking if I had any news. I would always frustrate her expectations with a painful "No." In deep isolation, she would lose her patience, blaming me for being a "pessoa dos direitos humanos" (one of the folks from human rights) that was not doing enough to help her. And to complete the troubling scenario, she would at times raise suspicions that I may be just another "advogado de porta de cadeia" (jail-door lawyer) interested in making money from her suffering. I hoped things would be different this time and that we would not leave empty handed.

On the day of the meeting, I took a two-hour ride from Dreaming City to downtown with Dona Maria and Sandrinha. Only then, sitting in the back of a crowded bus, did I begin to understand these women's relationship to the city. Trapped in the favela where Dona Maria had raised her children and where Sandrinha is now raising her own, they are strangers to São Paulo, similar to the many errant homeless people we met on our way to the offices of the public attorney, where the meeting was scheduled to take place. It was clear to me that Dona Maria's relation to the city was one of economic dispossession, political marginalization, and ontological displacement. Since her arrival in São Paulo from the neighboring state of Minas Gerais, she has moved from being a domestic servant in the houses of *paulistanos* to a floor cleaner in a supermarket, and finally to a jobless favelada. Sandrinha seemed to follow the same fate: she is now working to get a job and get her kids back from the state orphanage.

At the main gate, two black guards blocked the entryway and asked us where we were going. They demanded to see our identification but before we attended to their request, Dona Maria shouted at them and demanded they open the way as we were going to the office of the public attorney. Upstairs, we entered a large conference room where the public attorney, a white woman, warmly welcomed us. Instead of exchanging pleasantries, however, Dona Maria collapsed into her seat at the table with a torrent of anger and desperation. She unapologetically commandeered the meeting, complaining about the guards downstairs and announcing that she refused to deal with questions other than when she would have the body of her son: "Where is my son? I just want you to bring my son back. When will I have Betinho's body?" I feared that my efforts to organize the meeting were going to be dismantled in a few short minutes. I looked at her and sent some eye signals, trying to get her to be strategic and let the meeting simply happen, but she remained indifferent to the efforts of the task force and continued pressing for a rapid solution. When I tried to intervene, she desperately asked me to stop because she had been "waiting, waiting, and waiting. Until when?" As the lawyer from the black movement tried to calm her down, Dona

Maria insisted that she wanted a resolution to her case because she had been going back and forth for nothing while Betinho's body remained in a plastic bag waiting to be exhumed. "When are you bringing my son?" She started getting demanding, giving orders on where to go and how to make legal claims as if the experts in the room were unfamiliar with the state bureaucracy. Despite my worries that it would be the last chance to have the group together focusing on her case, I was deeply moved by Dona Maria's despair and remained silent at her side for most of it, hoping we would not leave the building empty handed. It is from this position of empathy for her pain and frustration over the state bureaucracy that I later tried to understand the tense exchange at the state attorney's office that afternoon.[1]

A deafening silence filled the room. All of us—the lawyer, the public defender, a representative from the Police Ombudsperson's Office, a psychologist/social worker, a representative of the Human Rights Council, and I—sat for a while in stunned silence as we witnessed her anxiety escalate while she demanded quick answers. Someone tried to explain the steps to making a claim for the exhumation of Betinho's body and where the trial of the Slaughters stood, but Dona Maria turned even more anxious when she heard the word "Slaughters," responding that she would not accept him as bones in a black plastic bag because Betinho had been taken alive by the Slaughters. Dona Maria seemed not to acknowledge Betinho's death and seemed to demand us to bring him back to life. How were we to respond to her despair? Fearful that we were in danger of losing the chance to create a unified strategy for the release of Betinho's remains and enrolling Dona Maria in the state pension program, I tried to interject. But as I began speaking, Dona Maria looked for my solidarity; she impatiently insisted that she had waited for too long and had seen "too much talk and too little action." The public attorney tried to help. "We will not bring back your son," she said, "and no one can compensate you for your pain, your health, your peace. But financial compensation is your right and we will fight for that." Dona Maria interjected yet again: "When? When?" Then, she insisted that the *carniceiros* (butchers) had taken Betinho alive, yet now he was in a black plastic bag waiting for exhumation. "I want my son." The social worker tried to calm her down by assuring her that we all shared her pain and that we were in solidarity with her suffering.

The public attorney reviewed the plan that they had agreed to, which included requests for the governor to release a pension and for the judge in charge of Betinho's case to release his body for a proper burial. The social worker promised to put her on the list for a visit, to file a petition to include her in the housing authority's rental stipend program. Just when it seemed like Dona Maria had calmed down and was beginning to engage with the bureaucratic procedures, she again demanded to know the specific date when she could bury her son: "When, when?"

The group grew impatient. The attorney asked her to wait. Then the human rights lawyer asked her to be reasonable, saying that the state bureaucracy does not work as fast as we may want and that all of us were on her side. The psychologist suggested that she participate in a therapy program to cope with anxiety and depression while waiting for the process to unfold. As we discussed strategies to help her overcome state bureaucracy, Dona Maria grew anxious. She stood up to light a cigarette, and responded from the window by lumping all of us in the room together into a generic *you*, "vocês," as if we were to be blamed for the death of Betinho: "I want my son. Who killed my son? *You* didn't take my son dead! So, now *you all* bring him back. And I will not accept him in a plastic bag. My son was taken alive!" Understandably, she used the generic "you" to refer to the state bureaucracy (that some of my colleagues were representing) as much as to the police. It was perhaps also a call to the societal structure of rights that granted legal protection to individuals like my friends (and to some extent, me myself) in the room (middle class, light skinned, and in my case, formally educated) at the expense of black favelados like her and her son. Within this structure of privilege and disavowal, the distinctions between the perpetrators of Betinho's murder and the bureaucrats in the room (who despite their good faith also benefited from the state's war against the favela) were irrelevant. For Dona Maria, the lethal force unleashed by the police and the "soft knife" of state bureaucracy came together in the kidnapping, killing, and withholding of her son's body.[2] We could not keep up with Dona Maria's demands, which shifted from refusing to accept that her son was dead in a plastic bag to asking for his remains. Just when she seemed to be calm and accept that we were trying to help her, she threw her overdue electricity and rent bills onto the table: "I don't care how you are going to do that, I have no money." The social worker filled out the form to put her on the list of visits, so she could have her situation assessed for entry into an assistance program. She wanted money to pay for her cigarettes, the bus fare, and the overdue rent right away. As I feared, Dona Maria left empty handed.

Dona Maria's survival depended not only on the material conditions she was desperately trying to improve but also on having the right to bury her son, thereby closing a circle of horror that had opened with Betinho's killing two years before. Her anger and unapologetic impatience with the bureaucratic procedures brings to the surface the unbridgeable gap between her personal experiences as a black woman from the favela and the middle-class white privilege of the human rights activists and state bureaucrats around the table. There was a structural positioning that made the conversation appear out of place and her demands irrational. While she insisted on demanding the state bring back (the remains of) her son, the bureaucrats insisted on seeing her as a *coitadinha* (poor thing) and Betinho's death as just another casualty in the Brazilian urban war. Was she demanding that the murderous state produce life? By shifting from demanding a proper funeral to refusing to acknowledge her son's death—"he was not taken in a plastic bag"— she challenged to the extreme the state's murky biopolitical narratives of rights. If the state were to sell the image of peace, human rights, and the fostering of life, then it should prove this capacity by bringing back her son. In the demand for life from a murderous machine, the state was laid bare and no one could respond to Dona Maria's inquiry. The incomprehensibility of her suffering could be seen in the white middle-class lawyers, human rights activists, and civil servants' silence on her inquiry. Her social location as a placeless subject in the anti-black city was reflected in the structure of rights that my friends represented.

In *Scenes of Subjection,* Saidiya Hartman writes that "the elusiveness of black suffering can be attributed to a racist optics in which black flesh is itself identified as the source of opacity, the denial of black humanity, and the effacement of sentience integral to wanton use of the captive body." Hartman asks, "Is not the difficulty of empathy related to both the devaluation and the valuation of black life?"[3] My white counterparts at the meeting with Dona Maria had enormous empathy for her suffering. The conversations before and after the meeting on how to help her secure financial compensation and a place to live attest to that. They were also understanding of her anxiety, particularly the white public attorney. Indeed, they tried hard to help her cope with the exceptional pain generated by Betinho's death. As Hartman forcefully argues, however, this empathetic response itself cancels black suffering as the relational empathy between black victims and white spectators and is only possible through the displacement of black experiences and the valuation of white humanity. It is not an "if I were you" but rather an "if you were me." This displacement also normalizes anti-black violence in that it entails a tacit denial of the implication of "the white community" in the ordinariness of racial terror. Indeed, it is the white subject's negation of its complicity with the structure of terror (and the reading of black death as an individual misfortune) that grants it power over other racialized bodies and allows the reproduction of whiteness in our presumed postracial moment.[4]

When the spectacular death-squad practices of torturing, dismembering, and disappearing black bodies become too grotesque to be ignored, the white subject responds (is confronted) with an empathy that reveals what Charles Mills calls "white blindness," which he conceptualizes as a "cognitive distortion" of the privileges conferred to whites by the unjust racial order.[5] Who do the police protect when they kill black individuals in the "illegal" city, anyway? The white inability to understand black suffering, regardless of white empathy for black pain, is made manifest in the fact that Dona Maria's unapologetic—apparently irrational—demands were the only way she could be noticed in a city where black women occupy invisible spaces as domestic workers, the unemployed, and faveladas. In the racialized regime of Brazilian citizenship, Dona Maria's dramatic appeal to its legal and humanitarian apparatuses was destined to fail. This is not because her demand—that the state bring back the dead—is irrational, but because, as Hartman has shown, the black body is in ontological opposition to the very definition of humanity around which notions of human rights, civil society, and the rule of law are defined. Both Dona Maria's and Betinho's fates were bound to an existential impossibility that allowed white bureaucrats to normalize violence against blacks while simultaneously condemning and detaching themselves from it. What kind of political action would be necessary for the pain of black individuals like Dona Maria to be made legible in the white-controlled political order?

Making Black Death Legible

Abolition Street, in downtown São Paulo, is the location of a task force named the Committee against the Genocide of the Black Population (hereafter the Committee), which serves as an umbrella for different black organizations such as UNEafro, AMPARAR (Association of Parents and Friends of Incarcerated Youth), MNU (Unified Black Movement), Mães de Maio, and the Tribunal Popular (or Popular Trial). The Committee meets sporadically around specific demands pertaining to police violence, mass incarceration, torture, and other human rights violations. A prominent tactic of theirs is to bring collective campaigns and legal claims against the state. The coalition provides spaces for discussing collective strategies against what the movement describes as the "genocide of the black population."

In 2010, I participated in the group's meetings. It was in the aftermath of the killing of two black men at the hands of the Military Police and of the police invasion of Paraisópolis.[6] Eduardo Pinheiro dos Santos, thirty years old, was arrested, tortured, and killed by a police battalion in the north side of the city, while Alexandre Santos, a twenty-five-year-old, was killed on his doorstep by two police officers as his mother, Cidinha, begged for his life. While the cases were not exceptions in Sao Paulo's rotten policing practices, they provided an opening to launch a campaign and, hopefully, to mobilize Brazilian civil society against the "anti-black genocidal state." Black activists articulated several demands, including the immediate resignation of the general commander of the Military Police and the São Paulo state secretary of public safety; the end of the legal classification of killings by the police under the rubric of "resisting arrests"; federal investigation of the May 2006 massacre, in which the police killed hundreds of civilians; the end of police raids in poor, predominantly black communities; and immediate financial compensation for the families of victims of police killings. At the organizational level, there were some tensions regarding the demands that had been laid out in the open letter sent to state authorities. Some activists thought we had set the bar too high since all the demands could not be met at the present but rather were utopian visions for the larger struggle. For instance, some suggested that we should strategically negotiate with the state and not demand the immediate firing of the police commander and the state secretary of public safety. These individuals argued that in demanding the firing of the police commander we were setting the terms of the debate and sending a message to other social movements that they were too naïve in trying to negotiate with the police. Everyone seemed to agree on one thing: we did not hold high hopes for a government whose main political platform was its iron-fist policies. Rather, we were waging an ideological battle over the meanings and rationality of state killings. The goal, many activists agreed, was to politicize black death, demystify state fantasies of "community polic- ing," and denounce the continuous genocide of black people.

Parallel to the endless discussions about political goals, we orga- nized sit-in demonstrations, released open letters, handed out flyers in metro entrances, and held street classes (*classes de cidadania*) about po- lice violence "so we could educate other Afro-Brazilians on the fraud of the Brazilian democratic state of rights," as one of the participants in the Committee stated. 2010 was an election year, and all of us agreed that the government could not afford to ignore our public agenda. And they did not. The state secretary of public safety sent an e-mail to the group asking for an emergency meeting to discuss our demands regard- ing police killings, his firing, and the firing of the Military Police com- mander. Again, we had to decide whether we should sit at the table with state authorities or continue to demand the firing of the police commander as a precondition to any conversation. As we discussed the circumstances and terms under which we should negotiate with the state, some contended that to accept the meeting would mean giving legitimacy to those "with blood on their hands." After heated discus- sion, the majority of us voted to refuse the meeting with the secretariat. Instead, we demanded a meeting with the big fish: the governor, or at least his secretariat of justice. Claudia, a longtime activist in the black movement, became a dissonant voice in the room: the state wanted to co-opt us with "cafezinho e promessas" (coffee and promises), she said. She contended that we would hear the same "conversa-mole" (bunch of hot air) with the government sending black police officers to attend the meeting and promising to investigate the deaths. We should not meet with the secretary of public safety, she commented. What we should do instead was go to the *quebrada* and bring the victims, parents, ex- prisoners, drug dealers, everyone to the discussion on police violence.

Popular education was the answer, she reasoned. "How is it that one day we demand the secretariat be fired and the next day we accept a meeting with him? No one here is a child and we know that if we accept this dialogue tomorrow it will appear in the newspaper's headlines, 'Secretariat dialogues with black movement.' Is that what we want?"

Then, Claudia surprised us by asking how many of us had talked with the PCC members in the *quebrada*. She told us that she had been negotiating with some of the brothers because her son was a drug addict. He had been harassed by the police and had received death threats from the local dealer. Without anyone to protect her son, Claudia went to talk with the Partido. The Partido controlled the periphery and attracted many young black men to its side even as we discussed negotiations with the state in a comfortable room downtown, she contended. Now she wanted to learn what was attracting young people to join PCC. "If the Partido is out there recruiting our sons, they may have something to offer them that we don't have. The problem is that we don't know how to talk with the youth in the *quebrada*. What if these youths want to tell us something but we are not willing to hear?"

As eloquent as it was, Claudia's question was not addressed in the meeting. The question bugged me, though. Although she did not suggest that PCC was a revolutionary pro-black organization, she did ask us to shift our approach from talking with the delinquent state to talking with a "criminal organization" that has been at the center of security concerns in the city. At the same time, the critique of our failure to communicate with the primary victims of police terror was well set. Perhaps we were too domesticated within civil society's politics to consider such a radical shift. To accept her call, we would have to dislodge ourselves from our "law-abidingness" and consider how police terror affects the ways black youth engaged in PCC's practices conceive of political action in the *quebrada*. This was exactly what Claudia asked for. I pressed this matter in many individual encounters with members of the black movement. The common answer was that we were already doing popular education with public meetings in the favela and weekly educational training workshops held in local cells of organizations such as UNEafro, which focus on preparing black youth for the entry exams of public universities. We were not talking with the Partido but were organically working in the community. That was right. Another member took a straightforward pragmatic approach contending that at both the practical and political levels, the movement still had to deal with the issue of how to charge the Brazilian state with genocide and, even more urgently, how to stop killings by the police. Self-defense was out of the question not because we disregarded that as a legitimate response to state terror but because "our first battle is to win the minds of the oppressed" who did not believe in the existence of racism in the first place. "If we are not able even to make the oppressed recognize himself as black, how are we to organize to face the police on the streets?" I shared my skepticism against PCC's agenda, and *neither Claudia nor any of us advocated violence against cops as a strategy for the black movement*. However, underlying Claudia's critiques of the limited effects of our activism was a question that spoke volumes about the shortfalls of black organizers' attempts to make black suffering legible, and subsequently redressed, by the Brazilian state. How could one expect legal protection from a state in which the penal system is designed for white protection? At the same time, we were aware that proximity to organizations like PCC would jeopardize the movement's efforts even more because PCC's violence quite often precipitated and "justified" police terror against black communities. On one occasion, one of the founders of MNU (Unified Black Movement) reprimanded me when I questioned him about PCC's politics: "Don't be naïve. They are part of the problem. You know what is PCC's political agenda? To secure power and make money." Although they did not admit it publicly, some black activists saw in PCC "a latent potential to be explored," as pointed out by another member of the Committee. While he held PCC accountable for some of the violence against the black community and condemned its violent means, he also told me we could not overlook the Partido's role in organizing marginalized youth against police terror even if it was in the criminal organization's own interest. The challenge for black organizers was how to mobilize enraged black youth against racial oppression, something lacking in the Partido's approach. "If PCC had racial consciousness," another lamented, "the periphery would be the most explosive place against racism."

The question was whether one could relate relying on retaliatory violence or on traditional politics of rights to the challenges Dona Maria faced in her legal battle to bring Betinho home. Although she avoided bringing this issue to our conversations and I kept it at bay, she admitted to me that her older son "corre com o Partido" (belongs to PCC) and that after Betinho's death he had considered going after the officers who killed him. Dona Maria discouraged him against doing so, fearing more retaliation from the police, and decided instead to fight the legal battle and bring the killers to justice. While she relied on the legal system, she was aware of the limits of the law in protecting her and her family against police terror; she, like others in the favela, kept the Partido at arm's length but did not condemn its urban riots in 2006. When I asked her about it, she sarcastically laughed and asked me if she needed to remind me who was her "nightmare."

Whether one of retaliatory violence or a larger project of black freedom, the question of armed black resistance is hardly new in Brazilian history. One only has to look at the almost-century-long Republic of Palmares, a complex of maroon communities economically and militarily organized against Portuguese colonizers in the seventeenth century, or the Revolta dos Malês, a Muslim-based slave revolt in the early nineteenth century in the state of Bahia, to demystify accounts of a passive black population waiting for white saviors. In face of white terrorism, blacks sometimes relied on violent acts to defend their lives.[7] A black radical tradition can also be identified in countless small "everyday revolts" by the enslaved (such as poisoning entire families, murdering their masters, freeing other slaves) throughout the colonial period. The fact that the Brazilian authorities had to create an expanded judicial system in the wake of the Haitian revolution to punish black criminality accounts for the growing (fear and) resistance embedded in acts ranging from organized revolts to killing, running away, poisoning masters, and committing suicide.[8] Luis Alberto Couceiro, for instance, tells the story of a spontaneous rebellion by a group of slaves in nineteenth-century Brazil. When Bonifácio, an old slave, was beaten and blinded by an overseer, his colleagues avenged him by beating the overseer to death and taking both his eyes out. The slaves continued to work until dawn; they left for the slave quarter where they ate, rested, and took the long walk to the police station to hand themselves in. Asked who the killer was and why they had killed the overseer, the slaves told the police officer that it was a collective act against the punishments by the overseer. Of this juridical case, one of many registered in the court of Rio de Janeiro by that time, Couceiro observes that the enslaved population relied on the justice system not because they believed in it but rather because they saw it as an opportunity to assert their humanity. Killing was the only way to be legible under the gaze of the state, even though such legibility meant *criminal liability*.[9]

The fundamental question of how to make legal claims in the face of an anti-black regime of law continues to be a historical headache for the modern Brazilian black movement. The very founding act of the leading black movement in the country (the MNU) illustrates this urgency. On July 7, 1978, black activists organized a demonstration in the stairways of the Municipal Theater to denounce the death of Robison Silveira da Luz, a twenty-one-year-old black man tortured in a police precinct in the city of São Paulo for stealing fruits from a truck while on his way home from a party. Brazil was at the highest point of its military dictatorship and the black movement had been swept away from the political scene. Public debate about racism was regarded as a threat to national security and black activists who dared to make public complaints were punished as enemies of the political regime. Tolerance for the black movement was given only insofar as the movement restrained its actions to the realm of culture, narrowly defined as samba schools, culinary festivals, community-level self-help programs, and so on. Black political resistance faced violent repression, death, and political exile.[10] In the second half of the 1970s, however, the modern Brazilian black movement began to embrace a critique of internal colonialism by focusing on what they named as the need for a second (slavery) abolition, influenced by the Black Power movement and the African independence movements.[11] Rampant police violence, poverty, and illiteracy became the urgent problems brought to public debate. Within that context, the death of Robison Luz marked the rebirth of the movement, as illustrated in the open letter from MNU: "Today we are in the streets in a campaign . . . against racial discrimination, against police oppression, against unemployment and marginalization. We are in the streets to denounce the bad conditions of living of the black community. Today is a historic day. A new day begins for black people. We are leaving the room meetings and conference rooms, to go to the streets. A new step has been given against racism."[12]

I exchanged many informal conversations with Miltão, one of the founders of MNU, to understand the motivations behind the founding of the modern black movement. Miltão explained to me that although the outrage generated by the death of Robison Luz was the main motivation in 1978, politicizing his death was an opportunity "to break the culturalist perspective" in black organizing and to mobilize the black population to occupy the streets against racial hostilities. I asked Miltão what we are to make of current waves of police violence despite black organizing back in the day. "The black movement has not been successful in curbing police brutality but at least it has unmasked the myth of racial democracy," Miltão contended, reasoning that black struggle is a "political process" rather than something to be achieved in a single event. He saw the foundation of MNU, and now the Committee against the Genocide of the Black Population, as part of a tireless struggle for black liberation that far preceded the 1970s and that "will continue after we are gone." Although conscious of its setbacks, Miltão reminded me that "if it were not for the black movement, the white elite would have already revoked the Lei Áurea," referring to the legislation that abolished slavery. Seeing black struggle as a political process helped Miltão and many other activists I worked with continue struggling against racism while also counting the bodies and grieving the dead. It also had a profound impact on the ways they dealt with the paradox of demanding rights from the state and denouncing it as a genocidal project.

While not rejecting Claudia's refusal to talk with state representatives—nor dismissing black youth's insurgent practices in the periphery—most of the members of the Committee saw the state not as a one-dimensional oppressive entity but rather as a multifaceted terrain of political disputes. Their political vision could be framed in terms of a "war of positions," in which they sought to transform the state and civil society by producing counterhegemonic narratives of racial relations and of the state as a racially neutral entity. Denouncing state violence and demanding state protection were material dimensions of the struggle to decolonize the nation; after all, as many black protests voiced, "we are also Brazilians." Black activists did not see this as a matter of choosing between a radical or compromising strategy. That is why the open letter of the Committee brought together demands such as banishing the Military Police and demanding affirmative action for black youth in public universities. The decision about attending the meeting with the secretariat of public safety was one of very few possibilities within the constrained terrain for black politics.[13] We did not attend the meeting with the secretariat but instead developed a two-part strategy: the first was to occupy the streets with a "campanha de concientização" (consciousness-raising campaign) to educate the public on how racism shortens black lives. The program included holding open classes on racism in subway stations and buses terminals and distributing flyers to inmates' relatives lining up outside the prison gates. This strategy was seen as very important because it would sustain the long-term project of strengthening the black movement to gain popular support for its more radical (and less palpable) demands. The second strategy was to keep pushing a legal battle through each step of the judiciary system, up to taking the Brazilian state to the international human rights system. Aware of the Brazilian state's ambition to become a global player in matters of human rights, the Committee denounced it, claiming that "a country that aims to become a protagonist and even a referee of the main international human rights concerns cannot promote the ethnocide of a population as it has done. . . . The Brazilian state, instead of promoting human rights, is an agent of violence and death."[14] In order to organize parents of the victims and push the legal battle further, we created a report combining personal accounts from parents of those killed by the police with data from newspapers, the police ombudsperson, and human rights organizations. Before launching a more aggressive campaign, we filed complaints against the government in the state court by sending the dossier to the high command of the Military Police, the Brazilian Ministry of Justice, and the National Secretary of Racial Equality. The document was also distributed to mainstream media outlets, religious groups, and left-wing social movements.

Using the language of rights did not take us too far, but the Committee was able to achieve some short-term goals. The first was to force government authorities to publicly recognize the "crisis" in public safety right in the middle of major electoral campaigns. As the black movement denounced the "new" wave of killings by the police, the Committee's demands for the resignation of the Military Police commander and the secretary of public safety intensified an institutional crisis, with the two state entities caught in the middle of a crossfire and with deputies of opposition parties demanding a response from then Governor

Alberto Goldman. With an eye on the votes of black youth agitators, left-wing candidates began to incorporate the issue of police violence into their campaigns. The Committee distributed the dossier to the state legislature, international human rights organizations, churches, and unions. The Committee also fed the press with information on killings by the police and disturbed everyday city life with continued protests. Although the mass media paid little attention to the Committee's activities, the open classes on police violence in strategic places of the periphery of the city and in the entrances of bus terminals became opportunities to dialogue with the large segment of the black population that, although discriminated against, did not participate in the formal black movement.[15] In particular, UNEafro-Brasil used this approach to protest against the police in strategic places while also collecting signatures to file a petition demanding affirmative action in the state's public universities. Focusing on everyday matters such as unemployment, poor public transportation, and lack of access to education would put forward a less contentious set of demands while also offering an indirect way to contest the myth of racial democracy and strategically play the game of civil society.

The constrained terrain of black protest affected the political lexicon used by black activists. The term *genocide* was especially contentious. If it exposed state terror on the one hand, on the other it put the black movement in an even more precarious position in terms of its capacity to mobilize large publics. The term was never taken seriously by state authorities, who refused even to hold meetings with us, by mainstream NGOs too afraid to be associated with radical politics, and by the white-dominated academy afraid for their intellectual reputation. They saw it as "a certain overstatement," as I heard from an important sociologist at an academic conference, even though the statistics unmistakably point to the orchestrated anti-black practices of the Brazilian state.[16] Abdias do Nascimento authored the first publication accusing the state of a "dissimulated and sophisticated schema of genocide" against Afro-Brazilians. In *Brazil: Mixture or Massacre,* Nascimento listed several genocidal practices ranging from official immigration policies that aimed to "improve the race" by bringing white Europeans to the country to discriminatory practices in access to education, housing, health care, the job market, and the denial of full rights of citizenship.[17]

More recently, an emerging field of black studies has recuperated his claim, addressing the theoretical problem posed by the use of the Jewish holocaust as *the* reference for its legal definition. Echoing the black movement, they center their critique not only on the overtly present practices of targeted assassination of blacks by the police but also on the mundane violence Nascimento identified in state-sanctioned practices that prevent and limit black life in Brazil.[18]

Within the black movement, the term "black genocide" has become a common ground for a diverse and multifaceted agenda that includes land rights, access to health care and education, the struggle against police brutality and mass incarceration, and so on. The broader political alliances united under the Committee in São Paulo was an example of how the term could be deployed to mobilize intersecting agendas around structural vulnerabilities while also putting police terrorism into sharp focus. Aware of the constraints posed by the legal definition of genocide as an "intentional" act of mass killing, the Committee backed up its claim by producing a dossier with names and statistics on deaths by the police in the periphery of the city. The document, which related police killings to spatial segregation, unemployment, and poverty, was presented at public events and released to state authorities and mainstream human rights organizations. The message was that anti-black genocide is not a historical event that one could point to on the calendar but rather the cumulative effect of everyday acts and institutionalized practices that produce *vulnerabilities* to death. It was a member of the Committee who provided an expanding perspective on the term during a protest:

> There is an ongoing genocide against black people. This genocide permanently manifests itself in our everyday, in the day-to-day of our people. It happens, for instance, in the lines of the emergency room, in the school system that *educa para o preconceito* [educates to prejudice]. The genocide is also in the job market, in low-paid jobs, in the negative perception of our culture, in the inefficiency of public policies; all that incarcerates, tortures, and kills our people. This is genocide. Here is the pretext of the main text: *pode matar, vão morrer de qualquer jeito* [go ahead and kill, they will die anyway]. The process of [the formation] of the white elite was itself a genocidal process.

Focusing on Brazil's history of racial terror, the black movement also questioned the narratives put forward by the state, in which racism is viewed only as a matter of individual behavior. If we were to consider such a narrow definition, we would also have to accept the individualized responses that state authorities usually give when the black movement denounces their anti-black policing practices. If these were acts of racism by individuals, then they could be redressed by taking racist officers off the streets. Although organizing against police killings was an urgent matter that required some pragmatism, members of the Committee determined that we also had to focus on the broad practices of racial domination that the state supported even when the state was not directly implicated in those practices. That is why focusing on racialized outcomes produced by the cumulative and mundane violence of everyday state practices was a better strategy than spending time going over the legal definition of what *genocide* entails. In Douglas Belchior's words, "this is the genocidal process . . . we are killed by diseases, unemployment, hunger, and by police bullets."[19] Put another way, while the state demanded a legal definition as a precondition for any conversation, the movement gave it the hungry, sick, wounded, caged, or killed bodies of its victims in return. The question then became: What to make of such an expanding and radical definition of black suffering—as black genocide—in line with the black movement's reliance on the state to redress state terror?

Occupying the Governor's Office

After long discussions about whether the group should attend the meeting with the secretary of public security, the Committee decided to protest in the palace of the state governor. The group was not optimistic about the results of this strategy, but there was a common understanding that if we wanted to call attention to our demands we would have to promote disorder. Unable to galvanize large publics around the movement's agenda, some members were worried about police repression while others reasoned that if we were to wait for solidarity from mainstream social movements, "the police would kill us before they woke up." The criticism, nicely put forth by one of the attendees, was not an overstatement. Although white-led human-rights-based NGOs were very vocal in denouncing police violence and expressed sympathy for black activists' claims at times, black mobilization against black genocide was a lonely enterprise. White-led NGOs went to the favela as part of the project of state control rather than to demand the end of policing.

Knowing well the place that the black agenda occupied in left-oriented social activism, and in the face of the urgency of "stopping the killings of our youth," we decided to cross the city and go to the governor's official residence in the fancy neighborhood of Morumbi to pressure him into receiving our dossier in person. We were about ten individuals. We had not planned on entering the building, but then someone had the idea to occupy the highly secure facility. The group split; some of us stood along the wall while others arrived at the main gate of the governor's residence under the pretext of needing to file a document with the public relations office. Although the general public has access to the protocol session, a group arriving together would draw the guards' attention. As the guard opened the gate, we jumped into the protocol session. The guards tried to block the second gate but we pressured them, arguing that we needed to see the governor's assistant secretary in order to follow up on a letter we had sent months earlier. After a long discussion and several phone calls, they let us into the main building where we demanded to be received not by the secretariat of public safety but by Governor Alberto Goldman or by Antonio Marrey, his secretary of justice. A black woman in military uniform was sent to tell us that the secretary of justice's agenda was full for days and that he could not see us. She promised us our letter had already been delivered to the governor and he would be answering it in writing soon. Bispo, one of the most eloquent among us, sarcastically told the woman that we were not in a rush. We were prepared to wait all night for someone from the governor's office to attend to us, he told her. As we occupied the room, sitting around a table, she went to tell the secretary of justice that we would stay until he met with us.

Meanwhile, we discussed what we wanted to get from the lone protest. Would it have any impact or would it weaken our powers of negotiation if the secretariat refused to receive us? If we accepted the woman's word that the governor was going to respond to our demands it would be an honorable withdrawal for the moment, but that also meant further delays from his office. We also worried about the obvious: an occupation of the building without media coverage or any kind of visibility would make us vulnerable to violence without any gain. Until then, the guards had been patient. The strategy of occupying public buildings was not new for any of us: we had all occupied shopping malls and public universities to denounce institutional racism. For instance, we had occupied the Law School of the University of São Paulo (USP) years earlier to demand affirmative action for black youth and we had occupied the office of the secretary of justice a year prior. The police harshly reprimanded the protests, but the demonstrations made news headlines, unveiling the racist practices of the USP and the governor. Now, at the governor's office, we were far fewer individuals; worse, we were behind closed doors away from public sight, which made us easy prey for the police.

Some members of the group wanted to stay and call the alternative media, announcing that we were in the governor's office and would not leave until the secretariat of public safety and the commander of the Military Police were fired. Soon, someone reasoned that the alternative media would have no impact in shaping public discourse and thus bring no political consequences for the moment. Others proposed that we "get the hell out of the office before things get hot" and reiterate our request for an official response to our demands. If the governor still refused to respond, that would not be a failure because we would have additional justification to take the legal battle a step further by asking for a federal investigation of the crimes committed by the police. An intermediate option was to push a little further, hoping the governor or at least the secretariat of justice would receive us, so that we could deliver the dossier and our list of demands. We decided to press a little further and continue waiting in the office.

Thirty minutes later, we were met by Walter, an overweight white man in his early sixties. He was a former state congressman and now served as special advisor to the governor. Visibly disturbed by our presence, he ordered someone to serve us coffee and tea and apologetically justified the governor's refusal to meet with us. The meeting turned out to be an interesting contrast between the black activists' politics of urgency and Walter's bureaucratic-rational narratives of state violence. Walter asked us to be patient because the governor's agenda was very busy. He introduced himself as someone who was sympathetic to the black movement's agenda because he had "many black friends" and was committed to finding an effective way to deal with our demands. Railda from AMPARAR (Association of Parents and Friends of Incarcerated Youth) recounted our unsuccessful attempts and frustrations going through endless bureaucracy just to file a request to schedule a meeting with state officials, "all to no avail." Pointing to Cidinha, the mother of Alexandre, a black young man who had been killed months earlier by the Military Police, Railda concluded: "Your government simply turned its head and pretended that the police are not killing black people in the favelas."

Marisa, the only white activist–researcher in the group, then updated Walter on the secretary of public safety's invitation to meet with the group. "The problem is that we do not want to talk with the secretary. We want him to be fired," she concluded. After he knew the secretary was willing to receive us, Walter changed his strategy and accused us of being difficult. "So the secretary is calling you to talk, and you don't want to talk? What kind of negotiators are you?" The group jumped at him. "Don't try to teach us how to do politics," someone shouted at him. Laughing nervously, Walter offered to distribute our dossier to the secretary of public safety and the secretariat of justice. The group refused to hand him the document, knowing it would soon be just another file on someone's desk. "If you give me the document, I will file it right away. Why do you want to fight with us? We are sensitive to this demand and we will help you with it," said Walter. Someone in the group replied, "We don't want to fight. The problem is that you are fighting with us. Your police are fighting with us." Then, Bispo gave him a final challenge: "We want to let you know that this is the last of a series of steps that will result in a UN petition. We are passing through each stage, trying to have a meeting to discuss this matter, and you guys are refusing to receive us. Open your eyes. I am not sure the governor would like to see this happen."

Not sure how to respond to Bispo's threat, Walter promised us he would try right away to have at least the secretary of justice to come down and receive us. We took our banners from our backpacks and hung them around the room while awaiting his return, hopefully with the secretary of justice. For a moment, the group was confident the protest inside the governor's own house would result in a small victory, that is, to be received by at least a senior official from the governor's cabinet who would hear our demands and hopefully release financial compensation for women like Dona Maria and Cidinha. "Let's not fool ourselves. This is not a matter of meeting with us or not. We need to be clear on that because if they meet us, it does not mean that our demands will be addressed," Bispo pointed out, making sure we were all on the same page regarding the demands put out by the committee. A few minutes later, Walter came back. He told us that our previous letter had been misplaced and that he had just located it. He also guaranteed us that it would be delivered to the governor and that he would suggest the creation of a work group to address our demands to the governor. "This sucker is bluffing trying to get us tired," I thought.

It was clear that Walter had not talked with his colleagues but was trying to extend the waiting time, perhaps in the hope that we would give up. As we began shouting that "we are not children," and "the governor is racist," Walter admitted that no one would be able to meet with us because the secretary of justice was "uncomfortable" that we were demanding the firing of one of his colleagues (the secretariat of public safety). "It is a real cause of discomfort, and neither the governor nor his secretary will receive the group if you don't take this demand off the table," he said. Railda interjected, "We have here someone who had a son killed by your troops. We have others whose sons are in your prisons, and we demand that the secretary has at least the good sense to hear the mothers." I intervened, saying that he was treating the firing of the secretary of public safety as if it were our main demand, and reminded him that the main point was the killings of black youth by the police. Walter disagreed, arguing that we were coming to the governor's house to establish the terms of the negotiation and that he and other government officials could not negotiate with "a knife at the neck." The urgent matter of police assassination of black individuals was nothing more than a minor problem from the point of view of the bureaucratic rationality that Walter represented. As Walter dismissed black victimization, our rage toward him grew. Pressed against the wall, he had no choice but to listen to our shouts of "your state" and "your government" that demarcated the political terrain in the same way that Dona Maria had done in our meeting in the state attorney's office. He shouted back, saying we "didn't know how to live under democracy" and that he was democratic enough to let us protest. Marisa asked him to "shut up and listen to a mother's cry," pointing to Cidinha. Perhaps appealing to a mother's pain would soften Walter's heart and let us have a conversation with the secretariat of justice. Cidinha, who had been quiet the whole time, told Walter about the moment when Alexandre was killed in front of her on her own doorstep just a few months earlier.

I had heard about Alexandre's death on the news. The case drew media attention because it had occurred soon after the killing of another black man Eduardo who had called the police to help him recover his son's stolen bicycle. Instead of looking for the bicycle, the police took Eduardo to the police battalion, tortured him, and killed him. Since the case was too abhorrent to be ignored and had been strongly denounced by eyewitnesses, it generated significant repercussions. The killing of Alexandre weeks later was seen as a continuation of the crisis in the police command. As usual, the newscasts portrayed Alexandre as a criminal suspect whose death had been precipitated by his alleged resistance against arrest.[20] According to the police, Alexandre evaded a checkpoint, resisted arrest, and eventually died while the police were transporting him to the hospital. But Dona Cidinha told me a different story when I paid her a visit.

It was late at night when she heard the police sirens at her front door. Then she heard Alexandre's voice: "Mom, mom!" She ran and opened the window, and saw a police officer beating Alexandre in his face, while another threw his motorcycle to the side as he kept crying out. "I don't know where I got the courage. I just know that I ran out to them, without sandals, wearing my sleeping clothes, and started crying out that he was my son." As she cried out, and as Alexandre struggled, the police officers kept kicking him in his back and in his face with their boots. They eventually stood him up and he fell to his knees, vomiting. Then one of them grabbed his neck and broke it in front of her. "I knew they had broken it because I saw he was trying to grab the gate and his hands stopped in the air . . . All that, right here, in front of me. Right there . . . Nobody on the street [at] two in the morning, only my son and I, struggling with the police . . ."

She resumed this story at the governor's office, pointing at Mr. Walter's face: "You are complicit with that, and you don't do anything to stop these killings. When is your government going to stop killing our sons?" Walter laughed and told Dona Cidinha that she was making "moral judgments." "Are you saying that the government is killing these people, that we are against human rights?" All of us cried out, saying "Yes!" He reminded us, then, that the government had expressed goodwill by offering us a meeting and we were the ones turning it down. Dona Cidinha asked, "I am sure that you haven't had a son even beaten by the police, have you?" To our surprise, Walter compared Dona Cidinha's loss with the kidnapping of his own son ten years earlier. "We had to negotiate for five hours with the criminals. So, it seems your opinion does not apply to everybody. My family was in a dangerous position as well." Angrily, Bispo responded, "Your son had the chance to negotiate with the criminal. Did these guys [black youth] in the favela have a chance to negotiate with the police?"

There was general outrage at Walter's attempt to equate the kidnapping of his son with the killing of Dona Cidinha's son by Military Police officers. His labeling of Dona Cidinha's assessment of police terror as simply a matter of "moral judgment" and his attempt to teach us how we should negotiate with the state illustrated the impossibility of establishing dialogue even on concrete topics such as the death of Alexandre. For Walter, the activists in the room were making biased judgments about state practices. It was clear to everyone else in the room, however, that the same state that protects Walter's son also (or because of that) produces dead bodies like that of Alexandre. It was also evident that the governor, Mr. Walter, and the police officers on the street all participate in the necropolitical dynamics of terror and bureaucracy under the service of state making. Not surprisingly, the state that had been depersonalized in the case of the Slaughters (according to Mr. Pontarelli, it was *individuals* rather than the *institution* who committed these crimes) was now anthropomorphized by Mr. Walter as a "being" to be defended against Dona Cidinha's moral judgments.[21] In deep frustration, Dona Cidinha started gathering her bag while saying, "In reality, we are here wasting our time. They will not meet with us, it will not change, and the police will keep killing. Today, right now, youth are dying, that does not matter to you, disappearing . . . When are we going to be heard, Mr. Walter? When? Next year?" As we made our way out, Marisa approached Walter, pointed at him, and said, "Look how foolish we were, bringing this mother to put this document in the governor's hands. Now he sent you as the *carrasco* [hangman] to receive us. You know that the secretary of public safety is an assassin." Walter tried to have a final word in his defense but we were already on our way out of the door. Then Bispo cried out to him, "Don't worry. Everyone has a role in this racist society. This is yours."

Black Mothering Politics

"I fight from my womb, a womb that was rooted out by the state" says Debora Silva, one of the main organizers of Mães de Maio (Mothers of May), the movement formed mostly by black mothers whose children had been killed by the police. When she dialed a radio station on the evening of May 16, 2006, Debora heard that her son, Edson Rogério da Silva, had been killed. It was Mother's Day in Brazil. The radio journalist started reading the names of sixteen youth killed just hours before and Edson, who had had the day off from his job as a garbage collector, was among them. She later learned that he was killed at a gas station soon after he had left her home, where he had come to celebrate Mother's Day. Like Debora, Railda told me of a "conhecimento vivido" (lived knowledge) that supersedes any academic explanation about the ways black women encounter the state. Railda has been actively working against mass incarceration since the late 1990s, when her teenage son was sent to the infamous Febem, the juvenile detention center. Like Debora, Railda funded AMPARAR, an organization of parents of prisoners fighting against mass incarceration. Railda and Debora's practices can be read through what Patricia Hill Collins calls the "dialectic of black motherhood," in which black women resist racial oppression by reclaiming their identities as (social) mothers. Their maternal activism is an "effort to retain power over motherhood so that it serves the legitimate needs of their communities."[22] Such a framework is particularly important in the context of urban violence in Brazil because, as the previous chapters make clear, regulating *black motherhood* and *black gender* is an essential aspect of the security strategies of the Brazilian state in its control of black geographies. In that sense, to situate the category "black mothering" within the realm of the struggle against racialized police terror is also to account for the dialectics of their gendered racial interpellation as "mothers of criminals" and for their self-making as social mothers. These dialectics are no better articulated than in the "lived experience" of terror that Railda points out and in the "fight from the wombs," as Debora reminds us.

In her struggle to bring her son home from prison, Railda also embarked on a journey of self-making. She educated herself about the penal system and began organizing other mothers whom she met at the prison gate. "We literally moved to prison with our sons. I was there the whole day, sometimes even slept there. After a while we were almost sixty mothers taking turns there," Railda recalls, referring to the permanent vigils to prevent abuses by prison agents in the overcrowded youth prison. Their protests at the prison gates received news coverage and the prison administration was forced to negotiate with the mothers for a solution to the "humanitarian crisis" generated by repeated rebellions in the prison system. The mothers took on a leadership position to prevent abuses such as the 1992 Carandiru Massacre—in which state troops invaded the prison of Carandiru and killed 111 prisoners—that was still fresh in their memories. From their common experience, they organized themselves as AMAR (Association of the Mothers of Imprisoned Adolescents), a word that in Portuguese also means *love*.[23] Their advocacy for forgotten prisoners and their demand for parents' rights to visit their children and to have them placed in facilities close to their homes resonated among the poor and predominantly black women who started joining them. Railda put it this way:

> We could not stay at home crying. We had to cope with our monsters and speak out in the street. That was when I decided to go after other mothers and starting organizing to bring our children home. Did I have another choice? Yes, I did. I could stay on my sofa crying, I could move to another place, I could even have revolted and start getting involved with all these stuffs out there [referring to the drug trafficking in the stairways of her housing project], but I decided to do something else. This is the way I found to not be consumed by angst and depression.

Debora also found in the Mães de Maio collective her "reason to continue living," after spending one month paralyzed in a hospital bed in state of shock over Edson's death. She first began a solitary journey trying to bring the officers responsible for Edson's death to trial, but soon recognized the institutional obstacles she would face as a favelada black woman. Then she began to call the mothers of other youth killed in the same bloody week of May 2006 and they started their own investigation to put together evidence linking the police to the massacre. "Nobody cared about us," Debora told me, remembering the long waits in the Police Ombudsperson's Office, at the information desk of the public attorney's office, and at the city council. Seen as "mothers of criminals"—in the news and in police discourses, the killed were PCC members and thus deserved to die—the women began a struggle based on their identity as *mothers*. The multiple ways they were interpellated before and after their children's death (through spatial segregation, police terror, and media-fed stereotypes) informed their resignification of their "motherhood" as a vehicle for radical politics. That is to say, mothering appeared as a political identity strategically forged under conditions not chosen by black women, but in which they were interpellated as such by the state and (white) civil society. This process of self-making is evident in Debora's discovering her own identity as a black woman. According to her, before Edson's death she had never thought of herself as black, as her friends referred to her as *moreninha* (little brunette), the euphemism that characterizes the everyday denial and enactment of racism in Brazil:

> When I learned that my son received the death penalty in the gas station *"morreu, voce é ladrão, neguinho"* [you're dead, you're a thug, blackie], I realized that I was not *morena*, that I was not *mulata*. . . . I was black because my son was of my skin color. I began to see openly that racism is the central factor for all violations of human rights in Brazil because racism throws you into poverty. . . . Then comes genocide, mass incarceration. . . . This is the reality because Brazil is a country that continues in slavery.

While inferring that Debora lacked racial awareness prior to Edson's death would be a problematic assertion—I doubt this was the only moment of racial interpellation she had faced as a favelada black woman— the deadly "invitation" to be black (a "call" she and her son could not refuse to "attend") is quite indicative of the "macabre form of certainty" that race provides in the supposedly ambiguous mode of Brazilian racial relations.[24] It also gives us a way to think about the intimate relation between death and black subjectivity, not only in terms of the dying conditions blacks live their lives but also in terms of the "productive" work of police terror in generating racial subjects. When she discovered the deadly interpellation of her son—"you dead, you are a blacky thug"—Debora's reasoning was that if her child was killed for being *neguinho,* then what was she? Pain, grief, and anger generated another sort of blackness, one that "speaks from the wombs" to promote black life. As Debora points out, "the struggle has resurrected my son . . . he demands justice and I cannot deny him that."

The political symbolism of the womb is self-evident in the context of the concerted assault on black reproductive labor by the state. Such violence is explicit in some of the Military Police's slogans that stress precisely the opposition between the mother giving birth and the police taking life. The slogan of ROTA, the São Paulo equivalent to the U.S. SWAT team, says: "God gives birth and the ROTA takes it away." To counteract the murderous state, Mães de Maio are very vocal in asserting their biological mothering—"we suffer nine months to give birth, then we give birth, we educate, and the state comes and take their lives as if they were a cockroach." And still, while their collective identity as "mothers" strategically reaffirmed their parental status and some cultural constructs of maternal love, it also questioned the heteronormative assumptions that reduce women to their bodies (equating mothering and childbearing with womanhood). The mothers call the victims of police and black youth in the movement "our children." Although very few in number, some men have also joined the movement, along with other relatives of the deceased. According to Debora, most of the victims' fathers did not participate because they were afraid of being targeted by the police. Other men, she complains, expected them to "go back home to take care of the family" or to return to their jobs to help with the family's needs, now further compromised by the killing of one family member.

Debora saw her activism as reproductive labor, and as such her fight was also against the structural violence of poverty, unemployment, and spatial segregation that prevents the cultural and economic sustainability of everyday black life. In fact, the political capital of Mães de Maio came from their ability to stress the connections between police terror and the reproduction of the city's unjust social order. "The police are fed by misery. The middle class is the one that funds these deaths

Protest against police violence in front of the secretariat of justice on the tenth anniversary of the 2006 May Massacre (Crimes de Maio). Photograph by Mães de Maio.

and the upper class advocates the peace of [the] cemetery to continue [being] rich," Debora says. By focusing on poverty, the movement was also able to launch a systemic critique of state violence and in doing so opened a space to speak to working-class parents who, although overwhelmingly black, were reluctant to join the racially loaded discourse of the traditional black movement.

The mothers from AMPARAR also embraced the intersectional categories of "favelada" or "from the periphery" as spatial referents to their antiprison struggle. Since the favela is a gendered spatiality constituted through processes of state carcerality—police violence, mass incarceration, and structural violence at large—their maternal activism was also an activism against the forces that produce the favela as prison. The capacity of Mães de Maio and AMPARAR to launch a systemic critique of police based on their identity as *mothers* while also mobilizing individuals under the general umbrella of the "poor favelada working class" resonates with organizing strategies similar to those scholars have noted in other contexts of the African Diaspora. Ruth Gilmore's work with "Mothers Reclaiming Our Children" (ROC) in Los Angeles is a case in point here. Ignited by the killing of a young black man by LAPD in November 1991, ROC sought to organize grieving black and working-class mothers, friends, and gang members against mass incarceration and racialized police brutality in Los Angeles' inner city. Gilmore argues that the shared social conditions created by the state in deindustrialized L.A. were the basis for a broad alliance to protect the common interest of their community and hold some autonomy over their lives. By contextualizing the killings and incarceration of their children within the larger context of economic and political crisis, ROC was also able to mobilize a large group of women whose reproductive and social labor was threatened by the restructuring neoliberal racial state. Gilmore notes that, "they remained at the fore, in the spaces created by intensified imprisonment of their loved ones, because they encountered many mothers and others in the same social locations eager to join the reclamation project. And they pushed further, because from those breaches they saw and tried to occupy positions from which collectively to challenge their political, economic and cultural de-development brought about by the individualized involuntary migration of 'urban surplus population,' and the potential values that go with that population, into rural prisons."[25]

While the Brazilian mothers embraced a radical political project "to demilitarize the police," "to bring the prisoners home," and "to transform Brazil into a true democracy," the structure of oppression in São Paulo—economic disempowerment, spatial segregation, collective police raids—severely limited their capacity to mobilize captive communities. The clear connection to the larger context notwithstanding, they faced great challenges in organizing disenfranchised individuals living in the shadow of death and incarceration. "To mobilize the mothers [Railda tells me], we need to focus on their urgent need first. Someone was arrested, someone was beaten by the police, and someone was killed. How are we going to respond? If we fail to support when they need most, they will not be with us fighting against the state." She was referring to the overwhelming demands from victims of police violence that inundated AMPARAR's unstaffed office and to the difficulties the mothers spatially dispersed in the urban sprawl of poverty and police violence faced in crossing the city to attend meetings in the east side. Railda's statement was also a critique of some activists who considered AMPARAR's approach not radical enough: instead of organizing carceral communities against penal abolitionism, AMPARAR spent most of its energy attending to individual calls from mothers desperately trying to free their sons from the hands of the police. In many instances, this critique was made by white activists who insisted on pushing AMPARAR to a more "radical approach against the state." To Railda, the abstract term "fight against the state" had to be translated into the everyday activism that helped depressed and disenfranchised faveladas get by. Radical changes would have to wait for them to rebuild their destroyed captive communities.

I worked closely with Railda in 2010 to help organize the annual Tribunal Popular (Popular Trial), a public forum in which the state is symbolically held accountable for its crimes.[26] Every year the Tribunal Popular, comprised of dozens of social movements, focuses on a pressing problem: its focus in 2010 was to mobilize the population against police terror and mass incarceration. In the days prior to the "trial" I joined Railda in talking with women who were waiting in the prison line for weekend visits. We also visited former prisoners and relatives of those killed by the police. I also took advantage of my work with the Advocacy Network to connect with prisoners in the detention center and with their families in the favelas. Since the elections were approaching, the group decided to mobilize people around a very specific injustice: the state's denial of prisoners' rights to vote. Besides the fact that it would give us an opportunity to speak directly to the large and dispersed population affected by São Paulo's criminal justice system, it would also help us make the point that the inmates were political prisoners because they were excluded from civil life in a country where supposedly anyone could vote and run for public office.

Advised by some activists who were lawyers, we filed legal petitions against the state government demanding that prisoners waiting for their trials be granted their right to vote, as mandated by the constitution. Although the Supreme Court of Justice ruled for the right of prisoners to vote—the right is granted only to predetainees, not sentenced prisoners—the state officials in São Paulo's predetention center ignored that decision by arguing that they could not guarantee a safe electoral process within the crowded prisons. Anticipating the judges' refusal of prisoners' rights, we filed petitions in several courts to increase the chances of having at least one case fall into the hands of a progressive judge. Of the more than fifty petitions that we filed with the courts, only one ruling supported our demand that the state authorities grant prisoners the right to vote. This decision was overturned days later based on a claim by state attorneys, who said that granting prisoners participation in the elections would endanger public safety and that the general interest of society should take priority over individual rights. All of the effort from prisoners filling out petitions and us mobilizing their families resulted in disappointment. As frustrating as this result was, the mobilization nonetheless opened a space for discussing mass incarceration and police terrorism in São Paulo from the perspective of the victims.

We set up the date for the Tribunal Popular on December 4, 2010, in downtown São Paulo. The date was strategically chosen to serve as a counterpoint to the celebration of the sixtieth anniversary of the Universal Declaration of Human Rights. The "Trial" brought together around one hundred individuals from a range of social movements (supporters of land rights and free bus fares alongside those fighting against housing discrimination, police violence, and mass incarceration) to symbolically judge the Brazilian state for the "concerted genocide" of black and poor youth. Mimicking a real trial, families of victims, lawyers, and activists took turns demanding the condemnation of the state as a genocidal machine while other individuals played the role of state bureaucrats and right-wing groups defending mass incarceration and police repression against the enemies of public order. This pedagogical approach proved to be a rich moment for designing strategies to fight back against the expanding penal state. One of the main concerns voiced by activists was the need to bring the discussion to the favelas and to prisons because "these two places are where we find the main victims of the assassin state," as one of the participants explained. By the end of the day, we had developed a working plan that included an extended alliance of progressive social movements, *aulas públicas* (open classes in the streets) to raise political consciousness, the distribution of flyers during visitation days at prisons, and a network of solidarity to support former prisoners in organizing themselves.

Although the forum attracted members of several social movements who generally did not express critiques against the state along the lines of racial justice, the most insightful moments in the discussions came from black women's analyses of their own encounters with police repression. A young black woman Angela who was arrested when selling pirated DVDs in downtown São Paulo, told us she always felt out of place in the city: "Imagine, black, woman, curly hair, from Capão Redondo (in the Fundão da Zona Zul), what is she doing here in downtown? Theft! Let's keep her locked for three years." Angela served time on three occasions in the infamous Febem (juvenile detention center), the same juvenile prison system Railda's son had served time in some years before. She thanked the organizers for trusting her and inviting her to speak about her experience without condemning the wrongdoings that she had been arrested for. Visibly moved to have the microphone to share her life trajectory, she asked us not to support civil society's rhetoric of respectability and to reclaim prisoners as part of the community instead. Angela asked us to embrace individuals like her and denounced the discrimination she felt even among social movements supposedly committed to antiprison practices: "Who see me tells, 'gosh, this girl is not an angel to have ended up in jail three times.' I did rob, I robbed a lot, dealt drugs a lot, was arrested few times . . . but I am here because some people believed in me."

The Trial also played the important role of bringing the invisible face of the criminal justice system to the discussion. Railda, for instance, brought up the struggle the mothers had to go through to visit their sons. According to her, many women were tired and had given up visiting because of the humiliation they had to pass through at the prison gates. Many women had to sleep at the prison gates to secure a slot to visit their children. When they were about to enter the prison, the prison guards would arbitrarily deny them access or take them for bodily cavity searches. The reason the women were giving up visiting their sons, Railda explained, was because it was emotionally overwhelming, bodily painful, and economically impossible to travel miles away from home and spend their limited money to be humiliated, raped, and denied access. "Our son is labeled as criminal and we are too. Your son is delinquent, marginal . . . this is what the family hears when visiting them." Other mothers and relatives of prisoners corroborated this experience, repeating the sentiment that they were arrested with their children, or, as they say, "puxando a cadeia junto" (doing time together). At the Tribunal Popular, they denounced the myriad ways the state punished them: the abusive prison guards, the lack of access to their children's judicial processes, the way the police treated everyone in the community as a criminal.

Their lived knowledge of "what it is like to have a child kidnapped by the state," in Railda's words, superseded the intellectual discussions that sometimes overshadowed their voices in the Tribunal. As some scholars engaged in fruitless debate on what "the state" means, they pointed to its outcomes in their lives and in the lives of the endangered youth in and out of prison. Meire, a young black activist from the hip-hop movement, urged the participants to consider the violence that plagued the city's periphery as programmatic violence against the poor. She concluded by warning us: "If we think it is an isolated event, we lose the chance to form a movement to resist this calamity . . . this genocide that is happening here in São Paulo." According to Meire, we underestimate the state's ability to fragment the struggle and destroy "our" communities. If we wanted to be effective in our strategy, she urged, we would have to change the ways we organize:

> My voice here is asking for help to unite ourselves—to strengthen these women that have their lives destroyed by the state, that haven't even the money to come here today. So, we need to review how to organize ourselves, not to be isolated but to have a collective understanding of what this violence is about and how it affects us all. We need to wake up as soon as possible to prevent more deaths by the assassin state.

The Cynical State

Timely as it was, the urgent action to stop mass incarceration and police terror found serious constraints such as the lack of financial support for impoverished families without money to even pay the bus fare to join the meetings. The Tribunal Popular in downtown São Paulo united people from different parts of the city, but this was an exceptional moment. As Railda voiced, the everyday struggle to make ends meet in the city's shrinking job market, the spatial isolation and fragmentation of the population in the hyperperiphery of the city, the high cost of bus fares, and the fear that the police imposed on the families of its victims were some of the challenges that activists faced in mobilizing the favelados. While mainstream human rights organizations could organize workshops and endless discussions about police violence (they were clever in securing funding from international NGOs and the government for this), organizations like AMPARAR and Mães de Maio counted on self-help campaigns to do their work. At AMPARAR, Railda was usually overwhelmed by calls to assist families of youth who had been imprisoned or kidnapped by the police, or with requests for help with food stamps or medical prescriptions. Understaffed and with minimal structure, the organization's headquarters is a small room in a two-story building that she shared with other grassroots organizations in Zona Leste, in the east side of the city. Several attempts to complete her bachelor's degree at a law school had collapsed in face of the urgency of mothers crying at her doorstep or her own need to protect her son from the police again and again. "At times I myself want to attend a call and run to the police station with a mother but I don't have money to pay for the bus." The mothers have no money even to visit their children in jail, let alone to attend a protest downtown, Railda reasoned.

Other mothers struggled with their deteriorating health after the arrest or killing of their children. Tonia, one of AMPARAR's organizers, was confined to a wheelchair after suffering two strokes, the most recent of which following the arrest of her twenty-eight-year-old son Antonio. Tonia had a speech impediment due to the stroke and spoke in an almost-unintelligible whisper. When I met her, she was living in a shack built below a bridge on the east edge of the city. Tonia and Railda had met in 1998 at the gates of the juvenile detention center. They both were among the parents in vigil at the prison gate to prevent the police from invading the facility. Tonia recalls a moment when the police tried to invade the detention center and they all decided to hold on to the gates in order to avoid the invasion: "It was a scary moment with these officers standing armed and stepping with their boots in front of us to make us get back. . . . But we couldn't cross our arms. . . . Our sons depended on us to do this or they would all be killed," she recalls. After that particular rebellion, Tonia and Railda began organizing other parents in the prison lines during their weekend visits; together they founded AMPARAR, the organization made up of the parents of incarcerated youth. Tonia recounted the days when she and Regina traveled around the state organizing mothers. She told me that she wanted to be back in the struggle because staying at home confined to a chair was "like being in another prison." Overcoming numerous obstacles, AMPARAR managed to free several individuals from prison and became an important group in the city's antiprison movement.

The two women recognized their achievements even as they complained that their work was like "drying ice." Although they had spent a considerable part of their lives organizing parents and trying to mobilize mainstream organizations around their demands, most of their claims were dismissed and the prisons continued to fill up with black bodies. Tonia and Railda reminisced about several of the children they had protected over the years, noting that some had been killed, some were back in prison, and others were now members of the PCC or drug dealers in the *quebrada*. Railda described these pitfalls as part of the patient and slow process of change. Tonia, on the other hand, saw this as an illustration of the triumph of the carceral state: "We worked hard all that time, and what have we got? When we look back, what we see is that there are more people in jail and more people killed by the police than when we began," Tonia contended.

Her frustration may have been bolstered by her own struggle to keep her own son out of the hands of the state. Back in the 1990s, Antonio was arrested and charged for drug trafficking as he was an addicted young man. She told the judge that her son did not have anything; she was the one paying for his clothes and food. If he were a dealer, he would at least have some money. She asked the judge to send her son to a health clinic instead of prison, but the judge would not be swayed. "She looked at me up down and said, 'Your son is a danger to society. He will stay in prison.'" Powerless, Tonia accepted the verdict and gave Antonio a hug before they took him away. She passed most of a decade struggling, with Antonio moving back-and-forth between prison and the outside, and now he was about to be killed by local dealers over the debt his addiction put him into. She complained that he had sold everything in their home to feed his addiction. He had also been very abusive and violent with family members and neighbors, and had received a death threat from other dealers for stealing in the favela.

Railda held out hope, but at times she felt isolated and depressed with no support for her work, and many times she thought of giving up. Railda states, "It is in that moment that you feel in your skin what it means to be a poor favela woman. You look back and you don't see anything, look forward and see no hope, no one to ask for help." Despite Railda's tireless efforts, her son continues to be addicted to crack and wanted by the police, a situation no better than that of Tonia's son. Railda recalls that bringing their sons home was supposed to have been a new beginning for their families, but the circle of violence had not been broken: "We fought to have them free, but when they came out, see what they find. There is a stigma of having been imprisoned, the family carries the stigma, and society doesn't give any opportunity. It closes the door. It is a lost generation." Because the mothers are the ones left to organize the community and resist state violence, they are also the most victimized by the violence of state bureaucracy and the psychological distress it produces. Railda voiced that several mothers were terminally ill:

> It is a horror. Today our situation is this, the parents are dying. There is a mom who had three strokes. There are mothers who go into a panic whenever they see a patrol car. There are some who have depression, and others who simply left their homes and abandoned everything. When we see a mother like Tonia, a brave woman who today cannot even walk by herself [because she is in a wheelchair], I think about what the prison system is doing to our families and our people.

This death-constraining space of maternal activism was produced by "the cynicism of the state" that continued to hold countless hearings to discuss human rights while turning the city into "a fantastic factory of cadavers," as Debora described it. In one of our meetings, I asked her what she thought of the campaigns the state was launching to "protect" children and women in the favelas from domestic violence. Debora, who had been invited to participate in a human rights program aiming to educate local leaders as human rights advocates, questioned why the state sought to prevent domestic violence while perpetrating targeted assassinations against their children at the same time. She denounced the state's hypocrisy: "I participated in this workshop where they are

training us to be *promotoras legais* [popular lawyers] against domestic violence. I said, "There is no violence against women worse than having a
son killed by the state. This is the worst violence that we have." Debora
reasoned that there was indeed domestic violence in the community,
but the state had no moral authority to face it because women were
"living incarcerated by the state" in their homes. The pain generated
by the killing of their children, she reasoned, placed mothers under a
permanent arrest. "This is a pain that these women carry for their whole
lives . . . depression, cancer, losing their mind." Debora was particularly
concerned with the number of mothers who are sick and without access to medical care. "They don't kill only our sons. They kill also the
mothers. We can't accept the mothers suffering that way . . ." Crying,
she began naming them: Dona Maria, still in depression; Vera, arrested and accused of drug trafficking; Rita, languishing with the cancer
in her womb spreading through her body. "You see, the mother loses
her son and the cancer appears in her reproduction organ. Does it tell
you something, hum?" According to Debora, the mothers were dying
of anguish from still having to cope with the "cynicism of the state"
despite having struggled for ten years (since the May 2006 massacres).
They lost every battle within the criminal justice system as the Crimes
of May were filed away for the "lack of evidence" linking the police
with the massacres. The mothers had not only been denied financial
compensation from the state, but had also lost their jobs and become
dependents solely on their husbands' incomes as they also took on the
responsibility of raising the children of the deceased. Left on their own,
the mothers had to be their own psychologists and continue standing
for their children even if they themselves resembled "cadáveres ambulan-
tes" (walking corpses), in Debora's words. The "cynicism of the state,"
therefore, comes from the state's ability to produce fantasies around
protecting favelada black women against favelado black men while at
the same time subjecting black communities to police terrorism. Instead of buying into the discourse of the state as savior—one prevalent
among NGOs and the mainstream media—black mothers denounced
depression, stroke, social marginalization, and abject poverty as part of
the state program of *governing through death* that I have outlined in the
previous chapters.

Occupy Downtown

On May 13, 2010, Brazil's Abolition of Slavery Day, the black movement organized a protest at the Patriarch Square in downtown São
Paulo to remember the fourth anniversary of the "Crimes of May." In
the middle of the square during rush hour, we found ourselves among
crosses and pictures of the young people who had been assassinated
by the police in the May 2006 massacre. A big banner reminded us
that "the abolition of slavery is unconcluded" and that this is "another
thirteenth of May with no justice." As he had done thirty years before,
Miltão from MNU evoked the memory of Robison Silveira da Luz,
the young black man whose death by the police in 1978 marked the
foundation of the modern black movement in São Paulo, to denounce
the continuous genocide of black youth. According to him, the deaths
at that time had made black activists mobilize to fight against racism
even under dictatorship, yet we were again protesting under democracy
in downtown São Paulo. Meanwhile, individuals from different organizations took the stage; many of us on the floor held cards with slogans
against the police and for affirmative action policies for black youth in
public universities. Mothers of the dead, from different parts of the city
held photographs of their children, creating a belt around the square. A
black young man held a Brazilian flag in white and black, with crosses
where there should have been stars.

Debora took her turn on the stage and reminded us all we were
there to speak out against the "assassin state" and that if we kept our
silence "it will kill us all." She then asked us to honor the dead by rejecting the label that the state put on them as "bandits." She also urged
us to reject calling the Crimes of May the "Crimes of PCC," as the state
and mainstream media did when referring to the massacre. This dispute
was not peripheral. The 505 civilians killed during the massacre were
said by state authorities to be "bandits from PCC" who therefore deserved to die. While right-wing groups called the massacre "the crimes
of PCC," Debora reasoned that "it was not PCC that killed our sons,
it was the state." She then invited us all to light our candles. In the
dusk, the photos of the dead and the candles turned the square into a
site of grief and sorrow. Some people stopped, trying to understand the

silence and the display of images of the dead in a public square during rush hour. While we all lit our candles, Douglas from UNEafro took the stage and named the different regions of the city and beyond where the massacres had taken place. We responded to each call by raising our left hand with a closed fist and saying "present." By naming the favelas and calling out to identify with the dead, we symbolically connected the dispersed geography of death and social suffering made up by police terror. Douglas stated that we were mourning the martyrs of the city. "They are martyrs because everyone who is killed by the police dies in the struggle. These are political murders," he concluded. Meanwhile, we listened to speeches at the square, and activists collected signatures on a petition that would be sent to the federal government to request the federalization of the investigation of the crimes, since the state police were themselves implicated in the crimes that they were investigating. According to the movement, it was the certainty of impunity that made the state police continue killing: because the organs of control were all part of the same corporatist culture, it would be nearly impossible to bring the officers to justice. Debora expressed frustration with the investigations, saying: "They killed my son, they killed these women's sons, and they are going to keep killing. It was so successful, the recipe, that they keep on killing."

The protest ended with a young black woman singing *O cantos das três racas* (The Chant of the Three Races), a well-known song by singer Clara Nunes and also a tribute to the forgotten black and indigenous warriors who resisted against Portuguese domination. The song stresses the national indifference with the "everlasting sorrow" of those fallen in the history of resistance against colonialism. "Nobody heard the sob of pain of those who whenever can sing sings in pain," the lyrics say. Her voice echoed in the square as she sang "the chant of rebellion" evoking the revolt of Palmares, the largest maroon community in seventeenth-century Brazil. The atmosphere created by the candles illuminating the photos of black youth killed by the police, combined with the voice of the young woman, caused me to place the current black condition in historical perspective. The history of racial terror on which Brazil was built resists time and Brazilian society resists coming to terms with its colonial past. The song concluded with the remarkable lyric: "This singing that should be a chanting of joy sounds just as a sob of pain."

If conventional political tactics—negotiating with the governor, sending press releases to journalists, calling for solidarity from civil society—seem to have failed (in light of continuing state terrorism), politicizing black death requires another order of discourses and practices. Retaliatory gang violence and self-serving acts of deviance by those in the world of crime were one, although controversial, attempt; appealing to "the suffering of the mothers" and occupying the public sphere aimed to be another. By bringing to downtown the terror that the police imposed on the edge of the city, the protestors aimed to make black death legible and to unmask the Brazilian state of rights as a terrocratic police state. It was black women who brought to the movement the strategy of converting black bodies into political symbols of black resistance. They did so by appealing to the social and biological category of "mothering" and by calling for a political community forged in the shared responsibility to honor the dead "from yesterday, from today and from tomorrow," as stated by one of the speakers. In opposition to state narratives claiming that those killed were criminals who deserved to die, the public mourning was an act of legitimizing the mothering category, politicizing its pain, and humanizing the dead.

The mothers demanded and managed to unify the set of demands put forth by the black movement—prison abolition activists, advocates of affirmative-action policies, reproductive rights, Afro-Brazilian religions, and hip-hop artists—around a politics of grief that asserted black political life in face of death. Luciane Oliveira Rocha observes in her work with black mothers in Rio de Janeiro that "if anti-blackness has black death as its defining feature, black maternity presents itself as an explicit alternative to such practices."[27] The mothers' motto points precisely to that: "We are the voice of the dead, our dead have a voice!" This politics focused on the dramatic appeal to all progressive forces to embrace the dead, regardless of their legal status, as members of the black community. In centering their loved ones' premature deaths and their own pain as the starting points for unmasking state terror, the Mães de Maio not only united the diverse demands of the black movement but also radicalized its practice, "using" the dead to bridge the world of crime with the other political worlds in which the black movement tried to have black voices heard.

This last observation requires some elaboration. Maternal activism has increasingly become an object of academic inquiry in Latin America, and in Brazil in particular. From human-rights-based movements against the dictatorship regime in the region (the "supermothers") to working-class women's grassroots-level struggles for public day care and against the cost of living in the periphery of São Paulo in the late 1970s (the "militant mothers"), and to the current "warrior mothers" against police violence in Brazilian major cities, the symbolic place of maternity has been strategically mobilized to open political spaces that redress "personal, moral, and political pain."[28] Very few scholars have explored the radical politics of black maternal activism in the Brazilian context. A neglected dimension in the scholarship is precisely the defiant difference of black maternal activism in relation to the forms outlined above; for example, black mothers' attempts to erase the line between black respectability and the *mundo do crime*.[29] In the context of my work, many black mothers have sons with criminal records. Yet, contrary to mainstream civil society that, at worst, hold that they deserve to be killed or, at best, claim the victims' "good" behavior in order to defend their right to live, Mães de Maio and AMPARAR unconditionally reclaim both the dead and the prisoner as theirs. The moral and legal status of victims was not up for debate; when it was, as in the case of Dona Maria's and Dona Cecilia's attempts to recuperate the spoiled biographies of the dead, it was a tactic for dealing with state bureaucracy. Another important dimension missing in this debate is the gendered differentials—or ungendering narratives—that deny black women's particular experience vis-à-vis the politics of mothering. Racial mythologies around what constitutes "womanhood" and the "ideal" mother put black women at a greater disadvantage within this very diverse range of maternal social politics. Suzan Franceschet, Jennifer Piscopo, and Gwynn Thomas make a very important point in that regard by noticing that "while motherhood as a cultural resource cross[es] social divides, lower-class and racially marginalized women often struggle to be recognized as good mothers and citizens."[30] The impossibility of black motherhood, decreed by the police's right to kill, demanded from black women a different kind of engagement with civil society. Thus, while in some cases—as in Argentina's dictatorship and to a lesser extent Brazil's—mothers struggled to democratize the public sphere, the favelada black mother questioned the very existence of democracy as a viable project because their children are the "victims of democracy," as Debora constantly reminded me.[31]

Certainly, the black movement has long fought to decolonize the Brazilian public sphere by bringing black matters to the larger public, as illustrated in the previous pages. It created alternative media to denounce black genocide, protested clandestinely during the dictatorship regime, deployed sit-in protests, chained them(our)selves to the gates of public universities, occupied public offices, disturbed public order, and produced cultural performances. Some of these strategies produced tangible results, particularly when the state recognized and adopted some affirmative-action policies to address longstanding racial inequalities in the 2000s. Working with Educafro and UNEafro, for instance, I learned that political pressure on the streets, lobbying Congress, and sending countless e-mails to presidents of public universities were effective strategies for securing the approval of the quota system granting access to black youth in institutions of higher learning. Also, thanks to the pressure of the black movement, President Lula da Silva's administration adopted some institutional moves that, at least symbolically, had an impact on the question of racial discrimination in Brazil. Think, for instance, about the adoption of Law 10639/03, which required the inclusion of the History of Africas in the national school curriculum, the creation of the Ministry of Racial Equality, and the appointment of the first black judge, Joaquim Barbosa (who later would become the Workers' Party's hangman), to the Brazilian Supreme Court of Justice. However, granting some rights while maintaining racial violence indicates the limits of the politics of rights in redressing anti-blackness.

The racial structure of the Brazilian public sphere, I argue, conditions the nature of black protest. That is true about the ways the black social movement compromises with the state in the hope of strategic gains, about *some* black youth who choose to drive their point home by engaging in criminal activities, and about the symbolic dimension of black mothers desperately appealing to their maternal condition when protesting in public squares. I do not argue one is better or more effective than the other, although the ethnographic data speaks for itself about which ones are acceptable in the domesticated public sphere. My point, rather, is that the multiple ways black protest takes place provide a diagnosis of the brutality of racism in the Brazilian polity. Within a context where entitlements to participation in the public sphere are racially defined, pain, rage, and crime appear as political resources that enable a repositioning of the black subject in relation to the city politics. That despite such struggles black death continues to define black urban life indicates the seemingly impossible endeavor to decolonize white civil society's zone of being.

The debate about the black public sphere is a recent one in Brazil. An incisive approach claims that there is no such thing as a "black public sphere" because of the structural condition that blacks bear as neither fully human nor fully citizen. In societies like Brazil, the public sphere is a white male heterosexual spatiality. This critique highlights the ontological position of black people as impossible contractual subjects by asking: If civil society were the materialization of the social contract between private citizens and the state, what is the place of those regarded as nonbeings, thus noncontractual subjects within this political space?[32] Some scholars prefer to highlight the agency of the black movement despite the indifference and racial hostility that characterize responses to black demands. Flavia Rios notes that in order to occupy the public sphere, the modern black movement had to fight on two fronts: to demystify the national celebration of May 13 as "the day of a false abolition" (and instead vindicate November 20 as the National Day of Racial Consciousness) and to dispute space with the leftist Brazilian political parties and unions. While in the first case black activists tried to integrate a critical black history into national narratives of "Brazilianness" (what one could regard in Gramscian terms as an attempt to create a new "national popular"), in the second case they tried to secure a place in the leftist agenda for social justice by embracing popular demands while seeking some autonomy from the Left because it refused to take race seriously. She locates different cycles of black protest in Brazil, from the "cultural" contestation of "racial democracy" to the attempts to "racialize" unions and social movements, to the strategic dialogue with the state as part of this war of positions.[33] While recognizing the existence of a black public life in Brazil, political scientist Michael Hanchard maintains that there is a "radical disjuncture" between Habermas's "ideal type" and the ways such a *public* domain becomes privatized in contexts of racialized access to citizenship. That explains, he argues, why Afro-Brazilians had to develop a "micro-public sphere" in their attempts to decolonize the white/bourgeois public sphere, expressed in cultural and religious practices of resistance (such as candomblé and black music).[34] Likewise, Kwame Dixon's rather optimistic approach to the Brazilian black movement's civic participation in electoral politics and its demands for affirmative-action policies is seen as indicative of an emerging "Afro-civil society" that marks democratic Brazil. According to him, "Afro-civil society challenges the normative underpinnings of traditional civil society while at the same time making it more conceptually and theoretically relevant to Black peoples and their forms of organization and culture."[35]

While it would be anachronistic to deny black civil participation within Brazil's current political life, the success of black demands is conditioned to the extent that black activists can mobilize large publics not in terms of black matters but in terms of poor, subaltern, working-class issues.[36] That is why black activists find themselves "praying to the priest" when mobilizing as blacks, as the saying goes. At least within the constrained space of traditional politics, black protest has not generated a "subaltern public sphere" because the subaltern public sphere is that

Black activists protest against police violence and demand affirmative action. Downtown São Paulo, May 2010. Photograph by UNEafro-Brazil.

of the poor working class, not one that would encompass the matters of those struggling to be recognized as humans in the first place. This critique can be located in the practices of those in the world of crime and also of those in the interstice position of claiming rights from within yet constantly being denied full membership in the world of citizenship. Nothing makes this precarious position clearer than the eloquent denouncement made by the Mães de Maio, who consider their sons the "victims of democracy."

Referring to the shutdown of public political life during the twenty-one years of Brazilian military dictatorship (1964–85), Debora argued that while civil society was very moved by the death of middle- and upper-class political activists at the hands of the military junta, the current victims of the police in the democratic regime of rights are forgotten because they are black and from the favelas. "The dictatorship was mild. True dictatorship is the one we live in now. Under democracy, Brazil is the largest producer of childless mothers," she contends:

> They can't say the military dictatorship ended, because it is a lie. It will end only when the Military Police has been banished. There is no way they think it is natural . . . that dictatorship ended in a country that kills more than a country in war. We are breaking this paradigm that dictatorship is over because it is not. It continues in the periphery. The dictatorship has color, class, and sex. If not, I would not be a Mães de Maio of a black kid, poor, favelado.

One of Mães de Maio's frustrations was that when the Workers' Party came to power, they held out hope that the presidents (Lula da Silva and Dilma Rousseff) would put an end to police terror because they were, respectively, a *nordestino* and a woman; both were victims of the military dictatorship. The mothers were particularly optimistic about President Dilma Rousseff, who had been tortured by the military. After several attempts to have a hearing with the president and several letters seeking to meet with the Ministry of Justice to bring the crimes committed by the state police to federal jurisdiction, the mothers gave up and created their own truth commission in February 2015, adding the term "democracy" to highlight the permanent state of exception that the urban peripheries have become. The Mães de Maio Truth Commission of Democracy made it explicit that they were responding to the National Truth Commission, created in 2012 by President Dilma Rousseff to investigate the crimes committed by the military regime during the state of exception in the 1960s. Rousseff had participated actively in the National Commission's creation. In 2015, the Commission concluded that 434 individuals had been killed and 200 had been "disappeared" by the military junta.[37] When receiving the final report, Rousseff cried and stated that "Brazil deserved the truth, the new generations deserve the truth, especially those who lost family, relatives, friends, companions, and who continue to suffer as they die again and always every day."[38]

In 2013, when President Rousseff's National Truth Commission was still investigating the crimes of the military regime, the Mães de Maio received the national award for human rights from the hands of the president. Debora did not miss the opportunity to tell President Rousseff how frustrated she was with the fact that the president was seeking justice for the victims of the 1964 coup and celebrating the end of dictatorship while the police killed black youth in the favelas. She said, "You as a gramma, a woman, a president, and a victim of the dictatorship . . . you should not be in a comfort zone seeing Brazilians assassinated. Where is the revolution?" Although her protest came two years before President Rousseff's moving remarks, Debora was incisive: the death of Debora's son did not count for as much as those of the victims of dictatorship, whom the president later referred to as those dying "again and always every day." In 2016, President Rousseff suffered a parliamentary coup by an evangelical right-wing male-dominated coalition that falsely accused her of mismanaging state-controlled banks to finance the Workers' Party's social programs. Impeached, she denounced the violation of her political rights and appealed to social movements to occupy the streets and defend the endangered Brazilian democracy. Social activists, including me, found themselves in an ambivalent position about standing with the left-wing parties against the nightmares to come while aware of the anti-black nature of the Brazilian state, including under the Workers' Party government. While I was furious and distressed with the jeopardizing of the forty-something-year-old Brazilian democracy, it was all crystal clear to Debora: "Don't be silly! Where is the *golpe* [coup], Jaime? The *golpe* has long been consummated in the favela."

CONCLUSION
BLACKPOLIS

> The fact is that power, in the postcolony, is *carnivorous*. It grips its subjects by the throat and squeezes them to the point of breaking their bones, making their eyes pop out of their sockets, making them weep blood. It cuts them in pieces and, sometimes, eats them raw.
>
> —Achille Mbembe, *On Postcolony*

"The freedom to make and remake ourselves and our cities is, I want to argue, one of the most precious yet most neglected of our human rights. How best then to exercise this right?" In response to his own question, geographer David Harvey argues that the struggle for the "right to the city" is inevitably an anticapitalist and citizenship-based one. Since urbanization is a predominantly capitalist phenomenon, to reclaim the city is also to reclaim control over the conditions and the means of its production. Thus, the potential for an urban revolution lies in the alliance between the *proletariat* and the *precariat*: for example, in identity-based social movements and the traditional working class demanding solutions to pressing everyday problems such as housing, public transportation, and so on.[1] If the premise of this book—that the city is constituted through and in black evisceration—is correct, then the urban revolution, at least in Brazil, has to move much beyond claiming control of the means of production and become a fundamental struggle for a radical reinvention of the city as a *blackpolis*.

To claim the city, as I have shown in this book, blacks have engaged in a multiplicity of political struggles that are not necessarily hierarchical in efficiency and radicalism: from black youth participating in the *mundo do crime* to retaliatory gang violence against the police, and to black mothers' efforts to decolonize the *politeia* (the community of *men*). While these spatial practices challenge fatalist narratives of blackness as dystopia, they also suggest the limits of even progressive urban politics in transforming the city into an inclusive polis. They are, nevertheless, attempts to generate what Katherine McKittrick has named "oppositional geography": to ontologically and spatially reposition the placeless subject in relation to a racial geography of domination.[2] Black women, I have argued, play a fundamental role in the struggle for a new ontology of space, place, and territory. Black mothering pedagogies of resistance represent a painfully creative attempt to decolonize the white zone of being and make the blackpolis possible. Their social-reproductive labor—fostering alternative community, nurturing life, bringing prisoners home, and honoring the dead—subverts pathological narratives of black urbanity, among them civil society's expectation of black women as disorganized, politically naïve, spatially confined favelada.

Perhaps a metaphor for understanding black women's spatial agency is the unfolding of the protests downtown (described in chapter 5), where "social mothers" from the city's edges took the Patriarch Square only meters away from City Hall to denounce the genocide of black youth. At the end of the demonstration the organizers decided to "baptize" the square and rename it. The square is named after Jose Bonifácio de Andrada e Silva, considered one of the founding fathers of the Brazilian nation for his prominent role in the movement for independence at the turn of the nineteenth century. The protesters aimed to baptize the square with the name of Dandara, the forgotten runaway female slave said to be one of the leaders of *Palmares,* the largest maroon community in colonial Brazil. As the participants held candles and pictures of the dead, a group of young women passed through the crowd; one of them climbed a ladder and covered the Patriarch statue with a flag of the black movement. The covering sealed the baptism of the square and the symbolic renaming from Jose Bonifácio de Andrada e Silva to Dandara. "From now on, this is the square of our leader, the Matriarch Dandara. This is the square for fighting for liberation, the square for denouncing the genocide of our people and our history!" shouted one of the participants.

Renaming the square was a political act to reclaim the place of black women in the history of the black radical tradition that quite often placed them in secondary roles, as the case of Dandara, better known as "the wife of Zumbi dos Palmares" than as the warrior for black liberation in seventeenth-century Brazil. It was also a "spatial praxis" to challenge their placelessness in a city in which they were virtually invisible. By infusing the Patriarch Square with a different narrative of space and time, black women confronted their political marginalization, denounced patriarchal domination, and retold a forgotten history that challenged the city's denial of gendered racial injustice. If we consider the place of black women in the nation (i.e., the ways the nation has been imagined as a heteropatriarchal project that requires racial and gendered subjugation), occupying the Patriarch Square becomes even more symbolic. Its renaming represents an attempt to resituate the black gendered subject in relation to the city and also in relation to the foundational violence that made Brazil. In the square on Abolition Day, the placeless black subject asserted, at least symbolically, a different relation to the Brazilian polity. By demanding a truly inclusive *koinonia* of *politai*, these subjects challenged the necropolis (the macabre spatial engineering created by state carcerality, police terror, and the daily soft killing of black lives), and demanded a city worth living in: the blackpolis.

No Ending

This book began with Dona Maria's painful experience of looking for Betinho's remains. Following Dona Maria's endeavor, the book crossed paths with other black victims of the delinquent Brazilian state. By shedding light on their lives, it sought to analyze a central aspect of state-led projects of domination: black Brazilians are enemies of the nation, and their killing is a constitutive aspect of Brazilian state making and its regime of rights. I argued that governing through death—as opposed to governing through community—is the dominant strategy for securing white (and nonblack) lives in the supposedly raceless city. It is also an economic and ideological underpinning for the production of the city as a white biopolis. Anti-black violence—segregation in favelas, exploitation in low-paying jobs, and killings by the police—is both functional and constitutive of the white polis, for white life is measured in relation to and must be protected against the black enemy. If the city were a *text*, black blood would be the ink.

This book has no happy ending. Following the politically engaged ethnographic tradition of recognizing the agency of the oppressed, I embarked on a journey to portray the individuals in this narrative as active agents in the struggle for rights and dignity. I tried to locate glimpses of hope in the vibrant black movement and in the outlawed, admittedly controversial practices of black individuals on the edges of the city. I regret that I have not been able to do justice to their strategies of resistance or to the meanings of their experience. Despite the effort to provide a "thick description" of what I saw and lived, ethnography is always incomplete, precarious, and ephemeral as an interpretative endeavor. And yet, regardless of what it means to each of these individuals, they would agree that the blackpolis is an aspirational and seemingly impossible project to make black life livable. Since the completion of the fieldwork for the book, thousands of black youth have been killed by the police and thousands of others have been incarcerated: Dona Júlia passed away without ever seeing Jairo return home; Eliseu was transferred to serve the remainder of his sentence in a penitentiary in the countryside; PCC continues to control the state prisons; Tonia remains trapped in a wheelchair and lives in an improvised home under the bridge while her now thirty-something-year-old son, Antonio, battles crack addiction. Serginho was killed by the police while evading a checkpoint at the entrance of the favela; Nina continues to make a living by selling drugs in a PCC-controlled *biqueira*; the favelas of the Fundão da Zona Sul continue to be terrorized by police-linked death squads; white-led and well-funded human-rights NGOs continue to release useless reports on police violence; and black activists like Debora, Douglas, Railda, Miltão, and Bispo continue in their herculean effort to make the underfunded black movement break the wall of white civil society and to make black lives matter.

My journeys back and forth across the city with Dona Maria to gather the paperwork for an official recognition of Betinho's death yielded no tangible results. Having gone through the official procedures and filed documents for claiming her son's body and obtaining a monthly stipend to pay her rent, Dona Maria received a denial from the government. She was told that in order to receive financial support, she must prove that Betinho had been working and contributing to the family income. Therefore, she had to start a new struggle to gather documents that proved Betinho was working as a car washer at the time he was killed by the police. Despite obtaining the documents from Betinho's former employer, Dona Maria received yet another denial from the government. Because the trial of the police officers accused of killing Betinho had yet to be scheduled, the government could not make a final decision on the compensation, and Dona Maria continued to wait.

The hardest part, however, was yet to come. The trial was finally held, and the six officers were found not guilty due to a "lack of consistent proof" linking them to death squads. Another three officers were indicted, but their lawyer appealed and the officers remained free pending a revision of their appeal. Dona Maria filed a petition in the civil court to demand that the state compensate her financially, but the judge denied the request, arguing that although there were signs of police participation in the killing of Betinho, "the officers did not act in the name of the state." Therefore, the judge concluded, "the state should not be penalized to compensate for individual actions." Betinho's body still waits to be exhumed and brought to the Luizão Cemetery in the Fundão da Zona Sul. Meanwhile, Dona Maria relies on psychotropic medication to make it through each day. She continues moving from place to place with Sandrinha, her niece, who keeps searching for a job in the formal economy in order to prove to social workers that she is "capable" of regaining custody of her three children. They were ultimately placed in an orphanage. The endless cycles of anxiety and panic endure. Dona Maria keeps holding the same old plastic folder filled with useless documents about Betinho's death, hoping they will one day help her bring the killers to justice. In one of my subsequent visits, she told me that she is not giving up on her mission to provide her son a proper burial.

In her acclaimed article "The Romance of Resistance," anthropologist Lila Abu-Lughod cautions anthropologists to be careful about placing too much emphasis on the question of "everyday agency" so as not to overlook everyday forms of oppression. Resistance, she argues, should be understood in relational rather than comprehensive terms, for sometimes what one reads as resistance could in fact be a "diagnostic of forms of power and how people are caught in them."[3] This relational approach recognizes the agency of the oppressed without "overdrama-tiz[ing] its reputation" (my inversion of James Scott's often-cited quota-tion), to the point of foreclosing possibilities of understanding the work of domination. Abu-Lughod's call is even more pertinent to the endless torment of the black individuals that this book highlights. My interloc-utors' empty hands after so many struggles remind me that despite the small everyday victories, oppressive power has an uncanny and grievous capacity to prevail. There are accounts of resistance here indeed. As you read these last pages, many black individuals continue to fight back and challenge state violence on the streets, attempt to fend off the state with urban riots, and try to make a living by selling cocaine on street corners. These acts of resistance are costly in terms of lost lives and limited in stopping the state machinery of death. Some might argue that I dis-miss the black movement's strategic gains and the cumulative everyday resistance embedded in acts such as drug dealing, sticking up, stealing electricity, and evading the police. No, I do not dismiss them. They are what keep us alive; in the words of a member of the Committee against Black Genocide, "if we stayed silent they would revoke the Lei Áurea," referring to the law of May 13, 1888, that abolished slavery in Brazil. Their political struggle is indeed a fissure in the urban concrete of op-pression, one that hopefully will gradually dismantle the city's insidious structure of power. Still, in the current political climate in which white nationalism and police terror gain new geopolitical configurations in Brazil and in the African Diaspora, it is worth asking ourselves the fol-lowing: How to translate dispersed insurgent practices into a collective struggle toward sustainable structural changes? How do we turn indi-vidual acts of black ungovernability into a "world of complete disor-der?" What does resistance look like, and how do we ethically respond to police terror, when the police kill to preserve the democratic regime of rights? These are critical inquiries for those who are truly committed to bringing the utopic black city—the blackpolis—into full existence.

ACKNOWLEDGMENTS

The Anti-Black City is not just a book. Humbly, it is also an exercise of political imagination in times of restructuring global white supremacy. As such, it is the product of many hands and minds, especially of those with whom I marched in the streets of São Paulo, those with whom I shared troubling times living in the favela of Vila Bahiana in the Baixada Santista, and those with whom I discussed most of the ideas presented here in conferences, graduate seminars, and study groups. This project would not have been possible without the support of a number of people, and I am deeply thankful. At the Department of Black Studies at the University of Texas, Austin, I am grateful for the emotional, political, and financial support of staff members, colleagues, and professors whose intellectual, political, and moral commitments continue to inspire me. During my years in graduate school, I was lucky enough to count on the support of Omi Jones, Kaushik Ghosh, Doug Foley, Maria Franklin, Jemima Pierre, Matt Richardson, Jafari Allen, Kali Gross, Shannon Speed, Kamran Ali, and Celeste Henery. I particularly appreciate my supportive dissertation-defense committee (Drs. Charlie Hale, Joy James, Simone Browne, Edmund Gordon, Christen Smith, and João Costa Vargas) for their guidance and resolute belief in this project.

I cannot overstate my gratitude for João Costa Vargas's mentorship, unwavering support, and moral commitment to increasing the number of Afro-Brazilian graduate students at the University of Texas,

Austin. At one given moment, thanks to his efforts, the Department of Black Studies at the University of Texas, Austin had more Afro-Brazilians than any graduate program in Brazil's highly segregated public universities. Vargas's insightful scholarship, his ties with diasporic black organizations, and his personal commitment to a young generation of Afro-Brazilian researchers has profoundly inspired my work and shaped my trajectory. Thank you, João, for opening doors and for being such a *parceiro de caminhada*!

I thank my passionate friends Elvia Mendoza, Hafeez Jamali, Sandra Cañas, Tathagatan Ravindran, and Barbara Abadia-Roxana, with whom I have closely shared anxieties, frustrations, and happiness preparing this manuscript over the years. Along with little Joakuin and Valerie, Elvia Mendoza provided me with food, shelter, and drinks in her warm home.

In the United States, Colombia, and Brazil, I extend my thanks to Diana Ojeda, Rosbelinda Cárdenas, Ted Rutland, Yanilda González, Andrea Lisboa, Steve Nicholas, Silvia Lorenço, Athayde Motta, Marisol Rivera, Mariana Mora, Damien Schnyder, Graham Denyer Willis, Paulo Paz de Lima, Edilene Machado, Rô Teixeira, Magnólia Santos, Paloma Diaz, Michelle Quinones, Vicenta Moreno, Andrea Moreno, Cristina Hurtado, Brenda Ramos, Anjoli Chadha, Pamela Calla, Carlos E. Castaño, Norris Gorris, Emidio Neto, Tia Didi, and Tia Licinha. I am thankful to Aurora Vergara-Figueroa, Jeronimo Botelho, Inge Valencia, and Henrique Caporalli at the Universidad Icesi for hosting me during a year-long visiting professorship and during several subsequent visits at the Centro de Estudios Afrodiaspóricos. Aurora Vergara's political vision and passionate engagement with racial justice continue to inspire me!

A postdoctoral fellowship at the Africana Research Center at Pennsylvania State University provided me additional support for the writing process. I thank Valerie King, Tracy Beckett, and Dawn Noren at Penn State for their critical support. There, I was also fortunate to count on the intellectual stimulation of Melissa Wright, who provided further insights on the reproductive work of police violence as I attended her graduate seminar in the Department of Geography. Finally, there are scholars whose theoretical work inspired this book and shaped my understanding of the black necropolis. Their inspiration merits recognition: Saidiya Hartman, Joy James, Hortense Spillers, João Costa Vargas, Frank Wilderson, Denise Ferreira da Silva, Dylan Rodríguez, Katherine McKittrick, Jared Sexton, Sharon Patricia Holland, and Fred Moten. I owe an intellectual debt to Charles Hale for his guidance and generous insights on the challenges and possibilities for doing activist anthropology in spaces of racial precarity. Our conversations helped me solidify my beliefs on the importance of an engaged analysis of police violence in São Paulo. The same could be said for two anonymous reviewers for *Antipode,* who pushed me to further consider the relation between the biopolis and necropolitical governance. Colleagues read parts of the manuscript and provided valuable suggestions: Graham Denyer Willis, Raquel de Souza, Elvia Mendoza, and Tathagatan Ravindran. One colleague went through the whole manuscript more than once: thank you, Keisha Blain. At the College of Staten Island, I counted on the critical emotional and political support of Rafael de la Dehesa, Ismael García Colón, Jean Halley, Saadia Toor, Don Selby, Jeffrey Bussolini, Hosu Kim, John Arena, Leigh Binford, Roslyn Bologh, Grace M. Cho, Kate Crehan, Ozlem Goner, Ananya Mukherjea, Phil S. Sigler, Thomas Volscho, and Franchesca Degiuli. Thanks also to Angela Ramos, Angela Chuppe, Alana Gaymon, and the other staff members at CSI. More than once, my faculty colleagues and staff reaffirmed their commitment to recruit and retain faculty of color as I slowly adjusted to my new position in the Sociology and Anthropology department at CSI/CUNY.

This book is dedicated to my sister, Dina Alves, who has been a source of inspiration for me. I devote most of the credit for this project to her: she was the one who visualized possibilities for breaking a circle of subordination as we spent our first years in São Paulo as Northeastern migrants working as domestic servants. My parents, José Ribeiro Alves and Celsa Paixão Amparo, taught me the first lessons on the meanings of *social justice* and *political anger* with their stubborn protests against the local elite, as they struggled to raise a demanding and always-sick little boy along with eight other children in Ipiaú, a small city in the Bahia countryside. I thank them and the many other community organizers who shared with me the last traces of a theology of liberation committed to a "preferential option for the poor" in the Bahia countryside. In the black movement in São Paulo, I am indebted to Luciana Soares, José Carlos Freire, Cleyton Wenceslau Borges, Rô Santos, Heber Fagundes,

Flávio Nogueira, Vanessa Nascimento, Rogerinho Santos, and Zezinho Botelho for providing me shelter, food, and friendship as I arrived in the cold and heartless concrete jungle. Our countless debates over black politics and our "saraus" were moments in which we nurtured utopia while facing the challenges of organizing black youth at Educafro and later at UNEafro-Brasil. I am deeply grateful to Frey David Raimundo dos Santos, Thiago Thobias, Amaro Braz, Dona Valdenir Barreto, Geraldo Gomes, Tita, Lurdinha IeloDore, Levino Fideli, and Lia Lopes, among others, who opened the door to my activism in São Paulo at Educafro.

During my fieldwork, I counted on the trusted support from people living under and struggling against state violence. Many of them may be happy to see this final product; others I regret will not agree with my interpretation of their politics. Among them are Indalécio Silva, Padre Jaime, Léa Gonçalves, Fabiana, Makarrão, Fábio, Jailson Silva, and many anonymous faces with whom I interacted in the *quebradas*. At Pastoral Carcerária, the Centro Santo Dias de Direitos Humanos, and the Police Ombudsperson's Office, I am thankful to Irmã Margareth, Dona Margarida, Cidinha, Leandro Siqueira, William Cardoso, Francisco, Bira, and André for their generous welcome, their work, and the insights they provided me from their critical readings of police killings and mass incarceration in São Paulo. With Leandro Siqueira, at the Centro Santo Dias de Direitos Humanos, I crafted important questions for this book as we pushed each other in the conversations about my race-centered perspective and what we named as a "generalized thanatopolitics of police terror." Most of this work could not have been done without the critical intervention of my activist friends at the Tribunal Popular and the Comitê Contra o Genocídio da População Negra in São Paulo: thank you, Milton and Regina Barbosa, Reginaldo Bispo, Marisa Ferfferman, Givanildo Santos, Railda Alves, Dona Kika, Flavinho, Soninha, Silvado Batista, Paulo Sampaio, and many other activists whose work has energized the current Black Movement in São Paulo. The Mães de Maio and AMPARAR not only agreed to talk about their painful experiences but also opened a new perspective of analysis and different strategies for reaffirming black life in the anti-black city. I am deeply grateful for their struggle and for their contribution to the conversations in this manuscript. *O maximo respeito às mães* Debora Silva,

Dona Irinéia, Dona Terezinha, Dona Cidinha, Dona Vera, Dona Dora, Railda, Dona Miriam, and many others who are, with their struggle, "giving birth to another Brazil."

During the writing process, I was fortunate to count on the editorial support of Keisha Blain in proofreading and copyediting different versions of my manuscript. I thank my colleagues at the College of Staten Island at the City University of New York (CUNY), the Centro de Estudios Afrodiaspóricos (CEAF) de la Universidad Icesi in Colombia, the International Network against Racism (RAIAR), and the Black Mothering Resisting Police Violence Network, supported by a FORD–LASA Special Project. Their insightful discussions provided an opportunity for me to reassess my ideas. The financial support of the Ford Foundation International Fellowship Program, DSD/SSRC and SSRC Summer Program, TIAA–CREF Ruth Simms Hamilton Research Fellowship, Inter-American Foundation Grassroots Fellowship Program, ARC–Penn State, and the PSC–CUNY Award made my graduate studies and this project possible. I am sure Fulvia Rosemberg (in memoriam) would be proud of me completing this project. Thanks, Fulvia!

Finally, I am deeply in debt to Erika Larkins and an anonymous reviewer of the manuscript, the anonymous reviewers of previously published articles that I draw on for concepts presented here, and my editor at the University of Minnesota Press, Jason Weidemann—as well as editorial team Erin Warholm-Wohlenhaus, Rachel Moeller, Gabriel Levin, and assistant managing editor Mike Stoffel and indexer Laurie Prendergast—for bringing this book into reality. Vladimir Carabali and Genylucia Andrade were an important source of support during this journey.

Lastly, I could not have finished this work without Raquel Luciana de Souza, Elvia Mendoza, and Tathagatan Ravindran's patience and generosity in the most critical moments when, hurt and depressed, I was about to give up the "academic business." Thank you!

The author's proceeds from the sale of this book will be donated to the anti-police violence campaign.

NOTES

Introduction

1. Sérgio Buarque de Holanda, *O homem cordial* (São Paulo: Editora Companhia das Letras, 2012).

2. Pierre Bourdieu and Jean-Claude Passeron, *Reproduction in Education, Society and Culture* (Thousand Oaks, Calif.: Sage, 1990); Jay MacLeod, *Ain't No Makin' It: Leveled Aspirations in a Low-Income Neighborhood* (Boulder, Colo.: Westview Press, 1987).

3. Cindi Katz, "Vagabond Capitalism and the Necessity of Social Reproduction," *Antipode* 33, no. 4 (2001): 709–28. Melissa Wright also challenges the "myth of disposability" by observing that in the *maquiladoras* of the Mexican–U.S. border the "disposable" third-world woman is regarded as a "living form of waste" while she "generates prosperity through her own destruction." Melissa Wright, *Disposable Women and Other Myths of Global Capitalism* (New York: Routledge, 2006), 3.

4. The Aristotelian definition of the *polis* is the object of intense academic debate. For an extensive discussion of the concept, see Mogens Herman Hansen, *Polis: An Introduction to the Ancient Greek City-State* (London: Oxford University Press, 2006).

5. Steve Martinot and Jared Sexton, "The Avant-Garde of White Supremacy," *Social Identities* 9, no. 2 (2003): 179. This critique has also been nicely articulated by Frank Wilderson in "The Prison Slave as Hegemony's (Silent) Scandal," *Social Justice* 30, no. 2 (2003): 18–27.

6. Tony Roshan Samara, *Cape Town after Apartheid: Crime and Governance in the Divided City* (Minneapolis: University of Minnesota Press, 2011), 5; Paul Amar, *The Security Archipelago: Human-Security States, Sexuality Politics, and the End of Neoliberalism* (Durham, N.C.: Duke University Press, 2013). For yet

another perspective on the relation of policing, blackness, and urban development, see John Collins, "Policing's Productive Folds: Secretism and Authenticity in Brazilian Cultural Heritage," *The Journal of Latin American and Caribbean Anthropology* 19, no. 3 (2014): 473–501.

7. Samara, *Cape Town after Apartheid*, 32.

8. Amar, *The Security Archipelago*, 7.

9. NEV-USP, "Os jovens, a escola e os direitos humanos." *Relatorio de Cidadania* (São Paulo: NE-CEPID, 2002).

10. In 2003, filmmaker Ana Paula produced a short documentary calling attention to the chaotic situation of the cemetery. The documentary can be seen at http://curtadoc.tv/curta/incluSão/cemiterio-São-luiz/.

11. William Cardoso, "Polícia de SP Mata Sempre nos Mesmos Lugares, nos Mais Pobres," *Ponte Jornalismo Oline*, February 12, 2016.

12. Andre Caramante and Joanna Brasileiro, "PMs de SP Mataram Mais de 10 mil en 19 Anos," *Ponte Jornalismo*, December 10, 2015.

13. Ministério da Justiça, "Censo Penitenciario Nacional/InfoPen," *Ministério da Justiça*, May 10, 2016.

14. A solid theoretical perspective on what the state means can be found in Philip Abrams, "Notes on the Difficulty of Studying the State," *Journal of Historical Sociology* 1, no. 1 (1988): 58–89; Timothy Mitchell, "The Limits of the State: Beyond Statist Approaches and Their Critics," *The American Political Science Review* 85, no. 1 (1991): 77–96.

15. In his analysis of colonial domination and black resistance, Fanon characterizes the colonial world as a "zone of being" in opposition to the "zone of non-being" occupied by the colonized. See Frantz Fanon, *The Wretched of the Earth*, trans. Constance Farrington (Harmondsworth, U.K.: Penguin, 1967), 8. To my knowledge, black feminist scholar Sueli Carneiro was the first in the Brazilian context to refer to a racial ontological condition she names as "non-being." This black nonbeing, she suggests, creates conditions of possibility to the (white) being. See Sueli Carneiro, "A Construção do Outro como Não-Ser como fundamento do Ser," (PhD dissertation, University of Sao Paulo, 2005). Also, "The Negation and Reassertion of Black Geographies in Brazil," *ACME: An International Journal for Critical Geographies* 14, no. 1 (2015): 324–43.

16. Denise Ferreira da Silva, "No-Bodies: Law, Raciality and Violence," *Griffith Law Review* 18, no. 2 (2009): 212–36 at 213.

17. Carl Schmitt, *Political Theology: Four Chapters on the Concept of Sovereignty* (Chicago: University of Chicago Press, 1985).

18. Michel Foucault, *The Birth of Biopolitics: Lectures at the Collège de France, 1978–1979*, ed. Michael Senellart, trans. Graham Burchell (Hampshire, U.K.: Palgrave Macmillan, 2008), 77.

19. Ibid., 13.

20. Michel Foucault, *The History of Sexuality, Vol. 1: An Introduction* (New York: Vintage Books, 1990), 81.

21. Ibid., 138.

22. Giorgio Agamben, *Homo Sacer: Sovereign Power and Bare Life*, trans. Daniel Heller-Roazen (Stanford, Calif.: Stanford University Press, 1998), 7.

23. Giorgio Agamben, *State of Exception*, trans. Kevin Attell (Chicago: University of Chicago Press, 2005), 14.

24. Ibid., 22.

25. Joy James contends that *spectatorship* continues to be the grammar of racial violence. "Foucault's assertion that the end of public executions represents a diminished focus on spectacle and the body fails to consider, as exemplified in death-penalty biases, that bodies matter differently in racialized systems." See Joy James, *Resisting State Violence: Radicalism, Gender, and Race in U.S. Culture* (Minneapolis: University of Minnesota Press, 1996), 34. Some critics highlight Foucault's "blindness" to the temporal overlapping of colonial terror and the *biopolitical* techniques of government that he identified in eighteenth-century Europe. See Jared Sexton, "People-of-Color-Blindness: Notes on the Afterlife of Slavery," *Social Text* 28, no. 2 (2010): 31–56; Silva, *No-Bodies*, 236; Alexander Weheliye, *Habeas Viscus: Racializing Assemblages, Biopolitics, and Black Feminist Theories of the Human* (Durham, N.C.: Duke University Press, 2014); Sharon Patricia Holland, *Raising the Dead: Readings of Death and (Black) Subjectivity* (Durham, N.C.: Duke University Press, 2000).

26. My take on Foucault's concept of "governmentality" is informed by two ethnographically grounded perspectives: Donald Moore presents a reading of Foucault's governmentality in relation to land struggle and postcolonial subject formation. Moore's analysis of the struggle of the Tangwena people to defend their territory—against eviction by white former rulers and against the Zimbabwean government's land policies—proposes revising Foucault's notion of governmentality by "grounding racialized rule in spatial practices." Importantly, Moore sees governmentality not as a coherent, unified project but rather as an entanglement of competing projects, "an assemblage of practices, apparatuses, and techniques" put in place by the "native," the government, local chiefs, and colonial history. See Donald Moore, *Suffering for Territory: Race, Place, and Power in Zimbabwe* (Durham, N.C.: Duke University Press, 2005), 8–31. In the same vein, in her study of "how programs of government are constituted and contested" in the highlands of Sulawesi/Indonesia, Tania Murray Li provides an expanding reading of Foucault's concept of governmentality, regarding it as a *constellation of programs*. Li proposes an "ethnography of government" that would enable us to locate and interpret the multiplicity of programs and the new subjectivities that emerge from such contexts. See Tania Murray Li, *The Will to Improve: Governmentality, Development, and the Practice of Politics* (Durham, N.C.: Duke University Press, 2007), 282–83. Like these authors, I aim to provide a *racialized* account of multiple, incoherent, and at times competing regimes of racial governmentality in São Paulo's periphery in my reading of Foucault.

27. Michel Foucault, *Society Must Be Defended: Lectures at the Collège*

de France, 1975–1976, trans. David Macey (New York: Picador, 2003), 254.

28. According to Barnor Hesse, the Jewish Holocaust is the referent to Western political thinking about racism. European thinking is caught in an "inescapable conceptual double bind" of denying colonial history while condemning domestic racism. Barnor Hesse, "Im/Plausible Deniability: Racism's Conceptual Double Bind," *Social Identities* 10, no. 1 (2004): 9–29 at 10.

29. A word of caution: to argue that black urban life is seemingly impossible may suggest an essentialist view that equates blackness and rurality. Likewise, the focus on the black urban experience may involuntarily deny the long struggle of black people to secure life in rural Brazil. Such dichotomy is rendered irrelevant when one considers that there is no safe space for black life, as police raids in favelas and the ongoing land dispossession of *quilombola* communities make clear. For an analysis of black struggle for traditional territories see Jan Hoffman French, *Legalizing Identities: Becoming Black or Indian in Brazil's Northeast* (Chapel Hill: University of North Carolina Press, 2009).

30. Achille Mbembe, *On the Postcolony* (Berkeley: University of California Press, 2001), 197.

31. Ibid., 29, 40.

32. Fred Moten, "The Case of Blackness," *Criticism* 50, no. 2 (2008): 177–218 at 178.

33. Ibid., 179. Likewise, Katherine McKittrick calls attention to the way some academic narratives may in fact "honor and repeat and cherish anti-black violence and black death." See Peter James Hudson, "Geographies of Blackness and Anti-Blackness: An Interview with K. McKittrick," *The CLR James Journal* 20, no. 2 (2014): 233–40.

34. Jared Sexton, "The Social Life of Social Death: On Afro-pessimism and Black Optimism." *InTensions* 5, no. 1 (2011), 1–47; Frank Wilderson III, "Gramsci's Black Marx: Whither the Slave in Civil Society?" *Social Identities* 9, no. 2 (2003): 225–40. These authors draw on the seminal works of Saidiya Hartman and Hortense Spillers on the original violence of slavery and its relation to black gendered subjectivity. Saidiya Hartman, *Scenes of Subjection: Terror, Slavery, and Self-Making in Nineteenth-Century America* (Oxford: Oxford University Press, 1997); Hortense J. Spillers, *Black, White, and in Color: Essays on American Literature and Culture* (Chicago: University of Chicago Press, 2003).

35. Sexton, "The Social Life of Social Death," 29.

36. Holland, *Raising the Dead,* 6.

37. Jaime Alves and João Costa Vargas, "On Deaf Ears: Anti-black Police Terror, Multiracial Protest, and White Loyalty to the State," *Identities* 43, no. 2 (2016): 23.

38. The expression *mundo do crime* is an emic category in the universe of urban violence in Brazil. The literature is very extensive. For reference works discussing the category *mundo do crime* in an ethnographic perspective, see Alba Zaluar,

A Máquina e a Revolta: as Organizações Populares e o Significado da Pobreza (Rio de Janeiro: Brasiliense, 2002); Gabriel de Santis Feltran, *Fronteiras de Tensão: Política e Violência nas Periferias de São Paulo* (São Paulo: Editora Unesp, 2011), 376; and Graham Denyer Willis, *The Killing Consensus: Police, Organized Crime, and the Regulation of Life and Death in Urban Brazil* (Berkeley: University of California Press, 2015). See also Michel Misse, "Sujeito, Crime e Sujeição Criminal," *Lua Nova 7*, no. 2 (2009), 12–38.

39. I should caution the reader that I am not invested in the moral judgment the expression conveys within mainstream society. As I will discuss later, the very category of "crime" must be interrogated. Rather than investing in the "black criminality" discourse, my interest relates to Cathy Cohen's assertion that "[o]nly by listening to their voices, trying to understand their motivations, and accurately centering their stories with all of the complexities in our work can we begin to understand and map the connection between deviant practice, defiant behavior, and political resistance." Cathy J. Cohen, "Deviance as Resistance: A New Research Agenda for the Study of Black Politics," *Du Bois Review* 1, no. 1 (2004): 33.

40. I rely on a critical distinction between lawbreakers and enemies provided by Paul Kahn, "Criminal and Enemy in the Political Imagination," *The Yale Review,* 99 (2011): 148–67; Alejandro Madrazo, *¿Criminales y Enemigos? El Narcotraficante Mexicano en el Discurso Oficial y en el Narcocorrido* (Buenos Aires: Libraria Ediciones, 2013).

41. Fanon, *The Wretched of the Earth,* 36.

42. As cited in Liane Camargo de Almeida Alves, "Os Passos de um Aventureiro," *Revista Terra,* Ano VI, nº 8, agosto 1997 no. 64: 34.

43. Darcy Ribeiro, *O Povo Brasileiro: a Formação e o Sentido do Brasil* (Rio de Janeiro: Global Editora, 2015). For a similar critique see also Marcelo Paixão, "Antropofagia e Racismo: Uma Crítica ao Modelo Brasileiro de Relações Raciais," in *Elemento Suspeito: Abordagem policial e discriminação na cidade do Rio de Janeiro,* eds. Silvia Ramos and Leonarda Musumeci (Rio de Janeiro: Civilização Brasileira, 2005), 1–45.

44. Oswald de Andrade's *Manifesto Antropofágico* is a remarkable attempt to resignify such mythologies by highlighting the Brazilian creativity in assimilating and cannibalizing other cultures around the world. See Oswald de Andrade, "Manifesto Antropofágico," *Correio da Manha.* http://www.ufrgs.br/cdrom/oandrade/oandrade.pdf.

45. Jacob Waiselfisz, *Mapa da Violencia: os Jovens do Brasil* (Brasilia: UNESCO, 2015), 82–85.

46. Ibid., 83–85.

47. This synthesis is far from a comprehensive view of the prolific and interdisciplinary field of studies on "urban violence" in Brazil. Anthropologist Alba Zaluar's chronological review from 1970–95 offers a comprehensive map of the scholarship on the subject. I draw from Zaluar's work to provide an obviously

274 Notes to Introduction

partial review. Likewise, my grouping of the scholarship into three lines of inquiry is limited and based on my theoretical and political interests. For a comprehensive review of "urban violence" as a category of analysis in Brazilian social sciences, see Alba Zaluar, "Violência e Crime. O que ler na Ciência Social Brasileira (1970–1995)," in *Antropologia 1* (1999): 13–107; Alba Zaluar, "Um Debate Disperso: Violência e Crime no Brasil da Redemocratização," *São Paulo em Perspectiva* 13, no. 3 (1999): 3–17.

48. Although the large body of work is too ample to cite here and many authors do not make an explicit poverty-criminality argument, the poverty-crime tension continues to haunt the "sociological imagination" in the Brazilian social sciences. See, for instance, Maria Fernanda Tourinho Peres, et al., "Homicídios, Desenvolvimento Socioeconômico e Violência Policial no Município de São Paulo, Brasil," *Rev Panam Salud Publica* 23, no. 4 (2008): 268–76; Lucio Kovarick, Cintia Ant, and Renato Boschi, "Violência: Reflexões sobre a Banalidade do Cotidiano em São Paulo," in *Violência e Cidade* ed. Renato Boschi and Ruben George Oliven (Rio de Janeiro: Zahar Editores, 1982); Alba Zaluar, "Violência e Criminalidade: Saída para os Excluídos ou Desafio para a Democracia?," in *O que ler para conhecer o Brasil*, ed. Sérgio Miceli (São Paulo: Anpocs, 1999). For a critical review of this enduring perspective, see Michel Misse, "Crime e Pobreza: Velhos Enfoques, Novos Problemas," in *O Brasil na Virada do Século*, ed. Marco Gonçalves and Gláucia Villas-Boas (Rio de Janeiro: Relume Dumará, 1995): 78–89.

49. Teresa Caldeira and James Holston, "Democracy and Violence in Brazil," *Comparative Studies in Society and History* 41, no. 4 (1999): 691–729.

50. Paulo Sergio Pinheiro, "Autoritarismo e Transição," *Revista da USP* 108, no. 5 (1991): 937–75; Sergio Adorno, "A Violência na Sociedade Brasileira: um Painel Inconcluso em uma Democracia não Consolidada," *Sociedade e Estado* 10, no. 2 (1995): 299–342; Alba Zaluar, "Unfinished Democratization: The Failure of Public Safety," *Estudos Avançados* 21, no. 61 (2007): 31–49.

51. Guillermo O'Donnell's chromatic classificatory approach—Latin America is divided into blue, green, and brown areas representing established, low-intense, and dysfunctional democracies respectively—is usually used as a referent for claiming that Latin American societies are "incomplete," "deficient," or "disjunctive" democracies.

52. Scholar Joy James provides a forceful analysis of the dialectics between slavery and democracy in the modern world. See Joy James, "Democracy and Captivity," in *The New Abolitionists: (Neo)Slave Narratives and Contemporary Prison Writings*, ed. Joy James (Albany: State University of New York Press, 2005), xxi–xlii. In the Brazilian context, O'Donnell's schema has been criticized by, among others, Donna Goldstein, *Laughter out of Place: Race, Class, Violence, and Sexuality in a Rio Shantytown* (Berkeley: University of California Press, 2003); Alves and Vargas, "On Deaf Ears," 1–21.

53. Luiz Machado da Silva, "Sociabilidade Violenta: Por uma Interpretação

da Criminalidade Contemporânea no Brasil Urbano," *Sociedade e Estado* 19, no. 1 (2004): 53–84; Ben Penglase, "States of Insecurity: Everyday Emergencies, Public Secrets, and Drug Trafficker Power in a Brazilian Favela," *PoLAR: Political and Legal Anthropology Review* 32, no. 1 (2009): 47–63; Alba Zaluar, "Para não dizer que não falei de samba," in *Historia da Vida Privada no Brasil*, ed. Lilia Moritz Schwarcz and Fernando Novais (São Paulo: Companhia das Letras, 1998), 311–35; Alba Zaluar, *Condomínio do Diabo* (Rio de Janeiro: Editora da UFRJ, 1994); Feltran, *Fronteiras de Tensão*, 376; Michel Misse, "Mercados ilegais, redes de proteção e organização local do crime no Rio de Janeiro," *Fronteiras de Tensão* 21, no. 61 (2007): 139–57; Vera da Silva Telles and Daniel Veloso Hirata, "Cidade e Práticas Urbanas: nas Fronteiras Incertas entre o Ilegal, o Informal e o Ilícito," *Estudos Avançados* 21, no. 61 (2007): 173–91.

54. Alba Zaluar situates herself in this perspective and provides a critique of such an approach. Alba Zaluar, "Juventude Violenta: Processos, Retrocessos e Novos Percursos," *Revista Dados* 55, no. 2 (2012): 327–65.

55. Among the inspiring efforts to *depathologize* black communities in the African Diaspora, see Khalil Gibran Muhammad, *The Condemnation of Blackness* (Cambridge, Mass.: Harvard University Press, 2011). Steven Gregory, *Black Corona: Race and the Politics of Place in an Urban Community* (New York: Columbia University Press, 1999); Keisha Khan Perry, *Black Women against the Land Grab* (Minneapolis: University of Minnesota Press, 2013).

56. According to some scholars, the myth of racial democracy is not only an ideology but also a form of "wish thinking." As a "dream," the myth helps black Brazilians to move through their daily lives while encountering racism. As an ideology, it enables whites to accumulate privilege while depoliticizing race as a category of struggle. See, for instance, Robin Sheriff, *Dreaming Equality: Color, Race, and Racism in Urban Brazil* (New Brunswick, N.J.: Rutgers University Press, 2001); France Windance Twine, *Racism in a Racial Democracy: The Maintenance of White Supremacy in Brazil* (New Brunswick, N.J.: Rutgers University Press, 1998).

57. João Costa Vargas, *Never Meant to Survive: Genocide and Utopias in Black Diaspora Communities* (Lanham, Md.: Rowman & Littlefield, 2010), 107; Robin Sheriff argues that despite the apparent abundance of categories to describe themselves, Brazilians "conceptualize racial being essentially as bipolar." Sheriff, *Dreaming Equality*, 30.

58. Revista Veja, "Rolezinho não é Problema de Polícia," *Revista Veja Online*, March 10, 2016. For a recent analysis of *Rolezinhos* see João Vargas, "Black Disidentification: The 2013 Protests, Rolezinhos, and Racial Antagonism in Post-Lula Brazil," *Critical Sociology* 42, no. 4–5 (2016): 1–15.

59. Douglas Belchior, "Rolezinhos," *Blog do Negro Belchior*, February 24, 2016, www.negrobelchior.com.

60. Devon Carbado, "Where and When Black Men Enter," in *Black Men*

on Race, Gender, and Sexuality: A Critical Reader, ed. Devon Carbado (New York: NYU Press, 1999), 9.

61. The Combahee River Collective represents a major critique of this androgynous perspective when it states, "we struggle together with black men against racism, while we also struggle with black men about sexism" (16). Underlining this argument is a call for an "integrated analysis and practice based upon the fact that the major systems of oppression are interlocking." Combahee River Collective, "The Combahee River Collective Statement," in *Home Girls: A Black Feminist Anthropology,* ed. Barbara Smith (New York: Kitchen Table Press, 1983), 63.

62. Emily Thomas, "Brazilian Women Fatally Dragged by the Police," *Huffington Post,* April 22, 2014.

63. Raquel Luciana de Souza, "Cruel Coexistence: Racial Violence and Black Disposability in the City of Blacks," (diss., University of Texas, Austin, 2016); Khan-Perry, *Black Women and the Land Grab;* Luciane Oliveira Rocha, "Black Mothers' Experiences of Violence in Rio de Janeiro," *Cultural Dynamics* 24, no. 1 (2012): 59–73; Sônia Beatriz do Santos, "Famílias Negras, Desigualdades, Saúde e Saneamento Básico no Brasil," *Tempus Actas de Saúde Coletiva* 7, no. 2 (2013): 41–53. See also Polly Wilding's compelling argument against the "ungendered" discussion about violence in urban Brazil. Polly Wilding, "New Violence: Silencing Women's Experiences in the Favelas of Brazil," *Journal of Latin American Studies* 42, no. 4 (2010): 719–47.

64. Jackeline Romio, "Homicídio de Mulheres Negras na Cidade de São Paulo," in *Retratos e Espelhos: Raça e Etnicidade no Brasil e nos Estados Unidos,* ed. Vinicius Vieria and Jacquelyn Jhonson (São Paulo: FEA/USP, 2009), 225–48; Maria Inês da Silva Barbosa, "É Mulher, Mas é Negra: Perfil da Mortalidade do 'Quarto de Despejo'," *Jornal da RedeSaúde* 23, no. 1 (2001): 12–32.

65. Satya Mohanty, "The Epistemic Status of Cultural Identity: On Beloved and the Postcolonial Condition," *Cultural Critique* 24 (1993): 41–80. I am also instructed by, among others, Joy James, *Transcending the Talented Tenth: Black Leaders and American Intellectuals* (New York: Routledge, 2014); Hortense Spillers, *Black, White, and In Color;* The Combahee River Collective, *A Black Feminist Statement* (New York: Women of Color Press, 1985).

66. It is not an overstatement to say that it was at Educafro's headquarters that one of the most comprehensive affirmative action policies in higher education (the ProUni) was developed and presented to the Workers' Party's government.

67. Arjun Appadurai, "Putting Hierarchy in Its Place," *Cultural Anthropology* 3, no. 1 (1988): 40. For a similar critique of how ethnography "position[s] subjects in spaces of confinement," see Donald Moore, *Suffering for Territory,* 18.

68. According to Mark-Anthony Falzon, "the very logic of contemporary understandings of space . . . requires that ethnographers take responsibility for their production of their field sites." Mark-Anthony Falzon, "Introduction," in *Multi-*

Sited Ethnography: Theory, Praxis and Locality in Contemporary Research, ed. Mark-Anthony Falzon (New York: Routledge, 2009), 10.

69. See, for instance, Carolyn Nordstrom and Antonius Robben, *Fieldwork under Fire: Contemporary Studies of Violence and Survival* (Berkeley: University of California Press, 1995).

70. Charles Hale, "Introduction," in *Engaging Contradictions: Theory, Politics, and Methods of Activist Scholarship* (Berkeley: University of California Press, 2008), 1–30; Shannon Speed, "Forged in Dialogue: Toward a Critically Engaged Activist Research," in *Engaging Contradictions: Theory, Politics, and Methods of Activist Scholarship*, ed. Charles Hale (Berkeley: University of California Press, 2008), 213–36.

71. Charles Hale, *Engaging Contradictions*, 21.

72. This critique has been part of a larger dialogue on the predicaments of activist scholarship in liminal spaces of racial oppression. I thank João Costa Vargas, Charles Hale, and Leith Mullings for their insightful engagement with this critique elsewhere (in personal communication).

73. Cathy J. Cohen, "Deviance as Resistance," 30.

74. Charles Hale, *Engaging Contradictions*, 3.

75. The critique put forward by the Afro-pessimist approach is that the black subject is alienated from participating in political life because his/her relation to politics is one of negation. The black subject is a *negative reference* from which political life itself is imagined and lived. For a reference on this debate see Saidiya Hartman, *Scenes of Subjection*; Wilderson, "Gramsci's Black Marx"; Sexton, "The Social Life of Social Death."

76. I came to realize that most of these tensions would not exist if I were merely doing *collaborative work* with the black movement. Doing collaborative work implies that one is not *from* the community; rather one comes and works *with* the community. Had my research been collaborative, I would have participated in the movement's daily activities, mapped its various strategies, documented its divergences, profiled the main actors, and offered an analysis of its structure and tactics. However, my work was more than collaborative. I was part of the political community under the name *movimento negro*.

77. Charles Hale observes that these contradictions are not necessarily bad, since "far from being deterrents, [these] tensions need to be understood as key sources of methodological sophistication and analytical insight." Charles Hale, "In Praise of Reckless Minds," in *Anthropology Put to Work*, ed. Les Field and Richard Fox (New York: Berg Editorial, 2007), 103–4.

78. Joy James and Edmund Gordon, "Afterwords," in Hale, *Engaging Contradictions*, 371.

79. My use of quotation marks here aims to highlight my interpretation of their skepticism with activists like myself who were suspicious for being too close to the state.

80. Robben and Nordstrom, *Fieldwork under Fire*, 12.

1. Macabre Spatialities

1. Tribunal Popular e ACAT-Brasil, "Mapa do Extermínio: Execuções Extra-judiciais e Mortes pela Omissão do Estado de São Paulo, São Paulo," *Dossie da Pena de Morte,* May 11, 2011.

2. Michael McIntyre and Heidi Nast, "Bio(necro)polis: Marx, Surplus Populations, and the Spatial Dialectics of Reproduction of Race" *Antipode* 43, no. 5 (2011): 1480.

3. The definition provided by Orlando Patterson emphasizes *dishonor* as a basic condition of the socially dead: "the permanent, violent domination of natally alienated and generally dishonored persons." Orlando Patterson, *Slavery and Social Death* (Cambridge, Mass.: Harvard University Press, 1982), 13. Patterson's reference to cultural alienation also resonates in the Herskovits–Frazier debate, which entailed the question of black cultural survival within the context of slavery and its aftermaths. Frazier advocated that blacks were not able to reproduce their social institutions because of the terror of slavery (the "problem" of black families would be a problem of culture). Herskovits, on the other hand, challenged this hypothesis, stressing the continuity of black heritage in the African American community and in African-based religion in Haiti. The implications of this debate should not be underestimated. The idea of a black culture, or the lack thereof, was and continues to be part of the narratives that pathologize black families and communities. See Franklin Frazier, "The Negro Family in Bahia, Brazil," *American Sociological Review* 7, no. 4 (1942): 465–78; Melville Herskovits, "The Negro in Bahia, Brazil: A Problem in Method," *American Sociological Review* 8, no. 4 (1943): 394–404.

4. Kia Caldwell argues that "[i]n contemporary Brazil, it is socially expected that Afro-Brazilian women will be servants, sexual objects, or social subordinates," Kia Caldwell, *Negras in Brazil: Re-envisioning Black Women, Citizenship, and the Politics of Identity* (New Brunswick, N.J.: Rutgers University Press, 2007), 57. Donna Goldstein proposes the concept of "color-blind erotic democracy" to account for the ways black women's bodies are commodified and devalued in Brazilian society. In this "economy of intersexual desire," the *mulata* becomes the subject of both the affirmation and negation of racism (Goldstein, *Laughter out of Place,* 568). On how "gendered antiblackness" is foundational to the Brazilian nation, see João Costa Vargas, "Gendered Antiblackness and the Impossible Brazilian Project: Emerging Critical Black Brazilian Studies," *Cultural Dynamics* 24, no. 1 (2012): 3–11.

5. Sueli Carneiro, "Black Women's Identity in Brazil," in *Race in Contemporary Brazil: From Indifference to Inequality,* ed. Rebecca Reichmann (University Park, Pa.: Penn State University Press, 2010), 218; Carneiro is also responding to Gilberto Freyre's assertion that in Brazilian society "white women are for marrying, *mulatas* for fornicating, black women for work." Gilberto Freyre, *Casa Grande & Senzala* (Rio de Janeiro: Record, 2000), 85.

6. Carneiro, "Black Women's Identity in Brazil," 218; Lorena Féres da Silva

Telles, *Libertas entre Sobrados: Mulheres Negras e Trabalho Doméstico em São Paulo* (São Paulo: Alameda, 2013); Celma Rosa Vieira, "Negra, Mulher e Doméstica; Considerações sobre as Relações Sociais no Emprego Doméstico," *Estudos Afro-Asiáticos* 14 (1987): 141–58. The intimate aspect of domination embedded in domestic work has been well documented by Goldstein, *Laughter out of Place*, 71–72, among others.

7. Fundação Seade, *Mulher e Trabalho: o Emprego Doméstico* (São Pulo: Seade, 2008).

8. Instituto de Pesquisa Econômica Aplicada, *Mulher Trabalhadora: Mais Emprego, Mais Igualdade* (Brasilia: Cadernos IPEA, 2016).

9. Chimamanda Ngozi Adichie, "The Danger of Single Stories" (TED talk, November 10, 2009).

10. Raquel Rolnik, *A Cidade e a Lei: Legislação, Política Urbana e Territórios na Cidade de São Paulo* (São Paulo: Studio Nobel, 1997); Paula Beiguelman, *A Crise do Escravismo e a Grande Imigração* (Rio de Janeiro: Brasiliense, 1981); Edgar Carone, *A Evolucão Industrial de São Paulo entre 1889 e 1930* (São Paulo: Editora Senac, 2001); José de Souza Martins, *O Cativeiro da Terra* (São Paulo: Hucitec, 1986); Lourdes Carril, *Quilombo, Favela e Periferia: a Longa Busca da Cidadania* (São Paulo: Annablume Editora, 2006).

11. George Andrews, *Negros e Brancos em São Paulo (1888–1988)* (Bauru: Edusc, 1998).

12. Emilia Viotti da Costa, *Da Senzala à Colônia* (São Paulo: UNESP, 1997); Rolnik, *A Cidade e a Lei*, 22–25.

13. Kabengele Munanga, *Rediscutindo a Mestiçagem no Brasil. Identidade Nacional versus Identidade Negra* (São Paulo: Editora Vozes, 1999); Thomas Skidmore, *Black into White: Race and Nationality in Brazilian Thought* (Durham, N.C.: Duke University Press, 1993).

14. Raquel Rolnik, "Territórios Negros: Etnicidade e Cidade em São Paulo e Rio de Janeiro," *Revista de Estudos Afroasiáticos* 17 (1989): 32 33; see also Carril, *Quilombo, Favela e Periferia*, 75–83.

15. Raquel Rolnik, "Territórios Negros," 32–33; Rolnik, *A Cidade e a Lei*, 73–79.

16. Luis Antônio Costa Maia, *O Ideário Urbano Paulista na Virada do Século: O Engenheiro Theodoro Sampaio e as Questões Territoriais e Urbanas Modernas em São Paulo* (São Carlos: Rima, 2003): 100–125.

17. Ibid., 120; Rolnik, *A Cidade e a Lei*, 73–79; Rolnik, "Territórios Negros, 32–33; Reinaldo José de Oliveira, *A Presença do Negro na Cidade: Memória e Território da Casa Verde em São Paulo* (master's thesis, Catholic University of São Paulo, 2008).

18. Caldeira, *City of Walls*, 213–55; Rolnik, *A Cidade e a Lei*, 181–216.

19. Teresa Caldeira also argues that as the proximity of the poorest and the richest increased (and as rising crime rates fed a moral panic), the new pattern of

urban occupation "not only exacerbated the separation of different social groups but also increased tensions and suspicions among them." Caldeira, *City of Walls*, 232, 254. Here, I do not do justice to the comprehensive literature on the spatial dynamics of social segregation in São Paulo. See, for instance, Haroldo da Gama Torres, Eduardo Marques, Maria Paula Ferreira, and Sandra Bitar, "Pobreza e Espaço: Padrões de Segregação em São Paulo," *Estudos Avançados* 17, no. 47 (2003): 97–128; Maria Ruth Amaral de Sampaio and Paulo Cesar Xavier Pereira, "Habitação em São Paulo," *Estudos Avançados* 17, no. 48 (2003): 167–83; Lucia Maria Machado Bógus and Maura Pardini Bicudo Véras, "A Reorganização Metropolitana de São Paulo: Espaços Sociais no Contexto da Globalização," *Cadernos Metrópole* 3 (2000): 81–98.

20. Carril, *Quilombo, Favela e Periferia*, 93. Carril rejects the idea of a *racial apartheid* in São Paulo even as she recognizes that "the lived territory is conceived as a picture of the reproduction of sociospatial and racial relations" (181). Surprisingly, the same ambiguous approach is present in Loïc Wacquant's analysis about Brazil. "O que é o Guetto? Construindo um Conceito Sociologico," *Revista de Sociologia e Política* 23 (November 2004):155–64.

21. Douglas Massey and Nancy Denton, *American Apartheid: Segregation and the Making of the Underclass* (Cambridge, Mass.: Harvard University Press, 1993); João Costa Vargas, "Apartheid Brasileiro: Raça e Segregação Residencial no Rio de Janeiro," *Revista de Antropologia* 48, no. 1 (2005): 75–131. For yet another dimension of the political economy of "ghetto making" in Latin America, see Zaire Dinzey-Flores, "Islands of Prestige, Gated Ghettos, and Nonurban Lifestyles in Puerto Rico," *Latin American Perspectives* 40, no. 2 (2013): 95–104.

22. Daniel Mariani, Murilo Roncolato, Simon Ducroquet e Ariel Tonglet, "Mapa da Segregacão Racial no Brasil," *Jornal Nexus*, March 15, 2016.

23. The reference parity for the US dollar (USD) and the Brazilian Real (BRL) was 1:3 as of October 2016. Data on family income, educational achievement, and violence are extracted from SMPIR, "Igualdade Racial em São Paulo: Avanços de desafios," *Secretaria Municipal de Promocão da Igualdade Racial*.

24. Ibid.

25. William Cardoso, "Polícia de São Paulo Mata nos Mesmos Lugares, os Mais Pobres," *Ponte Jornalismo Online*, September 10, 2014.

26. Jardim Angela is both a borough and a neighborhood within the borough that bears the same name. However, residents do not follow the formal borders created by the state. In everyday spatial references, the neighborhood is part of the Fundão da Zona Sul because it is located "da ponte pra cá" (meaning "on the other side of the bridge" that separates the Fundão from the prime areas bordered by the Pinheiros River).

27. "Jardim Angela Bate Cali em Homicídios," *Diário do Comércio*, March 4, 1997.

28. Folha de S. Paulo, "PM é recebida a Bala," *Caderno Cotidiano*, September 29, 1997.

29. "Drogas Assombram Jardim Angela," *Diário de S. Paulo*, March 4, 2004.

30. "Night of Blitz in Jardim Angela," *Jornal da Tarde*, October, 12, 1997.

31. Eyal Weizman, *Hollow Land: Israel's Architecture of Occupation* (New York: Verso 2007): 5.

32. Fanon, *Black Skin, White Masks*, 38.

33. Allen Feldman, *Formations of Violence: The Narrative of the Body and Political Terror in Northern Ireland* (Chicago: University of Chicago Press, 1991): 28.

34. Ibid., 73.

35. My claim here is deeply informed by Dylan Rodriguez's incisive work on the symbiotic relation between racial violence and the white subject of rights. Dylan Rodriguez, *Forced Passages: Imprisoned Radical Intellectuals and the U.S. Prison Regime* (Minneapolis: University of Minnesota Press, 2006). I am also informed by the work of Denise Ferreira da Silva, whose interventions outline a new research agenda on the economy of state making and black suffering in urban Brazil. As a "productive" technology, police terror not only produces death but also brings to life geographies of privilege and opportunity. As a space of social death, the favela is produced in these encounters with the police. For similar claims, see also Christen Smith, "Scenarios of Racial Contact: Police Violence and the Politics of Performance and Racial Formation in Brazil," *E-Misférica* 5, no. 2 (2008): 1–12; João Costa Vargas and Jaime Alves, "Geographies of Death: an Intersectional Analysis of Police Lethality and the Racialized Regimes of Citizenship in São Paulo," *Ethnic and Racial Studies* 33, no. 4 (2010): 611–36.

36. See, for example, Veena Das and Debora Poole, eds., *Anthropology in the Margins of the State* (Santa Fe, N.Mex.: School of American Research Press, 2004) and Thomas Blom Hansen and Finn Stepputat, "Sovereignty Revisited," *Annual Review of Anthropology* 35 (2006): 295–315; María Clemencia Ramírez, *Between the Guerrillas and the State: The Cocalero Movement, Citizenship, and Identity in the Colombian Amazon* (Durham, N.C.: Duke University Press, 2011).

37. João Costa Vargas, "Taking Back the Land: Police Operations and Sport Megaevents in Rio de Janeiro," *Souls* 15, no. 4 (2013): 275–303. Anthropologist Erika Larkins provides yet another interesting perspective on the deployment of spectacle as part of state making in Brazilian favelas. She analyzes the ways BOPE, the Brazilian version of SWART, uses spectacular operations to perform its power over and reclaim the favela. See Erika Larkins, *The Spectacular Favela: Violence in Modern Brazil* (Berkeley: University of California Press, 2015). Also, Vera Malaguti Batista, "O Alemão é muito mais complexo," *Revista Justiça e Sistema Criminal* 1, no. 1 (2009): 103–25.

38. This association appears in rap lyrics, poems, and public interventions by black activists. See, for instance, "Negro Drama" by singers Edi Rock and Mano Brown. Edi Rock and Mano Brown, "Negro Drama," in *Nada Como Um Dia Após o Outro* (São Paulo, Racionais MC's, 2001), compact disc.

39. He added, "Have you heard what happened to the two guys in Parelheiros?" The "two guys" whom my friend referred to had been recently kidnapped,

supposedly by Military Police, in the neighborhood of Parelheiros. Their families insisted that the youths were taken away by police officers from Rota (the police's special unit) after they had been searched at a checkpoint. Days after our conversation, the two burned bodies were found among shrubs in the favela my friend was referring to.

40. ACAT-Brasil, "Mapa do Extermínio: Execuções Extrajudiciais e Mortes pela Omissão do Estado de São Paulo," *Dossier Online*, May 10, 2011; "Pena de Morte Ilegal e Extrajudicial," *Observatório da Segurança Pública*, May 10, 2011.

41. Leandro Siqueira, at the Centro Santo Dias de Direitos Humanos, also called my attention to these cinematographic narratives. See also Jaime Alves and Leandro Siqueira, "Os Massacres se Tornaram Vitais: o terror policial como política de segurança em São Paulo" (unpublished manuscript, 2011), Microsoft Word file.

42. Michel Foucault, *Discipline and Punish: The Birth of the Prison*, trans. Alan Sheridan (New York: Vintage, 1977), 8.

43. Joy James, *Resisting State Violence*, 72. Contrary to what one may think, racial lynching is a recurrent practice in Brazil, whether committed by the police or by mob violence. The recent cases of young black men tied to poles and beaten to death in many Brazilian towns indicate the persistence of racial violence as spectacle. On July 8, 2015, for instance, Rio's *Newspaper Extra* showed the body of twenty-nine-year-old Cleidenilson Pereira da Silva on its front page. Accused of robbing a bar in the city of São Luis in northeast Brazil, he was tied to a pole in a public square and lynched. For news coverage of the case, see *Jornal Extra Online*, October 10, 2015.

44. The same can be said about news production. Crime journalists rely on the police report as the primary, and frequently the only, source of information. As in the police report, the dead appear in the news as agents of "unjust aggression" against the officers carrying out their "legal duty."

45. Human Rights Watch, "Lethal Force: Police Violence and Public Security in São Paulo and Brazil," *Executive Summary*, July 10, 2010.

46. See, for instance, Luis Eduardo Batista, *Pode o Estudo da Mortalidade Denunciar as Desigualdades Raciais?* (São Carlos: EdUFSCar, 2003); Dos Santos, "Famílias Negras, Desigualdades, Saúde," 41–53.

47. Andre Camarote, "Estribucha, diz PM a Baleado," *Folha de S. Paulo*, August 25, 2011.

48. Personal notes, Police Ombudsperson's Archives.

49. In Brazil, the ombudsperson's office and the internal affairs office oversee the military and civil police. The former files complaints from civilians and produces statistics for the secretariat of public safety. The latter investigates and presents persecution cases to the military and civilian courts.

50. Police Military Inquiry. Police Ombudsperson's Archives.

51. International Amnesty, "Você Matou meu Filho," *Executive Report*, December 10, 2015.

52. Maria Fro, "Promotor Sugere PM Atirar em Manifestantes," *Revista Fórum*, December 14, 2015.

53. Rio de Janeiro's secretariat of public safety, Jose Mariano Beltrame, made this remark justifying the slaughter of nineteen individuals in a military raid in one of Rio's favelas in 2007. The same rhetoric has been used ad nauseam by São Paulo's right-wing governor Geraldo Alckmin. In support of a police raid that killed nine individuals, he gave a public interview saying that "whoever didn't resist arrest is [still] alive." See Guillerme Voitch, "Alckmin Defende Ação da Rota," *O Globo Online*, September 9, 2012.

54. Two other former top military-police commanders hold seats in the city council of São Paulo. Likewise, at least twenty former officers serve as deputies in the Brazilian congress. See João Paulo Charleaux, "Brasil Pode Eleger Deputado que já Matou 40," *Revista Vice*, October 25, 2016; Brasil 247, "Com Trinta e Sete Mortes nas Costas Telhada vai para CDH," *Edição São Paulo 247*, May 9, 2015.

55. Mathieu Deflem, "The Ends of the State: Anarchy, Terror, and Police, 1851 to 9-11," *Comparative & Historical Sociology* 16, no. 1 (Fall 2004): 5.

56. Broadly, Michel Foucault conceptualizes the "police" as "a project for governing territory" or a "programme of government rationality." While Foucault is not referring to "officers" per se, his definition has informed many theories of policing that, although not exclusively about the uniformed branch of government, nonetheless includes it. In that sense, the claim I make here about *policing* as a means of social organizing and social reproduction is hardly new. It is in consonance with Foucault's broad understanding of policing as a rationality of power. See Michel Foucault, *The Foucault Reader*, ed. Paul Rabinow (New York: Pantheon, 1984), 241. An analysis of the concept of "police" in Foucault can be found in Colin Gordon, "Governmental Rationality," in *The Foucault Effect*, eds. Graham Burchell, Colin Gordon, and Peter Miller (Chicago: University of Chicago Press, 1991), 12.

57. Although there is no consensus among scholars about the "state," it is a well-established field of analysis. A reference in this regard is Philip Abrams's conceptualization of the state as "an ideological artifact." See Philip Abrams, "Notes on the Difficulty of Studying the State," *Journal of Historical Sociology* 1, no. 1 (March 1988): 81. Likewise, Begoña Aretxaga's understanding of the state in terms of its outcomes rather than its abstractions is an important contribution to the field. Begoña Aretxaga's "Maddening States," *Annual Review of Anthropology* 32, no. 1 (2003): 393–410.

58. Martha Huggins, Mika Fatouros, and Philip Zimbardo, *Violence Workers: Police Torturers and Murderers Reconstruct Brazilian Atrocities* (Berkeley: University of California Press, 2002), 248.

59. Rogerio Pagnan, "Metade do País acha que Bandido Bom é Bandido Morto," *Folha Cotidiano Online*, October 30, 2015. See also Willis, *The Killing*

Consensus; Pinheiro, "Autoritarismo e Transição"; Holston and Caldeira, "Democracy and Violence in Brazil."

60. Roque was a student at Educafro where, before joining the police force, he participated in an education project preparing black students for the admission exam to a public university.

61. Livio Sansone, "Fugindo para a força: cultura corporativista e 'cor' na polícia militar do estado do Rio de Janeiro," *Estudos Afro-Asiáticos*, vol. 24, no. 3 (2002): 513–32; Silvia Ramos and Leonarda Musumeci, *Elemento Suspeito: Abordagem Policial e Discriminação na Cidade do Rio de Janeiro* (Rio de Janeiro: Civilização Brasileira, 2005).

62. Miriam Wells, "Why do Brazilian Police Kill?," *InSight Crime*, November 21, 2013.

63. Fanon, *Black Skin, White Masks*, 111. An example: a recent *memorandum* from the higher commander of São Paulo Military Police in the city of Campinas instructed officers to focus attention "especially on black individuals ages 18–25." See Thaís Nunes, "PM Da Ordem para Abordar Negros e Pardos," *Diário de S. Paulo*, January 23, 2013.

64. María Victoria Uribe, *Matar, Rematar y Contramatar. Las Masacres de la Violencia en el Tolima* (Bogota: Centro de Investigación y Educación Popular, 1978), 168.

65. The duality *bandido* versus *trabalhador* (bandit versus worker) is a theme well-analyzed in Brazilian social sciences. See for instance, Zaluar, *A Máquina e a Revolta*; Feltran, *Fronteiras de Tensão*; Misse, "Sujeito, Crime e Sujeição Criminal."

66. For example, Caldeira and Holston, "Democracy and Violence in Brazil"; Pinheiro, "Autoritarismo e Transição."

67. James, *Transcending the Talented Tenth*, 121.

68. Holland, *Raising the Dead*, 15. The multiple ways blacks occupy *death worlds* can be synthesized in Achille Mbembe's forceful question: "But what does it mean to do violence to what is nothing?" Mbembe, *On the Postcolony*, 174.

69. Of course, the process of destroying black men's biographies is part of a much larger "controlling image" of black bodies in Brazil and beyond. Think, for example, on the fictional narratives of black men as *the* urban criminal. Brazilian popular movies such as *City of God* and *Elite Squad* invest heavily in such dehumanizing strategies by associating black youth with crime and violence. See Jaime Alves, "Narratives of Violence: the White Imagination and the Making of Black Masculinity in City of God," *CS* 13 (2014): 313–37.

70. Luciane Rocha, "De-matar: Maternidade Negra Como Ação Política na Pátria Mãe-Gentil," in *Antinegritude: o Impossível Sujeito Negro*, ed. João Costa Vargas and Osmundo Pinho (Cachoeira: Editora da UFRB, 2016), 177–92. This battle to counter criminalizing narratives of their children has been well documented in Brazil, particularly in the context of Rio de Janeiro, Bahia, and São Paulo. See Adriana Vieira and Juliana Farias, "A Guerra das Mães: Dor e Política em Situações

de Violência Institucional," *Cadernos Pagú* 37 (2016): 79–116; Vilma Reis, "Atucaiados pelo Estado: as Políticas de Segurança Pública Implementadas nos Bairros
Populares de Salvador e Suas Representações," (master's thesis, Universidade Federal da Bahia, 2005); Renata Gonçalves, "De Antigas e Velhas Loucas: Madres
e Mães de Maio contra a Violência de Estado," *Lutas Sociais* 29 (2012): 130–43.
    71. Fernanda da Escóssia, "Chacina de Costa Barros: Por que são as Famílias
que Têm de dar Explicações?," *BBC Brasil,* April 15, 2016.

2. "Police, Get Off My Back!"

    1. In fact, I would argue, institutional loyalty, depersonification, and bureau-
cratization make policing practices perhaps the most important exercise of state
sovereignty. For a detailed discussion on policing and bureaucracy see Mathieu
Deflem, "The Ends of the State," 3–5; Martha Huggins, Mika Haritos-Fatouros,
and Philip Zimbardo, *Violence Workers: Police Torturers and Murderers Reconstruct
Brazilian Atrocities* (Berkeley: University of California Press, 2002).
    2. Although still marginal, there is a growing literature on race and police
violence in Brazil. This scholarship suggests that an anti-black ideology of what
constitutes the urban threat, who deserves living, and whose lives are disposable
pervades both the state apparatus and Brazilian society at large. It also calls attention to how the everyday reality of anti-black racism informs policing practices
in Brazil. See, for instance, Jan Hoffman French, "Rethinking Police Violence in
Brazil: Unmasking the Public Secret of Race," *Latin American Politics and Society* 55, no. 4 (2013): 161–81; Jorge da Silva, "The Favelados in Rio de Janeiro,
Brazil," *Policing and Society: An International Journal* 10, no. 1 (2000): 121–30;
Vargas and Alves, "Geographies of Death," 611–36; Vilma Reis, *Atucaiados pelo
Estado*; Collins, "Policing's Productive Folds."
    3. For recent critical engagements with Foucault's concept of "governmen-
tality" in urban contexts, see Sally Engle Merry, "Spatial Governmentality and the
New Urban Social Order: Controlling Gender Violence through Law," *American
Anthropologist* 103, no. 1 (2001): 16–29; Steven Robins, "At the Limits of Spatial
Governmentality: A Message from the Tip of Africa," *Third World Quarterly* 23,
no. 4 (2002): 665–89; Jeff Garmany, "The Embodied State: Governmentality in a
Brazilian Favela," *Social & Cultural Geography* 10, no. 7 (2009): 721–39.
    4. Amar, *The Security Archipelago*, 16.
    5. Ibid.; Samara, *Cape Town after Apartheid*, 19; Swapna Banerjee-Guha,
"Neoliberalising the 'Urban': New Geographies of Power and Injustice in Indian
Cities," *Economic and Political Weekly* (2009): 95–107; Austin Zeiderman, "Living
Dangerously: Biopolitics and Urban Citizenship in Bogotá, Colombia," *American
Ethnologist* 40, no. 1 (2013): 71–87. Such security concerns pre-date neoliberal-
ism, but the restructuring of the economy has always been the backdrop for their
enforcement. In their analysis of Britain's 1970 fiscal crisis, Stuart Hall and his

colleagues argued that the British government's "tough" approach to crime was a response to its own failure to sustain consensus in addressing drastic economic changes. By targeting street crime and mugging, the state mobilized a *moral panic* and thus justified an internal war against racialized groups. "Managing the Crisis" (305) became a matter of creating fictional narratives about a society endangered by a black enemy. Hall et al. note that "black crime [became] the signifier of the crisis in the urban colonies." Stuart Hall, Chas Critcher, Tony Jefferson, John Clarke, and Brian Roberts, *Policing the Crisis: Mugging, the State, and Law and Order* (London: Palgrave-Macmillan, 1978), 339.

6. Granting rights, at least discursively, is part of the neoliberal state's strategy of accommodating political antagonisms without threatening the interests of national elites. It was under the neoliberal turn—from Cardoso's vociferous version to Lula da Silva's lighter model—that the Brazilian state officially recognized racism as a structural problem, adopted race-based affirmative-action policies, and implemented social policies that positively impact the lives of millions of Afro-Brazilians. The same period was marked by astonishing levels of black death. For an analysis of the Brazilian "contradiction" see João Costa Vargas, "Black Disidentification." The neoliberal "paradox" of granting rights and denying life is not unique to Brazil. In his analysis of the limits and possibility of neoliberal multiculturalism, Charles Hale observes that the recognition of cultural rights and the denial of economic rights are not contradictory but rather are the very feature of neoliberal governance. For a more detailed discussion on this point, see Charles Hale, "Does Multiculturalism Menace? Governance, Cultural Rights, and the Politics of Identity in Guatemala," *Journal of Latin American Studies* 34, no. 3 (2002): 485–524.

7. See Jamil Chade, "Conselho de Seguranca Sugere Fim da Policia Militar no Brasil," *Estadão Oline*, May 15, 2012.

8. Andre Caramante and Joanna Brasileiro, "PMs de SP Mataram Mais de 10 Mil em 19 Anos," *Ponte Jornalismo Online*, December 10, 2015.

9. This has also been the central argument of Tony Roshan Samara in his analysis of urban development and security governance in Cape Town, South Africa. See Samara, *Cape Town after Apartheid.* Similarly, scholars working on other racialized contexts have highlighted such connections; see, for instance, Keisha-Khan Perry, *Black Women against the Land Grab*; Cristina Rojas, "Securing the State and Developing Social Insecurities: The Securitisation of Citizenship in Contemporary Colombia," *Third World Quarterly* 30, no. 1 (2009): 227–45.

10. Helga Leitner, Eric Sheppard, Kristin Sziarto, and Annant Maringanti, "Contesting Urban Futures, Decentering Neoliberalism," in *Contesting Neoliberalism: Urban Frontiers*, ed. Helga Leitner, Jamie Peck, and Eric Sheppard (New York: Guilford Press, 2007), 10. The hyperpunitiveness of neoliberalism is well analyzed by Steve Herbert and Elizabeth Brown, "Conceptions of Space and Crime in the Punitive Neoliberal City," *Antipode* 38, no. 4 (2006): 755–77; Loïc Wacquant, "Crafting the Neoliberal State: Workfare, Prisonfare, and Social Insecurity," *Sociological Forum* 25, no. 2 (June 2010): 197–220.

11. Governo do Estado de S. Paulo, "Alckmin Assina Acordo para Formar Policiais Comunitários em Países da América Latina," *SP Noticias, Boletim Online,* March 29, 2012. The Japanese model was tested in 1999, and in 2005 the São Paulo Military Police signed an agreement with its Japanese counterpart to implement the model throughout the state of São Paulo. The project has also received several other awards, and has been a three-time winner of the Citizen Police Award by the Instituto Sou da Paz. Secretaria da Seguranca Publica, "Ações Comunitárias," www .ssp.sp.gov.br/acoes/lcAcoes.aspx?id=33362.

12. After the dictatorship period of 1964–85, the "new" Brazilian Constitution (1988) established several channels to grant popular participation in matters of public health, education, and security. Among those initiatives, a series of institutional mechanisms were created by the first democratically elected São Paulo governor, André Franco Montoro, to ensure popular participation at the local level: these included the community security councils. The councils were part of his progressive and ambitious "Plano Montoro," which aimed to create what he called a "new police" committed to the "rule of law" and human rights. Montoro's failure to reform the police has been the subject of several studies. Scholars suggest that middle-class Brazilians' fear of crime, the 1980s fiscal crisis, and corporatist resistance against police reform were the main reasons for the government's failure to create the "new police." The current configuration of the Consegs as a forum dominated by the police, NGOs, and local businessmen reflects the antagonistic forces against Montoro's plan. For an extended analysis of "Plano Montoro," see Ana Paula Galdeano, "Para Falar em Nome da Seguranca: O Que Pensam, Querem e Fazem os Representantes dos Conselhos Comunitários de Segurança," (dissertation, University of Campinas, 2009); Caldera, *City of Walls,* 165–71; Paulo Mesquita Neto, "Policiamento Comunitário: a Experiência em São Paulo," *Revista Brasileira de Ciências Criminais* 7, no. 25 (January–March 1999): 281–92.

13. This model, replicated in large Latin American cities such as Bogotá, Belo Horizonte, Mexico City, and Guatemala City, has received the support of international organizations such as the Inter-American Development Bank. For the international dynamics of police reform, see Hesta Groenewald and Gordon Peake, *Police Reform through Community-Based Policing* (New York: International Peace Academy and Safe World, 2004); For a comparative framework on community policing programs in the "developing world," see Robert Davis, Nicole Henderson, and Cybele Merrick, "Community Policing: Variations on the Western Model in the Developing World," *Police Practice and Research* 4, no. 3 (2003): 285–300. For a critique of the Western-orientalist model of policing in Africa, see Mike Brogden, "Commentary: Community Policing: A Panacea from the West," *African Affairs* 103, no. 413 (2004): 635–49.

14. Crime and insecurity are regarded as economic problems that, if solved, would enable economic growth and more inclusive societies. That is implicit, for example, in the UNPD's Executive Report, "Citizen Security with a Human Face," in which the organization offers a series of proposals for solving the problem of

"insecurity" in Latin America. The connection between security and development could be better understood as a "securing citizenship to securing capital" strategy, one that transforms citizenship into a security matter as much as it transforms security into a market matter, as seen in Brazil's preparation for the 2014 World Cup and in the Colombian "democratic security" strategy on crime and underdevelopment. See Vargas, "Taking Back the Land"; Diana Ojeda, "War and Tourism: The Banal Geographies of Security in Colombia's 'Retaking'," *Geopolitics* 18, no. 4 (2013): 759–78.

15. Robert Trojanowicz and Bonnie Bucqueroux, *Policiamento Comunitário: Como Começar* (São Paulo: Imprensa Oficial, 1999), 5.

16. As Nikolas Rose argues, "[I]n the institution of the community, a sector is brought into existence whose vectors and forces can be mobilized, enrolled, deployed in novel programs and techniques which encourage and harness active practices of self-management and identity construction, of personal ethics and collective allegiances." Nikolas Rose, *Powers of Freedom: Reframing Political Thought* (Cambridge: Cambridge University Press, 1999), 176. Many other authors have discussed this "new game of power" in terms of a "neoliberal governmentality." See Tomas Lemke, "'The Birth of Bio-Politics': Michel Foucault's Lecture at the Collège de France on Neo-liberal Governmentality," *Economy and Society* 30, no. 2 (2001): 190–207; Merry, "Spatial Governmentality and the New Urban Social Order." Tania Murray Li provides insightful discussion on the uses of *community* as a strategy of governing within the context of improvement programs pushed forward by the World Bank in Indonesia. See Tania Murray Li, *The Will to Improve,* 231–36.

17. Aaron Roussell, "Policing the Anticommunity: Race, Deterritorialization, and Labor Market Reorganization in South Los Angeles," *Law and Society Review* 49, no. 4: 816.

18. I am aware that such an affirmation may reinforce stereotypes about black urbanity. In *Black Corona,* Steven Gregory challenges the myth of black urban pathologies by showing how residents of Corona and East Elmhurst in New York City embrace community-based activism to demand their right to the city. Despite, or because of, racial hostilities, blacks were able to express their spatial agency through "community." See Gregory, *Black Corona,* 139–78.

19. Saidiya Hartman, *Scenes of Subjection,* 138.

20. It is interesting to note that even though the media are quite supportive of the police's tough actions against the favelas, police officers complain that the media misread their work. On the media's tactic of supporting police violence against poor and predominantly black communities in Brazil, see Maria Victoria Benevides, *Violência, Povo e Polícia* (São Paulo: Brasiliense, 1983); Danilo Angrimani, *Espreme que Sai Sangue: um Estudo do Sensacionalismo na Imprensa* (São Paulo: Summus Editorial, 1994).

21. I am aware of the difficulty (and political problems) of classifying individuals in the highly complex system of racial taxonomy in Brazil. When employing

the word "blacks," I am referring to the populations whose skin color puts them in greater vulnerability than other social groups. The category "nordestino" is tricky. Northeasterners are racially diverse and many of them are black or brown, including myself. I emphasize skin color for, as sociological studies have shown, race relations in Brazil are deeply informed by "pigmentocracy." While other cultural/biological traits certainly have a place in the ways race is conceived, the "symbolic purchase" of lighter skin color is a defining feature of racial privilege in Brazilian society. On *pigmentocracy* in Brazil and Latin America, see Edward Telles, René Flores, and Fernando Urrea-Giraldo, "Pigmentocracies: Educational Inequality, Skin Color, and Census Ethnoracial Identification in Eight Latin American Countries," *Research in Social Stratification and Mobility* 40 (2015): 39–58.

22. Caldeira, *City of Walls*, 87.

23. Although she does not identify the Conselho de Segurança as a racial formation, Ana Paula Galdeano's analysis of two different Consegs in the city of São Paulo (Campo Belo and Sapopemba) highlights similar sets of discourses. In the Consegs that Galdeano attended, categories such as disease, purity, favelado, and prostitute were coded to mean spatial disorder. See Galdeano, *Para Falar em Nome da Segurança*.

24. The racial imaginary around the *baile funk* is reproduced by the international press. In a news report from 2001, the *Washington Post* described the *baile funk* in the following way: "The 'funk balls' of Rio are pantheons of pleasure and violence that have gained international renown as the world's fiercest urban dance scene. Brazilian funk—inspired by the sounds and styles of American gangsta rap and hip-hop but far more extreme than either—and the balls where it is played are the most controversial craze yet in Latin America's largest nation." Anthony Faiola, "The Fierce Beat of Shantytown Chic: In Rio, Funk Scene Thrills and Alarms," *Washington Post*, July 11, 2001; Jessica Diaz-Hurtado, "Murder, Gangs and Hope. A Brief History of Criminalization of Baile Funk in Brazil," *Remezcla*, April 10, 2014, http://remezcla.com/features/music/murders-gangs.

25. A law approved by the city council of São Paulo in 2013 tried to prohibit *baile funks* on the grounds that they were the loci of drugs and violence. In 2015 the governor of the state of São Paulo Geraldo Alckmin signed a law prohibiting the *baile funks* and "pancadões." G1 São Paulo, "Alckmin Sanciona Lei que Proíbe Pancadões no Estado de São Paulo," *Portal G1 Online*, December 11, 2015.

26. Tatiana Santiago, "PM gasta R$ 1,5 milhão em 2015 no Combate a Pancadões," *Jornal O Globo Online*, May 17, 2015.

27. Hazel V. Carby, "Policing the Black Woman's Body in an Urban Context," *Critical Inquiry* 18, no. 4 (1992): 738–55; Kali Gross, *Colored Amazons: Crime, Violence, and Black Women in the City of Brotherly Love, 1880–1910* (Durham, N.C.: Duke University Press, 2014); Rocha, "Black Mothers Experience of Violence in Rio de Janeiro," 59–73; Dorothy Roberts, *Killing the Black Body: Race, Reproduction, and the Meanings of Liberty* (New York: Pantheon Books, 1997).

28. Ibid. Analyzing the migration of black women from rural areas to cities in the northern United States, Hazel Carby argues that the sexual behavior of black migrant women became a major moral concern for political and economic reasons. Such anxieties were not exclusive to white middle class; the urban black middle class embraced respectability as a way to achieve social mobility in the white supremacist world. As Hazel Carby notes, "Thus the migrating black woman could be variously situated as a threat to the progress of the race; as a threat to the establishment of a respectable urban black middle class; as a threat to congenial black-and white-middle-class relations; and as a threat to the formation of black masculinity in an urban environment." Carby, "Policing the Black Women's Body," 741.

29. The favelas pointed out by Cabral were under military supervision by the national army and by Rio's Special Unit (BOPE) as part of a "pacifying" program to "secure" the city in order to host international sports megaevents in 2014 and 2016. See Aluisio Freire, "Cabral Defende Aborto Contra Violência no Rio," *Portal G1 Online,* April 15, 2014.

30. As I discuss in chapter 4, the fall in homicide rates in the periphery of São Paulo has multicausal explanations. The Forum ignored both the presence of PCC and the fact that it was now the police who posed the main threat of homicidal violence in the periphery.

31. Their concern was not out of context: the Zona Sul has the largest population living in favelas localized in risky areas in the city of São Paulo. See SEMPLA, "Areas de Risco," *Prefeitura de São Paulo,* May 16, 2012.

32. Partha Chatterjee, *The Politics of the Governed: Reflections on Popular Politics in Most of the World* (New York: Columbia University Press, 2004), 135.

33. Many inquiries have been raised by scholars working on the politics of black legibility. For a reference, see João Vargas and Joy James, *Refusing Blackness-as-Victimization: Trayvon Martin and the Black Cyborgs* (unpublished manuscript, University of Texas at Austin, 2012); Rosbelinda Cárdenas, "Green Multiculturalism: Articulations of Ethnic and Environmental Politics in a Colombian 'Black Community,'" *The Journal of Peasant Studies* 39, no. 2 (2012): 309–33.

34. Ibid., 41.

35. For yet another alternative interpretation of the "practice of politics" as resistance to governmentality, see Li, *The Will to Improve,* 156–91.

36. I borrow the term from Charles Hale, although the framework developed here dialogues with the so-called Afro-pessimist perspective referenced above.

37. H. L. T. Quan, "Emancipatory Social Inquiry: Democratic Anarchism and the Robinsonian Method," *African Identities* 11, no. 2 (2013): 121. I also develop this argument in yet another starkly similar context in Jaime Alves, "Refusing to Be Governed: State Violence and the Politics of Black Ungovernability in a Colombian Shantytown" (unpublished manuscript).

38. According to my interlocutors, "the people from the Council *faz o jogo da polícia* [play the police game]."

39. Although my research pre-dates these new developments, the police continue to be linked to several slaughters in the peripheries of São Paulo. In 2015 alone there were fifteen slaughters in the peripheries of greater São Paulo, including Zona Sul. Human rights organizations have insisted that off-duty police officers are implicated in these massacres, but police investigations "fail" to draw connections to the police. See Jaime Alves, "Police Terror in Brazil," *Open Democracy*, January 10, 2015.

40. Fanon, *Black Skin, White Masks*, 111.

41. See Arthur Kleinman, "Introduction," in *Social Suffering*, ed. Arthur Kleinman, Veena Das, and Margaret Lock (Berkeley: University of California Press, 1997), vii. For another comprehensive discussion of the concept of structural violence, see Nancy Scheper-Hughes and Philippe Bourgois, "Introduction: Making Sense of Violence," in *Violence in War and Peace: An Anthology*, eds. Nancy Scheper-Hughes and Philippe I. Bourgois (Malden, Mass.: Blackwell, 2004), 1–31; Paul Farmer, *Pathologies of Power: Health, Human Rights, and the New War on the Poor* (Berkeley: University of California Press, 2004).

3. The Favela-Prison Pipeline

1. It was primarily in the capacity of antiprison activist that I had access to prison facilities. As a member of the Prisoners Advocacy Network group, I was allowed to visit prisoners every week, which I did for a year with four other colleagues. Usually, the group was divided into two; another colleague and I would visit a prison hall (where the inmates sunbathed) while others would visit inmates at the other side of the prison hall. Although the group took turns visiting the *raio* (prison courtyard) every week, I managed to continue (most of the time) visiting the same courtyard (at least every other week), which allowed me to have sustainable conversations with a small group of inmates. The Advocacy Network was not the only way I had access to the prison universe. Prisoners provided me useful information for contacting their families and former prisoners in the favelas. Also, at AMPARAR (Association of Parents and Friends of Incarcerated Youth) and UNEafro-Brasil's educational program, I had several opportunities to meet and interact with former prisoners and their relatives struggling for approval in the highly selective admission exams for public universities.

2. The indigenous population makes up less than 1 percent of the prison population and is subjected to an exclusive penal system. In the Brazilian complex of racial classification, "yellow" is a broad category that includes "Asian-Brazilian" and other foreigners who do not fall into the black, white, and *pardo* categories. For access to the prison racial census, see Conselho Nacional de Justiça, "Populacão Feminina cresce 567 percent em 15 anos," *CNJ Online Bulletin*, March 10, 2015; InfoPen, "Censo Penitenciário Nacional/ InfoPen," Ministério da Justiça, February 19, 2015.

3. Pastoral Carcerária, "Relatório Sobre Mulheres Encarceradas no Brasil," February 2007, http://asbrad.com.br/conteúdo/relatório_oea.pdf.

4. Angela Davis, "From the Prison of Slavery to the Slavery of Prison: Frederick Douglas and the Convict Lease System," in *The Angela Davis Reader*, ed. Joy James (New York: Wiley-Blackwell, 1998), 74–96.

5. Andrei Koerner, "Punição, Disciplina e Pensamento Penal no Brasil do Século XIX," *Lua Nova* 68 (2006): 205–42; Eugenio Raúl Zaffaroni and Nino Batista, *Direito Penal Brasileiro* (Rio de Janeiro: Revan, 2003).

6. José Henrique Pierangelli, *Códigos Penais do Brasil: Evolução Histórica* (São Paulo: Jolavi, 1980), 316. The Criminal Code of 1830 had already criminalized vangrancy, as discussed in Thomas Holloway, *Polícia no Rio de Janeiro: Repressão e Resistência numa Cidade do Século XIX* (Rio de Janeiro: Fundacão Getulio Vargas, 1997). Rural correctional facilities provided wageless labor to former slaveholders still struggling to be indemnified by the Brazilian state. Forced labor as a punishment for crime also disciplined urban life in the postslavery republic. See Karla Leal Luz de Souza, "A Atuação da Justiça e dos Políticos contra a Prática da Vadiagem: as Colônias Correcionais Agrícolas em Minas Gerais (1890–1940)" (master's thesis, Universidade Federal de Vicosa, 2006).

7. Clóvis Moura, *O Negro-de Bom Cidadão a Mau Escravo* (Rio de Janeiro: Conquista, 1977). Celia Maria Marinho de Azevedo provides a historical account of the feared black population migrating to the city in the wake of the abolition of slavery. The fear of the "freed negro" would inform the penal policies and urban design still in place in the city. Celia Maria Marinho de Azevedo, *Onda Negra, Medo Branco: o Negro no Imaginário das Elites do Século XIX* (São Paulo: Annablume, 1987).

8. Joy James, "Democracy and Capitivities," xxxv.

9. Zaffaroni and Batista, *Direito Penal Brasileiro*, 71; For the United States, see Carol Anderson, *White Rage: The Unspoken Truth of Our Racial Divide* (New York: Bloomsbury, 2016).

10. Joy James, "Democracy and Capitivities"; Angela Davis, "From the Prison of Slavery to the Slavery of Prison," 74–96; Manning Marable, "Black Radicalism and an Economy of Incarceration," in *States of Confinement: Policing, Detention, and Prisons*, ed. Joy James (Boston: Saint Martin's Press, 2000), 53–59; Anderson, *White Rage*. This seems to be an honest assessment for a country in which blacks and Latinos make up nearly 60 percent of those imprisoned and one out of fifteen black young males are behind bars (in opposition to one out of a hundred and six whites). Blacks and Latinos make up 30 percent of the U.S. population. See U.S. Department of Justice, "Prisoners in 2013," http://www.bjs.gov/content/pub/pdf/p13.pdf.

11. Aloysio Biondi, *O Brasil Privatizado: um Balance do Desmonte do Estado* (São Paulo: Editora da Fundacão Perseu Abramo, 2003); Francisco Anuatti-Neto, Milton Barossi-Filho, Antonio Gledson de Carvalho, and Roberto Macedo, "Os

Efeitos da Privatização sobre o Desempenho Econômico e Financeiro das Empresas Privatizadas," *Revista Brasileira de Economia* 59, no. 2 (2005): 151–75; Ricardo Antunes, *A Desertificação Neoliberal no Brasil: Collor, FHC e Lula* (São Paulo: Autores Associados, 2004).

12. See Paulo Roberto de Almeida, "Um Balanco Preliminary do Governo Lula: a Grande Mudanca Medida pelos Numeros," *Espaço Acadêmico*, Ano 5, no. 58 (2010): 38–45; Biondi, *O Brasil Privatizado*. As for unemployment under Cardoso's administration, the official unemployment rate was 11.7 percent. See Felipe Loreiro, "Desenvolvimentismo às Avessas: o Processo de Desindustrialização Brasileiro sob a Egide Neoliberal (1990–1999)," *Revista de Economia Política e História Econômica* 8 (July 2007): 33–62.

13. Antunes, *A Desertificação Neoliberal no Brasil*; Cristiano Monteiro da Silva, "Imperialismo e Dívida Externa nos Governos de Fernando Henrique Cardoso e Lula," *Ponto-e-Vírgula: Revista de Ciências Sociais* 2 (2007): 198–209; Edmilson Costa, "Os Vinte anos do Plano Real: uma heranca terrivel para os brasileiros," http://resistir.info/brasil/plano_real_20_anos.html.

14. See Sales Augusto dos Santos, Eliane Cavalleiro, Maria Inês da Silva Barbosa, and Matilde Ribeiro, "Affirmative Actions: Polemics and Possibility about Racial Equality and the Role of the State," *Revista Estudos Feministas* 16, no. 3 (2008): 913–29.

15. See "Dados Penitenciários," *Observatorio da Segurança Pública*, www.observatoriodeseguranca.org/dados/custos; IPEA, "Analise dos Custos e Consequencias Sociais da Violência no Brasil," Texto Para Discussao 1284, *Digital Repository IPEA*, June 2007, http://repositorio.ipea.gov.br/handle/11058/1824. Urban violence "eats" approximately 5 percent of the Brazilian GDP. In 2013 alone, the social and economic cost of violence in Brazil was 192 billion Brazilian Reais (approximately 70 billion USD). FBSP, "Anuario Brasileiro da Seguranca Publica (Brasilia: Fórum Brasileiro de Segurança Pública, 2014).

16. See Jorge Zaverucha, "(Des)Controle Civil sobre os Militares no Governo Fernando Henrique Cardoso," *Lusotopie* (2003): 399–418; Jorge Zaverucha, *Frágil Democracia: Collor, Itamar, FHC e os Militares* (Editora Record: Rio de Janeiro, 2000). Cardoso created a working group headed by his minister of justice, Jose Gregory, with the goal of crafting a new plan for public security that did not come to fruition until another crisis in public safety (a bus hostage crisis on June 12, 2006) under President Lula da Silva's administration. Folha de S. Paulo, "Assaltante Sequestra Onibus no Centro do Rio," *Folha Online*, June 12, 2000.

17. Zaverucha, "(Des)Controle Civil"; Luiz Eduardo Soares, "A Política Nacional de Segurança Pública: Histórico, Dilemas e Perspectivas," *Estudos Avançados* 21, no. 61 (2007): 77–97.

18. Marco Antonio Ferreira e Rafael Pinho Machado, "A Divida Pública do Estado de São Paulo," October 2012, http://marcopsol.blogspot.com.br/2014/08/a-divida-publica-do-estado-de-São-paulo.html.

19. By way of comparison, at the end of the 1980s the state of São Paulo's unemployment rate was already high at 8.7 percent. For the dynamics of employment in the 1990s, see Mário Rodarte, Thaiz Silveira Braga, and Lúcia Santos Garcia, "Desemprego de Longa Duração como Corolário da 'Década Neoliberal': a Evolução do Desemprego Metropolitano entre as Décadas de 1990 a 2000," *Anais do IX Encontro Nacional da Associação Brasileira de Estudos do Trabalho* (Recife: ABET, 2005), 1–25; Lilia Montali, "Relação Família-Trabalho: Reestruturação Produtiva e Desemprego," *São Paulo em Perspectiva* 17, no. 2 (2003): 123–35.

20. Rodarte, Braga, and Garcia, "Desemprego de Longa Duração," 1–15; Marcio Pochmann, *O trabalho sob fogo cruzado: Exclusão, desemprego e precarização no final do século* (São Paulo: Contexto, 1999).

21. *Mapa da População Negra no Mercado de Trabalho* (São Paulo: Fundacão DIEESE, 1998).

22. Loïc Wacquant, "Crafting the Neoliberal State: Workfare, Prisonfare, and Social Insecurity," *Sociological Forum* 25, no. 2 (June 2010): 198. Some scholars have contended that Wacquant's critique of the welfare state turned into prisonfare is very contextual to the United States because in some societies from the so-called Third World there was no welfare state to be dismantled in the first place. See, for instance, Elisa Brisola, "Estado Penal, Criminalização da Pobreza e Serviço Social," *Revista SER Social* 14, no. 30 (2012): 127–54.

23. As defined in David Harvey, *A Brief History of Neoliberalism* (New York: Oxford University Press, 2007), 188.

24. See Nicholas De Lissovoy, "Conceptualizing the Carceral Turn: Neoliberalism, Racism, and Violation," *Critical Sociology* 39, no. 5 (2012): 739–55; Also, Michael McIntyre and Heidi Nast, "Bio (necro) polis"; David Roberts, and Minelle Mahtani, "Neoliberalizing Race, Racing Neoliberalism: Placing Race in Neoliberal Discourses," *Antipode* 42, no. 2 (2010): 248–57.

25. As Jodi Melamed argues, under multicultural neoliberalism "the new racism deploys economic, ideological, cultural, and religious distinctions to produce lesser personhoods, laying these new categories of privilege and stigma across conventional racial categories, fracturing them into differential status groups." Jodi Melamed, "The Spirit of Neoliberalism from Racial Liberalism to Neoliberal Multiculturalism," *Social Text* 24, no. 4 (89) (2006): 14; Hale, "Does Multiculturalism Menace?"

26. Dylan Rodríguez Uguez, *Forced Passages*, 25.

27. While the state spends an annual average of R$16,000 with each inmate, it spends almost five times less (R$3,700) per student. See Wanderley Sobrinho, "Gestão Alckmin Gasta Quase 5 Vezes Mais com Detento do que com Aluno," *Revista Brasileiro*, October 15, 2015.

28. See Portaria Ministerial Portaria, n. 369 de 13 de maio de 1997. For an overview of São Paulo's public expenditure on the prison system, see "Dados Penitenciários," *Observatório da Segurança Pública* www.observatoriodesegu

ranca.org/dados/penitenciario (accessed March 30, 2013). For federal- and state- level budgets on the prison system, see INFOSEG, "São Paulo Amplia Prisão de Traficantes," Portal JusBrasil, June 10, 2007; PSDB, "Polícia Moderna e Equipada Reduz Criminalidade e Aumenta Prisões," *Plano de Governo*, June 10, 2011.

29. Andre Caramante, "Raio x das Prisões de São Paulo," *Portal R7*, September 9, 2014.

30. The increase in public spending on public security is expected to rise even more as the Brazilian congress is expected to approve the Proposal for Constitutional Amendment that was already approved by the Brazilian senate in 2007. This proposal mandates the increase in public expenditure on public security to 10 percent of the Brazilian gross domestic product (GDP). The proposal obligates states and municipalities alike to spend 7 percent and 1 percent of their annual budget, respectively, on public security. In comparison, the federal government's expansion of public security over the last decade has represented 1.5 percent of the Brazilian GDP. See IPEA, "Custos Sociais da Violencia, Texto para DiscusSão," *Boletim Ipea 1214*; IPEA, "Segurança Pública, Evolução da Conjuntura," *Boletim Ipea*, March 28, 2010. For public spending on public safety in 2014 see FSP, *Anuário Brasileiro da Segurança Pública* (São Paulo: Fórum de Segurança Pública, 2015), 53.

31. Like his predecessor, Lula da Silva designed a set of penal policies moved by popular outcries against urban violence. Responding to drug traffickers' shutdown of main avenues and the bus system in Rio de Janeiro, he created the National Police Force and the National Program of Public Safety and Citizenship (Pronasci). He also invested in the construction of high-security prisons. In 2006, the federal government released an amount of R$110 million to build new prison facilities in São Paulo's countryside. See *Observatório da Segurança Pública*, www .observatoriodeseguranca.org/dados/penitenciario.

32. Adriana Ferraz, "Mais 49 Prisões Previstas," Universo Online, April 15, 2012, www.agora.uol.com.br/policia/ult10104u613789.shtml; SAP, "Plano de Expansão," *Secretaria da Administração Penitenciária*, October 10, 2012, www.sap .sp.gov.br/noticias/not147.html.

33. Ruth Wilson Gilmore, *Golden Gulag: Prisons, Surplus, Crisis, and Opposition in Globalizing California* (Berkeley: University of California Press, 2007), 26.

34. In Portuguese, the term translates as "municipalidades solidarias." See Nélson Rodrigues, "Sistema Prisional Paulista Transformações e Perspectivas," *Revista de Criminologia e Ciências Penitenciárias* 1, no. 1 (August 2011): 1–45.

35. Geraldo Alckmin. "Governador's Speech," *SP Noticias*, February 2013. http://sãopaulo.sp.gov.br/spnoticias/lenoticia.php?id=225988&c=201.

36. William Cardoso and Chico Siqueira, "Corredor de Presídios faz, em 10 Anos, Criminalidade Dobrar no 'Texas Paulista'," Pastoral Carcerária, October 12, 2013.

37. This period covers the Workers' Party's administration. In 2010 the state

of Bahia registered an unemployment rate of 10.9 percent while the national rate was 7.6 percent. As for the expansion of prisons, Bahia is not the only state in the poorest regions of the country (the north and northeast) to undergo the privatization of prisons, but it is clearly one whose strategy is to boost the state economy with "carceral Keynesianism." Tatiana Spinola, *Aspectos do Mercado de Trabalho da Bahia no Período 2000–2010* (Salvador: Unifacs, 2014). Other corporations involved in the prison system in Ceará, Sergipe, and Amazonas are Humanitas, Inap, Montesinos, Conap, and Yumatá. See Folha de S. Paulo, "PPPs de Prisões Movimentam Empresas," *Folha Online*, February 7, 2008.

38. SAP, "Estatísticas, População Anual," *Secretaria da Administracão Penitenciária*, www.sap.sp.gov.br/common/dti/estatisticas.html.

39. Jonathan Simon, *Governing through Crime: How the War on Crime Transformed American Democracy and Created a Culture of Fear* (Oxford: Oxford University Press, 2007), 173.

40. Christian Parenti, *Lockdown America: Police and Prisons in the Age of Crisis* (London: Verso, 1999).

41. The literal translation reads: "O esforço paulista pela redução dos homicídios fica evidente quando são comparados os resultados da cidade de São Paulo com os obtidos pelo conhecido 'Tolerância Zero' de Nova York. A queda percentual dos homicídios dolosos nos primeiros trimestres dos últimos 8 anos (1999 a 2006) foi de -60%, praticamente o mesmo percentual obtido por Nova York durante a gestão do prefeito Rudolph W. Giuliani (1993 a 2000)." Estatísticas Anuais, *Secretaria da Segurança Pública*, December 12, 2006. More recently, Rudolph Guliani himself served as a security expert for the Brazilian government. See Gabriel Mascarenhas e Caudio Mota, "Giuliani Sera' Consultor da Copa," *Jornal Extra*, December 12, 2009.

42. Diaz-Hurtado, "Murder, Gangs, and Hope."

43. Willis, *The Killing Consensus*, 93. Overall, despite the increase in incarceration, homicide rates have in fact also increased in the last two decades in Brazil. Between 1990 and 2010, the number of homicides increased 63 percent from 31,989 to 52,260 violent deaths. Jacob Waiselfisz, *Mapa da Violência: os Jovens do Brasil* (Brasilia: Unesco, 2011), 127.

44. This trend has been identified by scholars of homicidal violence in the state of São Paulo. See, for instance, Luís Eduardo Batista, Maria Mercedes Loureiro Escuder, and Julio Cesar Rodrigues Pereira, "A Cor da Morte: Causas de Óbito Segundo Características de Raça no Estado de São Paulo, 1999 a 2001," *Revista de Saúde Pública* 38, no. 5 (2004): 630–36; Samuel Kilsztajn, Manuela Santos Nunes do Carmo, Gustavo Toshiaki Lopes Sugahara, and Erika de Souza Lopes, "Vítimas da Cor: Homicídios na Região Metropolitana de São Paulo, Brasil, 2000," *Cadernos de Saúde Pública* 21, no. 5 (2005): 1408–15; Paulo Borlina Maia, "Vinte Anos de Homicídios no Estado de São Paulo," *São Paulo em Perspectiva* 13, no. 4 (1999): 121–29.

45. Although homicides in general have decreased over the years, Jacob Waiselfisz has nonetheless shown there is a persistent pattern of black victimization, particularly of black youth. São Paulo's homicide rate for black youth, 103 percent higher than for white youth, is "not bad" compared to some Brazilian states where the rate is as high as 1,900 percent. For trends in homicide rates among black and whites, see Waiselfisz, *Mapa da Violencia*, 61.

46. Ibid.

47. This process is hardly unique to Brazil. Paul Chevigny has identified among politicians in countries like the United States, Mexico, and Argentina a strategy of creating consensus in a fractured society by appealing to a common public enemy. See Paul Chevigny, "The Populism of Fear and Politics of Crime in the Americas," *Punishment & Society* 5, no. 1 (2003): 77–96; Simon, *Governing through Crime*, 173–77.

48. A revealing shift in antidrug state policies is the fact that in 2001, the National Fund of Drug Prevention became the Anti-Drug Fund. The paradigm shift from prevention to punishment has been analyzed by, among others, Sérgio Adorno, "Lei e Ordem no Segundo Governo FHC," *Tempo Social* 15, no. 2 (2003): 103–40; Francisco Bastos, Redução de Danos e Saúde Coletiva: Reflexões a Propósito das Experiências Internacional e Brasileira," in *Drogas, Dignidade e Inclusão Social. A lei e a Prática de Redução de Danos*, ed. Cristiane Sampaio and Marcelo Campos (Rio de Janeiro: Associação Brasileira de Redutores de Danos, 2003), 15–41; Luciana Boiteux "Drugs and Prisons: The Repression of Drugs and the Increase of the Brazilian Penitentiary Population," in *Systems Overload: Drug Laws and Prisons in Latin America*, ed. Pien Metaal and Coletta Youngers (Washington, D.C.: WOLA, 2011), 30–39.

49. Boiteux, *Drugs and Prisons,* 35; Luciana Boiteux, "A Nova Lei Antidrogas e o Aumento da Pena do Delito de Tráfico de Entorpecentes," *Boletim IBCCrim* 14, no. 167 (2006): 4.

50. Secretaria da Seguranca Publica de São Paulo, "Estatisticas Criminais," www.ssp.sp.gov.br/Estatistica/Pesquisa.aspx; Luiz Flavio Gomes, "Nova Lei de Tóxico: Descriminalização de Posse de Drogas para Consumo Pessoal," *Revista Jus Navigandi,* Online Bulletin, https://jus.com.br/artigos/9180.

51. Infopen, "Levantamento de Informações Penitenciarias," Ministério da Justiça, www.dados.mj.gov.br/infopen.

52. Fundacão do Bem-Estar do Menor, *FEBEM-Internos* (São Paulo: Instituto Uniemp, 2006).

53. IBCCrim, "Mulheres Negras: As Mais Punidas nos Crimes de Roubo," *Boletim IBCCrim* 125 (2003):1–4; Sergio Adorno, "Discriminação Racial e Justiça Criminal em São Paulo," *Novos Estudos CEBRAP* 43, no. 2 (1995): 27–53. Although prisons are historically black spaces, the racial dynamics of incarceration in Brazil are still relatively neglected. Despite the silence on race, there is a growing literature on gender and incarceration. See Julita Lembruger, *Cemitério dos Vivos* (Rio

de Janeiro: Forense, 1999); Maria Gorete de Jesus and Denise Carvalho, "Mulheres e o Tráfico de Drogas: Um Retrato das Ocorrências de Flagrantes na Cidade de São Paulo," *Revista do Laboratório de Estudos da Violência* 9 no. 2: 177–92.

54. IBCCrim, "Mulheres Negras," 1–4.

55. Gross, *Colored Amazon,* 6.

56. Angela Davis, *Are Prisons Obsolete?* (New York: Seven Stories Press, 2011), 61.

57. Some of the main factors driving women into prison are abusive partners, child sexual abuse, economic marginalization, and the "war on drugs." See Meda Chesney-Lind, "Imprisoning Women: Unintended Victims of Mass Imprisonment," in *Invisible Punishment: The Collateral Consequences of Mass Imprisonment,* ed. Chesney-Lind Meda and Marc Mauer (New York: The New Press, 2002), 79–94.

58. Fred Moten, "The Case of Blackness," 171.

59. Assata Shakur, "Women in Prison: How We Are," in *The New Abolitionists: (Neo)Slave Narratives and the Contemporary Prison Writing,* ed. Joy James (Albany: State University of New York Press, 2005), 85.

60. Dylan Rodríguez, *Forced Passages,* 44.

61. The term draws on what scholars of education and prison refer to as the "school–prison pipeline." I am also in dialogue here with Loïc Wacquant's analysis of the dialectics between *prison* and *ghetto* in the United States. In the United States there is a large body of literature on the subject. See for instance Damien Schnyder, "Enclosures Abound: Black Cultural Autonomy, Prison Regime, and Public Education," *Race Ethnicity and Education* 13, no. 3 (2010): 349–65; Loïc Wacquant, "Deadly Symbiosis when Ghetto and Prison Meet and Mesh," *Punishment & Society* 3, no.1 (2001): 95–133. On the hyperpunitiveness of urban neoliberalism, see also Steve Herbert and Elizabeth Brown, "Conceptions of Space and Crime in the Punitive Neoliberal City," *Antipode* 38, no. 4 (2006): 755–77. The synchronicity between prison and favela in Brazil has been discussed by Edson Passeti, who proposes a reading of São Paulo's peripheries as "the camp." See "Ensaio Sobre um Abolicionismo Penal," *Revista Verve Nu-Sol* 9 (2006): 83–114.

62. Kenarik Boujikian, "Do Leblon às Favelas da Maré, Mandado Coletivo Nunca!" open letter, www.viomundo.com.br/denuncias/kenarik-boujikian -2.html.

63. Fabiana Marchezi, "PM Amplia Ocupacão de Paraisopolis e Marzagão vai a Favela," *Estadão Online,* February 3, 2009.

64. Polícia Militar do Estado de S. Paulo, "Operação Saturação Paraisópolis-Final," May 4, 2009, www.polmil.sp.gov.br/.

65. Carolina Garcia, "PM Fica em Paraisópolis," *Ultimo Segundo,* November 22, 2012.

66. Franciso, the law student and activist who helped us in dealing with the legal procedures at the Advocacy Network, ended up doing most of the work Dra

Fabiana was supposed to do. He assisted us with dozens of petition models and legal bids for inmates searching for a reduction of their penalties.

67. For some accounts of black men's complex position in relation to violence and victimization, see Edmund Gordon, "Cultural Politics of Black Masculinity," *Transforming Anthropology* 6 (1997): 36–53; bell hooks, *We Real Cool: Black Men and Masculinity* (New York: Routledge, 2004); Damien Schnyder, "Masculinity Lockdown: The Formation of Black Masculinity in a California Public High School," *Transforming Anthropology* 20, no. 1 (2012): 5–16; Carbado, "The Construction of O. J. Simpson as a Racial Victim," 159–93; Abby L. Ferber, "The Construction of Black Masculinity: White Supremacy Now and Then," *Journal of Sport & Social Issues* 31, no. 1 (2007): 11–24.

68. Ronald Jackson, *Scripting the Black Body: Identity, Discourse, and Racial Politics in Popular Media* (Albany: State University of New York Press, 2006).

69. Spillers, *Black, White, and in Color*; Davis, *Are Prisons Obsolete?*

70. Edward W Soja, "The Socio-Spatial Dialectic," *Annals of the Association of American Geographers* 70, no. 2 (1980): 207–25. I also draw on Katherine McKittrick's perspective on black geographies as spatialities constituted through racial violence and space-informed agency. Katherine McKittrick, "On Plantations, Prisons, and a Black Sense of Place," *Social & Cultural Geography* 12, no. 8 (2011): 947–63.

71. I never complained with colleagues from the Advocacy Network, as I was unsure if I were overreading the sensitive security matter that we should be familiar with as prisoner advocates.

72. McKittrick, "On Plantations, Prisons, and a Black Sense of Place."

73. According to the U.S. Department of State, "Brazil is a major transit and destination country for cocaine. . . . The majority of cocaine transiting through Brazil is destined for European markets, often via West Africa. See U.S. Department of State, "International Narcotics Control Strategy Report," *Bureau of International Narcotics*, 2016, www.state.gov/j/inl/rls/nrcrpt/2016/vol1/253244.htm.

74. See Julia Sudbury, "Celling Black Bodies: Black Women in the Global Prison Industrial Complex," *Feminist Review* (2002): 57–74, 57.

75. Jeremy Travis, "Invisible Punishment," 5–36; See also Joan Petersilia, *When Prisoners Come Home: Parole and Prisoner Reentry* (Oxford: Oxford University Press, 2003), 21–53.

76. Holly Foster and John Hagan, "Incarceration and Intergenerational Social Exclusion," Social Problems 54, no. 4 (2007): 399–433; Joseph Murray, "The Cycle of Punishment: Social Exclusion of Prisoners and Their Children," *Criminology and Criminal Justice* 7, no. 1 (2007): 55–81; James Forman, "Cops, and Citizenship: Why Conservatives Should Oppose Racial Profiling," in Invisible Punishment, 150–62. The relation between children and prison is very recent in the growing field of prison studies in Brazil. For some references (with a resounding silence on race) see Claudia Stella, "Filhos de mulheres presas: o papel materno

na socialização dos indivíduos," *Estudos e Pesquisas em Psicologia* 9, no. 2 (2009): 292–306; Ilka Franco Ferrari, "Mulheres encarceradas: elas, seus filhos, e nossas políticas," *Revista Mal-estar E Subjetividade* 10, no. 4 (2010): 1325–52; Miriam Ventura, Luciana Simas, and Bernard Larouzé, "Maternidade atrás das grades: em busca da cidadania e da saúde. Um estudo sobre a legislação brasileira," *Cad. Saúde Pública* 31, no. 3 (2015): 607–19.

77. The association between poor (and predominantly black) children, marginality, and crime informed the constitution of the Brazilian child-welfare and foster-care system. See Roberto da Silva, *Os filhos do Governo: a Formação da Identidade Criminosa em Crianças Orfãs e Abandonadas* (São Paulo: Pedagogia Social, 1997); Rinaldo Sérgio Vieira Arruda, *Pequenos Bandidos* (São Paulo: Global, 1993).

78. Donald Braman, "Families and Incarceration," 17–35.

79. Spillers, *Black, White, and in Color,* 207. For a forceful discussion of Spillers's concept of the pornotropic, see also Weheliye, *Habeas Viscus,* 89–91.

80. Spillers, *Black, White, and In Color,* 67.

81. Spillers, "Interstices," 76.

82. Drawing on Hortense Spillers and Sylvia Winter, Weheliye argues that "western Man [is] the mirror image of human life" (43). My thinking here is informed by a growing amount of literature on Spillers's critique of "humanity" in Western political thought. Weheliye, *Habeas Viscus*; Hartman, *Scenes of Subjection*; Holland, *Raising the Dead.* See also my discussion of Denise Ferreira da Silva's concept of *no-bodies* in relation to the Brazilian political order, in the Introduction of this book. Silva, "No-Bodies."

4. Sticking Up!

1. Presidência da República, "Relatório Sobre os Crimes de Maio," *Secretaria de Direitos Humanos,* May 10, 2016.

2. Monica Bergamo, "Burgesia tem que abrir a bolsa, diz Lembo," *Folha de S. Paulo,* Cotidiano, June 5, 2006.

3. Condepe, *Os Crimes de Maio* (São Paulo: Imprensa Oficial do Estado de São Paulo, 2006); Época, "Terror em São Paulo," *Edicão Especial* 418 (2006): 24–55; Fausto Salvadori, *Crimes de Maio, Crimes de Sempre* (São Paulo: Adusp, 2006), 65–69.

4. Folha de S. Paulo, "São Paulo sob Ataque," *Folha Online Especial,* May 15, 2006; Revista Veja, "Terror em São Paulo," *Veja Online,* May 24, 2006.

5. Black men continue to be incomprehensible sociological subjects vis-à-vis political agency. The incipient literature on black masculinity usually focuses on violence, public health, school performance, and sexuality. See Osmundo Pinho, "Etnografias do Brau: Corpo, Masculinidade e Raça na Reafricanização de Salvador," *Estudos Feministas* 13 no.1 (2005): 127–45; Edinilsa Ramos de Souza, "Masculinidade e Violência no Brasil: Contribuições para a Reflexão no Campo da

Saúde," *Ciência & Saúde Coletiva* 10, no. 1 (2005): 59–70; Raquel de Souza, "Rapazes Negros e Socialização de Gênero: Sentidos e Significados de Ser Homem," *Cadernos Pagu* 34 (2010): 107–42; Alves, "Narratives of Violence," 313–37.

6. David Marriot, *On Black Men* (New York: Columbia University Press, 2006), 15.

7. Paul Kahn, *Criminal and Enemy in the Political Imagination*.

8. Consider, for instance, the Brazilian–U.S. military exchange in counterinsurgency programs to "pacify" urban communities during Rio de Janeiro's preparation for the 2014 World Cup and the 2016 Olympic Games. See Patricia Campos Mello, "Paramilitares americanos treinam policia brasileira para a copa," *Folha de S. Paulo, Caderno Cotidiano,* April 21, 2014.

9. The distinction between violence and terror is not peripheral here. Frank Wilderson argues that "in its magnetizing of bullets the black body functions as the map of *gratuitous* [emphasis added] violence through which civil society is possible—namely those bodies for which violence is, or can be, contingent." Wilderson, "The Prison Slave as Hegemony's (Silent) Scandal," 25.

10. Fanon, *The Wretched of the Earth*, 8.

11. There is no data on the racial composition of its members. The participation of black men cannot be "proved" other than through ethnographic experience and through taking into consideration the racialized setting (spatial segregation, criminalization, and mass incarceration) in which they live and in which PCC operates. The debate about the racial composition of the Partido is trapped within the same debate on the weight of "race" in policing and incarceration practices in Brazil. Most of the work, of course, privileges class (or "the poor") rather than race as a category of analysis. For a contextual description of PCC's expansion in São Paulo's prisons, see Camila Caldeira Nunes Dias, "Da Guerra à Gestão: Trajetória do Primeiro Comando da Capital (PCC) nas Prisões de São Paulo," *Revista Percurso* (2009): 79–96; Bruno Paes Manso, *Homicide in São Paulo: An Examination of Trends from 1960–2010* (New York: Springer, 2016).

12. Based on my own encounters in the prison, the PCC is conceived as a horizontal community, or "a family," based on the ideal of equality. Although no one can deny its effects and its power, PCC is a "public secret." It is not clear who the real leaders are or who rules each *quebrada*. See also Karina Biondi, *Junto e Misturado: Imanência e Transcendência no PCC* (São Carlos: UFSCar, 2009), 77.

13. Marcola Camacho, PCC's main leader, has said, "We are all sons of poverty, we all are descendants of violence . . . We are forced to live in misery, violence. So, in any favela you will see bodies every day." Camara dos Deputados, interview, *Folha de S. Paulo*, Brasília, June 8, 2006, www1.folha.uol.br/folha/cotidiano/20060708-marcos_camacho.pdf.

14. For an account of the Carandiru Massacre, see Human Rights Watch, *Behind Bars in Brazil*, executive summary (Washington, D.C., December 1998); Drauzio Varella, *Estação Carandiru* (São Paulo: Editora Companhia das Letras, 2012).

15. Josmar Josino, *Cobras e Largatos* (Rio de Janeiro: Objetiva, 2004); Percival de Souza, *O Sindicato do Crime: PCC e Outros Grupos* (Rio de Janeiro: Ediouro Publicações, 2006); see also João de Barros, "A Construção do PCC," *Caros Amigos, Edição Especial,* May 28, 2006.

16. In 2016, a Brazilian court voided the conviction of seventy-three officers involved in the Carandiru Massacre on the basis that "there was no massacre. It was a self-defense." See Amnesty International, "Brazil Declares Carandiru Massacre Null." *Amnesty Americas,* www.amnesty.org/en/latest/news/2016/09/brazil-declares-trial-on-carandiru-massacre-null-in-shocking-blow-for-justice/.

17. Bruno Manso and Mariana Godoy, "20 Anos de PCC: Efeito Colateral da Política de Segurança Pública," *Revista Interesse Nacional,* Ano 6, no. 24 (2015): 1–12; Dias, "Da guerra à gestão," 79–96.

18. Although São Paulo's population represents 20 percent of the total Brazilian population, it houses a third of Brazil's six-hundred-thousand-and-counting prison population. São Paulo's prison population jumped from nearly sixty thousand in 1995 to the current count of two hundred thousand inmates, with drug trafficking (29 percent) and robbery/burglary (37 percent) being the leading reasons for imprisonment. São Paulo had selected small drug dealers as enemies of public order. See Afonso Benites, "Trafico de Drogas é Motivo de 24 percent das Prisoes," *Folha Online,* May 12, 2012.

19. There are no data on the real number of PCC members. Some scholars estimate a range from five thousand to thirty thousand individuals. For an estimate of PCC's membership, see Fabio Serapião, "Crime em Lugar do Estado," *Revista Carta Capital* 789 (2014): 18–23.

20. Caros Amigos, *PCC* (São Paulo: Casa Amarela, 2006).

21. Souza, *O Sindicato do Crime,* 2006.

22. For the first approach, see Elizabeth Leeds, "Serving States and Serving Citizens: Halting Steps towards Police Reform in Brazil and Implications for Donor Intervention," *Policing & Society* 17 (2007): 21–37; Sérgio Adorno and Fernando Salla, "Criminalidade Organizada nas Prisões e os Ataques do PCC," *Estudos Avançados* 21, no. 61 (2007): 7–29; Guaracy Minguardi, *O Estado e o Crime Organizado* (São Paulo: Complexo Damásio de Jesus, 1998). For an ethnography-based analysis see Zaluar, *Condominio do Diabo*; Willis, "Deadly Symbiosis? The PCC, the State, and the Institutionalization of Violence in São Paulo, Brazil," in *Youth Violence in Latin America,* ed. Gareth Jones (New York: Springer, 2009), 167–81.

23. Enrique Desmond Arias, "The Dynamics of Criminal Governance: Networks and Social Order in Rio de Janeiro," *Journal of Latin American Studies* 38, no. 2 (2006): 293–325.

24. In her analysis of a favela in Rio, anthropologist Erika Larkins observes that trafficker power relies on performance and violence (Larkins, *The Spectacular Favela,* 54). This unpredictability is also the core of Penglase's argument. See

Ben Penglase, *Living with Insecurity in a Brazilian Favela: Urban Violence and Daily Life* (New Brunswick, N.J.: Rutgers University Press, 2014).

25. The reference for most of the debate is the work of Charles Tilly, as well as recent anthropological interventions around the idea of the state as a historically situated and socially produced form of social organizing. See Charles Tilly, "State Formation as Organized Crime," in *Violence: A Reader*, ed. Catherine Besteman (New York: New York University Press, 2002), 35–60. See also the edited volume by Veena Das and Debora Poole, *Anthropology in the Margins of the State* (Santa Fe, N.Mex.: School of American Research Press, 2004).

26. She states: "If life is constantly patrolled by the state, then to transport life from the state's dominion, it is necessary to disengage from the state, *to break state addiction* [emphasis added] so to speak, in order to resource the terms of self-organized forms of life, however momentarily." H. L. T. Quan, "Emancipatory Social Inquiry," 121.

27. Hardly new, these have been driving questions in the scholarship on the "state" in different contexts. See, for instance, Abrams, "Notes on the Difficulty of Studying the State"; Mitchell, "The Limits of the State: Beyond Statistic Approaches and their Critics"; Das and Poole, *Anthropology in the Margins of the State*; Ramírez, *Between the Guerilla and the State*; James Ferguson and Akhil Gupta, "Spatializing State: Toward an Ethnography of Neoliberal Governmentality," *American Ethnologist* 29, no. 4 (1995): 981–1002.

28. Among those interventions is James Scott's theoretical proposition about "zones of escape," in which some groups refuse to be under state control even if they were unsuccessful in securing such independence. He argues that in many societies, groups of people (like maroon communities in colonial Latin America) "chose to place themselves out of the reach of the state" rather than "being left behind by the process of civilization." See James C. Scott, *The Art of Not Being Governed: An Anarchist History of Upland Southeast Asia* (New Haven, Conn.: Yale University Press, 2009), 22–23. Although I do not wish to transport Scott's rather contextual, historical, and controversial account of "Zomia" to the racialized context of urban violence in Brazil and Latin America, and the rich history of black resistance in the Americas is not necessarily articulated in terms of antistateness, *escaping from the state* is still certainly an important component of black resistance throughout the colonial period. For historical accounts of black radical tradition, see Richard Price, *Maroon Societies: Rebel Slave Communities in the Americas* (Baltimore: Johns Hopkins University Press, 1996); Franklin W. Knight, "The Haitian Revolution," *The American Historical Review* 105, no. 1 (2000): 103–15; João José Reis, "Quilombos e Revoltas Escravas no Brasil," *Revista Usp* 28 (1996): 14–39. I take on this question in an analysis of yet another ethnographic context in "Refusing to Be Governed: State Delinquency and the Politics of Black Ungovernability in a Colombian Shantytown" (unpublished manuscript).

29. Abdias do Nascimento, *Quilombismo: um Conceito Científico Emergente*

do Processo Historico-cultural das Massas Afrobrasileiras, digital repository, https://
baobavoador.noblogs.org/files/2016/01/O-QUILOMBISMO-Abdias-Do-Nasci
mento.pdf.

30. Scott, *The Art of Not Being Governed,* 22–26.

31. Willis, *The Killing Consensus,* 94.

32. According to a perspective, organizations like PCC lack a political project
and, given their ability to recruit soldiers and control favelas and prisons, it would
be more appropriate to regard them as "parallel" or "rogue" states. See Fiona Ma-
caulay, "Knowledge Production, Framing and Criminal Justice Reform in Latin
America," *Journal of Latin American Studies,* 39 (2007), 638; Sergio Adorno and
Fernando Sallas, "Criminalidade Organizada," 12.

33. James Scott names the strategies for evading state control as a "zone of insubordination" or "zone of refuge." And yet, according to Scott, the people's refusal
to comply with the state is also a *state effect* rather than a failure of integration into
the "civilized world." Scott, *The Art of Not Being Governed,* 328.

34. Sexton, "The Social Life of Social Death"; Wilderson, "Gramsci's Black
Marx"; Hartman, *Scenes of Subjection*; Vargas, "Black Disidentification."

35. Wilderson, "Gramsci's Black Marx," 230.

36. Hartman, *Scenes of Subjection,* 80.

37. André Caramante and Afonso Benites, "Um em cada 5 é vitima da PM,"
Cotidiano Folha Online, January 27, 2012.

38. An independent investigation by the Brazilian Ministry of Justice revealed
that only 6 percent of the individuals killed by the police in the May riot had a
criminal record. Presidência da República, "Crimes de Maio," *Secretaria de Direitos
Humanos,* July 8, 2016.

39. Donna Goldstein, *Laughing out of Place,* 180.

40. Machado Silva, "Sociabilidades Violentas," 55–85; Caldeira, *City of Walls,*
20. See Alba Zaluar, "Para Não Dizer Que Não Falei de Samba," in *Historia da
Vida Privada no Brasil,* ed. Lilia Moritz Schwarcz and Fernando Novais (São Paulo:
Companhia das Letras, 1998), 311–35.

41. Similar observations can be found in Ben Penglase's research in a favela
in Rio. Penglase notes that the favelados "experienced in their lives, a mixture of
both security and uncertainty, a sense of safety and yet a worry about the possible
appearance of lethal violence" (19). One can argue, unlike Penglase, that police are
the main agent of unpredictable violence in São Paulo's periphery. Like Penglase,
however, one can also argue that in São Paulo's periphery, fear is an experience
deeply marked by one's gender, class, and race. Penglase, *Living With Insecurity,* 19.

42. Taking into consideration that indiscriminate police killings in the favelas nullify the division between "criminals" versus "citizens" and "bandits" versus
"workers" in these territories, Serginho's claim can be understood in a broader context in which the category "favelado" signifies outlawness.

43. Vargas and James, *Refusing Blackness-as-Victimization,* 3.

44. Brazilian sociologist Clóvis Moura calls attention to the equation "from good slave to bad citizen" used by Brazilian civil society in the postabolition period. This discursive formation helped to consolidate a "new" criminal justice system to police the "bad" free blacks. See Clóvis Moura, *O negro de bom escravo a mau cidadão?* (Rio de Janeiro: Conquista, 1977).

45. Zaluar, *Condominio do Diabo*, 102; Marisa Feffermann, *Vidas Arriscadas: o Cotidiano de Jovens Trabalhadores do Tráfico* (Petrópolis, Brazil: Editora Vozes, 2006).

46. For a critical discussion of "spatial praxis" and "spatial transgressions," see Soja, "The Socio-Spatial Dialectic," 209; Lynn Staeheli, "Political Geography: Democracy and the Disorderly Public," *Progress in Human Geography* 34, no. 1 (2010): 67–78.

47. Katherine McKittrick, *Demonic Grounds: Black Women and the Cartographies of Struggle* (Minneapolis: University of Minnesota Press, 2006), xiv. See also McKittrick, "On Plantations, Prisons, and a Black Sense of Place."

48. Robin Kelley, *Race Rebels: Culture, Politics, and the Black Working Class* (New York: Simon and Schuster, 1994), 8.

49. My citations here do not do justice to the comprehensive body of literature on the question of criminality and black agency. See, for instance, Osmundo Pinho and Eduardo Rocha, "Racionais MC's: cultura afro-brasileira contemporanea como politica cultural," *Afro-Hispanic Review* (2011): 101–14; Trevor Gardner II, "Political Delinquent: Crime, Deviance, and Resistance in Black America," *Harvard Blackletter LJ* 20 (2004): 141; Peter McLaren, "Gangsta Pedagogy and Ghettocentricity: The Hip-Hop Nation as Counterpublic Sphere," *Counterpoints* 96 (1999): 19–64; Martin Lamotte, "Rebels without a Pause: Hip-hop and Resistance in the City," *International Journal of Urban and Regional Research* 38, no. 2 (2014): 686–94. Common to these works is an attempt to conceptualize black transgressive practices beyond pathological narratives that render black men as the urban criminal and beyond the class-based approach of political agency. Philipe Bourgois engages with James Scott's theory to make similar claims on everyday forms of resistance among marginalized Latino youth in New York City. See Philipe Bourgois, *In Search of Respect: Selling Crack in El Barrio* (Cambridge, Mass.: Cambridge University Press, 2003).

50. By using "tragic agency" I also aim to interrogate a tendency to portray black men as predators or victims without paying attention to the ways they respond to the forces that structure their lives. The adjective "tragic" calls attention to the ways their responses reinforce their subordination and help to further marginalize their communities. For a critique of the term "agency," see James Scott, *Domination and the Arts of Resistance: Hidden Transcripts* (New Haven: Yale University Press, 1990). For black men's investment in patriarchy, see Carbado "The Construction of O.J Simpson as a Racial Victim," 159–93; bell hooks, *We Real Cool*. And for the ways racial oppression and internal gender dynamics shift the

terms of resistance among racialized men, see also Bourgois, *In Search of Respect: Selling Crack in El Barrio.*

51. Although I was displeased with their justifications for domestic violence, I remained silent most of the time to avoid creating antagonism. Only later did I come to realize that my silence was a form of complicity and participation in the "brotherhood community." I was entitled to participate in their misogynistic conversations by virtue of being a man.

52. hooks, *We Real Cool,* 88; Ferber, "The Construction of Black Masculinity," 11–24.

53. Davis, *Are Prisons Obsolete?,* 77.

54. These accounts were tragically common in the carceral universe. They would spontaneously come up in conversation as we aided inmates with juridical assistance or monitored their process through the criminal system. It was under these conditions that my meeting with Elisa took place.

55. Sudbury, "Celling Black Bodies," 57.

56. For a rich analysis of PCC's system of justice, see Adalton Marques, "'Liderança,' 'Proceder,' e 'Igualdade': Uma Etnografia das Relações Políticas no Primeiro Comando da Capital," *Etnográfica, Revista do Centro em Rede de Investigação em Antropologia* 14, no. 2 (2010): 311–35; Camila Nunes Dias, "Ocupando as Brechas do Direito Formal: o PCC como instância alternativa de resolução de conflitos," *Dilemas* 2, no. 4 (April–June 2009): 83–106.

57. São Paulo has the lowest murder rates in the country: the Brazilian average is forty-five murders for every hundred thousand people; São Paulo's is eighteen. There is no consensus among scholars about the causes for the sharp downfall in homicide rates in São Paulo. Graham Denyer Willis, Paes Manso, and Gabriel Feltran corroborate with my findings that PCC plays an important role in the controlling of killings in the periphery of the city. See Willis, *The Killing Consensus,* 2015; Paes Manso, *Homicídio em São Paulo*; Gabriel Feltran, "Crime e Castigo na Cidade: Os Repertórios da Justiça e a Questão do Homicídio nas Periferias de São Paulo," *Caderno CRH* 23, no. 58 (2010): 59–73. Other scholars prefer a multicausal explanation that includes the aging population, the new gun statute, and the expansion of urban services, among other possible variables. See, for instance, Maria Fernanda Tourinho Peres, Diego Vicentin, and Marcelo Batista Nery, "Queda dos Homicídios em São Paulo, Brasil: uma Análise Descritiva," *Rev. Panam. Salud Pública* 29, no.1 (2011): 59–70.

58. While the Brazilian police force is responsible for an average of 4 percent of homicides, the state of São Paulo's Military Police is responsible for 20 percent of all homicides in the state. Sixty-five percent of those killed by the police are black young men. André Caramante and Afonso Benites, "Um em cada 5 é Vítima da PM," *Folha de S.Paulo,* January 27, 2012; Rachel Costa and Laura Daudén, "A Polícia Matadora," *Revista ISTOÉ,* August 24, 2012; Álvaro Magalhães, "Polícia Militar Mata mais Pardos e Negros," *Diario de S. Paulo,* March 26, 2014.

59. Willis, *The Killing Consensus*, 2015.

60. I borrow the term from Aldo Civico. I should note that he makes these remarks in the specific context of violence in urban Colombia. Aldo Civico, "We Are Illegal, but Not Illegitimate: Modes of Policing in Medellín, Colombia," *PoLAR: Political and Legal Anthropology Review* 35, no. 1 (2012): 77–93; Alves, "Refusing to Be Governed" (unpublished manuscript).

61. hooks, *We Real Cool*, 2004.

5. Bringing Back the Dead

1. My reconstitution of the exchange between Dona Maria and the other participants might raise objections. How would I translate her pain into words without portraying her behavior as irrational? How does one render state bureaucracy ethnographically visible in the face of my friends' goodwill to help her? Only later I revisited the details of the event. Back then, I was more concerned with dealing with the bureaucracy that hopefully would ameliorate her situation than in taking notes. There were other instances in which I mediated her encounter with state agents (for instance the public hearing on human rights and the visit to the office of the police ombudsperson). As Dona Maria's anguish grew further, so did my frustration with state bureaucracy. These multiple moments of frustration inform the ethnographic narrative presented here.

2. Kleinman, Das, and Lock, *Social Suffering*, vii.

3. Hartman, *Scenes of Subjection*, 21.

4. See Robyn Wiegman's discussion in "Whiteness Studies and the Paradox of Particularity," *Boundary* 2, no. 26 (1993): 115–50; also Charles Mills, "White Ignorance," in *Race and Epistemologies of Ignorance*, ed. Shannon Sullivan and Nancy Tuana (Albany: State University of New York Press, 2007), 13–38.

5. Ibid., 35.

6. On April 10, 2010, Eduardo Pinheiro dos Santos was tortured and killed by the Military Police on the north side of the city. Alexandre Menezes dos Santos was killed by the police on May 8, 2010.

7. Historian João Jose dos Reis warns scholars not to romanticize the *quilombos* as a progressive horizontal mode of social organizing. Palmares was a "complex social formation" with a strong, gendered social hierarchy. See Reis, "Quilombos e Revoltas Escravas no Brasil," 14–39.

8. Azevedo, *Onda Negra Medo Branco*.

9. Luiz Alberto Couceiro, "Demandas, Direitos e Entendimentos da Justiça: um estudo de caso da Sociedade Escravista do Império do Brasil," *Revista de Antropologia* 58, no. 2 (2015): 401. Saidiya Hartman argues that in the U.S. context, the state "recognized the slave's personhood only to the extent of her criminal liability." See Hartman, *Scenes of Subjection*, 126.

10. See Ivair Augusto dos Anjos, *O Movimento Negro e o Estado* (São Paulo:

Imprensa Oficial, 2006). Abdias do Nascimento left Brazil to live under exile in the United States for twelve years. He was hosted by the Fairfield Foundation. Abdias returned to Brazil in 1981 to become a federal deputy, the equivalent of a U.S. congressperson. See Sandra Almada, *Abdias Nascimento* (São Paulo: Selo Negro, 2009).

11. George Reid Andrews, "O Movimento Begro em São Paulo, 1888–1988," *Estudos Afro-Asiáticos* 21, no. 1 (1991): 37. A historic reconstitution of black protest in Brazil can be found in Flavia Rios, "O Protesto Negro Contemporâneo," *Lua Nova*, 85 (2012): 41–79.

12. Miltom Barbosa e Ivo Queiroz, "Movimento Negro Unificado: uma Crônica Inacabada do Combate ao Racismo," *Tambores Falantes,* http://tambores falantes.blogspot.com.br/.

13. I do not label these approaches as good or bad, reformist or revolutionary, because the very impasses we faced as organizers speak volumes about the hostile political environment for black activism in Brazil. Within the context of Brazil's longstanding discrimination, should affirmative action be regarded as a conservative integrationist political agenda?

14. UNEafro-Brasil, "Você Está Convocado," May 10, 2010, www.uneafro brasil.org.

15. In fact, the press in São Paulo ignored the report. Not only did the term "genocide" seem too radical, it would also have gone against a media establishment that has explicitly supported police operations in the favelas.

16. In the literature on genocide, the Jewish Holocaust is the universal measuring stick, so to speak, for studies on ethnic and political violence. Scholars and political commentators alike have contended that in defining an event as "genocide," one should pay attention to both the intentionality of the perpetrators and the intensity of the massacre. This would prevent the "trivialization" of the horrendous experiences of some groups in particular. See, among others, Leo Kuper, "Theoretical Issues Relating to Genocide: Uses and Abuses," in *Genocide: Conceptual and Historical Dimensions,* ed. George Andreopoulos (Philadelphia: University of Pennsylvania Press, 1994); Helen Fein, *Genocide: A Sociological Perspective* (London: Sage Publications, 1990); Frank Chalk, "Redefining Genocide," in *Genocide: Conceptual and Historical Dimensions,* ed. George Andreopoulos (Philadelphia: University of Pennsylvania Press, 1994), 47–63. However, João Costa Vargas argues that the legal term as approved by the Convention on the Prevention and Punishment of the Crime of Genocide (CPPCG) could easily be applied in African Diaspora communities such as those in the United States and Brazil, where black lives are prematurely shortened by police violence, malnutrition, health complications, and a host of other factors. Vargas argues that the debate over the applicability of the concept has very little to do with scientific criteria and more to do with the political perspectives of those working in the field. See João Costa Vargas, "Genocide in the African Diaspora: United States, Brazil, and the Need for a Holistic Research and Political Method," *Cultural Dynamics* 17, no. 3 (2005): 267–90.

17. Abdias do Nascimento, *Brazil, Mixture or Massacre? Essays in the Genocide of a Black People* (Dover, Mass.: Majority Press, 1989), 75.

18. Vargas, "Genocide in the African Diaspora," 267–90; Ana Luisa Flauzina, *Corpo Negro Caído no Chão: O Sistema Penal e Projeto Genocida do Estado Brasileiro* (Rio de Janeiro: Contraponto, 2008).

19. This is in line with João Costa Vargas's invitation to focus on the results (slow, cumulative, and premature death) instead of the legal definition of the term. See Vargas, "Genocide in the African Diaspora," 267–90.

20. In the language of Brazilian law enforcement bureaucracy, *legal police killing* is in line with military protocol and, therefore, a technical response to crime. In the Brazilian criminal justice system, the police incident report (Boletim de Ocorrências) is issued by the officer on duty at the police station. Therefore, it is the police that testify about the "death event." Usually, the police appear in the official records as the victims and the dead person appears as the violator of the law. Privileging the official report—filed by the police when a suspect is killed after allegedly resisting arrest—over witness accounts places the responsibility for proving the victim's innocence on the family of the deceased. Since January 2013, the state of São Paulo has banned the concept of "killed while resisting arrest" after the popular outcry following the police assassination of favela residents in São Paulo during yet another new wave of violence between September and November 2012.

21. These "human" qualities or vulnerabilities given to the state also indicate that the *mythic* state is performed, experienced, and lived through embodied forms of oppression and resistance. See Begoña Aretxaga, "Maddening States," *Annual Review of Anthropology* 32, no. 1 (2003): 393–410. For another perspective on the anthropomorphization of the state, see Adriana Viana and Juliana Farias, "A guerra das mães: dor e política em situações de violência institucional," *Cadernos Pagu* 37 (2016): 79–116.

22. Patricia Hill Collins, *Black Feminist Thought: Knowledge, Consciousness, and the Politics of Empowerment* (New York: Routledge, 2007), 377. Also Angela Davis contends that within the small range of possibilities for facing gendered racial terror on the plantation, black women found in mothering a way to redress institutional policies that deemed them genderless objects; mothering has historically been a site of both vulnerability and agency. In Angela Davis's words, "social life in the slave quarters was largely an extension of family life. Thus, women's roles within the family must have defined, to a greater extent, their social status within the slave community as a whole." Angela Davis, *Women, Race and Class* (New York: Vintage Books Editions, 1983), 16.

23. The organization was later renamed "AMPARAR" (Association of Parents and Friends of Incarcerated Youth).

24. In his elaboration on violence and racism, Arjun Appadurai argues that ethnic violence represents the "desperate effort to restore the validity of somatic markers of otherness in a world in which marks of difference such as race and

ethnicity have become a taboo." See Arjun Appadurai, "Dead Certainty: Ethnic Violence in the Era of Globalization," *Development and Change* 29, no. 4 (1998): 920.

25. As Ruth Gilmore writes, "the insistence on the rights of mothers to children and children to mothers was not a defense of traditional domesticity as a separate sphere, rather, it represented political activation around rising awareness of the specific ways that the contemporary working-class household is a site saturated by the neoliberal racial state." Gilmore, *Golden Gulag*, 239–40.

26. The Tribunal Popular was formed by a broad alliance of social movements, some of which also united under the Committee against the Genocide of the Black Population. Most of the activities and campaigns overlapped as activists organized the movement into an extended network. I worked as a member of UNEafro-Brasil.

27. Luciane Oliveira Rocha, "De-Matar," 185.

28. Adriana Viana and Juliana Farias, "A Guerra das Mães," 94; Sonia Alvarez, "Engendering Democracy," 89; Suzan Franceschet, Jennifer Piscopo, and Gwynn Thomas, "Supermadres, Maternal Legacies, and Womens' Political Participation in Contemporary Latin America," *Journal of Latin American Studies* 48, no. 2 (2016): 1–32.

29. Vilma Reis, *Atucaiados pelo Estado*, 2005; Rocha, "De-Matar."

30. Franceschet, Piscopo, and Thomas, "Supermadres," 7.

31. I thank Debora Silva, Joy James, and the other participants of a CSI–CUNY workshop on "Insurgencies: Black Mothering Politics and Pedagogies of Resistance in the Americas" in May 2015, for their critical perspectives on this subject. The Mães de Maio took inspiration for their struggle from the similar experience of the Madres de La Plaza de Mayo, the Argentinean activist group that denounced in public squares the disappearances of their loved ones during the Dirty War period. Like the Madres de La Plaza de Mayo, who are still active in their demands for "aparición con vida" (demanding that the state bring back their "disappeared" children) more than thirty years later, their Brazilian counterparts use their own suffering to denounce the disappearance of their loved ones by the Brazilian state. In her account of the strategies used by the Madres de la Plaza de Mayo, Diana Taylor presents a long critique of the strategies of resistance deployed by the Argentinean mothers to regain control of public space, such as public performance. One wonders how race complicates such an argument in the case of Brazil, where civil society was never meant for black women in the first place. See Diana Taylor, *Disappearing Acts: Spectacles of Gender and Nationalism in Argentina's Dirty War* (Durham, N.C.: Duke University Press, 1997).

32. Alves and Vargas, "On Deaf Ears," 7; Vargas, "Black Disidentification," 4–6. Although not explicitly stated, these critiques respond to Jürgen Habermas's normative definition of the public sphere. See Jürgen Habermas, *The Structural Transformation of the Public Sphere: An Inquiry into a Category of Bourgeois Society* (Cambridge, Mass.: MIT Press, 1991).

33. Flavia Rios, "O Protesto Negro Contemporâneo," 41–79.

34. Michael Hanchard, "Black Cinderella? Race and the Public Sphere in Brazil," *Public Culture* 7, no. 1 (1994): 165–85; Alexandre Emboaba da Costa, "Anti-Racism in Movement: Afro-Brazilian Afoxé and Contemporary Black Brazilian Struggles for Equality," *Journal of Historical Sociology* 23, no. 3 (2010): 372–97.

35. Kwame Dixon, *Afro-politics and Civil Society in Salvador da Bahia* (Tampa: University Press of Florida, 2016), 156.

36. This critique has been articulated by João Costa Vargas in relation to the waves of protests that swept Brazil in 2013. Vargas argues that in order to participate in the ephemeral public life opened up by the demonstrations that swept the country, blacks had to deny their blackness and participate as "workers," "students," or anything else but "blacks." The minimal black participation in the protest, he argues, illustrates black "deidentification" in the Brazilian public sphere. In his words, "the constitutive symbolic core that animates sociality [the polis itself] seems impermeable to external pressure." Vargas, "Deidentification," 12. A short discussion about the impossibility of the black subject in Brazilian public life can be seen in Milton Santos, "Ser Negro no Brasil Hoje," Caderno Mais, *Folha de S. Paulo*, May 7, 2000.

37. *Comissão Nacional da Verdade. Relatório Final* (Brasília: Presidência da República, December 2014).

38. UOL, "Dilma Recebe Relatorio da Comissão da Verdade e Chora ao Lembrar dos Mortos," *UOL Online*, December 12, 2014.

Conclusion

1. David Harvey, *Rebel Cities: From the Rights to the City to the Urban Revolution* (New York: Verso, 2013), xiv, 4–25. While Harvey argues for an inclusive understanding of the "right to the city," the political actors that emerge from his text are defined in relation to the world of labor. He writes, "the right to the city is not an exclusive individual right, but a focused collective right. It is inclusive not only of construction workers but also those who facilitate the reproduction of daily life: the caregivers and teachers, the sewer and subway repair men, the plumbers and electricians, the scaffold erectors and crane operators, the hospital workers and the truck, bus, and taxi drivers, the restaurant workers and the entailers, the bank clerks and the city administrators. It seeks a unity from within an incredible diversity of fragmented social spaces and locations within innumerable divisions of labor" (137).

2. McKittrick, *Demonic Grounds*, ix–xxxi.

3. Lila Abu-Lughod, "The Romance of Resistance: Tracing Transformations of Power through Bedouin Women," *American Ethnologist* 17, no. 1 (1990): 42. Complementing Abu-Lughod's critique, Kamala Sivaramakrishnan argues that because scholars using such frameworks have focused their attention on everyday

practices of resistance without considering their limits in challenging structures of domination, they have overlooked "an equally careful discussion of [the] everyday exercise of power." Kamala Sivaramakrishnan, "Some Intellectual Genealogies for the Concept of Everyday Resistance," *American Anthropologist* 107, no. 3 (2005): 351.

INDEX

Abrams, Philip, 283n57
Abu-Lughod, Lila, 261–62, 311n3
Adriana, 103–5, 106, 181
Afro-pessimism, 12–13, 29–30,
    178–79, 277n75, 290n36
Agamben, Giorgio, 9
agency, 305n50; black mothering
    and, 23–24, 194–95, 258–59;
    criminal, 136–37, 141–42,
    168–69, 197–207, 305n49; female
    criminal, 136–37; gender and,
    136–37, 305n50; hopelessness ver-
    sus, 11–12, 13–14, 38; resistance
    and, 194–95, 261–62, 300n5,
    305n50; social death and, 11–13;
    spatial dynamics and, 194–95,
    258–59, 288n18; tragic, 35,
    197–207, 305n50
Alckmin, Geraldo, 21, 127, 128, 145,
    283n53, 289nn24–25
AMAR (Association of the Mothers of
    Imprisoned Adolescents), 234
Amar, Paul, 5
Amaro, 110–13
AMPARAR. See Association of Parents
    and Friends of Incarcerated Youth
Andrade, Oswald de, 17, 273n44
Andrews, George, 47
antiblackness: baile funk and, 91–92;
    community security councils and,

89–95; gendered antiblackness,
    9, 42, 278n5; police terror and,
    66–71; spatial dynamics of, 2–5
Antonio, 243, 244, 260
Appadurai, Arjun, 26–27, 309n24
Aretxaga, Begoña, 283n57
Arias, Desmond, 177
Association of Parents and Friends of
    Incarcerated Youth (AMPARAR),
    216, 229, 233, 237–39, 243–44,
    250, 266, 291n1, 309n23

Bahia, 25, 129, 140, 220, 284n70,
    295n37
baile funk, 91–92, 131–32, 289n24
Baldwin, James, 25, 167
Belchior, Douglas, 21, 117, 226, 248,
    260
Beltrame, Jose Mariana, 283n53
Biondi, Karina, 171
biopolis, 41–43, 152, 162, 259–60.
    See also necropolitical governance
biqueira, 32, 94, 152–53, 192–95, 202
Bispo, 227–33, 260
black death, 161–62, 216–26, 233–34,
    237–38, 245–46, 249–51, 300n79.
    See also black necropolis, the
black men: criminalization of, 149–52,
    169; masculinity and, 151–59, 165,
    169, 198–202, 290n28; maternal

313

and, 171; prisons and, 127–29;
racial violence and, 18–21; spatiocarceral practices and, 125–35, 165;
urban development and, 51, 53
South Africa, 4, 50, 83, 286n9
Souza, Raquel Luciana de, 23
spatial dynamics: agency and, 23–24,
194–95, 258–59, 288n18; of
antiblackness, 2–5; apartheid and,
47–53, 280n20; of *biqueiras*, 32,
94, 152–53, 192–95, 202; black
geographies and, 299n70; black
masculinity and, 151–54; of
black mothering, 23–24, 194–95,
258–59; of the blackpolis, 151–54,
257–62; of black youth, 114–15;
community security councils
and, 289n23; consciousness and,
20–21, 114–15, 152–54; ghettos
as prisons, 298n61; oppositional
geography of, 258–59; police
violence and, 46, 53–58, 56–57,
114–15; resistance and, 194–95;
social segregation and, 279n19;
spatial praxis, 194, 259, 305n46;
urban development and, 279n19.
See also favelas
Special Unity, 110–11
spectacle, 9–10, 60, 214–15, 271n25,
282n43, 283n56
Spillers, Hortense, 161–62, 164,
272n34, 300n79, 300n82
state, the, 270n14, 283n57; affirmative
action policies and, 14, 25–26,
222–23, 247, 249, 251, 253,
276n66, 286n6; economy of state
making and, 281n35; as ideological
abstract, 283n57; the media and,
282n44; multicultural neoliberalism, 78–79, 126, 286n6, 294n25;
penal democracy and, 120–25,
295n31; relationship with police

and military, 282n49; rhetoric
of engagement, 6–7; social death
and, 281n35; as social organizing,
283n56; spectacle and, 209–15,
281n37; support for police violence, 58–66, 66–71, 170, 281n35,
285n1; zone of escape, 303n28

Taylor, Diana, 310n31
Thiago, 43, 44, 108
Thomas, Gwynn, 250
Tilly, Charles, 303n25
Tonia, 243–45, 260
Travis, Jeremy, 157, 158
Tribunal Popular (Popular Trial), 143,
239–42

UNEafro-Brasil, 25, 26, 195, 216,
218, 224, 251, 266, 291n1,
310n26
urban governance framework: apartheid and, 47–53, 279n19, 280n20;
community security councils and,
4–5, 34, 78–79; PCC and, 112;
Plano Montoro, 82, 287n12; police
violence, 53–58; prisons and,
127–29; "right to the city" and,
257–62; rurality and, 272n29; rural
migration and, 290n28; spatial
dynamics and, 77–78, 279n19
urban violence: Brazilian scholarship on, 273n47; criminalizing
narratives and, 284nn69–70; death-
worlds and, 11, 257, 284n68;
mundo do crime, 11–16, 190, 207,
250, 258, 272n38, 273n39
Uribe, María Victoria, 66–67

Vander, 174, 176
Vargas, João Costa, 308n16, 309n19
violence: black feminist analysis of,
23–24; domestic, 140, 199, 201–2,

Jaime Amparo Alves is assistant professor of sociology and anthropology at the College of Staten Island in the City University of New York. He is also research affiliate at the Centro de Estudios Afrodiaspóricos (CEAF) at Universidad Icesi (Colombia) and a member of UNEafro-Brasil.